15.00

c 47578

From UI to EI

LAW AND SOCIETY

Law and Society Series
W. Wesley Pue, General Editor

Appearing in 2004

Compulsory Compassion: A Critique of Restorative Justice
Annalise Acorn

Feminist Activism in the Supreme Court: Legal Mobilization and the
Women's Legal Education and Action Fund
Christopher P. Manfredi

The Heiress vs the Establishment: Mrs. Campbell's Campaign for
Legal Justice
Constance Backhouse and Nancy L. Backhouse

Tournament of Appeals: Granting Judicial Review in Canada
Roy B. Flemming

Gay Male Pornography: An Issue of Sex Discrimination
Christopher N. Kendall

The Courts and the Colonies: The Litigation of Hutterite Church Disputes
Alvin J. Esau

Despotic Dominion: Property Rights in British Settler Societies
Edited by John McLaren, Andrew Buck, and Nancy Wright

A list of other books in this series appears at the end of the book.

Georges Campeau

From UI to EI:
Waging War on the Welfare State

Translated by Richard Howard

UBC Press · Vancouver · Toronto

Originally published as *De l'assurance-chômage à l'assurance-emploi*
© Les Éditions du Boréal 2001

15   14   13   12   11   10   09   08   07   06   05   5   4   3   2   1

Printed in Canada on acid-free paper

Library and Archives Canada Cataloguing in Publication

Campeau, Georges
    From UI to EI : waging war on the welfare state / by Georges Campeau ; translated by Richard Howard.

    (Law and society, ISSN 1496-4953)
    Translation of: De l'assurance-chômage à l'assurance-emploi.
    Includes bibliographical references and index.
    ISBN 0-7748-1122-6

    1. Insurance, Unemployment – Canada – History. I. Howard, Richard, 1940- II. Title. III. Series: Law and society series (Vancouver, B.C.)

KE3459.C2313 2004   368.4'4'00971   C2004-904774-4   KF3675.C2313 2004

Canadä

UBC Press gratefully acknowledges the financial support for our publishing program of the Government of Canada through the Book Publishing Industry Development Program (BPIDP), and of the Canada Council for the Arts, and the British Columbia Arts Council.

The following organizations provided financial assistance for the English translation: Boag Foundation; Canada Employment and Immigration Union; Canadian Labour Congress; Canadian Union of Public Employees; Communications, Energy and Paperworkers Union of Canada; and the Douglas-Coldwell Foundation.

UBC Press
The University of British Columbia
2029 West Mall
Vancouver, BC V6T 1Z2
604-822-5959 / Fax: 604-822-6083
www.ubcpress.ca

Contents

Acronyms / vi

Introduction / vii

1 Why UI? / 1

2 The British Act of 1911 / 17

3 Developing a Canadian System / 31

4 The UI Act of 1940 / 56

5 UI Expansion, 1940-75 / 74

6 Vision under Siege, 1975-88 / 91

7 Rights Enshrined in Case Law, 1940-90 / 108

8 The System Hijacked, 1989-96 / 127

9 Onward to EI / 148

10 Case Law in the Neoliberal Riptide of the 1990s / 167

Conclusion / 178

Epilogue: Bill C-2, February 2001 / 182

Notes / 185

Selected Bibliography / 216

Index / 225

Acronyms

AALL	American Association for Labor Legislation
AIW	average industrial wage
CAP	Canada Assistance Plan
CCF	Co-operative Commonwealth Federation
CEIC	Canada Employment Insurance Commission
CFIB	Canadian Federation of Independent Businesses
CHST	Canada Health and Social Transfer
CLC	Canadian Labour Congress
CLFDB	Canadian Labour Force Development Board
CPC	Communist Party of Canada
CPQ	Conseil du Patronat du Québec
CRF	Consolidated Revenue Fund
CSN	Confédération des Syndicats Nationaux
CTCC	Confédération des Travailleurs Catholiques du Canada
CUB	*Canadian Unemployment Benefits*
EI	employment insurance
EPF	Established Programs Financing
FTA	Free Trade Agreement
GST	Goods and Services Tax
HRDC	Human Resources Development Canada
HRIF	Human Resources Investment Fund
ILO	International Labour Organization
MIE	maximum insurable earnings
NAFTA	North American Free Trade Agreement
NERE	new entrants or reentrants
OECD	Organisation for Economic Co-operation and Development
RCMP	Royal Canadian Mounted Police
RCWU	Relief Camp Worker's Union
SQDM	Société québécoise de développement de la main-d'oeuvre
TLCC	Trades and Labour Congress of Canada
UI	unemployment insurance
VER	variable entrance requirement

Introduction

The unemployment insurance (UI) scheme of 1940 came as a key component of Canada's social security net. Conceived against the social, economic, and political background of the Great Depression, the Canadian UI system began by recognizing rights to the jobless as it proceeded to define entrance requirements, a range of benefits that carried specific responsibilities, and an appeal process.

The Canadian plan drew on the existing British model, and its legal framework exhibited more or less the same basic features. In line with the social insurance approach, benefit payments were not discretionary but dictated by specific eligibility criteria. And the jurisprudence would confirm this acknowledgment of rights by holding that the purpose of the legislation was to pay benefits to the unemployed.

In the postwar period, the system evolved with Ottawa's new Keynesian bent. The federal government, wanting the scheme to play an economic multiplier role, favoured its expansion, and unemployment insurance thereby became one of the building blocks of the Canadian welfare state then under construction. This Keynesian strategy came with a social message that depicted unemployment as a collective responsibility and the government as an instrument of solidarity. By degrees, an increasing proportion of the workforce would be covered by unemployment insurance. The unemployed were the first beneficiaries of an interventionist strategy that reached its peak with the reform of 1971, when qualifying conditions were relaxed and the length and rate of benefits made more generous.

The mid-1970s saw the first stirrings of a counterattack as the Keynesian strategy came under siege. With other areas of government activity, social commitments were denounced by supporters of the neoliberal school as inflationary and unproductive. Employment was essentially a private sector responsibility, and the handling of the unemployed should reflect a free-market approach. This regressive movement culminated in the 1990s counterreforms that heralded a major policy shift. The term "counterreform" actually seems to be more appropriate than "reform" to describe a sweeping change that basically undermined the function of social protection that had typified UI up to that time. Thereafter the government reduced its direct involvement with the jobless to refocus on managing unemployment, primarily to serve the marketplace.

The rights that the system recognized to the jobless were radically challenged: qualifying conditions were tightened up, the length and rate of benefits were revised downward, and penalties for voluntary leaving and misconduct were toughened. The numbers of unemployed with access to benefits would drop by half during the 1990s.

The current status of the UI/EI (employment insurance) system, after the cutbacks and shrinkages in jobless rights of recent years, raises some basic questions about the scheme itself and the rights that it is supposed to stand for. Does the system still recognize genuine rights to the jobless? What are the nature and basis of the rights thus protected? Should not unemployment insurance, with its contributory principle, still guarantee the insured reasonable protection against the risk of unemployment?

How do we explain the government actually reducing the protection that the system affords to victims of a persistently high rate of unemployment just as the market is being restructured from top to bottom? Does the purpose originally enshrined in this legislation, to "provide benefits to the unemployed," still have valid meaning?

My working assumption is that the recognition of genuine jobless rights reflects the role taken by the government in dealing with the problems of employment and unemployment. I will attempt to validate this assumption by reviewing the historical development of unemployment insurance in Canada. I believe that the history of a law helps to reveal both its origins and its current focus.

This historical dimension helps us to see how industrialization produced mass unemployment over which the individual had almost no control. As a consequence of this, liberalism and its idea of unemployment as essentially an individual responsibility became less reputable. Bit by bit, unemployment came to be seen as a social problem and the jobless not as primarily responsible for their situation but as victims. The responsibilities of both the economic system and the government as our collective embodiment were called to account. Gradually, Canadians saw the need for ongoing state involvement.

Employment and unemployment then became social concerns that the government had to make its own. It was up to the government to create the right conditions for full employment or at least to compensate people whom the market could not keep at work. These new government responsibilities involved recognizing rights to the jobless: failing a genuine right to work, workers were granted a right to protection from unemployment.

Only insofar as the government accepted a direct responsibility for the social issue of employment, independent of dominant market interests, could the jobless hope for reasonable protection against unemployment accompanied by an array of genuine rights.

Although the need for an unemployment compensation plan gradually won minds, however, it was not easily carried into effect. Like any state intervention, the government's role in employment and unemployment was defined against the play of forces, political as well as economic, that quickened society. The extent of state involvement in the labour market was one of the main issues in this power play. Employers initially opposed the government initiative and then, when the UI principle won out, tried to limit its reach. Employer lobbies conjured up the costs of a future system that they would have to bear in part and the system's potential interference with the workings of a labour market in which, or so they claimed, unemployment insurance was a disincentive to work. At the same time, unions and grassroots movements were calling for vigorous government action to ensure reasonable social protection for the jobless and recognition of rights for victims of unemployment.

The extent of government involvement in the unemployment problem also reflected the influence of existing ideologies. On the one hand, liberalism, though weakened by the economic crisis of the 1930s, still proclaimed employment and unemployment as primarily personal responsibilities and challenged the state's role in economic life generally and in the labour market particularly. Once the unemployment insurance plan was up and running, the same liberals would try to curtail its coverage. On the other hand, the supporters of a more interventionist state maintained that government must not only play an active role in the economy but also deal with social issues stemming from the economic process, including jobs and joblessness. This interventionist movement spearheaded the introduction and development of a UI system with better protection for the jobless and acceptance of subjective rights to compensation.

Just as in Britain thirty years before, the Canadian unemployment compensation scheme of 1940 embodied a compromise on the type of state involvement reached by employers' associations, unions, and the ruling political class. Accordingly, elements of the UI system were borrowed from one or the other of these opposing ideologies.

This compromise would appear in the insurance feature of the scheme. Admittedly, the government assumed some responsibility for employment and unemployment by setting up and funding an arrangement based on the public right. The workers, however, through their own and, indirectly, their employers' contributions, had to pay the lion's share of the cost. Indeed, even though employers had to contribute financially, they sloughed off most of the cost on their employees.

Similarly, although the act's stated objective was always to compensate victims of unemployment, the system also pursued another and equally important economic goal from the outset. The establishment of an employment network to accompany the system, along with the various obligations that the law imposed on claimants to curb voluntary leaving, actually made UI an effective tool for controlling the workforce. Disregard for these obligations could result in penalties that went as far as forfeiture of entitlement. Since the message sent by these provisions was primarily for the employed, UI operated as a powerful workforce regulator.

If the social security aspect of the system reflected a social objective involving direct government action on behalf of the jobless, the workforce regulation aspect was intended to satisfy market imperatives. And the use of social insurance techniques helped to preserve the individual aspect of unemployment, which rationalized the regulatory notion of "voluntary unemployment": the unemployed, becoming insured, must not cause the risk of unemployment to occur.

Behind these two dimensions of unemployment insurance, the compensatory and the regulatory, loomed two concepts of social insurance as a method of indemnifying the unemployed. On the one hand, a social vision of unemployment insurance called for more government involvement to guarantee the jobless easier access to the system, better protection, and entrenchment of their rights. On the other hand, an actuarial concept of social insurance drew on the commercial insurance model that limited government involvement and, in the name of financial integrity, tried to limit the coverage provided by the system. Naturally, this second concept underscored individual responsibility for the occurrence of unemployment and controlling its effects.

The same protagonists for and against the unemployment insurance project would support one concept of UI or the other when the system was in place. This debate between the social and actuarial visions of unemployment insurance would haunt its entire development.

Finally, the system's legal structure also reflected the compromise that lay at its origin. Although the recognition of rights was a substantial advance compared to earlier systems based on handouts, it came with a retinue of obligations, especially regarding voluntary unemployment and labour disputes. Here again the delicate balance between claimants' rights and responsibilities would reflect the role taken by the government: as soon as the government extricated itself from its responsibilities for employment and unemployment and began treating them as essentially the products of market forces, claimants' obligations were strengthened and their rights undermined.

Some have seen the contributory model as a more secure basis for asserting the rights of the unemployed than a noncontributory scheme funded completely out of taxes. With premiums, was the worker not "buying" entitlement to benefit just as he or she bought private insurance? Would this model not be a better guarantee of his or her rights? Although the analogy with commercial insurance could have a positive psychological effect by lending benefits the colour of entitlements purchased through premiums, the contributory formula cannot be used as the ground for a right to unemployment insurance. Unlike a contract that is binding on both parties, a law can always be amended by the lawmaker alone. The real basis of the right to benefit was the law, which set out the procedures and reflected the responsibility that the government willingly assumed for employment and unemployment, not an alleged contractual relationship between the insured and the state that would generate the payment of premiums.

The system evolved in two phases that reflected differing government roles in the economy as well as differing ideologies and, above all, differing government involvements in unemployment and its casualties. Initially, the Keynesian approach that argued for direct and ongoing state involvement in running the system would positively affect the development and recognition of jobless rights. However, the neoliberal approach steered by free-market principles taken up by the government in the mid-1970s would spell a decline in these rights.

These two phases are also seen, though in mitigated form, in the relevant jurisprudence. The umpires, as the chief arbiters of the act in its early days, would increasingly favour a liberal approach and thereby, bit by bit, a jurisdictional recognition of claimants' rights. A more restrictive interpretation was still placed on certain provisions in the act, however, especially those for disentitlement due to labour disputes.

The Supreme Court confirmed in 1983 that the act should be given a liberal reading that favoured recognition of the rights of the unemployed. In 1988, the court went on to stipulate that this liberal interpretation was based mainly on the contributory nature of the system. These decisions announced a period of liberalized jurisprudence that affected a number of provisions in the act, including the ones for voluntary unemployment. This trend, asserting the primacy of the act's social purpose of paying benefits to the unemployed, would clearly be favourable to the jobless and, for the most part, continue until the 1990s.

Like the legislation itself, the jurisprudence saw a wave of conservatism after 1990 that took the form of a restrictive reading of certain provisions affecting voluntary unemployment. Although not generalized, this trend marked a setback compared with the type of interpretation favoured by Supreme Court decisions in the 1980s.

Although this study of the Canadian UI system deals more specifically with jobless rights, I thought it essential as well to look at the system's history and the Canadian government's record of managing unemployment.

As often happens in social law, consideration of these broader aspects is essential for a detailed understanding of the legislative story.

My viewpoint has been clearly stated. This book follows from a number of years of legal practice defending the rights of the unemployed in the company of jobless defence movements and union organizations. Obviously, this professional experience has influenced the book and been a major source of much of the thinking embodied in it. So this work is an extension of a professional commitment. My thinking highlights the jobless perspective by assuming that the primary aim of any UI scheme is to compensate workers affected by the occurrence of the risk of unemployment. I weigh the various aspects of the system's history from the standpoint most favourable to the rights of the unemployed. I take a critical look at the system, and more specifically at its legal aspects, to determine whether the Canadian version of UI is the one most likely to afford workers effective protection against unemployment.

This book also includes a number of references to works in disciplines other than law. I have not attempted to write in the guise of a historian, political scientist, or economist but simply to use these materials for the light that they can shed on my review of the legal rules. This approach strikes me as essential in terms of the right to social security, which is so closely tied to political struggles, economic doctrines, and the evolution of societies.

This book has ten chapters. The first two deal with UI's conceptual aspects and their application when the first government system emerged in Britain. The British reference is especially useful in that the Canadian act of 1940 was basically copied from its British precursor.

Chapters 3 to 7 focus on the process of creating the Canadian system and outline its development to 1988. The period after the system was introduced, generally favourable to the interests of the jobless, was marked by recognition of their rights. My review here deals mainly with the scope and meaning of legislative amendments, but the trend in the jurisprudence, also generally favourable to jobless rights, is also noted.

Chapters 8 to 10 offer a review of the system's evolution from 1989 to 2000. This period was typified by successive waves of counterreforms that profoundly altered the philosophy of the system. My review attempts to highlight the legislative substance of the various amendments to the system as well as the motives of the lawmaker. Jurisprudential developments in this period were not impervious to these motives: on certain significant issues, I find a tendency to break with the interpretation established at the close of the preceding period. The signs of this break are put back into their conjunctural context. Finally, I thought it appropriate to include a brief epilogue reviewing Bill C-2, which was tabled in the House of Commons in February 2001. Following from the counterreforms of the 1990s, this bill passed without much change.

We need to be mindful of a few comments about legislation and jurisprudence. First, I have given more space to the legislative than the jurisprudential process in appraising the rights of the jobless. In fact, the various legislative changes have had much more decisive impacts on the actual status of jobless rights than interpretations given to the act in appeal instances or the courts. I have therefore elected to review the jurisprudence in two separate periods that basically correspond to the episodes of growth and shrinkage in the system. This approach helps to convey a clearer idea of certain legislative amendments that started occurring in 1990 and were closely related to earlier jurisprudence.

Second, in view of the breadth and wealth of detail in the legislative and regulatory texts on UI, I have elected to make the provisions on voluntary unemployment and labour disputes my primary target. I made this choice because of the large number of appeals that these rules have always generated and because they reflect the power relationships and ideological movements in society and, ultimately, the question of responsibility for unemployment in a free-market system. I also devote a lot of attention to evolving ideas and legal texts on vocational training seen as a component of unemployment insurance, especially because of the importance that this component has assumed in the system's development from the 1990s on.

And third, I stress that the book reflects the state of unemployment insurance legislation as of 30 September 2002.

I could not conclude this introduction without thanking Professor Pierre Issalys from the Faculty of Law, Laval University, a recognized expert in social security law. Our many discussions on the subject's legal aspects and, more generally, the role of social security in our society have greatly enriched this book. Also, my colleague in the law, Jean-Guy Ouellet. His advice on various legal and political aspects of the work has been very useful, especially as it was grounded in more than fifteen years of experience in defending the rights of the jobless.

But above all, thanks to my companion, Brigitte Lahellec, who has given me her unceasing support and encouragement during this lengthy project.

From UI to EI

1
Why UI?

The basis of Canada's unemployment insurance system was the British scheme introduced in 1911. As the name suggests, its purpose was to compensate the jobless. Yet the unemployment insurance concept raises a number of questions. Why did the British lawmaker choose the insurance approach over a model funded from the general tax base? And even more basically, what prompted the British to create the first government-run UI scheme?

Britain had been hearing calls for a system of protection from unemployment since the nineteenth century. Worsening social problems associated with industrial growth caught the country's ruling political class off guard. It was becoming harder and harder to persuade the public that the rise of unemployment was basically an individual responsibility. Popular discontent did not stop at questioning the failure of the ruling class to act: it went after the capitalist system itself.

How were grassroots grumbling and the socialist menace to be neutralized? Liberalism would use social insurance as one response to these problems. The various hazards of life were now perceived from the standpoint of risk, which replaced the paradigm of individual responsibility. Unemployment became a "social risk" to be borne by society as a whole, thereby disposing of the capitalist system's liability in the matter.

Britain's socioeconomic context in the nineteenth century had been that of the unfolding industrial revolution. The advent of industrialism and its associated work organization yielded amazing gains in productivity. Britain saw its gross domestic product quadruple in that century.[1] However, the adjustment came at immense social cost.

Industrialization arose in a legal context in which the right of property and its corollary, freedom of contract, reigned supreme. This legal framework served the interests of the ruling classes, which could then impose working conditions on their employees. Child labour, derisory wages, and miserable, often dangerous working conditions were typical of the unbridled capitalism of that era. This industrialization had a price, and the ones who paid it, as is so often the case, were not those who reaped its benefits.

These deplorable working conditions came with living conditions that were just as bad. The change in production processes was coupled with urban growth. More and more people left the countryside to settle in cities, close to factories and jobs. This migration only intensified the dependence of these new workers on their bosses. And since the workers were ill paid, their living standards plummeted. More and more of them were trapped in unhealthy surroundings, sickness, and hardship.[2]

Inadequate wages were not the only cause of this impoverishment. Income lost to unemployment also loomed large. By degrees, the production system would require a workforce that was not only cheap but biddable as well. The pursuit of these objectives would lead to the formation of a surplus labour pool for new industrial needs and thus create downward pressure on wages. The swelling numbers of workers and cyclical fluctuations in demand for their labour would result in unemployment that affected unskilled workers as well as those better placed in the production chain. By the 1880s, Britain's industrial revolution was looking for its second wind, and unemployment ballooned.

To handle these problems of unemployment and poverty, all Britain had was the Poor Laws assistance system set up in the seventeenth century. Distinguishing the disabled poor from those able to work, these laws originally obliged petitioners to accept employment in workhouses run by local governments and prohibited them from changing their addresses.[3]

In 1795, Parliament's "Speenhamland Act" transformed the system.[4] Benefits would thereafter be paid to everyone without employment or whose employment income was inadequate, an immense leap forward for that era: "Passed amid economic crisis and a strong resurgence of pauperism, [this law] recognized the right of every man to minimal subsistence: if he could earn only part of this by his labour, society had to provide the balance."[5] This legislation, with its benefits that reflected criteria other than work itself, was diametrically opposed to the liberal ideology. The domicile law and the "generosity" of this system would be contested. By curbing the mobility and availability of the workforce needed by industries that were mainly concentrated in cities, the new system was unduly favourable to the rural economy. Some saw this law as merely slowing the development of a modern economy that would lend impetus to the forces of social progress.[6]

Britain's social policies, then, would adjust to the surrounding economic realities. The 1834 Poor Law reform put an end to the domicile law but tightened conditions for obtaining assistance. The "less eligibility" principle made the situation of the poor much less advantageous than that of the lowest-paid workers.[7] By clearly endorsing this principle, the 1834 reform[8] became the starting point for modern social policy in Britain. Assistance was now conditional on the indigents' acceptance of the wretched conditions in the workhouses. Poor people should always find ill-paid employment more attractive than the workhouse.[9] Workers should be fully available to the economic system. In this sense, the Poor Law reform facilitated the development of industrial capitalism.

Amid the prevailing liberalism of Victorian England, both poverty and financial success were personal matters and unemployment merely evidence of an imbalance between labour supply and demand. Either the worker was asking for wages higher than the market could bear, or the job supply was too restrictive in terms of working conditions or mobility: good working conditions actually created unemployment. Finally, assistance under the Poor Laws was strongly stigmatized, with poverty viewed as a moral flaw: poor people were lazy, the authors of their own destitution. This puritanical talk was digested by the working classes, who came to see accepting the help provided by the Poor Laws as something to be ashamed of.

Nonetheless, growing numbers of jobless were forced to accept this assistance in the deteriorating economy of the late nineteenth century. The institution's repressiveness finally created unrest. In 1886 and 1887, jobless riots broke out in the poor districts of London. These events raised the profile of the problems of poverty and unemployment. Thereafter, poverty evoked more fear of violence than pity in the upper classes. At the same time, the well-to-do rubbing shoulders with the unemployed realized that not all of them were lazy and irresponsible. The unemployed themselves also grew more aware of their political strength. In 1884, the electoral law was amended[10] by lowering the poll tax. This meant that most men now had the right to vote, and the unemployed could vent their dissatisfaction at the polls. Socialist ideas would find fertile ground in this new electorate.

In an increasingly unstable labour market, perceptions of unemployment evolved. It became obvious to many observers that every worker was likely to lose a job at some point, especially in industrial areas. Moreover, industrial requirements for workforce mobility and availability were causing a proliferation of casual employment. Workers would often have to round up several employers to put a full workweek together. By degrees, unemployment emerged as an integral cog in the capitalist system.[11]

This being the case, how could unemployment still be seen as an individual responsibility, and why rail at its victims? British social policy for the jobless would seek an alternative to the rigidity of the system introduced in 1834. A second phase began to offset the strictness of the Poor Laws, though at first without great success. Not until the passage of the 1911 National Insurance Act[12] did this process reach its culmination.

The economic recession that settled over the country in 1903 wrung action from the authorities. The 1905 Unemployed Workmen Act[13] attempted to occupy the jobless by creating public works projects funded almost wholly by private charities. Local committees were asked to choose unemployed men to take part in these projects. This was the beginning of the public labour exchange network formalized in 1909. The new law was a failure, however, attacked for doing nothing to improve things for the casual unemployed or to deal with the structural work shortage. In fact, the 1905 act reflected the thinking of the Poor Laws. The distinction between "good" and "bad" unemployed was still around, and projects were concerned more with keeping the jobless busy than with solving the unemployment problem.

The British system's inability to afford reasonable protection for the unemployed reflects a darker trend that involved a number of the negative aspects of industrialization. Difficult and sometimes dangerous working conditions, low wages, and insecurity associated with lost earnings as a result of unemployment, illness, and old age were creating hotbeds of popular unrest and political agitation. These years saw the birth of trade-based and political organizations dedicated to the defence of working-class interests and aspirations. The political and economic authorities felt threatened by the energy of these crusades. They were afraid of losing power to the left-leaning parties advocating the overthrow of the capitalist system or at least calling for vigorous state involvement in the economic process to curb the most flagrant injustices and inequalities.

Governments reacted to this movement in two ways. To begin with, the classic arsenal of repression swung into action: a ban on workers' parties and movements, the arrest of their leaders, demonstrations broken up, political censorship, et cetera. Some governments, however, wanted to enlist subtler tactics to curb the socialist threat and reap advantage from worker claims that they saw as acceptable and compatible with market economics. The classic example of this was Germany's introduction of the first social insurance systems during the 1880s. Chancellor Bismarck wanted to preempt his country's social democrats and seize the political credit that these programs had with ordinary people: "The democrats," he would say in his memoirs, "will fiddle in vain when the people realize the princes are concerned with their welfare."[14]

Similar motives inspired the liberal reformers crafting social reforms in early-twentieth-century Britain. A desire for social peace combined with political opportunism to steer the course of their governments. Yet the creation of the initial social insurance schemes was much more than a pragmatic response to cyclical political problems: it breathed a new liberal approach. With the advent of social insurance, liberal thinking moved away from its traditional credo.

Nineteenth-century liberal social engineering was founded on individual responsibility. Individuals were solely responsible for their actions and lives. This responsibility covered not just their dealings with others but any coincidences that might befall them. Illness, accidents, job loss, and old age were all misfortunes inherent in the human condition. It was up to the individual to guard against them, prepare for them. Unemployment and poverty were basically accounted for by personal factors. Poor and unemployed people had only themselves to blame. In this way, individual responsibility acted as a social regulatory mechanism.

In legal terms, this liberalism took on the forms of civil liability in both its contractual and its tortious dimensions. Its first component, freedom of contract, was an affirmation of individual will. Assuming that all were equal before the law, it denied the social and economic inequalities among individuals. Freedom of contract provided the legal framework for the market system.

The labour market was rapidly changing. With industrialization, work that had been done independently at home gave way to work for wages. The wage earner was free to accept or reject the work offered to him. Since the economy was supposed to generate work for everyone, unemployment would be explained by the refusal of some workers to accept the conditions that the market had to offer.

The second component of civil liability was the tort, the individual wrongful act. Responsible for his or her acts, the individual had to bear the consequences. Here liability stemmed from the concept of the tort. To justify a conclusion of liability, the damage suffered by the victim had to result from a tort committed by someone else. And it was obviously up to the person alleging wrongful conduct to produce the evidence. Just as obviously, civil liability could not cover all misfortunes: it excluded accidents in which no liability could be proven. This form of responsibility could not grow as dramatically as freedom of contract.[15] The reason for the lag lay in the respective functions of the two legal mechanisms. Freedom of contract, by fostering the development of the right of property for the benefit of commercial companies, served capitalism well. However, tort liability was perceived as slowing growth. By seeking the cause of the damage and, potentially, the tort, civil liability was a hindrance to market operation compared to freedom of contract, which was unconcerned about the quality of the contractual relationship as long as it maintained certain minimal standards of public order.

The social problems arising from industrialization would challenge these regulatory mechanisms. The deteriorating working and living conditions that crept into more and more people's lives helped to undermine the legitimacy of individual responsibility as the ground of social consensus.

First, the laissez-faire attitude to labour relations was seriously contested.

For many nonunion workers, the power relationship between the parties to the contract was so lopsided that the ideas of personal independence and freedom of contract became synonymous with injustice and exploitation: "The 'free employment contract' seems to have been imposed on workers in a relationship of political domination."[16] Workers' organizations would claim the right to collective bargaining for their conditions. Labour legislation would take the place of the contract in determining the rights and obligations of wage earners. Thereafter, collective agreements largely replaced personal independence in contracting matters – "the statute vs. the contract"[17] – at least as far as the latter's substance went.

Second, the liberal approach to the hazards of the human condition came under fire as well. This challenge was aimed mainly at the argument that poverty and unemployment were problems caused by individuals to be solved by individuals. The rise of mass unemployment prompted observers to recognize the phenomenon as intrinsic to the market economy. Suddenly, the reasoning from personal responsibility promoted by liberal ideologues could no longer stand.

Legally speaking, the principles of civil liability would prove unequal to the conflicts that were becoming more and more frequent and virulent with advancing industrialization. The challenge to civil liability for work accidents reflected the inability of the legal system to develop solutions based on social consensus. Productivity increased with industrialization, but so did work accidents. The legal remedies of injured workers based on the employer's civil liability were necessarily time-consuming and expensive. Injured parties could never be sure of collecting compensation when they had to prove their boss's wrongful act plus the causal connection between this act and the damage that they had suffered. On the other hand, a judgment for damages could sometimes represent a significant amount for an employer, especially a small-business person. A major source of discord between bosses and workers, work accidents urgently required a new legal framework to get past all of this dysfunction: "The law is not made to exacerbate war but to end it. This conflict of liabilities called for a solution that began with a challenge to the liberal diagram of liability."[18]

Beyond the work accident issue, the very legitimacy of the system was being challenged. If work accidents were the dark side of industrial progress, why should the victim have to bear the cost? Should accidents not be subject to automatic compensation by the people who reaped the profits, the bosses? Beyond civil liability, the very bedrock of free enterprise was coming under fire. Capitalism had come to a crossroads. Not only the economic system but also liberal doctrine and its regulatory mechanisms were being challenged. Liberalism was on the lookout for new solutions. Could an alternative be suggested to socialism and the interventionist state that would be compatible with the market economy?

Social insurance would be one of capitalism's responses to the social problems of industrialization.

The insurance approach featured a new way of perceiving society, that of risk. Developed in a private context, it could be applied to a range of events, including risks arising more from social relations, such as work accidents and unemployment. But insurance techniques, even before social insurance was invented, were already based on a collective concept of society.

Mathematical advances produced the first "actuarial science"[19] in late-eighteenth-century Europe, inspired by the idea that reality could be understood by calculating probabilities with data collected by the statistical method. It then became possible to determine certain constants in events ascribed to chance. Founded on the concepts of chance and accident, the rationale for insurance revolved around the idea of risk. The calculation of probabilities helped to usher in a new compensation system described by François Ewald as "risk technology." The definition of insurance highlights the central role played by risk in the compensation system: "Insurance is an operation by which one party, the insured, is promised for remuneration, the premium, for himself or a third party in case a risk comes to pass, a benefit from another party, the insurer, who, taking over a set of risks, compensates them in accordance with the laws of statistics."[20] Risk therefore replaced liability as a source of compensation. Insurance innovated by sharing the cost of this compensation, dividing it up among the policy holders. It became a collective exercise. The division of costs now reflected not liability but the probabilities of a risk occurring in any situation.

This new risk technology came as a challenge to the liberal paradigm of personal responsibility. First, the concept of risk was substituted for tort or causality as the source of compensation. Insurance compensated an individual when the risk occurred, regardless of liability. Second, the socialization of risk came as a challenge to the foresight that each individual previously had to show when it came to the hazards of life. Personal liability was much alleviated by a collective system for spreading the apprehended costs, and the foresight of the insured was now limited to the price of the premium.

The evolving legal framework at the turn of the twentieth century shows this conversion to the risk theory. In terms of civil liability, many businesses found insurance an economical way of solving potential compensation problems by reckoning the cost in advance. Since the purchase of insurance was voluntary, it could only benefit businesses using it and thus foster the growth of the capitalist economy. Moreover, although insurance viewed risk as the source of compensation, personal responsibility was still very present in the system: "Responsibility did not disappear: it was now perceived in terms of risk spreading."[21]

The insured person would now be compensated regardless of wrong-doing, yet was still obliged to avoid causing the occurrence of the risk. Risk being defined as a fortuitous event, its occurrence could not depend solely on the will of the parties and especially not of the insured. Arising from the insurance contract, the obligations of the insured were now contractual rather than tortious. Penalties for transgression now reflected not the wrongful act behind the damage but types of behaviour found to be reprehensible: "These offences were defined less as contraventions of law than as standards of behaviour. Their punishment would be less concerned with reforming the offender than with imposing a certain regularity of conduct."[22] Although these behavioural standards may have seemed harmless in the world of commercial insurance, like the obligation to lock a car as protection against theft, they would take on a whole new dimension in social insurance systems for the labour market. In the case of unemployment insurance, for example, the obligation of the insured not to deliberately court the risk would be used to inculcate into the workforce, unemployed and still employed, various behavioural standards for curtailing voluntary unemployment. By penalizing voluntary unemployment, the system could influence the decision of an employee dissatisfied with working conditions to leave or keep a job.

As for the collective aspect of risk technology, the liberal ideology would turn it to advantage, ensuring that it posed no threat to the very foundation of the system, namely the right of property. Commercial insurance contracts had to comply with strict actuarial rules. Premiums were calculated to reflect the risk in each specific situation. The total benefit paid, including administration costs, could not exceed the total premiums, and any surplus was to be prorated on the same basis. Redistributing costs between groups of individuals would offend the principles of individual property and responsibility and was prohibited. There would be no question of social redistribution, for example to benefit the most vulnerable groups. Even so, its collective face meant that commercial insurance still brought a form of solidarity to the contract: "A worker does not take out insurance to show solidarity with the other contributors, but he does anyway. His interest is bound up with that of the other members of the collective formed by the insured, and vice versa."[23]

Finally, insurance would emerge as a very useful device for protecting an economic and ideological system in crisis. By defining the various hazards of life as social risks ranging from illness to unemployment, social insurance virtually abandoned the issue of liability or causality. The theory was highly attractive in a context of class confrontation. Indeed, as had been seen in Germany, the use of insurance techniques for these social problems made it possible to reconcile opposing interests and thus gain political support from the workers.

Becoming social, insurance could then socialize certain risks to be recognized as shared by the society. Initially used for work accidents, this model saw rapid growth as it was extended to cover other social risks such as unemployment. Generally associated with paid employment, social insurance would become an integral facet of the wage structure.[24]

To play its new social and political role, insurance would exchange its initial private setting for a government environment. Since the purpose of these new systems was to protect whole communities against social risks, costs could not be spread according to the actuarial principles shaped by commercial insurance. As the risk was social, the distribution of its cost must be social as well.

At first, social insurance took the form of compulsory systems that the insured were legally obliged to join. Premiums were collected from low-risk as well as high-risk participants to put these systems on a sound financial footing. The need for all insured persons to unite against the social risk was used to justify compulsory membership. Afterward, the social perspective on risk might involve transfers to the more vulnerable insured groups. The cost of the risk was redistributed to reflect not strictly equal obligations among private citizens but social choices. Premiums largely ceased to reflect the likelihood of the risk in everyone's situation. In some cases, however (especially when, as with work accidents, the employer was the source of the risk being covered), contributions could be weighted to reflect the incidence of a risk.

Social insurance could also, for social risks such as unemployment, be funded in part by the government. For designers of social insurance such as William Henry Beveridge[25] or, later, Leonard Marsh, the financial participation of the insured themselves was not a basic factor: "The understanding of social insurance, however, is still confused because too much emphasis is placed on the second word and too little on the first word of the phrase. Social insurance brings in the resources of the state, i.e., the resources of the community as a whole, or in a particular case that part of the resources which may be garnered together through taxes or contributions."[26] Social insurance was further discovered to be a powerful regulatory mechanism. In addition to neutralizing potential conflicts between social players, it would command the loyalty of the vast majority of the people.

Social insurance was an idea whose time had come. It asserted a collective liability for social risks and the need for government involvement to cover them. For risks such as work accidents, health, and unemployment, the government imposed standards on the private sector. It used the compulsory contribution system to meddle in labour relations. The employment contract would thereafter be subject to rules beyond what the parties wanted. With some problems, unemployment being one, government involvement would go even farther. Not only did the government impose contribution levels, but, by helping to fund the system, it also accepted some responsibility for the unemployment problem itself.[27]

The first social insurance systems emerged in an area directly connected with civil liability: work accidents. Embodying mutual concessions by employers and wage earners, these compensation plans were based on an implicit transaction. This transactional aspect, as contemporary writers stressed, stemmed from the fact that civil liability was central to these systems: "The employer promised to pay up to 50% of the wages of injured workers. In exchange, the injured worker waived compensation for his actual losses, even in cases where the employer's liability would have been upheld by the courts under common law."[28] Designed initially as a political response to urgent social problems, social insurance was a compromise that went far beyond the law as such to reflect a new political and ideological balance.

The introduction of social insurance would meet with strong initial resistance from a number of market economy supporters. Rejecting any compromise to ease the social tensions stirred up by industrialization, they saw social insurance as unacceptable state interference in a liberal economy. The idea gradually spread in the political class anyway, however, and was finally given effect in Germany, then in Britain. Looming as an enormous social compromise, a concession on the state's role in the marketplace poised between collectivism and individualism, social insurance blended the principles of public and private law.

To begin with, social insurance used a collective solution for a social problem while minimizing state involvement. Admittedly, the imposition of compulsory contributions meant official interference with market systems, but the system was basically funded by the insured, not the taxpayer. The contributory formula also expressed the puritanical virtues of the work ethic and personal responsibility. Social insurance was based on a transaction between the state and the worker in which the benefit depended on previous employment.

The emergence of social insurance was also evidence of a compromise between private and public concepts of social security.[29] Some government benefits, health insurance being one example, would be delivered by the private sector. The analogy with commercial insurance, especially in terms of financial self-sufficiency, was often used against the interests of the beneficiaries. In the case of unemployment insurance, the actuarial process would be enlisted to justify state disengagement and thus limit entitlement.[30]

Social insurance legislation tended to move away from the traditional approach in which assistance was extended unilaterally, often on a discretionary basis. The new systems provided clearly defined rights, although as always the lawmaker could limit their effects.[31] The legal framework for social insurance showed the effects of its transactional dimension – for example, social insurance law borrowed some ideas from private contract and property legislation. The influence of private law also emerged in the survival of a form of individual responsibility – the obligation of each insured person not to cause the occurrence of the risk. This obligation was a perfect fit with market economy imperatives about workforce management and the traditional precepts of the work ethic.

Used initially for work accidents, where it replaced the old liability system, social insurance did raise some rather different questions in its adjustment to the social risk of unemployment. For one thing, unemployment presented social insurance with some special management problems. There was even concern about whether the unemployment risk could be handled by the insurance approach. In the mid-nineteenth-century debate over France's first social insurance legislation, some French lawmakers answered in the negative.[32] The German pioneers of government-run social insurance systems also thought that they could not handle unemployment.[33]

Once the decision was made to apply risk technology to unemployment, the question of funding arose. Compulsory systems already existed for work accidents, though funded by the employers and not the wage earners. In these insurance systems, the bosses rather than the workers could be seen as the primary beneficiaries.[34] Moreover, although unemployment could represent an industrial risk, no prior legal link could be inferred between the damage and its cause. There was recognition early in the twentieth century that mass unemployment was intrinsic to the market economy and therefore a collective responsibility. However, unlike workmen's compensation, compensation for unemployment could not be based on civil liability: lack of work might be the result of many factors that were often beyond the employer's control.[35]

For this reason, formulas for spreading the cost of unemployment compensation would evolve to reflect political and not legal criteria. The lawmaker's choice would recognize various political and ideological influences and power relationships between opposing social and economic groups. For example, the British lawmaker chose a tripartite funding formula, thus implicitly recognizing a government responsibility for the problems of employment and underemployment. The American system, on the other hand, would make contributions payable solely by employers.[36]

In all countries, the assertion of the rights of the jobless depended on the government's willingness to adopt a policy that expressly supported them. This policy was based on the premise that employment and unemployment were occurrences that involved collective responsibility, with the state acting on the community's behalf. The recognition, extent, and effectiveness of the rights of the unemployed would be real insofar as the exercise of this government responsibility made their interests a priority.

The contributory principle on which the British system was based lent strength to the belief of workers that they were now the holders of a genuine right that could be claimed through regular legal channels. In a context in which government involvement in social matters was virtually nonexistent and individual rights were basically derived from the right of property, the payment of unemployment insurance premiums would help to legitimize the system for the workers. In fact, the advantage of the contributory feature was mainly psychological: workers believed that they had a right to benefit because they were paying their premiums. Admittedly, this was a major advantage that would enable larger numbers of workers to claim and exercise the right to benefit: "I am entitled because I have paid." And this psychology would be used to defend the right to benefit and claim a vested right to maintain it when there were moves to cut coverage in UI systems.

However, the argument that the rights of the jobless would fare better under an insurance system because of the financial contributions made by the insured had more to do with an insurer's fantasies than any real basis in law. Likening this system to private insurance, with its legal foundation the contract and, ultimately, the right of property, some have held that economic and social rights inspired by contracts and property would be more substantial than those that stemmed from unilateral government funding.[37] However, recent developments in a number of countries, including Canada, suggest that arguments relying on the analogy between these systems and insurance contracts have little legal weight: the contract and property concepts cannot provide a legal basis for these social rights.[38] Rights to social insurance are vested in the law, not in a contract: "The main difference between the two is that the entitlement of state social welfare claimants derives from the relevant statute and not from any contract, express or implied, between them and the state."[39]

The contributory system in social insurance can no more guarantee these rights than a benefit system with no financial consideration from the claimant, as in a welfare scheme. Since Parliament is sovereign and these laws are not constitutional, they can be amended and the rights of the unemployed restricted or even abolished without any particular formality.[40]

One right that came up constantly in debates on legislation was the right to work. When the British act of 1911 was going through Parliament, Labour MPs faulted the government position that limited state liability for employment to compensation for the lack of it. They thought that the state should act first to guarantee employment for everyone and expressed regret that "no promise has been made of a bill establishing the right to work by placing upon the state the responsibility of directly providing employment or maintenance for the genuine unemployed."[41]

The right-to-work principle was clearly not upheld by the British lawmaker of 1911, who would limit involvement to the creation of an unemployment insurance plan coupled with a public labour exchange network. This right would have involved a much more pervasive state presence in the economy that was thought to be incompatible with liberal values. Moreover, its enforcement would have involved a government commitment to provide a job for every citizen wanting to work. From the liberal perspective, this obligation would mean a challenge to the right of property: "Above all, however, the recognition of the right to work, apart from giving one class a right with no corresponding obligation, would have made the state the big production planner: since how was work to be ensured for everyone unless the state itself gradually took charge of hiring, then production and, finally, remuneration? The right to work embodied a complete challenge to trade and industry and the prerogatives of the manager or employer, with the nationalization of all production."[42]

Later on, the Depression of the 1930s would see the beginnings of a meaningful commitment to employment by governments. The concept of full employment as developed by Beveridge and others[43] relied on vigorous government involvement in economic life, though still within a free-market system. An expression of Keynesian economics, the official commitment to full employment found its way into international instruments.[44] Clearly, however, this policy was not as binding as the recognition of the right to work for which British Labour MPs had called. It left the state with an obligation to edge toward the objective of full employment instead of a duty to guarantee employment for everyone able to work or, failing this, an appropriate compensatory benefit.

For some, however, creating an unemployment insurance plan, even with contributory funding, implied official recognition of a right to work.[45] In international law, protection against unemployment would be closely connected with this very right. The 1948 *Universal Declaration of Human Rights* speaks to this link between the two concepts: "23(1) Everyone has the right to work, to free choice of employment, to just and favourable conditions of work and to protection against unemployment."[46]

The British law was passed just a few years before the International Labour Organization was founded in 1919. From the outset, this body would associate protection of the unemployed with promotion of employment, as indicated by the goal of "prevention of unemployment" in the preamble to its constitution.[47] As well, the British trade unions had long associated prevention of unemployment with the right to work, as attested by their union funds.

The turn of the twentieth century saw a number of experimental unemployment insurance schemes. Launched by trade unions, employer groups, and governments, some of these experiments were more successful than others.

During the nineteenth century, unions, mainly British, had set up "friendly societies" that indemnified members becoming unemployed.[48] A portion of union dues went to these societies for this purpose. The aim was to assist jobless members and give them an incentive in hard times to reject jobs paying less than the standard wage that the union stipulated for particular types of work. The compensation was payable for unemployment due to lack of work or labour disputes.

As a rule, benefits were paid when a member was jobless unless the situation was self-created. And the amount of compensation would vary greatly from union to union. In 1864, for example, weekly dues were around a shilling, unskilled workers collected ten shillings in wages, and their skilled brethren took home thirty to forty shillings. Known for having one of the most generous arrangements of the day, the Amalgamated Society of Engineers paid its members ten shillings in benefits for the first fourteen weeks of unemployment followed by a smaller amount *sine die*. Generally speaking, the average benefit paid in 1907 was ten to twelve shillings to begin with[49] and decreasing amounts thereafter. In most cases, benefits extended for two years or more. However, the amount of dues limited access to the system almost exclusively to a minority of unionized workers who tended to be skilled and better paid.

The right to benefit was based on membership at the time of application, not earlier dues payments. As a result, anyone expelled from a union lost all benefit entitlement, whatever he or she might have paid beforehand. The system was run by union labour exchanges in which unemployed members had to report regularly to collect their benefits. Workers leaving employment that met union standards voluntarily and without just cause forfeited their benefits. When jobs were lost through misconduct, the penalty varied from more or less lengthy suspension in some unions to complete loss of entitlement in others. Some unions obliged these people to work for a specified number of weeks to requalify for benefits, whereas other unions could even expel them. When an unemployed worker refused a job offered by the labour exchange, the benefit entitlement was generally suspended in full.

This formula was very popular with unionized workers. In 1906, 747 British trade unions representing nearly 1.5 million members, or 69 percent of the unionized workforce, provided this type of compensation for their unemployed members. These systems exhibited the main features of unemployment insurance: "a defined level of compensation, a test to establish the availability of the insured for work and a connection to a system for finding work."[50] They would be a major source of ideas for the Board of Trade designers setting Britain's state system up in 1911, especially on the matter of voluntary unemployment.

Other unemployment funds were initiated by the bosses. In some industrial sectors, especially in Germany and the United States, employers created unemployment funds for their own workers. Their objective was to keep the workforce that they had trained on call during economic downturns. Every year the employer paid an amount into the fund that represented or was based on a percentage of wages or benefits. Benefits were paid to company workers during temporary layoffs, redundancies, and partial unemployment. Much fewer in number than the union funds, these experiments were no less significant: "The appearance of the employer funds denoted at least indirect recognition of the principle by which the cost of protection against unemployment could not fall on the workers – either exclusively or largely – but had to be borne by the consumers as a factor in the cost of production."[51]

The first unemployment insurance fund created by a public authority was set up by the City of Bern in 1893. This was a subsidized voluntary association open to all workers, unionized or not. The model would enjoy some success in Switzerland and Germany. However, as these plans were voluntary, there was a problem with getting high- and low-risk contributors to join the same risk-sharing fund. The comfortably employed were reluctant to put money into a plan that they were unlikely to use. Financial problems stemming from a predominance of bad risks eventually closed most of these funds down.

The first compulsory unemployment insurance scheme was introduced in 1895 by the Swiss canton of St. Gallen. This experiment was short-lived. An unexpected leap in the unemployment rate that prompted a rush of compensation claims, combined with lax management, piled up a major deficit. Since the dues were not collected by the employer, they were not always paid. A claim for benefit would frequently coincide with retroactive payment of dues.[52] A referendum put an end to the experiment within two years. Its main opponents were workers in stable employment, resentful at having to contribute for the benefit of the unemployed. Similar schemes in Basel and Zurich met the same fate.

Alerted by the unfortunate St. Gallen experiment, the Belgian commune of Ghent tried another approach. Abandoning the compulsory angle, it set up a communal fund in 1902 that subsidized private funds run mainly by unions. The subsidies made it possible to increase by a set percentage the amounts paid to the unemployed by each fund during the previous year. At the same time, the unions continued to manage these funds and were left to make sure that claimants were actually looking for work. This experiment turned out to be a success.[53] Less than six years later, the main Belgian communes had started similar plans. The Ghent model was so popular that it was soon taken up by a number of major European cities, including Milan and Amsterdam. Nor was the example long in attracting whole countries. In 1905, France became the first to adopt the Ghent model nationwide.[54] This type of scheme was based on state grants to unemployment insurance funds with optional membership. Norway, Denmark, and the Netherlands soon followed suit. Not until much later did these countries set up compulsory plans.[55]

The British, however, drew different conclusions from voluntary experiments, most of them purely local. According to the Board of Trade, which would be asked to develop Britain's first UI scheme, the optional aspect of the Ghent model would limit the future system to workers already covered by trade union funds: the vast majority of workers, who were nonunion, would be unable to avail themselves of this protection.[56] In 1911, as a result, Britain was the first country to set up a compulsory national plan.

The design of the British plan also drew on the experience of the social insurance schemes that Chancellor Bismarck had set up in Germany during the 1880s. The advent of social insurance for work accidents, sickness, and old age denoted recognition of the government's social responsibility. As well, compulsory membership was an innovation compared to existing social insurance systems, including those of the British trade unions. Here was a government intervening in the employment contract and forcing employers and employees to help fund these systems.

They were immensely popular. Although the German authorities saw the application of the social insurance model to unemployment as impractical, the governmental and compulsory aspects of these schemes seemed to yield excellent results. These aspects of the German experiment would be the ones adopted by the designers of British unemployment insurance.[57]

2
The British Act of 1911

The United Kingdom's 1905 Unemployed Workmen Act with its failed public works program really brought no improvement to the lot of the jobless. The issues of poverty and unemployment still loomed just as large. The British government attempted a response by setting up the Poor Laws Commission. William Henry Beveridge, who was involved in its labours, saw joblessness as due not to lack of work but to underemployment. The personal moral problem of unemployment now became an objective industrial event. Beveridge recommended, as the cure, a UI system coupled with a labour exchange network.

The Liberal team that gained office in 1906 embraced Beveridge's ideas. Pressured by the Labour opposition, it enacted social reforms that included the introduction of an unemployment insurance program in 1911. The government that set up and partly funded this system was implicitly acknowledging a responsibility for unemployment. Although the British act of 1911 recognized the right of the jobless to benefits, it also imposed a number of obligations stemming essentially from the concept of voluntary unemployment. Before things got to that stage, however, the whole issue had to come into focus.

In 1905, the powerlessness of the Unemployed Workmen Act to address the problem of unemployment prompted the Conservative government to create a Royal Commission of Inquiry on the Poor Laws. Its members included Beatrice Webb, the wife of Sidney, with whom she had done some authoritative work on social policy. The Webbs belonged to the Fabian movement that wanted to usher socialism in by a gradual process of state entrenchment in the economy. The objective was not to reform the capitalist system but to supplant it.[1]

The unemployment issue was thus central to the work of the commission, with Beveridge, already a recognized expert in this field, its appointed secretary. An Oxford graduate, he was a member of the London Central Unemployed Committee, an agency responsible for applying the 1905 act.

He denounced the new legislation as ineffective because of its failure to deal with the basic problem in the economy, underemployment.[2] The Poor Laws system with its air of stigma was not much use to the new class of industrial unemployed. Thus far seen in personal and moral terms, unemployment now became an "objective social, industrial phenomenon."[3]

For Beveridge, the problem was underemployment, not the unemployed. Many workers were jobless due to a malfunction in the labour market system. Casual unemployment was the result of poor articulation between the demand for labour and the needs of production. Beveridge called for the initial establishment of a public network of labour exchanges to tell workers about available jobs and fill them quickly. And this more functionally organized labour market would have to accommodate a new system to help jobless workers: compulsory unemployment insurance. It would be run by the labour exchanges in which the jobless had to register to prove their availability for work and collect their benefits. For Beveridge, the labour market would be more efficient if workers and employers were informed about labour demand and supply, and the administration of unemployment insurance would be facilitated by being able to identify those of the unemployed who were actually looking for work.

The commission's 1909 report was not unanimous. Areas of disagreement included different approaches to the phenomenon of poverty. For the majority, poverty, though possibly economic or industrial in origin, could also be ascribed to personal failure. However, the minority report by Beatrice and Sidney Webb argued that the basic cause of poverty was the economic system itself. In line with their political ideas, the Webbs called for change in this system rather than reform. Their report recommended a system of assistance for the employable poor run by a more powerful Ministry of Labour. This ministry would be responsible for organizing the labour market by various measures, such as improved use of labour exchanges and the introduction of training and public works programs. Although the commission's report recognized the usefulness of a labour exchange network, the minority remained opposed to the principle of compulsory social insurance, favouring instead a system based on the Ghent experiment in which the government would be asked to subsidize systems run by trade unions. Registration with labour exchanges should be compulsory, but unemployment insurance itself should be optional and voluntary.[4]

The commission's report would have little legislative sequel since, in the meantime, the British political landscape had changed. The 1906 election had returned a Liberal majority government and sent fifty-three MPs to Parliament on a Labour platform. Unemployment became a major political concern. In 1907, Labour tabled a bill recognizing a right to work for the jobless.[5] Under the banners of the right to work and its corollary, work or maintenance, the government should provide jobs for the unemployed or, failing that, provide benefits. The bill was defeated,[6] but the unemployment debate lost none of its urgency. The new Liberal team felt the need to act, but how?

Beginning in 1908, the debate on social reform quickened with the arrival in Prime Minister Asquith's Cabinet of Lloyd George as chancellor of the Exchequer and Winston Churchill as president of the Board of Trade. A renegade from the Conservative Party, Churchill was heralded as a progressive tonic for the Liberals. The Webbs persuaded him of the need for social reform, and through them he met Beveridge, another key reformer who saw Churchill's role as essential to the passage of the UI scheme.[7] Lloyd George, a politician of working-class origins, was identified with the party's left wing.[8] As new members of Cabinet, Lloyd George and Churchill were bent on transforming British social policy. In addition to health insurance and unemployment insurance, social measures such as old-age pensions, school meal programs, and medical examinations for the disadvantaged were among their government's achievements.

For the Liberals, the social insurance system offered a number of advantages. First, it was of electoral interest to the people who favoured social reform and usually supported Labour. Second, it involved competition with Germany – a foreign policy bauble calculated to win over certain right-wing elements of the party. Some reckoned that the social insurance programs, by enhancing the country's social cohesiveness, helped to expand its economic capacity. Not only would social reform serve the interests of the Liberal Party, but it would also serve the interests of the nation.[9] Above all, however, the Liberals saw in social insurance an ideological avenue, an alternative to the Fabians' socialist vision. It showed the possibility of reforming the capitalist system by harkening to worker demands. Its contributory principle and association with a labour exchange network meant that unemployment insurance did not break with the rules of the market economy. On the contrary, it fit right into the market system. Social insurance became the market's response to the problems of poverty and unemployment.

In the British social context, UI enabled its proponents to distance themselves from the much disparaged principles of the Poor Laws and thus broaden their popular support. The unemployed could now see collecting benefits not as degrading but as the exercise of a right acquired through work. Lastly, the Liberals saw unemployment insurance as a way of ensuring social peace in a jobless population seething with demonstrations and political agitation. Moreover, its passage would help to contain socialist influence by appropriating a social instrument put in place by the trade unions. This made unemployment insurance not a step towards socialism but in fact a way of curbing it.

In 1908, Churchill, now chancellor of the Exchequer, asked Beveridge and his own deputy minister, Llewellyn Smith, to draw up a draft UI scheme. Union organizations would oppose the project as developed at that time, especially the labour exchanges to be wrested from their stewardship. They were afraid of these exchanges being used by the bosses as strike-breaking agencies and worried that the state's creation of social insurance systems would erode their hold on their members. Beveridge and Smith were against the unions' approach, chiefly because the vast majority of the workforce was not unionized at that time and would thus not have access to the protection of the union systems.

Churchill engaged in talks with the trade unions, and the final bill would reflect a mutual compromise. For example, unlike the initial draft, in which benefits were proportionate to earnings, the final version provided a flat-rate benefit and, what is more, maintained the trade union systems for later integration with the new scheme. The bill from the Board of Trade team was thus essentially an original administrative creation, although some elements drew on earlier experience.

For reasons stemming from the political conjuncture, the labour exchange network and unemployment insurance system would be brought in by two separate enactments. The Liberal government put the labour exchange law through first, in September 1909.[10] Unemployment insurance needed supplementary appropriations and so would have to wait until the Liberals were reelected in 1910. For tactical reasons to facilitate its passage, the unemployment insurance bill would be paired with a bill on health insurance and finally presented to the House of Commons on 4 May 1911. Unlike Part 1, dealing with health insurance, which met with strong opposition from private insurance companies,[11] Part 2, on unemployment insurance, went through without a hitch. Beveridge ascribed the lack of resistance to the fact that few people outside the Board of Trade team were familiar enough with the bill to offer detailed criticism.[12] The National Insurance Act finally came into force in December 1911.[13]

This act contained the broad principles reflecting the compromise behind the UI system, including its integration with the labour market. For Beveridge, unemployment was primarily an occasional event arising from labour market dysfunction, and its solution began with setting up a labour exchange network. From this standpoint, the failure of the St. Gallen experiment as the first system with compulsory contributions had been partly a result of lack of attention to the employment side,[14] which would have helped to verify the merits of claims. Now, by tying the compensation of the jobless to their market integration, unemployment insurance made the workforce supply and demand systems more effective. For example, the scheme compensated the involuntary unemployed who were looking for jobs. Described as a job-search facilitation tool for claimants, this employment system would prove to be a powerful means of controlling the workforce, especially when bristling with penalties.

The main doubts about the feasibility of a social insurance system for unemployment had to do with the nature of the risk. Since unemployment is primarily the outcome of a general economic context, its cost is difficult to pin down. The insurance rationale therefore had to be rethought to accommodate this new social risk that was so highly dependent on impersonal factors. Indeed, the conceptual approach of insurance for the unemployment risk is very different from the approach suited to other social risks, such as disease or old age. These risks are covered with a linear insurance model. The wage earner who is physically able to work pays into the system for potential benefits in a later period of life when he or she is inactive due to sickness or advanced age. The accumulation of funds paid in over periods of employment will eventually be used to support later episodes of inactivity. From this standpoint, the insurance dynamic is based primarily on the individual.

Since the occurrence of the unemployment risk does not depend on personal factors, the trend is more toward a lateral insurance concept. Wage earners working in a given period contribute for the ones who are jobless during that period. The transfer occurs not between different periods in an individual's life but between different groups of individuals unevenly affected by unemployment. From this standpoint, the premiums of one group have to be enough to cover the benefits of the other. By substituting the risk-spreading approach for individual accumulation, this concept moves away from traditional insurance principles and has more to do with ideas of solidarity and social justice.

However, for reasons involving the innovative nature of the system, coverage was limited to a certain number of industries in which it was easier to anticipate the occurrence of the risk and then expanded as more complete data became available. Finally, the lateral concept of insurance would warrant the government's financial participation, especially to create an initial fund to pay the first benefits while waiting for enough returns from contributions.[15]

As it developed, then, this system moved away from the strict insurance principles used in the private sector. For one thing, premiums were compulsory. As well, not only were premiums unrelated to individual risks, but the system also allowed transfers between groups of individuals affected differently by unemployment. And, finally, the government partly funded as well as managed the system. This new insurance rationale raised major issues for the jobless, including the respective responsibilities for unemployment of government and the unemployed. The plan developed by Smith and Beveridge represented a major breach with the liberalism of the day. It reflected the values of the market economy, of course, but it assigned a major role to the government in an area formerly resonant to none but market forces.

It will be remembered that the state-run approach met with initial opposition from the unions. One of the arguments that Churchill used to win unionists over to his bill was the funding formula. The workers would not bear the cost alone: bosses too would have to contribute. Subsidized union-run systems would have made it hard to persuade employers to contribute. Employer objections would obviously not be as stubborn if the government managed the system. Moreover, the problem did not affect employers only, since the government would also provide part of the funding. All of these arguments were in favour of a government plan. At any rate, the law would make it possible to incorporate the existing trade union systems.

The project's architects were convinced of the value of having employers fund the system. They defended this involvement by citing advantages that employers would derive, especially in terms of controlling the workforce:

The insurance scheme will benefit the employers indirectly as well as the men in so far as

(a) it will help to prevent deterioration during periods of unemployment;
(b) it will discourage misconduct and irresponsibility since men throwing up work without cause or dismissed for misconduct will forfeit the benefits for which they have been made to pay;
(c) (in conjunction with the Labour Exchange) it will tend to sift the better workmen from the worse and make the former immediately available for the employer.[16]

Furthermore, employers would be able to pass part of the cost of their participation on to the consumers.[17]

However, these arguments failed to convince the bosses. They were chafing at a change that has to be recognized as radical for that era. Business circles denounced the bill as an unacceptable intrusion on the market system. They saw the compulsory contribution as a tax on industry that would push prices up and create unemployment.[18] Reacting to this charge, Churchill said that the objection did not stick because, in the final analysis, the workers would actually pay all of the contributions, employer as well as employee, from their own wages: "I believe that the whole system will prove to be nothing more or less than wages-spreading."[19]

And the government too was being tapped to fund the system. The tripartite funding formula typified the compromise of the early days of social insurance. Initially, the government refused to get involved in an active

right-to-work policy. Instead of guaranteeing work for the jobless, its obligation was limited to compensating for loss of employment. Moreover, the
social insurance system helped to separate responsibility for unemployment from responsibility for compensation. Unemployment, for which
there was agreement that the capitalist economic system was basically
responsible, became an inherent social risk of industrialization, a risk that
had to be borne by all the social stakeholders since the whole population
reaped the benefits of industrial expansion.

The definition of the legal framework that the law provided for the jobless focused on two poles, both of which reflected the commercial insurance philosophy. On the one hand, the system recognized rights to the
class of unemployed that it covered. Anyone who contributed to the system was entitled to benefit if he or she became unemployed and met the
conditions. The exercise of this right was protected by a specific legal
framework that included an appeal mechanism for claimants. On the
other hand, this right came with obligations, most of them involving voluntary unemployment. Since the system compensated only involuntary
unemployment, the unemployed became insured people who had to
refrain from deliberately causing the occurrence of the risk. The legal
framework for insurance therefore reflected the various functions of the
system, covering both compensation for unemployment and control of
the workforce.

A primary concern of the bill's architects was to get away from the Poor
Laws system in which assistance had a moral connotation. The Webbs
shared this vision of conditional assistance to control the social and economic behaviour of the jobless. For this reason, they were against uncon-
ditional payments.[20] Churchill was radically opposed to their approach. To
his mind, unemployment insurance, like any other kind of insurance, had
to be based solely on premiums and not reflect any moral consideration
attempting to judge or influence individual behaviour. For Churchill, benefits could not be denied to a worker who was personally responsible for the
loss of employment, for example due to a problem with alcohol: "He has
paid his contributions; he has insured himself against the fact of unemployment and I think it arguable that his foresight should be rewarded
irrespective of the cause of his dismissal whether he lost his situation
through his own habits of intemperance or through his employer's habits
of intemperance. I do not like mixing up moralities and mathematics."[21]

Through the social insurance system, the unemployed applying for
benefits would not have to feel degraded anymore. Anyone who had contributed to the system was entitled to its benefits: "It is obviously contrary
to sense and justice to deprive the workman of the accommodation for
which he has paid. The power to change his situation for private reasons
when he chooses, and to be found another through the Labour Exchange,

drawing benefits meanwhile, is, in my judgment, a new freedom which he will have purchased; a freedom which, if abused, will quickly cease, and which, if not abused, will add to the self-respect and responsibility and independence of the worker ... The qualification for insurance must be actuarial. You qualify, we pay."[22]

The benefit was not charity anymore: it had become an entitlement. The conditions for exercising this right were stated – type of insurable employment, number of weeks worked, premium rate, et cetera – and the unemployed who met them would be entitled to benefits. However, for this to be a genuine right, claimants had to be able to take their case before a tribunal. And here the situation revealed the limits of the analogy with private insurance. Unlike what goes on in private insurance, the basis for this right to benefit stemmed not from a contract but from a statute. This made it imperative for the system to provide an appeal instance in which claimants could argue their rights. The act provided for an administrative tribunal made up of employer and worker representatives and chaired by an independent jurist. Beveridge and Llewellyn Smith attached a great deal of importance to this legal challenge mechanism.

However, the act did not contain rights alone: there were also claimant obligations that essentially reflected labour market management objectives. Also raised was the issue of voluntary unemployment, which enabled the system, despite its recognition of collective responsibility, to retain an element of the individual variety. It had to encourage people to keep their jobs if they were working and not refuse available work if they were jobless. This disciplinary role was one of the arguments to get employers to support the bill.[23] Over time, in fact, unemployment insurance would become a powerful workforce regulator.

The primary obligation that the act imposed on the insured was not to unduly cause the occurrence of the risk. The initial loss of employment should not be voluntary. And once entitlement was recognized, the claimant had to be available for work. After some lobbying by the trade unions, however, fearful that their members would be forced to accept jobs under conditions that did not meet union standards, this obligation was further defined. Workers would not be forced to accept jobs under working conditions inferior to those generally offered by the local market.[24] Similarly, they would not be forced to accept jobs that were vacant due to a labour dispute.

But before this obligation to be available arose, the claimant first had to prove that the loss of employment was involuntary. This issue involved a collision between two opposing ideas, both of them claiming to represent the insurance rationale. This debate, with Llewellyn Smith pitted against Churchill, was a high point in the discussions that accompanied the drafting of the bill. The reasoning developed on both sides, and the victory of the arguments against the unemployed, would have far-reaching ramifications for jobless rights.

Llewellyn Smith, arguing that the system should cover only economic unemployment, held that people who were voluntarily unemployed should not be entitled to benefits. But unlike the approach taken by the Poor Laws, his case was not founded on moralizing considerations: he was using actuarial logic. To his mind, it was impossible to assess and compensate unemployment that depended on personal factors.[25] In support of his position, he cited most of the trade union schemes, with their penalties for members who left jobs that met recognized union standards or were let go for misconduct. Churchill, who was fiercely opposed to the moralizing of the Poor Laws, advocated an automatic entitlement for claimants. As in private insurance, the workers' contributions entitled them to benefits. We should not wonder about the causes of contributors' unemployment but simply compensate them when the risk occurred. This meant that a worker who quit a job would be entitled to benefits. The same applied to a worker dismissed for cause: was it not the ultimate purpose of insurance to guard us against our mistakes? "Our concern is with the evil, not with the causes, with the fact of unemployment, not with the character of the unemployed. In my judgment, if a man has paid to the fund for six months he should have his benefit in all circumstances, including dismissal for personal fault even of the gravest character."[26]

For Churchill, a contributory system with a low benefit rate afforded sufficient protection against "moral hazard."[27] It would go against the logic of insurance to deny the right to benefit in these cases. His position was clearly bound to meet with opposition in the business community. Reaching Cabinet, the business viewpoint would finally win out: the final act contained a six-week disqualification in cases of voluntary leaving without just cause or dismissal for misconduct. This six-week period was chosen after a survey of jobs then available in the market. It was assumed that, if a worker had not found a new job after this time, the unemployment could no longer be ascribed to the termination: rather, it reflected poor labour market conditions.[28]

It was between these two poles, then (the right to benefit and the obligations of voluntary unemployment), that the legislative framework and jurisprudence for jobless rights would evolve.[29]

Like the penalties for voluntary leaving and dismissal for misconduct, the low benefit rate was a concession to the employers in return for their coming into the system. At seven shillings, the benefit proposed was lower than the average initial benefit of ten to twelve shillings paid out by unions at that time. The provision that prohibited workers involved in a labour dispute from collecting benefits was part of the same effort to sell the scheme to the bosses.[30]

If the disqualification for voluntary leaving and dismissal for misconduct reflected the insurance rationale with its obligation not to deliberately cause the occurrence of the risk, it was otherwise with the provision
disentitling claimants who had lost their jobs due to a labour dispute. In
these cases, the disqualification was collective, involving neither the insured's personal responsibility for unemployment nor the liability of the
parties to the dispute. Nonetheless, the refusal to pay benefits in such cases
owed much to the idea of voluntary unemployment. In fact, automatic
disqualification in labour disputes went back to a strike that had occurred
a decade earlier.

In 1898, miners from the Powell Duffryn Steam Coal Company at Merthyr
Tydfil in Wales walked off the job. A number of striking miners and other
mine workers would request and receive assistance from the local authority or "union" in charge of Poor Law relief. At the company's behest, the
attorney general went to court for an injunction to prohibit the union
from helping the strikers. The Court of Appeal ruled that able-bodied men
refusing to work due to the strike or for any other reason were not entitled
to the assistance provided by the Poor Laws. This judgment did say, however, that the strikers' families were still entitled to assistance.[31] This decision was a clear setback at the time.[32] The last-ditch relief dispensed by the
Poor Laws would now be subject to considerations beyond the person of
the applicant that had more to do with industrial power relationships.
Assistance was refused because of the strike's association with the concept
of voluntary unemployment. When the bill was debated, however, the
refusal to pay benefits during a labour dispute was not defended on these
grounds: a new principle came into play, that of government neutrality.

The unions supporting the government bill would end in reluctant
agreement with this provision. In penalizing unemployment due to labour
disputes, the new system differed appreciably from the one then used by
the trade unions, which actually paid higher benefits when unemployment was caused by a dispute.[33] The act categorized the unemployed,
and workers involved in labour disputes would no longer be entitled to
benefits.

To avoid repeating the mistakes of earlier experiments, the future system was to have a solid financial basis. The system was compulsory and
contributory, but by dint of caution its reach was limited to industry segments already largely covered by trade unions. The act applied only to
building and construction, shipbuilding, mechanical and metallurgical
industries, vehicle manufacturing, and sawmills. Finally, taking a cue from
the St. Gallen experience, the act provided that both worker and employer
contributions be collected by the employers.

The protection afforded by this system was relatively limited. A minimum twenty-six weeks of work over the past five years was required for

the right to benefit. Length of benefit depended on the number of full weeks of contributions: one week of benefit was payable for each period of five weeks of work, and a maximum fifteen weeks of benefit were provided for a complete year of work. Payment of these benefits was preceded by a one-week waiting period. The benefit level under the act was low: a flat rate of seven shillings. The variable wage-based rate would not be introduced until 1975.[34]

A number of the ideas found in the 1911 act were to crucially influence the future of the concept of unemployment insurance. First, the act explicitly recognized the right to benefit of an employee who had worked enough weeks in the industries covered before being laid off.[35] Second, it provided a right of appeal from the decisions of the insurance officer and set up administrative tribunals to rule on these appeals.[36]

A Court of Referees sitting in each district was made up of employer and employee representatives with a neutral chair who generally had some background in the law. The employee representative was elected by all of the insured persons in the district, the employer representative was chosen by the Board of Trade after consultation with employer associations, and the chair was appointed by the Board of Trade as well. The official who ruled on initial claims came under the authority of the Board of Trade, but this authority did not extend to the appeal instances: the minister could not interfere with their operation in any way. The senior level of appeal was to an umpire who enjoyed judicial independence and was responsible for stating the law – "a judge of a specialized kind, whose rulings bound the Court of Referees and from whom there was no appeal."[37]

A claimant who was dissatisfied with the insurance officer's ruling could appeal to the Court of Referees. If the officer's position was upheld at that level, the decision was final. However, if the court allowed the claimant's appeal, the officer could appeal to the umpire. Meanwhile, the regulations provided that a claimant winning his or her case in the Court of Referees would continue to collect benefits until a final decision was reached.[38] If the umpire reversed the court's decision, the claimant did not have to repay the benefits, since there was no legislative provision to this effect.[39] The umpire was also responsible for ruling on matters involving the insurability of employment.

Proof of availability for work was obtained by signing a register for this purpose at the labour exchange.[40] Breach of this obligation resulted in disqualification from benefit until the situation was rectified. The penalty for refusing suitable employment reflected the insured person's more general obligation to be available for work. The act's definition of "unsuitable" extended to jobs that were vacant due to a labour dispute or where conditions were inferior to those of the job that had determined the right to benefit. In 1927, this provision, thought to be overly generous, was amended to place a reasonable time limit on the right to refuse such employment.[41] Not until 1930 was refusal of suitable employment made subject to a maximum disqualification of six weeks instead of *sine die*.[42]

In cases of voluntary leaving and dismissal for misconduct, the British lawmakers of 1920 would replace this set six-week period with a discretionary disqualification ranging from one to six weeks.[43] And in 1934, the minimum disqualification period was reduced to one day,[44] later extended to a week in the British counterreform of 1995.[45]

Of all the provisions affecting the rights of the unemployed, disqualification due to a labour dispute was the one that sparked the liveliest debates in Parliament. In the initial bill, the claimant had to be directly involved in a strike or lockout to be disentitled: "A workman who loses employment by reason of a trade dispute involving a strike or lockout by which he is directly affected shall be disqualified for receiving unemployment benefit so long as the strike or lockout continues."[46]

When the bill came before the House of Commons, the government amended it considerably. The final text no longer referred to the claimant's direct involvement in the dispute. The Liberal government was now reaching beyond the workers directly involved in a dispute to include those taking part in sympathy strikes. Although they agreed with the general principle of disqualification, Labour MPs mounted an unsuccessful attack on the amendment. And an opposition amendment to qualify the use of disqualification in lockouts was rejected on the ground that it would be excessive to ask the insurance officer to rule on the merits of the employer's decision.[47] The final text made no distinction between strikes and lockouts: the use of disqualification was therefore very extensive.

This practice was defended on the ground of government neutrality in labour disputes. The reference to the idea of "trade dispute"[48] also allowed the claimant to refuse employment as a strike breaker, thereby legitimizing the disqualification rule: "This section [the one limiting the obligation to be available] is complementary to proviso (a) in section 86. Thus the Unemployment Fund cannot be used either to assist workmen to strike or to enable employers to procure strike breakers."[49] According to the commentators of the day, "When work is resumed any workman who is not taken back will be entitled to benefit."[50]

The refusal to consider the merits of the positions of the parties to a dispute would later attract a steady stream of criticism. In 1924, a Parliament now led by a Labour government passed a measure to water down the use of disqualification based on employer liability in a dispute.[51] Unfortunately, this provision would be short-lived:[52] the Conservatives hastily repealed it on returning to office in 1927.[53] Although government neutrality was also used to justify a claimant's freedom to refuse work as a strike breaker, it was actually much more useful to the employer interest. By refusing to question the merits of the parties' positions, the government chose to make the worker accountable for labour disputes. By refusing to question the parties' liability, the system worked automatically against the worker, whatever his or her responsibility may have been for the outbreak of the dispute. There was no consideration for the inequality of the opposing forces in most labour disputes.[54]

Moreover, since no attempt was made to find out whether the claimant was actually responsible for the unemployment, disqualification was incompatible with an insurance approach. How could this collective measure be reconciled with a social insurance program that had to rule on whether loss of employment was voluntary in every case? The worker contributing to the system was entitled to receive benefits as soon as the "social risk" of loss of employment occurred. To refuse the claim, the officer had to review the worker's responsibility for losing employment. In fact, except for the brief legislative episode of 1924, this factor was not taken into account in rulings on disqualification due to labour disputes. Similarly, how can we not see a parallel between this disqualification and the disqualification imposed in cases of voluntary leaving and dismissal for misconduct? The claimant with just cause to quit a job, or whose dismissal was not due to misconduct, would not be penalized. However, if the loss of employment was part of a work stoppage due to a labour dispute, the claimant was disqualified no matter what his or her responsibility for unemployment may have been.

The British system saw a number of amendments between 1911 and 1935.[55] In the latter year, a legislative consolidation[56] retained most of the provisions affecting voluntary unemployment, disqualification in the event of a labour dispute, and the appeal mechanism. This meant that the key elements of claimant rights in the 1911 act would also be in the system introduced to Canada in 1940. Moreover, the British system and the ideas that it embodied were not slow to make their influence felt internationally. Britain's contributory, compulsory version of UI would be imitated by many countries with very uneven levels of industrialization, including Poland (1924), Bulgaria (1925), Germany (1927), the United States (1935), and South Africa (1937).[57]

On the world scene, the International Labour Organization passed its 1919 Convention (no. 2) on unemployment,[58] which involved the obligation of contracting states to set up systems of public employment offices, and Recommendation (no. 1) Concerning Unemployment,[59] urging member states to organize systems of insurance against unemployment. As the first instrument of international law to set out certain minimum standards for the operation of systems of compensation for unemployment, the 1934 Convention (no. 44) on Unemployment[60] contains the main elements of claimant rights and responsibilities already present in the 1911 act, including the provisions for voluntary unemployment and labour disputes. So these international instruments, as references for governments wanting to set up such systems,[61] would ensure the influence of concepts initially developed in Britain's 1911 legislation.

Although the Canadian UI system would not come into force until 1940, the relationship to the British system was clear. The flow of information and even of advisors between the two countries would influence the passage of a UI scheme virtually identical to the British model. When developing the first unemployment insurance bill, which was passed in 1935, the architects of the Canadian system were briefed by their British counterparts on changes being considered in their own imminent reform of that year: the Canadian bill took these into account.[62]

Britain's 1911 legislation was essentially an administrative creation of the Board of Trade team. With its principles expressing a compromise between marketplace and state, the system apportioned the responsibility for unemployment and its compensation among government, employers, and workers. Although the 1911 act recognized rights to the jobless, it also imposed a set of claimant obligations that were mainly concerned to penalize voluntary unemployment and legitimized by the responsibility of all insured persons not to deliberately cause the occurrence of the risk. These initial concepts around which claimant rights and obligations were organized would later be incorporated almost unaltered into the Canadian UI system.

3
Developing a Canadian System

The introduction of a UI scheme raises two major questions for any government – first, the type of unemployment that it wants to compensate and, second, the system with which it wants to do it. The first has to do with the country's economic structure and, specifically, the status of its labour market, while the second centres on the system's organization and its legal and, ultimately, constitutional face. In Canada, these issues would reflect a very special focus.

The Canada of the early twentieth century had particular qualities that set it apart from the Britain of the day. Its harsh climate made seasonal unemployment a significant feature of the Canadian labour market. Yet its constitutional status undoubtedly set the Canadian experience apart even more. Although the Canadian constitution gave provinces jurisdiction over matters of civil law and help for the indigent, the federal government was the level with the bulk of the financial resources. Very early, and until the UI system was introduced in 1940, the same questions kept coming up. What level of government was to be responsible for the unemployed? What level was to bear the cost of compensating them?

Although the influence of the British model was being felt in Canada by 1914, it was only with the crisis of the 1930s that the debate on UI really got under way. Joblessness was reaching record levels, and its persistence was a reproach to laissez-faire economics. In these years, however, Prime Ministers R.B. Bennett and Mackenzie King in turn cited constitutional problems as justifying a waiting game in the matter of unemployment insurance.

Unions and jobless groups kept calling for unemployment insurance, and employers, though divided, kept opposing the idea. Recognizing the influence and popularity of the US New Deal, however, Bennett would radically change his tone to opt for an interventionist economic policy that included the establishment of a UI system.

Climate has played a predominant role in the development of Canada's economy. The country has seasonal periods of inactivity in a number of economic sectors such as agriculture, fisheries, and forestry. Historically, large numbers of workers have regularly gone jobless for the winter months. In fact, seasonal unemployment was the main cause of poverty in the Canadian economy of the first half of the nineteenth century.[1] At the same time, Canada's industrial development lagged somewhat compared with the United States, due mainly to the country's overdependence on exports. Until the Second World War, the whole Canadian economy was reliant on work done outdoors, making seasonal joblessness a national characteristic.

Other types of unemployment were also present in Canada at that time. Considering the complexity of the phenomenon, we may usefully look at a few subsets of the general concept.[2]

The term "structural unemployment" is used when there is a connection with perennial features of an economy or economic sector. It can surface cyclically or in a swirl of economic restructuring when an activity has become impossible or demand for its products has ceased. For example, the declining activity in the Canadian textile industry stems from restructuring due to competition from developing countries. Under free trade, the outcome is the relocation of businesses to countries where the labour component is a lot cheaper. "Conjunctural unemployment" arises in episodes of adversity such as recessions. Some sectors may be more affected than others by an economic slowdown. For example, sagging purchasing power in a recession may have negative repercussions on industries such as home building. Finally, "frictional unemployment" is the result of an imbalance in labour supply and demand. In fact, William Henry Beveridge saw unemployment as the result of a poor link between labour supply and production requirements.[3] The term "frictional unemployment" is used today to describe the period of inactivity between the time that someone leaves a job and the time that he or she has another one. This unemployment is often seen as normal because it is inherent in the freedom of the individual, as an "economic player," to choose work.

Seasonal unemployment bears a natural resemblance to structural unemployment, though conjunctural factors, especially those affecting demand for finished goods, can modify its extent. For example, the Canadian hotel industry, its activities often seasonal anyway, might be further hit by reduced consumer purchasing power in a recession. Typical of the Canadian economy, seasonal employment and unemployment would be a constant concern for both the designers and the administrators of a Canadian UI system.[4] Even today, despite the fact that Canada is an industrialized country, seasonal unemployment affects a significant percentage of its workforce and several of its regions.[5]

As in Britain, however, it was industrialization with its growing appetite for labour that, paradoxically, unleashed the first massive waves of unemployment on Canada and prompted governments to rethink their approach to this problem. Industrial development came with generalized urbanization in which country folk, drawn by the hope of better times, settled in cities close to job-creating factories. The thirst for workers would also bring major influxes of immigrants.

This new population of wage earners was typified by economic dependence that was heightened by the concentration of workforces in bigger and bigger businesses. The shutdown of a large company impacts a large number of workers. The interdependence among the various economic sectors would increase this insecurity. Vulnerability to unemployment became increasingly collective. When the first major convulsions appeared in this industrial economy, the result was massive unemployment that reached a peak on the eve of the First World War. In January 1914, according to Wilfrid Laurier, the leader of the Liberal opposition in Ottawa, Canada had more than 100,000 unemployed people.[6]

At that time, assistance to victims of unemployment was handled locally. True to our Poor Laws heritage, unemployment and the attendant poverty were primarily individual responsibilities. It was therefore up to the private sector to solve the problems of poverty induced by unemployment. The family, then the local community (i.e., the municipality or parish), had to take care of the poor. These local institutions were under provincial jurisdiction. When industrial unemployment made its appearance, however, the economic system became accountable. As in Britain, the central government was asked to help contain the damage, including the impoverishment of the working class.[7] And, as a result, the idea of an unemployment insurance scheme began to make headway in the political class. Drawing on the British experience, Newton Rowell, then Liberal opposition leader in the Ontario legislature, called in 1914 for the creation of a public labour exchange system with unemployment insurance. The federal government, however, refused to take any responsibility for unemployment. For Prime Minister Robert Borden, solutions to this problem fell under the jurisdiction of the provinces.

However, high prewar unemployment levels made people fear the worst for the period after demobilization. The Ontario government was moved to set up a commission of inquiry on unemployment whose report would not be published until 1916,[8] when the economic stimulation generated by the war effort had made unemployment a much less urgent problem. The commission resisted the idea of introducing a UI system based on the British model. This was seen as a rash move: at that time, Canada had nothing in the way of labour exchanges or statistical data on employment and unemployment. Instead, the Ontario commission recommended borrowing from Ghent, where the government funded private systems managed by volunteer associations – generally, unions – for their memberships. This meant that the vast majority of workers would be left unprotected. Except for the establishment of a provincial network of public employment offices, the Ontario report had little sequel. It did represent an advance, however, in the way that unemployment was perceived as an inherent problem of industrialization: "For unemployment resulting from trade depression, or the temporary dislocation of business, workingmen are not responsible."[9]

The First World War contributed to the growing role of government in the Canadian economy. Laissez-faire had yielded for a time to an economy in which the government had become a major player. When hostilities ended, however, demobilization and the ensuing economic slowdown made the authorities more than concerned. The rise of revolutionary movements and their seizure of power in Russia helped to fuel apprehension.[10]

Concerned that unemployment swollen by demobilization might result in unrest, the federal government passed legislation in 1918 to create a national network of public employment offices.[11] Half of the cost of these offices, which came under provincial authority, was funded by the federal government, which also provided coordination. Here was the first federal involvement in manpower issues. This initiative, though responding to a particular conjuncture – the problem of returning veterans – was nonetheless an initial step toward introducing UI. Its first director was Bryce Stewart, a liberal economist and Beveridge convert hired by the Department of Labour in 1914. He saw the new service as presaging a general system to combat unemployment, including an unemployment insurance system.

The year 1919 was marked by a series of events that would propel the notion of unemployment insurance into the political limelight. First, a Canadian delegation including Newton Rowell, now a member of Prime Minister Borden's Union government, went to Washington for the opening conference of the International Labour Organization. Canada voted with the majority at that conference for a recommendation that governments actively encourage the introduction of unemployment insurance schemes.[12] They could take the form of government plans, as in Britain, or state-subsidized systems, as in Ghent.[13] At home, meanwhile, the country was gripped by political agitation. The working class protested the rapid rise in the cost of living while wages stagnated. With high unemployment due to demobilization and the postwar economic slowdown, strikes and lockouts came in rapid succession. This turmoil would peak with the Winnipeg General Strike. Although their demands did not include unemployment insurance, the Winnipeg strikers called for a six-hour working day in industries affected by layoffs.[14]

In the wake of the strike, Ottawa created a royal commission of inquiry on industrial relations with a mandate to deal with worker agitation. Testifying before this commission, union representatives called for an unemployment insurance system funded wholly by employers. The commission's majority report recommended the establishment of a government social insurance system to cover various social risks, unemployment included.[15]

A few weeks after the commission published its report, the first national convention of the Liberal Party of Canada endorsed the principle of a UI system. This policy move breathed the influence of Mackenzie King, already a dominant party figure. A former labour relations advisor to the Rockefeller empire,[16] King had published a book the year before in which he explored industrial disputes from a moral perspective. The unemployment insurance issue was summarily canvassed in that book: "Insurance against unemployment recognizes that an isolated human being, not less than a machine, must be cared for when idle."[17]

The plan for an unemployment insurance system also began to build solid public support.[18] Prime Minister Borden asked the Department of Labour to look into the feasibility of such a scheme. A draft system resembling the 1911 British version was submitted to the government in 1920. However, there were doubts about its constitutionality. Had Parliament not recognized, in its 1918 act concerning the public employment offices, provincial jurisdiction in labour force management?

The advisors to the federal Department of Justice decided that the plan was constitutional. In their view, federal jurisdiction stemmed from the treaty-making power. Jurisdiction would also derive from the social clauses of the Treaty of Versailles that Canada had signed as a dominion of the British Empire. According to these jurists, the constitutionality of such a system could also be founded on the power of Parliament to make laws for the peace, order, and good government of Canada. Not until 1928 would the department change its constitutional ruling. Testifying at that time before the House of Commons Committee on Industrial and International Relations, Deputy Minister Edwards opined that contributory social insurance systems came under the domain of property and civil rights and thus under the provinces.[19] The committee, while supporting an unemployment insurance system in principle, deferred to the Department of Justice and confirmed provincial jurisdiction in this matter. Its report was to receive unanimous approval by the House of Commons in 1929.[20]

The prehistory of effective unemployment insurance in Canada was one of dodging responsibility, and Canadian federalism might as well have been crafted for this purpose. In 1920, Borden resigned and was succeeded by Arthur Meighen as prime minister and Conservative leader. Meighen would try to rid himself of his predecessor's entanglement in the unemployment problem. This was no easy task, however: postwar Ottawa was already involved in assisting the unemployed. Demobilization found a lot of soldiers joining the jobless ranks, and the municipalities had to take care of them. In view of concerns about agitation voiced by authorities in some cities, the federal government agreed to provide assistance to these ex-soldiers during the winter of 1919-20 through a veterans' organization called the Patriotic Fund. Come the following winter, the problem survived intact, but there was no repetition of the direct assistance. This time, arguing that the unemployment was being generated by a postwar recession, the Meighen government agreed to defray one-third of the costs borne by municipalities for that winter's jobless assistance.[21] The government was saving money, since this plan was much cheaper than its predecessor, but it was still an important precedent: for the first time in North America, a nonlocal government admitted a financial liability for the jobless.

Meighen was in a dilemma. He wanted to reduce Ottawa's financial involvement in assistance to the unemployed, but he also wanted to court the voters. Therefore, a few months before the 1921 election, his government, while renewing its contribution to the jobless winter fund, charted the new course of federal policy. Ottawa's commitment was only temporary for the conjuncture: unemployment was and remained a municipal and provincial responsibility. This policy would be renewed by his successor.

In December of the same year, in fact, the new Liberal Party leader, Mackenzie King, was elected as the head of a minority government. To govern, he had to rely on the support of sixty-five MPs under the Progressive banner. They basically represented the interests of the rural community, not supportive of assistance to the unemployed and even less supportive of unemployment insurance. The sole exception in their political agenda was made for government assistance to people whose unemployment was due to the end of hostilities.[22] King's policy on unemployment would reflect the new parliamentary configuration.

For these rural representatives, largely unaware of the problem of industrial unemployment, assistance encouraged the unemployed to refuse farm work for wages seen as too low. The help would then have the effect of creating ... unemployment! Obviously, these positions would buttress the opposition to social measures in the business community.[23] On the unemployment insurance issue, the business people actually went one better. According to them, UI would rule out any competition with the United States, which was not saddled with such a system.

As a result, despite the Liberal commitment to create an insurance system, King would continue Meighen's move to back off on unemployment. In 1922, he convened a federal-provincial conference on unemployment that concluded the federal commitment was merely conjunctural in an area of provincial jurisdiction. With the end of the postwar period, Ottawa terminated its financial support to the unemployed in the summer of

1922. Continuing Meighen's policy over the decade that followed, King would refuse any responsibility for this issue, insisting that it was primarily a matter for the provinces. The timely about-face by the Department of Justice in 1928 before the House of Commons Committee on Industrial and International Relations enabled King to come out in favour of unemployment insurance in principle while struggling free of any responsibility for giving it effect. The ball was now in the provincial court.

Another outcome of the federal withdrawal was that the budget of the Employment Service fell significantly between 1922 and 1924. It stopped doing research on unemployment. In 1922, its director, Bryce Stewart, left his job to do research in the United States, where he would play an active role in setting up the American UI system. He did not come back to Canada until 1939, to work as deputy minister of labour to establish the Canadian model.

In fact, King's inertia on unemployment suited the ideological mood of the period. The early 1920s found the working class at a low ebb. Worker agitation had more or less collapsed, and the socialist threat presented by the Winnipeg General Strike had melted away. Everyone went back to business as usual. The mild aspirations to state interventionism conjured up by the British example were succeeded by a wave of conservatism that scoured the whole North American continent. Plans to introduce unemployment insurance would feel its effects in both the United States[24] and Canada.

Less state control and more room for the marketplace: Canada's federal government, which had seen substantial growth during the war, had to resume more modest dimensions. The market viewed unemployment insurance as more counterproductive government meddling: unemployment would ultimately end if the market economy was left to operate unimpeded.

In this ideological context, the workers' movement had serious difficulty making its case. It would have a chance, however, in the 1928 hearings of the House of Commons Committee on Industrial and International Relations. While voicing his preference for a federal scheme in which provinces could participate, CTCC[25] president Pierre Beaulé commented that, if a province refused to join the program, Ottawa should go ahead with a system that it would fund with the employers and employees.[26] The president of the TLCC,[27] Tom Moore, was also in favour of federally administered UI. The system would be funded initially by the employers, but, in view of the fact that it shared the responsibility for the employment situation, the government could contribute as well. This insurance would not require worker contributions: obliging workers to contribute would be tantamount to making them pay twice, since they already participated in production on the same basis as their employers.

The social insurance system would confer a right to benefit on workers even if they did not contribute.[28]

Although unemployment remained a significant problem during the 1920s,[29] it would not be a major concern for politicians until 1929, when an economic crisis broke out on an astonishing scale. In the years 1929-33, Canada's gross domestic product plummeted from $6.2 billion to $3.5 billion.[30] The numbers of unemployed wage earners went from 107,000 in 1929 to 341,000 in 1930 and reached a record 646,000 in 1933,[31] when nearly 15 percent of the population was relying on unemployment assistance programs.[32] Unemployment and poverty were generalized and penetrating new social strata. Even the provident would ultimately be obliged to go begging when their savings ran out.

The crisis hit as a challenge to the laissez-faire credo. Yet free-enterprise principles had deep roots in America. Politicians such as US president Hoover maintained an unshakable confidence in capitalism. For them, the crisis was ephemeral, and the economic mill would start up again on its own. The Hoover administration refused overinvolvement in the economy, preferring to go after a balanced budget. As the crisis and unemployment worsened, however, there were demonstrations in a number of US cities, often led by Communists.[33] Despite growing agitation, Hoover stuck to his guns. But his successful opponent in the 1932 presidential campaign, F.D. Roosevelt, had understood the turmoil that was overwhelming the American people. He offered them a "new deal" that included a number of interventionist measures, unemployment insurance among them.

In Canada, the 1930 election handed power to new Conservative leader R.B. Bennett. A lawyer identified with the business community,[34] Bennett still grasped, better than King did, the voters' sensitivity to the effects of the crisis. On the hustings, he proclaimed that unemployment was now a national issue and promised to give the unemployed jobs instead of relief. Despite the hopes enticed by his victory, however, Bennett's response to the unemployment problem was appreciably the same as King's: both men subscribed to the same ideology. Admittedly, Bennett said in April 1931 that his government would soon be submitting an unemployment insurance model,[35] but the plan would not move ahead until 1935. Like US president Hoover, Bennett saw the crisis as ephemeral. So Ottawa's position went unchanged: no direct intervention in an area of provincial responsibility.

To confront the political disaster created by the Depression, Bennett, like Bismarck before him, adopted the strategy of the carrot and the stick. With one hand, he gave money to the provinces for their jobless assistance programs; with the other, he took savage action against any who threatened to disturb the social peace.

At first, since the crisis was assumed to be temporary, federal funding to unemployed assistance programs took emergency form. In 1930, Parliament passed an initial stopgap piece of legislation[36] to fund locally operated relief and public works programs. The act was careful to define unemployment as a provincial and municipal responsibility: this new funding did not portend that Ottawa was assuming new constitutional obligations.

Then the crisis began to have its effects on the finances of municipalities and provincial governments. The recession gave them less income with which to shoulder increasingly heavy costs, especially for assistance to the unemployed. Their treasuries were severely stressed,[37] and this problem affected their credit in financial circles. In 1932, following a federal-provincial conference, the government passed legislation that made a priority of funding direct assistance. The "dole," which required a means test, was cheaper than public works programs. Given the scale of the recession, this policy would loom large in the years 1932-36.[38] Payouts were small, often in the form of coupons. Coupled with the means test, these handouts were perceived as humiliating and stigmatizing by the unemployed. Although he had promised work and not charity, Bennett took precisely the opposite tack.

As the crisis dragged on, these federal measures began to wear an air of permanence.[39] The federal commitment to these programs was also dictated by fear of political unrest. With this inadequate response, however, more and more of the jobless were wandering the country on freight cars to look for work. Their numbers were growing steadily, and they were highly receptive to revolutionary ideas. The cities complained about these people, who were not their ratepayers but their responsibility nonetheless. To solve the problem, governments created work camps that both assuaged the cities and isolated the unemployed. The camps were intended for young unmarried males, homeless and broke.[40] Although they were not forced to live in them, these men would be disqualified for any government assistance if they did not. In 1931, the first work camps were seen in British Columbia. The federal government set up its own network the next year under Department of National Defence control, and it would continue to operate until 1936. In 1935, these camps held more than 20,000 unemployed, 1,900 of them at Valcartier, Quebec, alone. Their military setting and marginal living conditions were not appreciated by these denizens. With their pay of twenty cents a day, "they felt they were in concentration camps doing forced labour."[41]

All of these measures were clearly going to arouse opposition. The jobless banded together to defend their interests. The 1930s saw no fewer than nine such associations founded in Saskatoon alone.[42] A number of jobless groups also made their appearance in Quebec. The movement grew, and several cities saw unemployed demonstrations. Not all of these associations were led by Communist militants, but they were in the forefront of activity.[43]

Nationally, the CCF[44] and especially the CPC[45] harnessed this discontent. The crisis quadrupled CPC membership to some 16,000 by 1933. Its contribution to the jobless struggle was twofold. First, the Communists created organizations of workers and the unemployed to build resistance and solidarity in these groups. The Worker's Unity League was founded, then the National Unemployed Worker's Association addressed specifically to the unemployed. Jobless demonstrations staged by Communists were frequently broken up. Second, the Communists developed political positions to oppose the dominant messages about the crisis and unemployment. The Worker's Unity League drew up a model plan called the Working Class Unemployment Insurance Bill. Its noncontributory funding would come from a tax on wealth and transfers from military budgets. People with annual incomes of more than $5,000 would pay a progressive tax to fund the plan. It would guarantee universal coverage to the unemployed, with no waiting period. The plan even included maternity benefits. It would basically be run by unions and jobless committees.[46] Communist organizations stirred up a lot of solidarity behind this demand. It was part of a petition that travelled across Canada in the spring of 1931, collecting more than 94,000 signatures before it was finally handed to Prime Minister Bennett.

The CCF's involvement was very different. This party had MPs who brought the unemployment debate to Parliament. Its platform included dismantling the unemployed camps and establishing noncontributory social insurance with coverage to include the risk of unemployment. In the House of Commons, CCF leader J.S. Woodsworth, having called for a contributory plan in 1932, would be advocating a noncontributory system in 1935.[47]

From 1933 on, the UI debate turned up more regularly on the government's order paper. Pressure grew, especially from the working class. The TLCC and CTCC declared their support for a contributory scheme funded by workers, employers, and the government and "preferably" created within the federal government apparatus.[48] Appointed by the Quebec government as the crisis broke, the Social Insurance Commission chaired by Édouard Montpetit came to the identical conclusion on pragmatic grounds. The commission saw it as imperative, if unemployment insurance were to come under the provincial authority, to harmonize provincial schemes and rule out unfair competition between provinces over the level of employer contributions. Yet the simultaneous establishment of provincial schemes seemed highly improbable, if not impossible. These considerations prompted the Montpetit Commission to come out in favour of a federal system as well. Meanwhile, pressure for unemployment insurance was also coming from other circles. Canada's western provinces, where the crisis hit particularly hard, were in deep financial difficulty. In addition to more federal funding, they called for the creation of unemployment insurance to reduce the assistance paid out to the jobless.

Although the unions were generally supportive of unemployment insurance, the employer associations, despite a small fraction that approved the principle, were opposed. The spearhead of this opposition was the Canadian Manufacturers' Association.[49] As the Depression dragged on, however, opposition to unemployment insurance in the business community began to crumble. There was concern about the repercussions of provincial indebtedness on Canada's credit. The banks came to look favourably on a measure that, enlisting employers and employees, would alleviate the financial burden on municipalities and provinces. Merchant associations also came out in favour of UI.[50]

A federal-provincial conference was called in January 1933. On unemployment insurance, Bennett asked the provinces if they would agree to waive their jurisdiction in that area and were prepared to participate financially in such a system. When Premier Taschereau of Quebec wondered about the potential cost, Bennett replied that no plan had yet been worked out. Speaking in support of his proposal, he maintained the only reason that warranted setting up an unemployment insurance system was Canada's determination to honour its commitments under the Treaty of Versailles. With arguments as thin as this, Quebec and Ontario declined to back a constitutional amendment.

In the summer of 1933, Bennett and the clerk of the Privy Council, R.K. Finlayson, went off to the Imperial Economic Conference in London, where they canvassed the unemployment insurance issue with senior officials from the British Ministry of Labour. The prime minister came home convinced that such a system was feasible in Canada and prepared to draft UI legislation. He presented his plan to the business community as the lesser evil in view of the revolutionary threat. The ideological bias of the move was glaringly obvious. Here is how Bennett broached the plan to Sir Thomas White, then president of the Canadian Bank of Commerce:[51] "Great Britain has avoided revolution when other countries have had to face practically civil war, because Great Britain is so far ahead of other countries in socialist legislation. I am not unmindful of the differences between Great Britain and Canada, but I have not forgotten the circumstances under which Bismarck introduced the legislation in Germany and the effect of such legislation in Australia."[52]

The team assembled to draft the bill was made up of R.K. Finlayson; F.G. Price, a British official retained as a consultant; A.D. Watson, the government's chief actuary; H. Wolfenden, a consulting actuary; and Leonard Marsh, a well-known economist, a McGill University researcher, and an authority on unemployment statistics.[53] The dominant figures on the team, actuaries Watson and Wolfenden, were there to safeguard the "solid financial basis" of the future scheme. The draft bill was completed in April 1934. Few amendments would be made before it became the Employment and Social Insurance Act[54] of 1935.

Bennett convened a new federal-provincial conference for the fall of 1934. In August, he sent his provincial counterparts a letter in which he announced the main item on the agenda: "Are the provinces prepared to surrender their exclusive jurisdiction over legislation dealing with such social problems as old-age pensions, unemployment and social insurance, hours and conditions for work, minimum wages, etc. to the Dominion Parliament? If so, on what terms and conditions?"[55] Following some by-election losses, however, Bennett decided that he now lacked sufficient public support, cancelled the conference, and opted for another strategy.

The year 1935 was decisive for Bennett's unemployment insurance plans. US president F.D. Roosevelt was riding high on his social legislation. Having found on taking office in March 1933 that the crisis had reached catastrophic proportions, with a number of banks closed down, one-quarter of the American population jobless, and unemployed relief organizations completely swamped,[56] he had moved swiftly on his election promises. The many laws passed in the first 100 days of his administration included reforms of the banking sector and labour relations. And to persuade the voters of the merits of his policies, Roosevelt spoke to them directly in "fireside" radio talks. Half-term elections in April 1934 confirmed the popularity of his New Deal policy. In early 1935, a bill that encompassed a number of social security measures, including unemployment insurance, was tabled in the House of Representatives and became law in August of that year.[57] The voting in favour of the bill in both the House of Representatives (371 to 3) and the Senate (76 to 6) reflected the measure's hold on public opinion.

Canadian prime minister Bennett ended by taking an interest in President Roosevelt's New Deal. His brother-in-law, W.D. Herridge, whom he had made ambassador to Washington, tried to persuade him to buy into the policy as a way of staying in power. Noting the New Deal's popularity with the American people, Bennett decided to take this advice, and his conversion was dramatic. Like Paul on the road to Damascus, Bennett abruptly discovered the glories of the interventionist state and progressive social legislation. Laissez-faire had failed: now he had to move fast. Emulating Roosevelt's style, Bennett addressed the Canadian public in a series of radio talks in early January 1935. For the man in the street, his message was surprising, to say the least, coming from an unbridled capitalist. In one of these talks, he said, "And, in my mind, reform means government intervention. It means the end of laissez-faire. Reform heralds certain recovery. There can be no permanent recovery without reform. Reform or no reform! I raise that issue squarely. I nail the flag of progress to the masthead. I summon the power of the State to its support."[58]

When Parliament convened on 17 January 1935, Bennett expanded on this in the speech from the throne:

> In the anxious years through which you have passed, you have been the witnesses of grave defects and abuses in the capitalist system. Unemployment and want are the proof of these. Great changes are taking place. New conditions prevail. These require modifications in the capitalist system to enable that system more effectively to serve the people. Reform measures will therefore be submitted to you as part of a comprehensive plan designed to remedy the social and economic injustices now prevailing, and to ensure to all classes and to all parts of the country a greater degree of equality in the distribution of the benefits of the capitalist system.[59]

The apostle of laissez-faire was transformed into the nemesis of capitalism. Defending his initiative from a constitutional standpoint, Bennett, while acknowledging the formal jurisdiction of the provinces, asserted that Parliament could pass this legislation under its powers to make laws for Canada's "peace, order and good government." He also cited the jurisdiction conferred on the federal government, as representing a dominion of the British Empire, by the social clauses of the 1919 Treaty of Versailles.

Meanwhile, the political turmoil went on. The marginal living conditions in the work camps made them hotbeds of unrest. The Communists had created an organization, the Relief Camp Worker's Union (RCWU), specifically to defend their unemployed inhabitants.[60] On 4 April 1935, a strike broke out in the BC camps, with demands that included a noncontributory UI system. Getting no response from the authorities, the strike leaders set out on 30 May to tighten the pressure on the federal government: this was the On to Ottawa March. Climbing aboard freight cars, the marchers paused in a number of cities, where they were welcomed by sympathizers. As the march progressed, the numbers grew. From 1,000 leaving Vancouver, they were 2,000 when they reached Regina. Bennett looked for an excuse to end this march, which was getting too much publicity. On 22 June, however, under pressure from CCF MPs, he agreed to meet two delegates of the marchers, then in Regina. His attitude was arrogant, the meeting was cut short, and the marchers' representatives left empty-handed. The justice minister, however, issued strict orders to the RCMP to prevent the striker mob from getting to Ottawa. A rally staged in a Regina park was upset by the preventive arrest of the leaders, who were supposed to speak. A riot broke out in which a plainclothes police officer was killed and about fifty people injured. Bennett's and Justice Minister Guthrie's instigator roles were painfully obvious. But in truth, the On to Ottawa March had petered out anyway.

Although repressing the militant jobless, Bennett did propose an unemployment insurance scheme. He counted on this to win over part of the workers' movement while undermining the Communist influence that he did not discount. He defended his new policy to a representative of the business community: "[Communist leader] Tim Buck has today a very strong position in the province of Ontario and he openly demands the abolition of the capitalist system. A good deal of pruning is sometimes necessary to save a tree and it would be well for us in Canada to remember that there is considerable pruning to be done if we want to preserve the fabric of the capitalist system."[61]

Bennett's New Deal ushered Canada into a new era of state interventionism. The Canadian initiative, like the US New Deal, was consistent with an ideology that commanded support in more and more industrialized countries. Influenced by Keynes, politicians were discovering the economic stimulator role that various types of government intervention could play. Public works policies would again be priorities because of their effect on sustaining demand. The same applied to income security programs, including UI: "The current singling out of unemployment insurance for government attention in many countries is dictated by the appalling costs of direct relief and the hope that unemployment insurance benefits will give some protection to public treasuries in future depressions and will, by sustaining purchasing power, tend to mitigate these depressions."[62] In addition to creating an unemployment insurance system, Bennett's program included legislation for a minimum wage, limits on working hours, and the weekly rest period, all of which was passed.[63]

The 1935 Employment and Social Insurance Act was passed by the Commons with the support of all but three MPs[64] – an indication of the public support for the measure. Although Mackenzie King voted for the bill, he maintained that the system fell within the jurisdiction of the provinces. As it happened, public opinion did not swallow Bennett's political conversion. People sensed political opportunism instead. Bennett would have to yield power to King in that year's election. And one of the victor's first official acts would be to refer all of the New Deal legislation to the Supreme Court.

Although the prevailing political mood of our neighbours to the south had had something to do with Bennett's decision to offer his homemade New Deal, his actual UI bill drew on the existing British legislation. In contrast to the United States, where the employers waded into the debate to push for solutions that maximized their role and minimized state intervention, the discussions in Canada began with the idea of a government system and dealt mainly with matters of detail. While acknowledging the role of the state, the Bennett team tried to limit its influence, for example by insisting on the need to put the future scheme on a "solid actuarial basis." Yet the reference to the British model was never in doubt; nor was the government's responsibility in the battle against unemployment. Introduced in a federal political framework, the 1935 act was not destined to survive the review of its constitutionality ordered by King's government.

The significance of US influence on the later development of the Canadian system, the geographic proximity of the United States, and the economic rivalry between the two countries give us reason to dwell on the context in which the American unemployment insurance system was enacted. In that country, the UI debate gained impetus with the Depression and intensified in the shadow of the legislation promised by Roosevelt. However, some US states had already seen attempts to set up insurance schemes drawing on the British experience.[65] The Massachusetts legislature had debated a bill to this effect in 1916[66] that was rejected in large part because of its compulsory nature, seen as too coercive for employers. Behind this and other US initiatives was an academic reform group called the American Association for Labor Legislation (AALL) that wanted to adapt European-style social insurance models for home use.

In the early 1920s, the AALL revised its unemployment protection demands. Thereafter, it campaigned not for British-style social insurance but for a prevention-based system that gave employers a central role in system management as well as risk prevention. The AALL's change of tone in favour of an unemployment insurance scheme framed primarily for the employers instead of the jobless was influenced by the shift in the play of political forces that occurred in both the US and Canada during the early 1920s: "This about turn was typical of the political defeat of 'progressivism' and the success of the employer offensive that put an end to the social crises of the immediate postwar period."[67] Modelled on workmen's compensation schemes, this idea of "prevention" involved stabilizing production and employment. That stabilization could be achieved by setting up an unemployment fund in each business for the employer to pay benefits to its laid-off employees. The approach was inspired by experiments conducted by "progressive" employers wanting to stabilize their workforces. It was characterized as a workforce management device in an industrial strategy for modern big business.

It should be remembered that, at the time, even wheeler-dealer US union leaders such as Samuel Gompers opposed unemployment insurance.[68] The American Federation of Labor's 1932 convention condemned UI as "contrary to our way of life."[69]

After a number of attempts and some tinkering with the initial concept, a law reflecting the prevention theory was passed by the State of Wisconsin in 1932.[70] It obliged employers to form "unemployment reserves" with individual accounts into which each employer paid compulsory contribu-tions. When an account reached a certain level, the employer could stop paying contributions so long as it did not have to pay out benefits to its workers. The system was wholly funded by the employers, and beyond a minimum level the amount of contributions was based on actual layoffs.[71] This variable contribution system would later be dubbed "experience rat-ing" or "merit rating." These features of private insurance – contributions paid only by employers to reflect a philosophy of individual responsibility for unemployment and a variable contribution (premium) rate based on the risk represented by each employer – would become the pillars of US unemployment insurance legislation.

The prevention theory made unemployment an individual problem to be managed by each employer, with the state playing a very secondary role. Identified with the Wisconsin experiment, this theory would be chal-lenged by a school of thought that called for a return to the fundamentals of social insurance. In 1932, a commission appointed by the governor of Ohio called for a state-run fund with contributions from employers and employees.[72] It also suggested that the government operate an employ-ment service. Unlike the Wisconsin system, this one would give insured workers the right to benefit regardless of their employers' contributions, thus creating a "general right of the unemployed on the fund."[73] In this insurance approach, obviously, unemployment became a social problem exceeding the responsibility of just the employer.

Let us note, however, that, for all their differing approaches, the pre-vention and insurance theories exhibited a number of similarities: the employer's obligation to pay into a reserve fund, the lack of public dollars in the system, and, finally, comparable contributions and compensation. The noteworthy difference between the two doctrines had to do with con-trol of the system. Whereas, in the prevention theory, the employer paid only for its employees, in the insurance system it contributed without dis-tinction for all potential claimants. These two concepts would dominate the American debate, and the US federal bill of 1935 contained elements of both.

Coincidentally with this debate on the form of a future unemployment insurance scheme, a movement arose demanding unemployment com-pensation based on a right to work. Demonstrations across the country called on governments to fight unemployment and compensate its vic-tims.[74] In 1931, a national march organized by Unemployed Councils close to the American Communist Party campaigned for noncontributory unemployment compensation.[75] As in Canada, the Unemployed Councils played a major role in the movement. In 1934, Ernest Lundeen, a con-gressman from the Farmer-Labor Party of Minnesota,[76] tabled his Lundeen Bill,[77] which in many ways resembled the one promoted in Canada by the

Worker's Unity League. It called for a noncontributory unemployment compensation system locally administered by committees of the jobless and farmers. The bill was the subject of hearings before a subcommittee of the House of Representatives Labor Committee[78] but was ultimately defeated despite its public appeal.[79] Although it stood as proof that substantial elements of the union movement and unemployed organizations were opposed to a payroll-funded unemployment insurance plan, the Lundeen Bill had no sequel.

Among US employers, positions changed quickly as federal legislative intervention became inevitable. This group had always favoured voluntary action to deal with the unemployment problem, but beginning in 1933 the employer organizations were simply trying to see that the future system was drawn up in the way most consistent with their interests. They were opposed to a uniform national system and pleaded for the least coercive standards possible for the states that would have to run it. In the months leading up to the passage of the federal legislation, some employer organizations failed in an attempt to have the bill include a compulsory employee contribution. However, they said they were satisfied with the freedom left to states to use contribution methods of the experience-rating variety.[80]

Although the Social Security Act was a product of compromise by the social stakeholders as well as the experts and politicians who had a hand in its development, it also reflected its constitutional setting. Like Canada, the United States was a federal country. Setting up a system there involved the same dilemma: should the system be under federal jurisdiction or be run cooperatively by both levels of government? For the bill's framers and the politicians, the final text had to be as immune as possible from a court challenge to its constitutionality. Some Supreme Court decisions against early New Deal legislation[81] made constitutionality a core issue. This problem pointed to the use of a federal law to frame a system managed by the states:

> Everyone assumed that the Court would cast a skeptical eye on any unemployment insurance law that centered great power in the federal government at the expense of the states. Miss Perkins, moreover, had heard from Justice Harlan Fiske Stone that use of the taxing power to establish a jobless insurance system would be a legitimate exercise of federal power. With this in mind she and Witte effectively argued that the Wagner-Lewis tax-offset plan would be likely to receive a favorable opinion from the Court. And even if it were struck down, the state laws would remain, ensuring the continuation of the system whatever the verdict of the High Court.[82]

In contrast to what happened in Canada, then, this constitutional focus prompted the Roosevelt administration to opt for a system involving both levels of government. The Social Security Act became law in August 1935, and the first unemployment insurance contributions became payable in 1936. The act also set up systems for the elderly, children of disadvantaged families, and the blind and disabled.

The Social Security Act indirectly obliged states to introduce UI systems by imposing a 3 percent federal tax on employer payrolls to be phased in gradually, starting in 1936. Employers would be credited (the tax credit or tax offset principle) up to the equivalent of 90 percent of this tax for any contribution to a state-run unemployment compensation system that met minimal requirements. State benefits were to be paid through public employment offices.[83]

The federal law thus imposed a uniform contribution rate for the whole country, avoiding the downward pressure that a difference in rates might have caused. However, states had considerable freedom to define the type of system that they wanted. The varying power relationships in each state would produce a variety of solutions. Despite the overwhelming prevalence of single funds, a number of states would use variants of experience rating borrowed from the prevention theory.[84] As well, the federal law did not prohibit states from collecting contributions from wage earners. With the reelection of the Roosevelt administration in 1936, however, the unions saw their political influence rise in the country. The workers benefited from this favourable new power conjuncture. Very few states set up systems that obliged wage earners to contribute.[85]

As for the rights of the jobless, the Social Security Act imposed no minimum standard on states as far as benefits were concerned. The only standards affecting claimants that states were obliged to meet had to do with the right to refuse unsuitable employment: strike breaking, work under conditions appreciably lower than market standards, and work involving an obligation to belong to a union dominated by the employer or in which accepting employment would prevent the worker from joining a union organization.[86]

Finally, the Social Security Act would be challenged in the courts. Did the US Constitution allow Congress to impose the compulsory collection of contributions on states? The Supreme Court would rule in favour of the constitutionality of both the federal legislation and state laws.[87] The majority on that court found that the federal law was not really coercive on states but aimed at cooperation between the states and the national government to promote the general well-being.[88]

The American process clearly differed from the one used in Canada, especially in constitutional terms, and so separate systems emerged.[89] This distinction applied not only to their features but also, and especially, to their basic policies.

The Canadian system's development owed little to the American experiment despite the factor of proximity. There were many reasons for this. First was the direct influence of the British experience: Canada, as Bennett recalled in his argument supporting the constitutionality of the 1935 act, was still part of the British Empire. And unlike the United States, Canada had seen few voluntary initiatives.

The main difference between the debates in the two countries had to do with the role that government should play in the system. What Canadian employers actually opposed was the principle of unemployment insurance. Only at the last minute did they suggest private systems as alternatives to a state-run one. Although the framers wanted to ensure that the system was set on a sound actuarial footing, there was universal agreement that the government should play a major role in administering and funding it. In the United States, employer opposition to all government involvement in social policies ran deep. The land of free enterprise fiercely rejected government intervention: "What was at stake in the debate surrounding the Social Security Act was the nature of the state itself."[90]

In contrast to what happened in Canada, where employers opposed only the plan for a contributory state system, American employers advanced private alternatives or systems derived from private models. Unable to stymie the system itself, they would do their utmost to wrest control and exert their influence for more "privatization." In Canada, the fact that Ottawa was running and helping to fund the system did not raise any particular objection from employers, whereas the American antagonists would do everything they could to keep the federal authorities as far from unemployment insurance as possible. Their full payment of contributions gave the US employers more control over the systems' administration and substance – not to mention the fact that they could pass their costs on to the workers[91] and consumers.[92]

Finally, whereas the system's administration at the federal level met with little employer opposition in Canada, the American opponents insisted on handing administration to the states. In this way, local economic forces would have much more power over a system's day-to-day parameters, especially when it was wholly funded by the bosses.

The only major US influence on the Canadian legislation would not be seen until 1940, when the principle of flat-rate benefits was abandoned for a system in which benefits reflected previous wage levels. Here the US footprint was unmistakable. Walter James Couper offers this comment on the flat-rate benefit principle in the act of 1935: "From the American point of view ... this seems to break the direct connection between the contributions payable and the benefits receivable by any individual, and to introduce an element of payment according to need, which, however admirable, is alien to our present economic system."[93]

With this sole exception, the Canadian UI system would be based on British legislation that had seen a number of major amendments since its first passage in 1911.[94] Almost right away, the workforce protected by the system grew substantially from 2,250,000 in 1911 to over 12,000,000 in 1920. The initial scheme, created when unemployment was seen as an ephemeral phenomenon, was seriously affected by the recession that settled over Britain in 1920. Jobless numbers quadrupled to more than 2,000,000 in 1920-21.

As unemployment gradually assumed an air of permanence, the British government adjusted the system to these new circumstances. An extended benefits system was set up to assist unemployed workers who failed to meet the eligibility requirements. Due to the deteriorating economic conjuncture, the proportion of resources allocated for this type of benefit assumed increasing importance compared with standard benefits and by 1925 represented half of all benefits paid. Clearly, this system could not function unless a large share of its funding came from the government. These extended benefits, initially paid on a discretionary basis, were later paid by entitlement on the same basis as standard benefits, though they became discretionary again in 1925. The scale and persistence of unemployment caused a deficit in the UI fund that reached £75 million in 1931. Arising from the recommendations of the Gregory Commission, which began its work in 1932, a major 1934 amendment split the system into two separate components: a contributory insurance scheme and a system of assistance with a means test for jobless aged sixteen to sixty-five who failed to qualify for standard benefits.

The British UI system in force at the time that the Canadian government tabled its bill in early 1935 had the following general features. Most jobs held under contracts of employment were covered, and thirty weeks of contributions over the past two years were required for entitlement to benefits for a maximum period of twenty-six weeks. To receive benefits again the following year, only ten weeks of contributions were needed. The waiting period was six days.

With a few variations, the Canadian law was a copy of this British legislation. Departures stemmed mainly from the concern of the Canadian framers, uneasy about the problems afflicting the British system, not to overcommit general revenues for unemployment relief. The Canadian system would be administered by a relatively independent commission, a tripartite body with two of its commissioners appointed after consultation with organizations representing employers and workers. The system's funding would also be tripartite.

Like the British system, the 1935 act provided flat-rate benefits. The amount of basic compensation was adjusted to reflect the age and sex of the insured. Males over twenty-one were entitled to a weekly unemployment benefit of $6.00 and women of the same age to compensation of $5.10, while the younger jobless of both sexes were compensated at a lower rate. Obviously, the act reflected working-class income inequalities between employees of different ages and sexes. Additional benefits were provided for "insured contributors" with dependants at a rate of $2.70 for each adult and 90 cents for children. This benefit still fell short of what was needed. For example, a worker with four dependants would receive only $11.40 a week, much less than the minimum required for their basic needs, estimated as $17.30 at that time.[95]

Moreover, the coverage was limited. It ruled out a number of normally seasonal fishing, farming, and logging jobs. Basic eligibility required contributions for a minimum of forty weeks over the previous two years. The maximum benefit period was seventy-eight days but could be extended for people who had paid in for more than two years out of the previous five. The right to benefit was clearly asserted for people meeting the conditions set out in the act, people who also had a right of appeal from benefit allocation rulings.[96]

The system of 1935 would never come into force. King's government packed it off to the Supreme Court. The commissioners appointed by the Bennett government received no direction from the new regime, and their duties remained exiguous. When the Privy Council confirmed the act as unconstitutional, the commission was dismantled. In any case, the act would have been of no use to the vast majority of the unemployed, who in 1935 could not have found work for enough weeks to qualify for benefits.

No sooner was Mackenzie King elected, in fact, than he submitted not just the unemployment scheme but the whole Canadian New Deal to the country's Supreme Court. References were requested for seven other laws, including three on labour relations. Yet King, even though he had voiced reservations about the constitutionality of a federal system, was on record as favouring the principle of unemployment insurance. His attitude suggested a lack of haste to implement the New Deal, as his parliamentary majority would have allowed him to do. The referral to the Supreme Court looked like a way of playing for time.[97] Yet there are those who thought that the position of King's government in defence of the New Deal had gradually progressed, with King himself wishing "quite clearly that the courts would rule in favour of its constitutionality."[98] It was a fact that the Keynesian approach had gained ground in Ottawa's corridors of power.

The choice of lawyers to appear for the federal government was a matter of some delicacy. Since the New Deal was definitely popular and the government was the instigator in shipping the legislation to the court, there was an attempt to choose counsel who could lend the process credibility with the public. The team appearing before the Supreme Court was made up of Newton Rowell, Louis St. Laurent, and C.P. Plaxton. A well-known constitutional lawyer, Rowell was familiar with the unemployment insurance file. After arguing the case before the Supreme Court, he would be appointed chief justice of Ontario and later co-chair the Royal Commission of Inquiry into the Relations between the Dominion and the Provinces – the Rowell-Sirois Commission. Future prime minister St. Laurent was an expert in corporate law and looked credible from the employer standpoint. Plaxton represented the Department of Justice before both the Supreme Court and the Privy Council.

The government arguments for federal jurisdiction in unemployment insurance echoed the preamble to the act of 1935. Such jurisdiction stemmed first from section 132 of the BNA Act[99] conferring the treaty-making power. This involved the social provisions of the Treaty of Versailles and the obligations to its workers that fell to the Dominion of Canada as a part of the British Empire.[100] As the king's sole representative in Canada, the federal government was empowered to have Parliament pass laws to ensure compliance with the international conventions that it signed. Now, although Canada had voted for the ILO's Recommendation No. 1 in 1919, it had not ratified Convention No. 2 on unemployment. Consequently, while the federal government could cite its accession to ILO conventions for New Deal components involving labour law, it could not for the law establishing unemployment insurance. The preamble to the act referred instead to the general intent of sections 23 and 427 of the Treaty of Versailles. The argument based on BNA section 132 was thus attenuated. Realizing its weakness, the federal lawyers relegated it to silence.

The federal government also cited Parliament's residual powers under the BNA Act. No program like unemployment insurance had existed in 1867 and so could not have entered into the division of powers created by that act. Moreover, although unemployment may once have been a local problem, it was anything but local anymore. Unemployment had assumed such proportions as to become a national problem that required a national solution. With the onslaught of the Depression, the unemployment situation in Canada called for urgent action by the federal government.

Finally, the federal government cited Parliament's general powers to levy taxes and regulate trade and commerce. Unemployment insurance would be funded through its power to spend in the public interest. The compulsory contributions to the Unemployment Insurance Fund provided by the act were described as a payroll tax that Parliament, which had free rein on systems of taxation, could collect for public purposes. Furthermore, the imposition of a flat "tax" to fund the system would have a regulatory effect on trade across Canada, preventing the provinces from "bidding down" in their unemployment compensation systems.

Following the King government's request for a reference, a number of provinces jumped into the debate. Their positions, however, were not in seamless agreement. Only Quebec and New Brunswick[101] opposed the New Deal root and branch. Quebec maintained that it exceeded the powers of Parliament since these matters fell within the purview of "civil rights" and were "local and private" in nature. Although most provinces intervened to ask that the 1935 act be found unconstitutional, Ontario supported its validity based on the residual powers of Parliament.

Both the Supreme Court and the Privy Council would find the 1935 act unconstitutional. The Supreme Court thus endorsed the majority provincial position. Speaking for the majority on the court, Mr. Justice Rinfret compared the social insurance system created by the 1935 act to a private insurance plan. This similarity made the act's unconstitutionality self-evident: "Insurances of all sorts, including insurance against unemployment and health insurance, have always been recognized as being exclusively provincial matters under the head 'Property and Civil Rights,' or under the head 'Matters of a merely local or private nature in the Province.'"[102] As for the urgency of the situation of generalized unemployment in Canada that would have justified the use of the residual clause, the Supreme Court pointed out that unemployment was a permanent problem and that the proposed legislative solution was permanent as well.

Mr. Justice Rinfret also used the comparison of social and private insurance to refute the argument based on the general taxing power of Parliament. Without ruling on the issue of whether contributions could constitute taxation, the judge voiced his doubts on this point: "I doubt whether the contribution received from the employee can properly be described as a tax. In fact, it would seem to me to partake more of the nature of an insurance premium or of a payment for services and individual benefits which are to be returned to the employee in proportion to his payments."[103]

The decision delivered by Lord Atkin for the Privy Council found the act of 1935 unconstitutional for appreciably the same reasons as Mr. Justice Rinfret for the Supreme Court of Canada. Unemployment insurance was similar to private insurance and thus came under exclusive provincial jurisdiction in matters of property and civil rights. Nor was the act intended to relieve an urgent situation. The argument based on Parliament's taxing power was not accepted either. Without ruling on whether contributions constituted taxation, the Privy Council was of the opinion that, even if they did, areas of provincial jurisdiction could not thereby be placed in the federal domain.[104]

These decisions came under heavy fire. The courts' finding that the unemployment situation in Canada was not urgent at that time and so did not warrant the use of Parliament's residual powers would move eminent Canadian jurist F.R. Scott to ridicule the Privy Council decision:

Outside of the Great War there has been only one national crisis in Canada which has been held to justify the use of the residuary clause, and that was the degree of drunkenness existing at the time the Canada Temperance Act was adopted in 1878. According to the noble Lords of the Privy Council, the evil of intemperance at that date presented a greater emergency than did the unemployment and sweated labour conditions in Canada which prompted the *Employment and Social Insurance Act,* since the Canada Temperance Act was considered as a valid exercise of residuary powers and the latter Act was not. Such interpretations of Canadian history add to the law of the constitution an element of burlesque which would be merely humorous if the issues at stake were not so serious.[105]

The essence of the argument developed by the courts hinged on the contributory system of social insurance. The act's provision for compulsory payroll deductions was changing the contract of employment, an area of provincial jurisdiction. These opinions were therefore well founded in law.

Apart from the courts' refusal to consider the unemployment crisis then rampant in Canada as an emergency, it was the analogy with commercial insurance that undoubtedly stirred up the biggest controversy. Many people thought that the courts' comparison of social with commercial insurance failed to account for both the basic differences between the two systems and the nobly social purpose of an unemployment insurance scheme. Unlike private insurance, the contributory system in social insurance was compulsory, a fundamental difference from a private plan in which, under the freedom of contract principle, subscriptions would be voluntary. What is more, the nature of the risk covered, the collective responsibility for compensation, and the state's involvement in running the system were all features differentiating unemployment insurance from the commercial variety. Unquestionably, these two opinions, confusing insurance techniques with the objectives of private insurance, downplayed the social purpose of UI and reflected a commitment to a narrowly actuarial vision.

Moreover, by comparing unemployment insurance with the commercial variety, these decisions planted the seed of a legal definition of the new concept of social insurance. For what was the nub of this legal challenge if not the contributory nature of the system? While refusing to rule on the federal government's contention that its jurisdiction in the matter of UI was authorized by its taxing power, the courts held that there was no distinction between the contributory systems of social and private insurance. True to general insurance practice, admittedly, contributions (premiums) were deducted to compensate victims when the risk occurred. Social insurance therefore stood out by its contributory character from other collection methods then available to the state. Social insurance was something other than a tax imposed by the lawmaker to collect money that could then be spent as desired: insurance practice ensured that contributions and benefits were intrinsically linked. Just as in commercial insurance, the contributions were deducted for a specific purpose, namely the payment of benefits when the risk of unemployment occurred. As a result, the unemployment insurance system, even if it differed from private insurance in a number of respects, including its social and redistributive dimensions, still retained a feature in common with commercial insurance – a contributory system for deducting money to be spent for a specific purpose. If this seemed obvious in 1937, it was still a perceptible gain for the unemployed. If this social insurance system compelled workers and employers to contribute, the government should logically be compelled to use these amounts solely to compensate the insured unemployed.

The unemployment insurance debate in Canada took on a shape of its own. The employer-union confrontation was joined by difficulties connected with the seasonal nature of the Canadian economy and the constitutional formalities of Canadian federalism. Despite the high unemployment generated by the Depression, the federal government maintained a wait-and-see strategy with UI, citing the provincial responsibility in like matters. Not until late in the day, noting the popularity of the US New Deal, did Bennett take the initiative of creating a federal unemployment insurance system. Submitted to the courts, the 1935 act was found unconstitutional. When the Privy Council delivered its reference, the UI debates would resume in the political arena.

4
The UI Act of 1940

The aftermath of the Privy Council's invalidation of the 1935 act in January 1937 saw positive change in Mackenzie King's government on the UI front. Keynesianism was gaining ground in its corridors, and the UI cause would gradually be included in the new interventionist role that the Canadian state was preparing to play. King attempted to get the provinces to agree to a constitutional amendment, though without success: despite continuing high unemployment, the parties stuck to their positions. In the end, Canada's entry into the Second World War and some shifts in the provincial political landscape would make it possible to bring all of the provinces to confer exclusive jurisdiction in the area of unemployment insurance on the federal government. The system finally began operations in 1940.

The 1940 Unemployment Insurance Act contained virtually all the features of the system then in force in Britain. Although the Canadian system included an acknowledgment of a right to benefit, its legal framework still reflected its transactional quality as a contributory system in which the rights of the unemployed were coupled with obligations, mainly around voluntary unemployment.

The system's implementation process reflected Ottawa's compromise between the union and employer positions. And behind this duality stood two concepts of the economic system's responsibility for unemployment. The first had a social bias, asserting the basic responsibility of that system and calling for a plan with broad coverage and better benefits. The second embodied a vision of UI that owed more to the private model and would attempt to prevent the government role from being too redistributive. Nonetheless, the 1940 act, especially in its funding arrangements, enshrined the government's political commitment to unemployment and its victims, thus making it the champion of jobless rights.

In 1935, when King asked the Supreme Court for a reference, he was convening a new federal-provincial conference on the issue of funding

assistance to the unemployed. For the provinces, the question of a constitutional amendment was tied to the issues of financial relations between
the two levels of government and the funding of unemployed assistance.
As for the amendment itself, the only consensus reached in this conference was a commitment to keep talking. On the issue of funding the relief
delivered by provinces, Ontario called for federal government participation comparable to the arrangement in place for old-age pensions since
1931: 75 percent of the cost of benefits paid out by the provinces. Shortly
after the conference, Ottawa agreed to this demand but in return insisted
on a provincial commitment to cooperate with a new federal commission
to review how the provinces were actually administering this relief.

With this commitment from the provinces, the National Employment
Commission Act received the royal assent on 8 April 1936.[1] The minister
of labour overseeing the relief commission was Norman Rogers, a former
Queen's University political science professor with a reputation as a progressive force in Cabinet. He was in regular touch with Harry Cassidy and
Frank Scott of the League for Social Reconstruction that was ideologically
close to the CCF.[2] Except for the appointment of his Queen's colleague and
economist W.A. Mackintosh, Rogers filled the commissioner positions to
reflect economic or regional interests. The chair went to Arthur Purvis, an
influential Montreal industrialist.[3]

Mackintosh played a major role in developing the Purvis Commission's
policy on unemployment. He saw Canada as basically an exporting country: the ongoing economic recession stemmed from outside factors, and
little could be done domestically to reduce unemployment other than
increase trade. The government's monetary and tariff policies should
therefore include measures to promote trade and private investment. Economic recovery would come from the marketplace, and the government
should encourage private initiative instead of usurping its role. The recovery was already happening, so unemployment was essentially a result of
lack of training, which prevented job seekers from getting the jobs created
by the private sector. The burden of unemployment was not the fault of
the capitalist system, as ex-Prime Minister Bennett had insisted, but lack
of proper training for the unemployed. The problem was not a shortage of
demand but an imbalance in the labour supply. State intervention must
therefore target individuals. The concept of "employability" had just joined
the roster of Canadian social policies: "The NEC's role would be to 'see ...
that employables are brought into jobs which have been opened for
them.' Since recovery was already under way, the chief concern of the
commission should not be employment but employability."[4]

The premise of this argument was that the private sector, if encouraged
by the state, would create full employment. The Depression had proved,
however, that the market could not create jobs for everyone, and, despite

the economic recovery cited by Mackintosh, more than a million Canadi-ans were collecting direct relief in September 1936.[5] That was the year when the King government ordered the work camps shut down. Viewed as fertile ground for Communist agitation, they would be replaced by tem-porary job-creation projects in railways and agriculture.

On 28 January 1937, the Privy Council delivered its reference on the con-stitutionality of the New Deal legislation.[6] Despite the fact that the gov-ernment had defended the 1935 act's constitutionality, the Privy Council ruling backed King's earlier positions on the matter. King expected the decision to make the provinces more demanding, especially since Maurice Duplessis, a proponent of greater provincial autonomy, now held office in Quebec. Nonetheless, the Department of Labour undertook to develop a new unemployment insurance bill that would be completed the follow-ing year.

Meanwhile, the Purvis Commission continued its work. Supporting Mac-kintosh's argument, it pointed out that the economic recovery, though beginning, was not creating jobs. In February 1937, when the national income had recorded 10 percent growth in one year, the employment level had risen by only 5 percent. The commission reasoned from this that unemployment was not a temporary problem but a structural one. This approach was diametrically opposed to the views held by King, for whom the economic recession and its joblessness were but passing phenomena. To curtail this structural unemployment, the government had to support the private sector, on which job creation depended. Unemployed workers must be made employable. The commission asked for appropriations to develop manpower training, including a youth program. After discussions in Cabinet, the amount requested for this program was cut substantially from $2.5 million to $1 million. King defended the cut by recalling that the program was primarily in provincial jurisdiction. The next year, how-ever, its appropriation would be increased to the level first requested.[7] This was the first major federal government incursion into the area of man-power training.

In July 1937, the Purvis Commission submitted an interim report to the minister of labour.[8] It criticized the public works programs as helping to corroborate the notion that the government had to provide employment for everyone able to work and make the unemployed dependent on the state. Maintaining that the Depression was due to an inadequately trained workforce, the report shifted the responsibility for unemployment to the unemployed themselves: "The moral terms of the debate shifted dramati-cally from an emphasis upon society's responsibility to provide work to an emphasis upon the individual's willingness to do it."[9]

In August, King announced the creation of a Royal Commission of In-quiry into the Relations between the Dominion and the Provinces that would focus, *inter alia*, on the unemployment insurance issue. The chair of this commission was initially given to Newton Rowell, at that time chief justice of Ontario, and then to the jurist Joseph Sirois when Rowell fell ill.

That 5 November, King wrote to the premiers asking them to support a constitutional amendment giving Parliament exclusive jurisdiction over unemployment insurance, including a national employment service. Six provinces agreed in principle, but Alberta, New Brunswick, and Quebec were against it. The first two called for a review of all outstanding federal-provincial issues before getting into the matter of UI. Quebec premier Duplessis did not see the need for a constitutional amendment. He called instead, using the existing old-age pension plan as his model, for an unemployment insurance program funded jointly by the federal government and the provinces but administered by the latter.

In December 1937, the Purvis Commission presented its final report to King's government. It differed substantially from the interim report, which had seen Ottawa playing an essentially unobtrusive role in support of private sector initiatives. Now the commission wanted the state to play a conspicuous part in addressing the unemployment problem. In addition to federal unemployment insurance and a national employment service, it wanted Ottawa to assume full responsibility for employable people by creating a nationwide unemployment assistance scheme.[10] It was clear to the commission that only the federal government had the financial means and competent bureaucracy to take over this file.

King did not buy all of the Purvis Commission's recommendations. Having delayed publication of the report, he announced that he would postpone his decision on the unemployment insurance issue until the Rowell-Sirois report came out. On 6 June 1938, he said that further planning on the constitutional amendment required an agreement with the provinces. Meanwhile, the unemployment insurance case was making progress in a Cabinet that was increasingly converted to Keynesian thinking. The intellectuals around the government made their influence felt. Rogers, Mackintosh, and W.C. Clark, the deputy minister of finance, all graduates of Queen's University, were receptive to Keynes's ideas. The debates in Cabinet reflected a struggle between the classic liberal position and the Keynesian approach. At the outset, King maintained the position on unemployment insurance that he had argued in his first term, trying only to balance his budget. Keynesian thinking was very different: budget deficits could be used in economic slowdowns to restart the economy. And the Rowell-Sirois Commission's report, published in 1940, summarized this role of budgets in the Keynesian vision to justify an exclusive federal jurisdiction over unemployment: "The Dominion is the only government which can meet, in an equitable and efficient manner, the large fluctuating expenditures due to unemployment ... The monetary and taxation powers of the Dominion would enable it to follow a planned budgetary policy of deficits during depressions, and surpluses and repayment during prosperity – a policy which is generally impracticable for provinces and municipalities."[11] Clearly, the creation of an unemployment insurance system fit the Keynesian framework perfectly. A plan that built up surpluses from contributions in periods of prosperity that were later redistributed as benefits in periods of recession would stimulate the economy.

The Quebec government was against the introduction of a federal unemployment insurance system. However, the Duplessis regime, noting developments on the federal scene, passed an Unemployment Insurance Act in 1939 that, in its preamble, proposed "that a system of unemployment insurance be established in co-operation by the federal and provincial authorities, within the bounds of the constitution of Canada and respecting the autonomy of the provinces."[12] This legislation was to remain a dead letter. Although Quebec's national petty bourgeoisie endorsed Duplessis's position,[13] the CTCC maintained its call for federal UI.[14]

When Canada went to war in September 1939, King turned into a keen supporter of UI. In his view, new circumstances made its introduction necessary, among them anticipated social unrest with the end of hostilities and demobilization. As well, the draft unemployment insurance legislation developed the year before could not pay benefits for two years. The recovery and full employment brought about by the war meant that there would be no problem filling the Unemployment Insurance Fund, a reserve that could be tapped to back the war effort. With all this in mind, any provincial opposition to the constitutional amendment that Ottawa was asking for could be labelled as unpatriotic.[15] King also thought that the CCF should not be left to monopolize the electoral rewards that came with a plan for social reform.

Moreover, the political climate was now more accommodating of King's aims. In Quebec City, Adélard Godbout and his Liberals had succeeded Duplessis. Unlike his predecessor, Godbout was in favour of unemployment insurance, though he was also aware of the anger that recognizing federal jurisdiction was bound to arouse in Quebec. The list of UI's foes was led by Duplessis and a crowd of nationalists but included the business community as well. Yet labour circles were for it, and the Quebec Liberals had embraced the Montpetit Commission's recommendation in this regard at their 1938 convention.[16] And to thwart the nationalist opposition, Godbout held a trump card: Henri Bourassa himself had championed just such a plan in the House of Commons in 1929.[17] Like Duplessis, however, Godbout had reservations about the amendment, preferring concurrent jurisdiction instead. The federal authorities would argue in rebuttal that the risk of provinces bidding to please the bosses made separate provincial schemes unworkable: lowering contribution rates would undermine their financial footing.[18] In the end, Godbout let himself be persuaded.[19]

In the throne speech of 16 May 1940, the federal government announced its intention of moving quickly on the constitutional amendment and bringing in a UI system. Employer antagonism to this plan had coalesced, however, with the economic recovery generated by the outbreak of war. Speaking to the House of Commons committee studying the bill, a Canadian Chamber of Commerce representative summed up the stand of most employers: they would fight this new payroll deduction on the ground that they were already overtaxed. They further argued that collecting contributions from employees would prompt calls for higher wages, the tax would ultimately be passed on to the consumers in price increases that slashed their buying power, and, finally, this increase in production costs would undermine their competitive position in outside markets.[20]

With the bill's passage looming, the employers came up with various forms of private or mixed UI schemes. One proposal included a variant of the experience-rating system in which the employer's contribution would reflect its layoff record. The King government paid no heed to these suggestions. And the unions, while calling for improvements in the bill, especially with regard to coverage, were still resolute in their support.[21]

Coincidentally with the throne speech, the Rowell-Sirois report was published. Although appearing too late to significantly affect the UI bill, the report echoed the Purvis Commission's final message in recommending that the federal government assume responsibility for all able-bodied unemployed Canadians by creating a national unemployment insurance and unemployment assistance system.[22]

In June 1940, the federal government, having secured the agreement of all nine provinces, petitioned Westminster for the constitutional amendment. On 12 July, the British Parliament amended the British North America Act to give Canada's Parliament an exclusive jurisdiction that was limited to unemployment insurance.[23] King had told the House of Commons that this was a condition of the provinces' agreeing to the constitutional amendment: "May I say that, if we had ventured to go beyond unemployment insurance, we would probably have met with further objections on the part of some, if not all, of the provinces. As the correspondence will show, one of the circumstances which enabled us to get the approval of all of the provinces was the fact that we were asking for only one amendment, related to unemployment insurance."[24] On 15 July, the Unemployment Insurance Bill was tabled for its first reading in the House of Commons, becoming law on 7 August. The first contributions to the system would be collected on 1 July 1941.

This 1940 Unemployment Insurance Act[25] was essentially based on the

Canadian act of 1935. However, it departed from its British model on one point:[26] the basic benefit was not flat but reflected the last wage earned. Why this change, since the 1935 act never came into force and the government had not been able to gauge its effects? The rationale for the change was outlined in 1940 by Eric Stangroom, a Department of Labour spokesman who testified before the special House of Commons committee studying the UI bill. During the five-year interval, the Canadian government had learned from the experience of a number of countries, including the United States, that had just developed UI schemes. In the United States, benefits reflected previous earnings.[27] Emphasizing that the 1935 act provided different benefits to reflect age and sex and that such a system could have been hard to administer, Stangroom acknowledged that the main reason for the change was to encourage low-income workers to get jobs: "Any flat benefit must be fixed at the low earnings of any worker in any part of the country; otherwise the benefits would exceed wages. If the benefit exceeds wages you get a tendency to malingering; men will prefer unemployment benefits to a job."[28] With this system, the incentive to work was maintained for both low-income and better-paid employees.

As to coverage, the act applied only to employment contracts – a feature common to all forms of unemployment insurance: "Only those who work for wages or a salary, who are at liberty to quit their jobs yet who may also be deprived of them by someone else, can become unemployed."[29] But the lawmaker would provide exceptions to this rule. Insurable employment exercised under a contract of employment could be "excepted" by regulations and vice versa: noninsurable employment could become insurable by the reverse process. With this idea of "excepted" employment, the 1940 act excluded a large number of workers, including people in farming, fishing, logging, permanent federal or provincial public service employment, or employment with annual earnings of more than $2,000. The commission could exempt people from contributions who were in seasonal jobs for fewer than twenty weeks a year and had no other insurable employment and exclude seasonal workers from benefits during the off season. This afforded little protection for the seasonal work that typified the Canadian economy. At this time, only 42 percent of Canada's labour force was covered by the new system.[30]

To meet the entrance requirement, the claimant had to have been in insurable employment for a period of at least 180 days during the two years immediately preceding the benefit claim. To establish a subsequent claim, an added condition had to be met: sixty days of work since the last day that the claimant received a benefit from the previous claim. The required length of employment, however, was shorter than in the 1935 act, which had insisted on at least forty weeks. The normal working week considered by the new legislation was then six days.[31]

The act explicitly provided a right to benefit: "27. Every person who being insured under this Act is unemployed and in whose case the conditions laid down by this Act (in this Act referred to as 'statutory conditions') are fulfilled, shall, subject to the provisions of this Act, be entitled to receive payments ... so long as the statutory conditions continue to be fulfilled and so long as he is not disqualified under this Act for the receipt of benefit." Recognition of the right to payment thus went with an array of obligations intended to check the claimant's labour market status. Claimants had to prove that they were ready and available for work but could not find suitable employment. This was the central obligation of the system. The 1940 plan addressed only able-bodied people, since no type of benefit was available at that time for sickness, injury, or maternity. As evidence of availability for work, the commission could require the claimant to report to its office and sign a register for this purpose.[32] Claimants were relieved of this obligation on proving that they were regularly attending a course of instruction or training approved by the commission. No doubt this new provision,[33] not present in the 1935 act, was a response to the Purvis Commission's recommendations on vocational training. Note, however, that this measure was also in the British act of 1935.[34]

Corollary to the duty of availability were various types of penalties for violations. Thus, someone who deliberately quit a job without just cause or was fired for misconduct could forfeit the right to benefit for a period not exceeding six weeks. Since, however, the insured person had one year to collect full benefits and would frequently not have worked long enough to claim the one-year maximum, the penalty would often merely have the effect of delaying their payment.

A comparable penalty was generally imposed in cases of nonavailability or in which a claimant, without good cause, neglected or refused to accept suitable employment or obey an official's directives to do so. As in the British act, the idea of suitable employment referred to the market. For example, the claimant beginning a benefit year could not be forced to accept a job in his or her usual occupation but with lower pay or less favourable conditions than those found in the market, or another type of job with lower pay or less favourable conditions than those of his or her usual occupation. However, after a reasonable time not stipulated in the act, the claimant could be forced to accept employment other than the usual employment with lower pay or less favourable conditions so long as these were not less favourable than the conditions found in the market. The claimant's right to insist on employment of the same type as his or her former occupation or with equivalent working conditions disappeared over time.

Some union-related reasons were also accepted as justifying refusal of employment. For example, no insured person could be forced to accept a job that was vacant because of a "work stoppage due to a labour dispute" or if the result of accepting the job would be to lose the right to become or continue to be a member of a trade union. Both the British[35] and the American legislation contained similar mechanisms to protect union membership and activities.[36] However, the right to refuse a job involving mandatory union membership or, conversely, the obligation not to join a union[37] was not part of the British legislation: it stemmed from the American law.[38] As a result of labour pressure, a final provision not in the 1935 act extended protection for union activities to someone who had been dismissed for the same reasons.[39]

These provisions, more or less copied from the British act of 1935, were designed to impose discipline on the workforce and addressed the conduct of the claimant. They did not cover the total forfeiture of the right to benefit by a claimant who lost a job as a result of a "work stoppage" due to a labour dispute. In this case, the conduct of the individual claimant was not the issue, but the industrial power relationship was: the responsibility was collective. Entitlement was then forfeited for as long as the work stoppage lasted or until the claimant found other employment in compliance with the act's requirements.[40]

The provisions affecting voluntary unemployment sparked little debate, but there was the testimony to the special House of Commons committee studying the bill by TLCC president Tom Moore. He was able to support the voluntary unemployment provisions because they included various mechanisms that guaranteed the rights of claimants, like the employer's (and not the employee's) obligation to bear the burden of proof in misconduct cases.[41] There was much discussion, however, of the particular provision dealing with labour disputes. Testifying before the committee, Moore stated his agreement with the principle of the provision, which, despite some shortcomings, he found acceptable.[42] CTCC president Alfred Charpentier was more critical, believing that disqualification should not be applied indiscriminately without considering the merits of the parties to the dispute.[43] When this debate reached the House of Commons, speakers on the government side gleefully pointed out that the provision was not only analogous to the British act but also had actually been approved by Moore and other labour leaders![44] There was still criticism of the refusal to consider the merits of the parties' positions when testing for disqualification: "In the first place, the section assumes that the worker is responsible for strikes. I say that because under this section he is penalized. However, my experience has been the reverse ... Provision should be made for some sort of investigation in order to determine the responsibility for strikes, lockouts and so forth. Why should one side be penalized and not the other?"[45] Notwithstanding, no amendment was made to the labour disputes provision.

Along with recognition of the right to benefit, the act provided for an appeal procedure to Courts of Referees and then to umpires. The composition of a Court of Referees was tripartite: a chairman appointed by the governor in council and an equal number of representatives of employers and insured persons, with the latter chosen from union organizations. Umpires were chosen from the judges of the Exchequer Court and provincial superior courts.

Where issues involved insurability of employment, the only appeal from decisions made by the UI commission was to the umpire. In other cases, in which a claim for benefit was refused by an insurance officer, the claimant could appeal first to a Court of Referees. Note that in cases of breach of the obligation of availability or its corollaries, such as nonattendance of a course without good reason, or in cases of refusal of employment, dismissal for misconduct, or voluntary leaving, the insurance officer could not disallow a claim: it had to be referred to a Court of Referees.[46] The claimant was entitled to benefit until this tribunal delivered its ruling,[47] which had to include a statement of its findings based on the essential matters of fact.

The claimant had a right of appeal from a Court of Referees decision to the umpire that was automatic in the presence of a dissenting opinion. To appeal in all other circumstances, the claimant needed permission from the chair of the Court of Referees. In all cases, however, a commission official or employee association of which the claimant was a member could appeal a Court of Referees decision to the umpire. In authorizing appeals as of right by union members, the lawmaker seems to have wanted to avoid a landslide of dissenting opinions in Court of Referees decisions by union-endorsed claimant representatives. The umpire's decision was final, although the UI commission, Court of Referees, or umpire could revoke or amend an earlier decision if new facts came to light.

The act imposed a nine-day waiting period during which no benefit was paid. At that time, the British act provided a six-day waiting period.[48] Length of benefit was established at one day for each five-day period of contributions paid over the past five years. One day was deducted from this period for each three-day period in the previous three years when a claimant had collected benefits. This had the effect of cutting the benefit entitlements of frequent claimants, including seasonal workers. The maximum length of benefit was one year for someone paying into the system for five years and therefore could not be paid out until ... 1946!

The act of 1940 substituted benefits of variable duration, depending on the worker's employment history, for the fixed thirteen-week base period in the act of 1935. The rate of benefit was thirty-four times the average weekly contribution paid over the previous two years. When the claimant had dependants, this factor was raised to forty. The exact amount of benefit was determined, as with contributions, by sorting claimants into seven categories by wage level, with an added special classification for anyone earning less than ninety cents a day or under age sixteen, in which cases the full premium was paid by the employer. The minimum weekly benefit varied by category from $4.08 to $12.24 for a single person and $4.40 to $14.40 for a claimant with one dependant. These benefits were low compared to the cost of living. Leonard Marsh, in his 1943 report on Canadian social security, would call for their increase from these patently inadequate levels: "None of the categories (based also on the two-person unit) reaches the 'desirable' minimum or 'living wage' standard."[49]

The system was to be run by a commission created by the act. Reporting to the minister of labour, the Unemployment Insurance Commission was made up of three commissioners, two of whom were appointed after consultations with organizations representing workers and employers. Its tripartite makeup reflected the system's funding. In fact, the Unemployment Insurance Fund was financed equally by employers and workers, with the government adding a supplementary contribution equal to 20 percent of the combined employer and worker amounts.[50] The cost of operating the system, however, was borne by the federal government.[51] Like the act of 1935,[52] the 1940 legislation stated that the Unemployment Insurance Fund, kept as a special account in the Consolidated Revenue Fund, could not be used for any purpose other than paying benefits or refunding contributions:[53] "78(1) Notwithstanding the provisions of *The Consolidated Revenue and Audit Act, 1931*, the Minister of Finance may ... pay out of the Fund claims for insurance benefits and refunds of contributions as provided for by this Act but no other payments shall be made a charge on the Fund."

The act of 1940 provided a system to ensure that the Unemployment Insurance Fund was transparent and managed in line with the system's objectives.[54] Compulsory contribution rates were fixed and expressly provided in the act.[55] Although the total contributions of employers and employees to the fund were equal, this proportion would vary by wage level. Like benefits, contribution rates were tied to a classification of eight claimant categories by wage. Employer and employee contributions were respectively 21 and 12 cents for the lowest category earning $5.40 to $7.50 a week, whereas they were 27 and 36 cents for the top category earning $26.00 to $38.50 a week. While bosses paid in more than their employees from the six lowest wage groups, they contributed less than the workers in the top two. As Yves Vaillancourt emphasizes,[56] the impression of overfunding by employers was misleading, as these last two categories totalled 71.1 percent of the insured workforce in fiscal 1943-44.[57]

Payment of contributions was confirmed by unemployment insurance stamps that the employer stuck in a special booklet attesting to the number of days worked. Although this method was not in use for very long, the expression survived in the language of ordinary people, especially in eastern Canada, where "unemployment stamps" stand for the weeks of work needed to establish a benefit period.

In addition to the unemployment insurance plan, the UI commission was responsible for organizing and maintaining a national employment service to operate in conjunction with its insurance services. The existing employment offices, though federally funded, were run by the provinces. From now on, given the new constitutional order, they came wholly under federal jurisdiction. Indeed, this jurisdiction over unemployment insurance and employment enabled the federal government to enter fully into an area hitherto sacred to the provinces. This was a major issue, as the Gill Report later emphasized: "The record seems clear that the primary purpose of the *Unemployment Insurance Act* of 1940 was the positive one of establishing and maintaining an effective National Employment Service."[58]

Canada's UI system stemmed from a compromise between opposing socioeconomic forces but also between two visions of the state role in employment and unemployment. The first held, in the liberal tradition, that responsibility for finding work and dealing with unemployment fell primarily to the individual functioning in the market economy. The state must not get involved except to support individual activities. The second maintained, in the socialist tradition, that responsibility for employment and unemployment fell primarily to the market economy, and state involvement was imperative. This involvement could take the form of a highly socialized economy (state socialism) or be limited to regulation of the market economy as in Britain and Canada. It is of paramount importance to grasp the positions of both sides during the system's development, as basically the same points of view would later be used to justify expanding or cutting the coverage offered by the system.

First, the social vision – and here we have the entire Canadian grassroots labour movement calling for an unemployment compensation scheme that recognized jobless rights. Various views were voiced, however, on the form that this future scheme should take, especially when it came to funding. Should it be a contributory system? The majority union tendency in the 1920s had been to call for a noncontributory one. Since unemployment was a problem intrinsic to industry, it fell to industry to bear the cost. Given the sheer scale of unemployment in the 1930s, however, the vast majority of unionists would take a more pragmatic view and get behind the contributory plan to hasten its introduction.

The supporters of the contributory model stressed its positive side. They held that contributing to the fund would give the workers leverage to control it in their own interests. It was also argued that, compared to the beneficiaries of the old assistance system, the unemployed would be in a better position to claim benefits as a right since, as in commercial insurance, they were paid-up contributors. This meant that paying benefits would cease to be seen as an act of official charity, humiliating for the recipient.

However, the argument for a noncontributory scheme was still very much part of the debate. The main case was based on the responsibility for unemployment as developed in a book by Jacob Lawrence Cohen[59] on the political and ideological bases of a UI system.[60] Published in 1935, this work reviewed the grounds for applying social insurance techniques to the unemployment risk in that year's new legislation. Exploring a parallel with worker's compensation schemes, Cohen argued that no worker should bear the responsibility for the unemployment risk personally since that person had no control over the causes of unemployment, which was generated by the operation of the economy. This meant that it was not an individual but a social risk and should be managed socially. Unemployment insurance only cloaked the real responsibility for unemployment and afforded a pretext to have its potential victims contribute to its cost.

On the other hand, the principle of a noncontributory system involved recognizing unemployment as a concern for the whole society. This concern gave rise to a claim that was "not for more relief, but for the right to work. By recognizing that claim in terms of non-contributory insurance, the state accepts the responsibility, either of paying unemployment compensation, or of shaping economy and productivity in such a manner as to absorb all capacity for labour."[61] Cohen further maintained that the contributory approach was rife with drawbacks for workers and the unemployed. After helping to fund the system, people qualifying for benefits could not collect them for the total duration of their unemployment since the benefit period was finite. Furthermore, the disciplinary controls tilted the balance of power against the workers in their campaign for better wages.

Responding to the argument that only a contributory scheme could guarantee jobless rights without a means test, Cohen maintained that the right to benefit was based not on the worker's contributions but on the legislation recognizing this right. He quoted William Henry Beveridge to support his claims: "The collective bearing of risks is insurance. It is insurance, whether the individual contributes specific premiums to meet each specific risk or whether he receives free insurance out of general resources of the community or an industry. It is insurance whether the contributions are voluntary or compulsory. On the other hand, it is not insurance if the receipt of benefits depends in any way upon the discretion of some authority, if it is given not as a right but as a favour, if it can be withheld because an individual otherwise entitled has other means."[62] Cohen advocated a noncontributory system in which the sole eligibility requirement would be unemployment itself. This system would recognize the right to benefit for the entire period of unemployment and be funded mainly by a national tax on wealth. A number of Cohen's ideas turned up in the UI model advanced by the Communist-led Worker's Unity League.[63]

As a social insurance system, UI subscribed to the rationale for all insurance by pooling the cost of a risk, in this case unemployment. However, the objectives were clearly social due to the very nature of the unemployment risk, which involved the responsibility of a society. Given this social dimension, unemployment compensation would entail a much more collective form of risk sharing as a government program.

On the other hand, such state fiddling with the labour market was unacceptable to the supporters of liberalism, who fiercely opposed the very principle of unemployment compensation. Several of their arguments revolved around the prohibitive expense of the scheme and what they feared would be its deterrent effect on the workforce. As the idea of unemployment insurance gained popularity in the industrialized world, however, opposition to state involvement in this compensation took a subtle turn: the insurance medium itself would be used to limit state intervention.

Comparing unemployment insurance to private insurance, some would advocate various measures to limit coverage for the sake of the system's financial integrity. Inasmuch as this argument was essentially about more financial autonomy for the system, actuaries would be invited to play a leading role. This happened in Canada, where actuaries A.D. Watson and H. Wolfenden were on the team that put together the act of 1935. That is why their concept of insurance, built on the premise of financial integrity, has been described by Leslie A. Pal as the "actuarial ideology." It would play a major role in the development of the Canadian scheme: "The term reflects the importance of actuarial considerations in designing and evaluating UI, though the ideology also incorporates administrative and political aspects. It became the dominant way of understanding UI, at least for the commission. Employers, trade unions, and other experts suggested different visions, perhaps equally valid, but to little avail. The actuarial ideology became the administrative touchstone of UI and remained so for years."[64]

The most frequent role of the actuarial ideology would be to call for cutting coverage in the face of the interests of the jobless. According to this ideology, modelled on private insurance, the system had to be financially self-sufficient and open to more privatization. Not only should it not be funded by the government, but also its administration had to be kept as far from the government as possible. Otherwise, political leaders might be tempted to expand its coverage under pressure from their voters, as happened in Britain, and this might mean additional costs. The real predicament of the jobless was clearly not a major concern for this school of thought.

Bryce Stewart, who as deputy minister of labour would later supervise the launch of Ottawa's UI scheme, summed up the essence of this approach in 1933 as "the desirability of keeping government out of the financing of unemployment insurance, and further, keeping the administration of unemployment insurance as far away from government departments as possible."[65] This attitude was not unconnected with the fact that Stewart was then a US resident. In any event, it was a viewpoint that resonated with the supporters of the actuarial ideology. Facing the imminent creation of an unemployment insurance scheme, the Canadian Life Underwriters Association offered its expertise to the Bennett government. Actuary Wolfenden, later a member of the team asked to draft the first unemployment insurance bill, was mandated by that association to conduct studies on the subject. His view of social insurance was unambiguous: "All forms of social insurance are largely incompatible with the spirit of individual freedom, responsibility, and initiative which is so largely characteristic of North America."[66]

Immersed in the North American world of commercial insurance, Wolfenden borrowed these comments on UI by an American analyst: "It is not insurance, since no insurance principles, in the strict sense of the term, apply as regards the payments of benefits in exact proportion to the contributions paid, but is rather a measure of taxation, of compulsory levies upon both labor and industry, amplified by ever-increasing grants-in-aid or financial subsidies on the part of the State."[67] Once the principle of state financial participation was established, the state would then be asked to limit its contribution in the name of sound financial management, the underlying aim being to make the system self-financing.

The absence or inadequacy of state funding would have serious consequences for the jobless. First of all, it meant a corresponding decline in the system's capacity to act as an agent for redistributing the national wealth. As a result, no distinction could be made between those profiting from the economic system and those who were its victims. The distinction existed instead, as in commercial insurance, among the insured themselves. And the same financial concerns would be used to argue for reducing the coverage of the system. Projecting its costs involved defining and isolating the portion of the unemployment risk to be insured. Only temporary, involuntary, and unpredictable unemployment could qualify. Many in cyclical employment, including seasonal workers, would be excluded from the system.

Admittedly, the actuarial ideology was not an exclusive club for the adversaries of an expanded UI system. A number of bureaucrats subscribed to its objective of enlisting commercial insurance principles to put the system on a sound financial footing. From this standpoint, the system would also be an effective tool for promoting employer interests. In the name of sound financial management, the actuarial ideology grafted onto the system some typical elements of a privatizing view of unemployment and insurance. Numerous references to individual responsibility for the occurrence of unemployment were defended on the ground of better control of the system's expense. Individual responsibility, the cornerstone of the protection afforded by private coverage, thus became a major component of unemployment insurance. The system would have to avoid being overly generous and alluring for the jobless and inducing them to unduly cause the occurrence of the risk. Effective action would be needed to curb voluntary unemployment.

The 1930s, with the British system established, saw the spread of a theory that unemployment insurance actually created unemployment. Based on the notion of "moral hazard" and arguing that the chance to collect benefits might actually induce workers to quit work or stop looking for jobs, this theory would be the keystone of the actuarial ideology. Developed by the economist J. Rueff in France,[68] it was widely taken up by UI's opponents. Rueff saw the "abnormally high" rate of unemployment then prevailing in Britain (1931) as the consequence of "abnormally high" wages that were themselves a result of a policy of "subsidies to the unemployed": in the final analysis, therefore, unemployment insurance could be held liable for unemployment.[69] The theory soon found promoters in Canada. A.D. Watson, one of the actuaries on the team for the 1935 bill, was one of them: "Unemployment insurance in itself increases in a marked manner the unemployment which will be recorded for benefit purposes."[70]

The use of the moral hazard concept in connection with unemployment lent credence to the classic liberal belief in individual responsibility for that condition. The insurance debate would now ally the objectives of workforce discipline and control with the underwriter's art. It became imperative to enrich the legislation with provisions limiting its application to involuntary unemployment and instituting penalties for voluntary leavers. In this way, the actuarial ideology legitimized most of the obligations to be met by claimants, including availability for work. Yet by refusing to acknowledge a social liability for unemployment, this ideology denied the right of the jobless to fair compensation. For Cohen, the background of the British system demonstrated this conflict: "The history of its thirty-five amending acts in twenty-four years ... [testifies] to the struggle between adherence to a 'sound' insurance scheme and recognition of the basic social fact of chronic unemployment."[71]

The actuarial ideology would often be depicted as the only way of creating social insurance. By seizing on the insurer's method and identifying it with private coverage, the ideologues sowed confusion about the real nature of social insurance. An example is found in this comment from

Gary Dingledine on the rationale for the waiting period: "Short periods of unemployment each year were regarded as a near certainty for the majority of people in insurable employment. This safeguard was regarded as comparable to the deductible feature in automobile insurance."[72] Here we have the confusion of private with social insurance and not a thought about the liability for the event being compensated for. Would the driver who did not cause an accident be made to pay the deductible? Why would things be otherwise for the unemployed? All this confusion only obscured the basic issue of responsibility for unemployment.

The UI system thus looked like a compromise, not only between opposing interests, but also between two views of work. The labour movement was calling for an income security plan and jobless rights, while the employers insisted that the system would be an incentive not to work. This is why the law's recognition of a right to benefit was accompanied by labour market obligations. Finally, the conciliator role formed part of the redefined economic duties of the Canadian state.

State involvement in unemployment took two forms. One was an attempt to boost the economy by promoting the public's purchasing power. The other was an attempt to afford a degree of income security to people becoming unemployed. The UI system reflected both of these objectives.

The system's place in Ottawa's Keynesian strategy is well known. Leonard Marsh, one of its framers, cited this explanation of its function in the economy: "On the other hand, from the standpoint of the economic system as a whole, social insurance can aid in maintaining consumer purchasing power if national income exhibits a tendency to shrink and thus can assist in maintaining employment at high levels."[73] From this standpoint, social programs such as unemployment insurance acted as "automatic stabilizers" of the economy.[74] Amid prosperity, the UI fund filled up with money from premiums that would then be available for less prosperous times. The system therefore had an anticyclical effect, especially in periods of economic recession.

As the system came into effect in Canada, unemployment was finally recognized as intrinsic to the market economy. Despite its limited reach, which would leave thousands of workers and unemployed without protection, the act of 1940 was still a genuine advance compared to earlier legislation providing the jobless with relief at the discretion of officials: "The insured person knows 'what he is entitled to'; his benefit comes as of right, and not from charity. Further than this, there is a proper machinery for adjudication in the event of doubt or dispute ... These are the advantages of social insurance which meet the psychology of the dependency situation."[75]

The underside of this recognition of the right to benefit was the imposition of a set of obligations on claimants, mainly to discourage "voluntary unemployment." Realizing the impact these penalties had on working conditions, the unions succeeded in persuading the Canadian lawmakers to limit their scope. They held that the maximum six-week penalty often merely delayed benefit payments. What was more, the insurance officer could not impose these penalties on his own initiative. Nevertheless, the 1940 act legitimized the principle of penalizing such cases. Once the assumption was entrenched, it would be easier to amend its substance.

Finally, the act confirmed a state liability for unemployment and its victims, especially by its funding formula. And this very political commitment made the government the guarantor of jobless rights.

The act of 1940 was the child of compromise between interest groups and opposing ideologies about the government's role in the issues of employment and unemployment. As the right to benefit stemmed from the government's attitude to unemployment and the unemployed, the balance of rights versus obligations was a delicate one. The system's development is evidence of this.

5
UI Expansion, 1940-75

From the time that it was introduced, the UI system saw progressive expansion through to 1975. This period, imbued with the Keynesian spirit that attended the emergence of the Canadian welfare state, was conducive to the acknowledgment and growth of jobless rights. It also saw two sweeping reforms. The reform of 1955 squared away the gains of a system fated to play an increasing role as economic prod. The reform of 1971 harnessed this momentum to liberalize the system and make its social mission more explicit. Together these reforms created an unambiguous public responsibility for jobs and joblessness.

Yet the ideological debate over the system's role did not slacken. The 1962 Gill Report[1] and the 1970 white paper, *Unemployment Insurance in the 70s*,[2] were distillations of the two rival schools, with the ideology of the actuaries opposing a more social vision of UI. However, the criticisms of this social bias as expressed in the Gill Report would return with a vengeance after the 1971 reform and, in the end, support the turnaround begun by the lawmaker of 1975.

UI had been introduced in a wartime economy running at full tilt. Low unemployment helped to fill the coffers of a fund that was little used: it was there to back the war effort and emerge as "a salutary stabilizing factor during the postwar period."[3]

The end of hostilities in Europe did not bring the business slowdown that many feared. The economy found fresh stimulus in the international conjuncture: first the Marshall Plan in Europe and then, in the early 1950s, the Korean conflict. In Canada, the government made full employment one of the objectives of its postwar economic policy: "The reconstruction program has to begin by making a smooth and orderly transition from the economic conditions prevailing in wartime to the ones that will emerge with the return of peace, and maintain work and revenue at a high, stable level. The government is adopting this as the primary aim of its policy ... In making a high, stable level of work and revenue its goal, the government is aiming at nothing less than 'full employment.'"[4]

With unemployment still marginal and a surplus in the UI fund, Ottawa used these auspicious circumstances to assign the system a major economic role as a building block for the construction of the Canadian welfare state. In addition to acting as an economic stabilizer, UI would play a significant redistributive role, not only between groups of workers but also between the country's regions. Most changes up to the early 1970s were designed to increase coverage and benefit levels. Two major issues emerged, however: the inclusion of seasonal workers and discrimination against married women. After a brief outline of the main amendments in this period, I will return to these issues at greater length.

Gradually, coverage was extended to jobs that had originally been excluded – for example, stevedoring in 1946 and certain logging contract jobs in 1950.[5] The proportion of the workforce getting coverage rose from 42 percent in 1941 to over 59 percent in 1954.[6] In 1943 and then in 1950, the special qualifying condition for the cyclically unemployed was relaxed. The act of 1940 originally provided that 60 of the 180 days of work in the past two years needed to establish a benefit period had to follow the final payment made under the claimant's last claim. Beginning in 1950, the requirement was met when forty-five daily contributions had been paid in the six months preceding the new claim or since the beginning of the previous benefit year. After 1953, claimants who fell ill could keep collecting benefits even when unable to fulfill their obligation to be available for work.[7]

The 1940 act saw an initial reform in 1955[8] that basically entrenched the gains of previous years. Thereafter, contributions were recorded on a weekly rather than a daily basis. This amendment reflected the changing workweek as it inched back from six days to five. Similarly, the requisite length of previous employment would now be shorter and calculated in weeks: thirty weeks over the past two years would be enough to secure the right to benefit, with eight of these weeks in the year immediately preceding the claim. Finally, the waiting period went up from five days to six.

Benefits remained low until the 1971 reform. In 1959, for example, the maximum single benefit was $27 (or $115.39 in constant 1986 dollars), and the maximum for claimants with dependants was $36 ($153.85).[9] In 1968, these benefits would be, respectively, $42 ($146.35) and $53 ($184.67). The average benefit paid out was $27.57 ($92.58) at a time when average weekly earnings were $100.54 ($350.51). The incentive to work was still significant.

In the years 1945-56, the rate of unemployment fluctuated between 2.6 percent and 4.6 percent.[10] The cost of service expansion was offset by a low unemployment rate, a bigger contributor pool, and low benefits: the fund built up substantial surpluses to reach $927 million by late 1956.[11] The provisions affecting voluntary unemployment and labour disputes saw some change in this period. Insurance officers could now impose disqualification periods themselves. As well, the union protection allowing claimants to refuse work if acceptance meant losing the right to union membership would now apply equally to resignation for the same reasons. Finally, the UI commission was authorized to pass regulations to determine the beginning and the end of work stoppages in labour disputes.[12]

Seasonal work began to make inroads in terms of coverage, though a 1946 regulation prohibited the payment of benefits to these workers in the off season.[13] Thereafter, they were eligible for benefits except during their seasonal slack periods.

In 1950, an unfavourable economic conjuncture produced a spike in unemployment. Thousands of jobless failed to qualify for benefits.[14] The impact of this recession and the presence of an accumulated surplus in the fund prompted the government to introduce additional benefits for those who could not qualify for regular benefits or had exhausted their entitlement. Recipients must have paid premiums for half of the period required for regular benefits. They could collect these benefits during a set period, generally from 1 January to 31 March, at about 80 percent of the regular rate. The additional benefits were funded through a general increase of one cent a day in employer and employee contributions and a government contribution representing 20 percent of the product of this increase. Should the cost of these additional benefits exceed the receipts accumulated for this purpose, the government was committed to covering the shortfall.

Another economic recession settled in during 1954 that was triggered by falling exports after hostilities ended in Korea. The federal government tried to stem this wave of unemployment by further liberalizing the UI system. This 1955 reform replaced additional benefits with seasonal benefits that were now paid at the regular benefit rate. To qualify for these benefits, payable between 1 January and 15 April, claimants must have contributed for fifteen weeks before the previous 31 March or completed their benefit period after the 15 April preceding their claim for seasonal benefit. The introduction of this seasonal benefit system meant repealing the regulatory provisions for the off season. In the wake of this reform, the government would ultimately stop funding this type of benefit: its cost was not recorded separately anymore. Seasonal expansion proved to be an expensive business, representing, for fiscal 1958-59, $116.5 million out of a total of nearly $479 million paid out in benefits.[15]

Married women became subject to special regulatory requirements under a 1950 amendment. Commission officials suspected these women of collecting benefits when they were not really unemployed or able to accept work. A new regulation imposed additional qualifying conditions on this group.[16] Women claiming benefits in the first two years of marriage had to prove that they had not left the labour market as a result of their union. The regulation obliged them to prove that they had worked for fifteen weeks after their marriage or after the first separation following the same event. In 1952, this period was reduced to ten weeks.[17] At the time, the Unemployment Insurance Commission had this comment: "That the regulations were justified was shown in the first month after they came into effect by the large percentage of married women who, on finding their claims disallowed thereby, made no further effort to keep alive their applications for employment. Out of 8,884 married women who were disqualified because of these regulations during that period, approximately 18 per cent kept alive their application for employment, 5 per cent reported that they had found work, and 77 per cent allowed their application for employment to lapse."[18] Following a wave of protest from unions and women's organizations,[19] the offending regulation was finally revoked in 1957. In the period 1950-57, these provisions disqualified 12,000 to 14,000 women every year. The savings achieved at their expense were estimated at about $2.5 million.[20]

Those highly restrictive provisions reflected the prejudices of the day against women's labour market integration. The same women who had been invited to participate in the war effort[21] were now expected to stay home. By creating additional qualifying conditions that applied solely to married women, the lawmaker was working on the assumption that unemployment was voluntary for many of them. Unfortunately, this legal presumption of unavailability exclusive to women would not be the last, as we shall see in the reform of 1971.

The year 1956 saw a major change that indirectly affected the system. After a lot of skating around on its responsibility for the jobless shut out from UI, the federal government passed the Unemployment Assistance Act.[22] A vehicle for joint federal-provincial funding of assistance administered by provinces, this act targeted[23] the needy unemployed. It was replaced in 1966 by the Canada Assistance Plan Act[24] designed for all needy people, the jobless included. Like unemployment assistance, the Canada Assistance Plan (CAP) was a tied-funding program. To get federal money amounting to 50 percent of the total bill, provinces had to sign undertakings with Ottawa to set up social assistance schemes that met certain standards set out in the act: they included determining the amount of benefit based solely on need, recognizing a right of appeal by welfare recipients, and ruling out a residence requirement for collecting assistance. The CAP also prohibited provinces from requiring welfare recipients to perform any kind of work as a condition of collecting assistance.[25] In

1967, Quebec signed one of these agreements, and its 1969 Social Aid Act[26] would form part of this new funding framework.

The late 1950s saw another economic downturn, and unemployment once more became a major concern. In fiscal 1960-61, the unemployment rate reached 7.2 percent,[27] a level unknown since the end of the Second World War. Demand for unemployment insurance was heavy, and the fund's surplus was quickly used up. The positive balance of $927 million in 1956 had shrunk to $20 million by 31 May 1962.[28]

John Diefenbaker's Conservative government convened a committee to come up with some solutions. The Gill Report, named for its chairman, was permeated by the actuarial ideology. It laid much of the system's financial predicament at the door of its recent "liberal" policies, criticizing its departures from basic insurance principles.

The membership of the Committee of Inquiry into the Unemployment Insurance Act reflected the privatizing view of UI favoured by the government. Two of them came from the insurance community: Ernest C. Gill, president of the Canada Life Insurance Company, and Étienne Crevier, president of La Prévoyance Compagnie d'Assurances. The other two were economists: John J. Deutsch, vice principal of Queen's University, and Joseph Richards Petrie, a Montreal consultant. The committee's mandate was far-ranging and covered both the basic principles of the system and the full array of legislation. However, its more specific task was to look at what was needed to deal with seasonal unemployment, correct the abuses and inadequacies of the system, and, finally, harmonize the relationship between unemployment assistance and other social security programs.

The committee's deliberations began with a concept developed by the UI commission according to which, to prove kinship with the insurance business, the system had to be placed on an actuarial footing – that is, be able to set the amount of premiums needed for settling all possible claims. The compensable event had to be limited to the unexpected, and the loss had to be real for people to have an insurable interest. These conditions, which ruled out anyone who was "not normally in insurable employment most of the time," would determine whether a loss fell "within the purview of the insurance contract."[29] The idea had first been expressed in 1931 by Frederick H. Ecker, then president of the Metropolitan Life Insurance Company, to describe the basis of a "sound insurance" plan.[30] Applied to social insurance and especially unemployment insurance, it would later turn up in various studies.[31] It showed clearly how the actuaries were attempting to liken social insurance to private insurance with the latter as the standard.

References to the actuarial ideology occurred in both the report's findings and its recommendations. The UI system had to be self-sufficient, with no redistributive mechanism or state funding. Yet the committee's

consultations had yielded memoranda suggesting other ways of compensating unemployment, for instance replacing insurance with a tax-funded
benefit program lasting until claimants found suitable work. This proposal
was dismissed as unrealistic and largely ignored. Compared to the 1930s,
after all, Canadian jobless movements[32] were in disarray, and their influence showed it.[33] As for the Confédération des Syndicats Nationaux (CSN),
it was opposed to the "principle of a distinction between seasonal risks
and non-seasonal risks."[34]

For the report's authors, the poor employment situation of recent years
was not the only cause of the financial crisis in the system. This crisis
stemmed in part from amendments offensive to actuarial standards: "It is
apparent that the many changes that have been effected in the plan over
its history have led to a gradual dissipation of the sound actuarial basis on
which the original plan was founded. This, together with the change
in the economic climate, has resulted in the virtual bankruptcy of the
Fund."[35] In this connection, the report cited the creation of first additional
and then seasonal benefits. Not only had the compensation of seasonal
employment proved expensive, but it also violated actuarial principles.
After all, the purpose of insurance was to compensate for loss, in this case
an interruption of earnings due to lack of work. The fact that someone
had not worked in the off season simply meant that that person "cannot
be said to lose what he never had."[36] Seasonal benefits were income supplements, not insurance payouts: they could not be part of an insurance
plan.[37] These positions, conditioned by the actuarial ideology, denied the
redistributive function of social insurance.

Confident that the system's financial crisis could be blamed largely on
noncompliance with actuarial principles, the report advocated bringing
UI back to a more actuarial vision of social insurance and recommended
structural alterations: jobless compensation should be broken down into
three separate systems.

First, the country needed a basic system to cover predictable, short-term
unemployment – or frictional unemployment. Universal insurability would
allow this system to be fully funded, except for operating costs, by the
employers and workers. Claimants would qualify for benefits after twenty
full weeks of work in the past year and, to solve the problem of "new entrants and persons who move into and out of insured employment frequently,"[38] a total of thirty weeks over the preceding two years. One week
of benefit would be paid for each full two-week period of contributions
in the past year to a maximum of twenty-six benefit weeks. The rate of
benefit would fluctuate between 45 percent and 60 percent of earnings to
reflect family responsibilities. When it came to funding, however, the American "experience-rating" approach was discarded. The report emphasized
the absence of proof that this weighting could reduce unemployment.[39]

Second, the report recommended the creation of an extended benefit system paid out of general government revenue and accessible only when regular insurance benefits had run out. The long-term unemployed who could prove a prolonged labour market attachment would be able to collect these benefits, as, in some cases, would seasonal workers. The rate of benefit would be the same as for regular benefits and could be collected for a maximum of one and a half times as long, fifteen to thirty-nine weeks.

And third, to compensate residual unemployment, the report recommended a needs-based assistance scheme run by local or regional authorities. The existing unemployment assistance program should be improved and expanded for this purpose.

In passing, let me note what the report had to say about vocational training. Claimants in training courses should receive not UI benefits but special training allowances: "Retraining of the work force is a matter of community interest and can reasonably be expected to be carried out at the expense of the community rather than at the expense of the Unemployment Insurance Fund ... We recommend, therefore, that where claimants are directed to training, living allowances be provided as part of the general vocational training program and unemployment insurance benefits be discontinued."[40]

The Gill Report's comments on abuse of the system revealed the same actuarial logic: "Many examples of abuses were placed before us in submissions and testimony ... Some of these abuses constitute fraud, but, in a formal sense, most are legal under the existing system, though morally questionable and socially undesirable."[41] Concerning fraud, which would be cited frequently to justify cuts and restrictions in coverage, the report was at pains to point out that provably fraudulent claims in fiscal 1960-61 amounted to $2.3 million of the total $514 million paid out in benefits for that year. The writers hastened to add that this low percentage (0.4 percent) could not cover all of the abuses since it took "no account of undiscovered fraud or payments in circumstances that could not be classed as fraudulent and yet where the payment is contrary to the spirit of the Act."[42] Obviously, the most prominent of these circumstances contravening "the spirit of the Act" was voluntary unemployment. And here, in line with the actuarial ideology, the moral hazard theory came up: "Unemployment insurance suffers particular difficulties in this regard because the event insured against – unemployment – is not always undesired by the insured person."[43] Among the classes of people most likely to abuse the system, married women were again singled out: "Accurate reporting ... would do much to correct abuses arising from certain groups, particularly married women."[44] Although disavowing the suggestion that women required special regulatory attention, the report did recommend "more vigorous monitoring" of their claims.

At the time that the Gill Report was written, there was a UI commission directive that pregnant women were assumed to be unavailable for a six-week period prior to their presumed confinement and up to six weeks thereafter.[45] They could produce proof of availability, but few were successful. The report suggested extending this period to eight weeks before and after confinement. It further recommended that mothers of small children be considered unavailable until they could prove otherwise to the commission's satisfaction and make the necessary arrangements for their children's care if jobs were offered to them. Here again the rationale was to maintain the system as an insurance plan: if the lawmaker wanted to pay maternity benefits, they should be paid through another social security program.[46] Finally, married women who were not the sole supports of their families would be excluded from the extended benefits offered by the commission. The following reflects contemporary prejudice about the male breadwinner role: "The extended benefits plan would not provide for payment of benefits to a married woman who is not the sole support of her household ... The community may reasonably undertake to assist the head of a household after he or she has been subjected to a period of unemployment beyond the duration of insurance benefits but we do not think that there is the same obligation to a married woman who is not the sole support of the household, at least without proof of need."[47]

The idea of complete disqualification for voluntary leaving was discarded on the ground that it would infringe the worker's freedom to change jobs in our economic system.[48] The report did recommend, however, that the penalty for voluntary leaving and refusing work, which then delayed benefit payments for six weeks, be replaced by a real loss of entitlement for the same period.

With regard to labour disputes, the least that could be said about the report's recommendations is that they did not reflect the principle legitimizing worker disqualification, namely the neutrality of the state. An example was the recommendation that refusal to cross a picket line, for any reason, be viewed as connivance in the dispute. Not even threats or violence could justify such refusal: paying benefits in these cases would be tantamount to condoning an unlawful act.[49] The report also called for the regional disqualification of all workers in industries such as construction who belonged to the same class or category as workers who honoured picket lines.

Most of the Gill Report's major recommendations went nowhere. However, supporters of a less generous scheme would get a lot of mileage out of a number of its proposals or thoughts, mainly to attack the payment of benefits to people on the fringe of the labour market, led by the seasonal workers but also including much bigger groups such as women and youth.

The 1960s saw little in the way of changes to the act. Insurability was extended to new categories such as nonowner taxi drivers.[50] Benefit rates were raised. As of October 1966, the employment service came under the newly minted Department of Manpower and Immigration. In 1967, the Adult Occupational Training Act was passed.[51] Its programs were wholly funded by the federal government, and trainee allowances were deducted from UI benefits.

When the Conservatives, now the opposition, called on the government to pronounce on the Gill recommendations, the ruling Liberals deferred debate. In any case, the employment situation had stabilized, and the system's financial crunch had abated.[52] Besides, apart from making the system universal, the reform bruited by the Liberals as that decade closed would be contrary to the thrust of the Gill Report.

In fact, the white paper on *Unemployment Insurance in the 70s* tabled by Minister Bryce Mackasey in June 1970 embodied a very different approach. Whereas the earlier report seemed to have been composed in a vacuum with the primary aim of making the system self-financing, the white paper placed the role of UI in a more general social and economic context. And, to be sure, the political setting was now very different. Internationally as well as domestically, a wind of challenge was forcing governments to embrace more "generous" policies that included poverty reduction. The Canadian government did not want to be left behind. Its white paper was part of a strategy for reorganizing the country's social security system.

At this time, the United States, mired in the Vietnamese disaster, was fighting another type of war at home: a war on poverty. President Johnson's campaign under that banner was waged amid a riptide of grassroots defiance and solidarity that soon reached Canada and Quebec. Populist and union movements saw renewed activity.[53] The government of Canada soon declared its own war on poverty in the form of the "just society" dominating the 1968 election campaign that swept Pierre Trudeau's Liberals into office. The new government weighed various options for social reform. The idea of a negative tax and the suggestion of a guaranteed annual income were rejected in turn. Apart from its outlandish expense, the latter would have required provincial consent. A proposal for expanded and more generous UI was finally chosen as the easiest to implement. For one thing, there was no constitutional problem. And, above all, the project would not generate additional long-term costs for the federal government. The increased cost of access to benefits would be offset by making the system universal. On the assumption that unemployment rates would remain appreciably the same as in past years, the system was expected to be self-financing.[54]

In tandem with the movement to reform UI, a constitutional review process began in Canada during 1968. As part of this process, the federal government suggested a shared jurisdiction with provinces over income security and social services that would enable it to guarantee a uniform level of services across the country. Quebec was opposed, claiming legislative supremacy in these areas and demanding compensatory tax transfers for "opting out." The failure of the 1971 Victoria conference came as confirmation that the two positions were irreconcilable. The constitutional review process petered out.[55]

The 1970 white paper was the second of three government of Canada publications issued at this time that affected unemployment insurance. The year before, a paper titled *Income Security and Social Services* had suggested redefining provincial and federal jurisdictions in the broader context of renewed Canadian federalism. This paper clearly affirmed exclusive federal jurisdiction over unemployment insurance.[56] The third document, *Income Security for Canadians*, was issued in late 1970 by the Department of National Health and Welfare. It echoed the white paper's general thrust and the role of UI in the war on poverty: "Increasing benefits will enable unemployment insurance to more effectively reduce the dependency of the unemployed on social assistance."[57] Only the white paper, however, would have immediate, tangible results: reform of UI was the centrepiece of Trudeau's "just society."

The system set up by the 1971 Unemployment Insurance Act basically embodied the proposals of 1970. Unlike the Gill Report, primarily concerned with money, the white paper had built its vision of UI on humanity. It embraced an optimism about the future and technical advance that could only find increased prosperity around the corner. At the same time, its writers stressed that Canada was not looking solely for technical progress but human progress as well: "The country believes at least as much in a more equitable distribution of our national wealth and the fulfilment of the expectations and potential of all our people."[58] Social programs such as UI had to contribute to this distribution of wealth. With this objective, the war on poverty became a priority, and the paper recalled a factor often lacking in studies on unemployment insurance: "It is important to constantly bear in mind the human element behind the plan."[59]

The white paper cited the insecurity that afflicted so many employees as more and more jobs fell vulnerable to the spread of automation and new technologies. Fewer and fewer people were shielded from unemployment. Technological changes were coupled with profound transformations in a labour market adjusting to the reality of temporary employment. The UI system was incapable of dealing effectively with all of this. For example, it was not generous enough: the requirement of seven months (thirty weeks) of employment was seen as much too high when so many active workers were failing to qualify. Moreover, benefit levels were too low, forcing large numbers of claimants to go on welfare. This situation prompted the white paper's proposal to substantially reduce the weeks of work needed for benefits and raise benefits to an appreciably higher level. Not only would the system improve the financial situation of low-income workers, but it would also enable people on the fringe of the labour market to join in: "Persons with a short work history may have even greater problems than those who have a long labour force attachment. Allowing workers to take early advantage of an unemployment insurance program prevents them from falling into unstable work patterns. Instead, they are effectively integrated into the productive mainstream."[60] Longer benefit periods would reflect individual work histories as well as national and regional unemployment rates. The system would also include new sickness, maternity, and retirement benefits to bring it into sync with overall social policy. This new and more generous scheme clearly needed more contributors. It would therefore be made into a universal plan covering 96 percent of the workforce. This reform was introduced as a mark of solidarity with marginal and low-income workers. The luckier workers were called to the rescue.

The government also had to become part of the funding solution. The proposed threshold for its financial involvement was a 4 percent unemployment rate. Below this level, the system should pay for itself, with employers and employees bearing almost the full expense. Above this level, the federal government would be obliged to defray the cost of benefits stemming from unusually high unemployment. With this new provision obliging it to cover the costs of the increase, the government acknowledged its responsibility for jobs and joblessness: "It clearly establishes the government's responsibility for the financial support of a national unemployment insurance program over and above the self-financing aspect."[61] This financial obligation was indeed a major commitment to UI and the issue of unemployment generally. Although the white paper stopped short of actually saying so, the 4 percent rate apparently "approximated full employment."[62]

This formal commitment by the government of Canada also helped to distance the Canadian system from its American counterpart, in which the state role was much more limited and policies were defined mainly by the bosses who picked up the tab. The 1970 white paper took aim at the US model. The state could not effectively stand up for the workers without participating financially: "In some other countries, unemployment insurance is financed largely by the employers. As a result, the employers are reluctant to enlarge benefits or reorient the plan to meet the changing needs of workers."[63]

As in the Gill Report, universality was the key to the system. There, however, the resemblance tended to stop. The white paper stood clearly apart from the principles of the actuarial ideology that opposed too much redistribution among the insured. The treatment meted out to casual and seasonal workers speaks volumes in this regard. For the Gill Report, these "persons on the fringe of the labour force"[64] did not have much to offer a self-financing insurance scheme: they were accordingly disqualified and relegated to second-rate plans. The white paper took a completely different approach: these workers were not to blame for a labour market marginalization that was partly due to their harsh treatment by the UI system.[65] By suggesting that they be brought into the system, the white paper was recognizing that they had virtually the same rights as claimants with longer labour market attachment.

This debate held considerable significance for the jobless. The question was fundamentally this: should we classify the unemployed by their jobless status or their labour market status? If their unemployment was not voluntary, why place them in different systems, reserving premium protection for the unemployed coming from the best jobs and reduced protection for the more marginal workers and thus creating a two-tiered compensation plan? In the end, the Gill proposal kept offloading the responsibility for unemployment from the economic system onto the individual sufferers. But what was the problem if workers with more regular jobs showed some solidarity through their premiums with workers who were not so lucky or were suffering from the insecurity of seasonal work? This approach strikes me as perfectly compatible with the Beveridge or Marsh concept of social insurance.[66]

The white paper took the perspective of an interventionist state in managing unemployment, and the primary beneficiaries of this approach would be those on the fringes of the labour market who held unstable, low-paying jobs. It was a category in which women and youth were overrepresented.

The 1971 Unemployment Insurance Act[67] embodied a complete overhaul of the legislation then in force. Coverage was extended to 96 percent of the workforce, now swelled by teachers and government employees. The contribution period needed to qualify for benefit, formerly thirty weeks in the past two years of employment, now became eight weeks in the past year alone. Maximum benefits ranged from $53 to $100. This was a major increase indeed: in 1968, the average weekly benefit stood at $26.57, and the average insurable weekly wage was $100.54, while in 1972 the same benefit was $61.79, and the average insurable weekly wage was $136.49.[68] Maximum insurable earnings, and hence benefits, would be adjusted every year to reflect increases in the average wage. Although benefits became taxable as income, premiums, now collected by the Department of National Revenue, were tax deductible. Change also affected the way in which the premium rate was established. Formerly set by explicit provisions, premiums would now be calculated from a rate set by the commission to reflect the "adjusted basic cost of benefit." The act provided for the downward or upward adjustment of this rate to reflect benefits actually paid over the past three years, depending on whether the Unemployment Insurance Account was showing a deficit or a surplus.[69] Finally, the act provided for a regulatory experience rating of premiums for some businesses: however, this capacity was repealed in 1975 without even being used.

Benefits were established at a rate of 66 2/3 percent of insurable earnings for single claimants and 75 percent for claimants with dependants. In the latter case, an adjustment was made to reflect the previous wage or length of unemployment. In no case, however, could the minimum benefit be greater than $100 or less than $20. Claimants were divided into two classes: the first group had a major labour market attachment – that is, more than twenty weeks of insurable employment, while everyone else was in the second group. The new special sickness, maternity, and retirement benefits were available only to major attachment claimants. The system became more accessible, and more unemployed had the right to longer benefit periods, but the waiting period was increased to two weeks. In 1975, these two weeks made Canada's the longest waiting period of any UI system in the world.[70]

This complex piece of legislation provided for a sequence of benefits in five phases. The first phase lasted eight to fifteen weeks to reflect weeks of insurable employment. The second phase lasted ten weeks, also available to everyone. The other phases were extension periods. The third, based on length of previous employment, was accessible only to major attachment claimants and provided a maximum of eighteen weeks of benefit. The last two were tied to the rate of unemployment. The fourth lasted four weeks when the national unemployment rate rose above 4 percent but remained under 5 percent and eight weeks if the national rate exceeded 5 percent. The fifth and final phase, based on the regional unemployment rate, paid six weeks of benefit if this rate exceeded the national rate by 1 percent, twelve weeks if this overage became 2 percent, and eighteen weeks when it exceeded 3 percent. Total benefits collected, however, could not exceed fifty-one weeks. This system enabled an insured person who built up the minimum weeks of insurable employment to qualify and lived in a region with a high rate of unemployment to collect benefits for a fairly long time.

Liberalization of benefit access was belied only by the rules for claimants over age seventy and those over sixty-five who applied for benefits under the Canada or Quebec Pension Plan. These people lost their entitlement to regular benefits, but if they were major attachment claimants they received a lump sum equal to three weeks of benefits. The white paper defended this discriminatory treatment[71] on the ground of wanting to coordinate the UI system with other social security systems.

The act provided a new sickness benefit lasting fifteen weeks for major attachment claimants even if the medical problem was the cause of their termination. Ground was lost in other cases of sickness, however, since the sick unemployed had never seen their benefit period limited before. Eligibility for maternity benefits, also reserved for major attachment claimants, included an added condition in the form of the "ten magic weeks" rule. Of the requisite twenty weeks of employment, ten had to fall between the thirtieth week and the fiftieth week preceding the expected date of confinement. This was simply more evidence of prejudice against women, who were now suspected of taking jobs for the sole purpose of collecting these benefits and must therefore have their access restricted.[72] These benefits lasted for fifteen weeks around the expected date of confinement. Maternity and sickness benefits could not total more than fifteen weeks per benefit period.

Although maternity benefits filled a serious gap in the social security net and were so popular that they enhanced the system's overall legitimacy, this new type of benefit was not without its critics. Some maintained[73] that UI was not the appropriate vehicle for this type of benefit, since its status as social insurance implied benefits stemming primarily from a claimant's former labour market attachment. Doubt was also cast on the constitutionality of these benefits.[74] Was it consistent with its jurisdiction over unemployment insurance for the federal government to enact a maternity benefit plan? Was this type of benefit not a family assistance program that should come under provincial jurisdiction? The act also stated that, when a province set up a sickness or maternity benefit scheme, the corresponding UI benefits would cease to be payable in that province, and contributions to the federal system would be reduced accordingly to fund the provincial scheme.[75] Quebec would cite this exception in 1997 to launch its own parental benefit program.[76]

The matter of women's availability while pregnant was dealt with explicitly in the 1971 act. Whereas women in the major attachment class were entitled to maternity benefits, minor attachment women were disqualified for fifteen weeks around the date of confinement with no opportunity to prove their availability during this period. The previous system had disentitled them for six weeks before and after confinement. The Gill Report, which rejected the principle of maternity benefits, had recommended increasing this period to eight weeks before and after confinement. Women who had suffered discrimination from 1950 to 1957 for being married were now discriminated against after 1971 for being mothers. This provision would form the subject of a major court challenge in *Bliss*.[77]

The disciplinary component of the system underwent a complete overhaul. Where the old law penalized voluntary leaving by delaying benefit payments, the new act stripped claimants of their benefits altogether. The new disqualification would also apply in cases of dismissal due to misconduct, refusal of suitable employment, refusal to obey a summons by the UI commission or comply with one of its directives, or failure to attend a training course. However, the maximum length of penalty was reduced to three weeks. The 1971 act also provided a new form of penalty called "disentitlement."[78] This idea incorporated while varying some of the old rules. Disentitlement delayed the payment of benefits for an indeterminate period within a benefit period as long as the circumstances for its use persisted. It could also involve their irrevocable loss if claimants did not have enough available weeks in their initial benefit period or returned to work before disentitlement ended. Disentitlement would be used mainly in cases of nonavailability for work but also in situations such as labour disputes.

For cases of voluntary leaving and dismissal due to misconduct, the act now contained the idea of "last employment." The regulations[79] stipulated that no job terminated by claimants more than thirteen weeks before their benefit claims could represent a loss of employment subject to penalty. This meant that someone quitting a job could elect to wait thirteen weeks before filing a benefit claim instead of being disqualified. The thinking behind this provision was apparently that a thirteen-week claimant should not be disqualified because this interval after loss of employment meant that a causal connection between the voluntary termination and the unemployment could no longer be assumed.[80] This is reminiscent of the reason for the British provision of 1911 limiting the length of disqualification in similar cases to six weeks, after which the worker's unemployment had to be blamed on a poor labour market instead of the circumstances of separation.[81] This provision, which passed almost unnoticed as the act went through, would prove to be an effective though, unfortunately, little-known defence.[82] When it came to labour disputes, the UI commission was now able to regulate the meaning of "bona fide hiring" within the claimant's usual occupation so that disentitlement could be avoided.[83]

Finally, the 1971 act contained a provision that reflected the system's transactional quality. In return for relaxing the system for workers, the lawmaker recognized the employer's right to appeal UI commission decisions on the same basis.[84] This was a formidable weapon that employers could turn to their own advantage in, for example, cases involving voluntary unemployment or labour disputes. And having fired someone, an employer could now challenge the UI commission's decision not to disqualify the former worker for misconduct. The possibility of being deprived of benefits for a time could be an incentive for a claimant to accept an offer of settlement from other authorities, such as grievance adjudicators.

Generally speaking, the 1971 reform was positive for jobless rights, especially in terms of UI access for the most marginal workers. The result was a substantial drop in the numbers of unemployed forced to go on welfare.[85] This policy would continue until 1975. The system saw few legislative changes during this period, although in 1972 the administration of its benefit component was transferred from the minister of labour to the minister of manpower and immigration.[86]

Hopes of self-financing were deceived. The premiums from the enlarged contributor base failed to cover the added cost of the system's expansion, and Ottawa had to pick up a growing share of UI funding. This federal proportion went from 19 percent of total spending in 1971 to 42 percent in 1973 and 51 percent in 1975.[87] As the state's bill for the system spiralled upward, employer criticisms of UI found ready listeners. Employers were hostile to relaxed conditions for collecting benefits, claiming that they allowed temporary and intermittent workers into the system with resultant abuse. The rise in disqualifications for voluntary leaving after 1971 came as grist for their mill, although the connection between this increase and the 1971 reform enactments is far from clear.[88] Indeed, according to a study on the first half of 1974, 90 percent of people leaving employment voluntarily were not claiming UI.[89] However, these criticisms reached the Canadian public, and there was a proliferation of charges of abuse blamed on the reform. A number of observers would attribute the 1972 Liberal election losses that forced Pierre Trudeau to form a minority government to a backlash against UI reform.[90]

The narrowly reelected Liberals saw the expediency of answering these critics by tightening up the system: all they had to do was go after the "bad" unemployed. In 1973, the government brought in Bill C-125[91] to strengthen deterrents against voluntary unemployment. This bill provided an additional contribution period in cases of voluntary leaving, dismissal due to misconduct, and refusal of suitable employment: claimants losing their jobs in such circumstances must have accumulated eight additional weeks of insurable employment, and the maximum length of disqualification would be extended from three weeks to eight. The bill ran into a lot of opposition at a time when many jobless were already having trouble qualifying for benefits. The minority Liberal government had to withdraw its bill when it failed to win the support of MPs from the New Democratic Party.

Despite this setback, the policy shift was increasingly noticeable. The government's strategy was subtly to prepare public opinion for the need to place restrictions on the system. In 1974, it commissioned an initial survey of public attitudes. Although most Canadians "found the system acceptable in terms of basic social requirements," one-third voiced concern about abuse. Naturally, this part of the survey was the one that people remembered. In the same year, an election brought the Liberals back into office with a majority in the House of Commons.

In 1975, administrative controls were tightened radically, and a second survey revealed a substantial rise in concern about UI abuse. In short, controls and surveys were used to prepare public opinion, initially in favour of the system's social thrust, for potential cutbacks. It would not be the last time this tactic was used to prepare the public for changes that would ultimately be to their detriment. Now everything was in position for an about-face.

Despite this reversal, how can we sum up the system's first thirty-five years? There is no doubt that they had been good to the jobless. As an arm of the federal government's Keynesian strategy, the UI system was called on to play a growing economic role, first as an automatic stabilizer between periods of growth and then to mitigate regional disparities. Seasonal workers and then marginal workers in general were the primary beneficiaries of the system's expansion.

6
Vision under Siege, 1975-88

The later 1970s saw an international backlash against Keynesian economics that soon spilled over into Canada. Neoliberals won support with their
call for a freer market to curb new economic problems such as stagflation.
One of their favourite targets was UI, where the focus on income support
would shift to labour market management. Although the main reason for
tinkering with the system in this period was to cut Ottawa's outlay, the
influence of the new thinking was felt as well. Legislative amendments
would actually take rights away from the unemployed.

In the early 1980s, however, an economic recession had politicians mark-
ing time. There would be little in the way of legislative movement until
late in that decade, when some changes favoured the jobless. The most
conspicuous products of the 1980s were reports that revealed mounting
neoliberal influence and a commitment to fine-tune the system to the
reality of free trade with the United States. The reports were used to persuade the public that the coming counterreforms were inevitable. These
changes were put on hold, however: the economic conjuncture, with job
markets deteriorating, made any proposal for radical cuts in unemployment protection a political powder keg.

The period opens with a general loss of confidence. The oil crises that
erupted in 1973 created good openings for attacking the Keynesian strategy. The traditional right, stymied in the 1960s by the emergence of a state
with policies that eluded its control, was now bent on revenge. And the
new economic conjuncture, typified by stagflation that combined high
unemployment with inflation, offered fertile ground for that crop. Neoliberal ideas, always lurking in the spectrum of economic theory despite
the triumph of Keynesianism, came back into fashion.[1] Developed mainly
by the Chicago School and its most illustrious champion, Milton Friedman,[2] these ideas won increasing influence with Canadian governments.
The new orthodoxy would call on governments to minimize their involvement in market regulation, stepping aside in all areas that could be

handled by free enterprise. They should instead support and accommodate market forces and practise laissez-faire to let markets work in the best
conditions. The appearance of stagflation lent credibility to the neoliberal
case against Keynes.

Heavy government involvement in the economy brought charges of creating inflation and thus helping to maintain a high unemployment rate.
A "natural" or "basic" unemployment rate was apparently needed to forestall renewed inflation. Since the fight against inflation was now ranked
ahead of the fight against unemployment, jobless rates once seen as high
came to be accepted as necessary for economic growth.[3] Naturally, a primary outcome of this thinking was to cast doubt on the objective of full
employment, that old colour bearer for John Maynard Keynes:

> Over most of the postwar period, there was a widespread consensus
> among politicians and the professional economics community that a rel-
> atively low level of unemployment could be achieved and sustained with-
> out accelerating inflation.
>
> Over the course of the 1970s, this consensus largely disappeared. The
> experience of the late 1960s and 1970s led to doubts that unemployment
> could be significantly and permanently affected without a concurrent rise
> in the rate of inflation. Economists have generally agreed that develop-
> ments in labour markets have tended to increase the unemployment rate
> independently of cyclical factors. These developments related to ... in-
> creased eligibility for and size of unemployment insurance benefits.[4]

By a curious turnabout in perspective, these economists blamed the
failure of full employment in part on the existence of UI or at least some
of its features. Another noteworthy paradox in this doctrine was that, just
as high unemployment rates were being recognized as intrinsic to the
workings of a liberal economy, there was a growing tendency to see the
unemployed as responsible for their own joblessness. In this respect,
neoliberal economic thinking meant a shift in focus from demand to
supply. To counteract unemployment, then, government should work on
the labour supply, not the demand. Its focus should be on the individual
who was responsible for the labour supply and therefore, ultimately, for
unemployment. The jobless should be trained and given more incentives
to work: the marketplace would take it from there. Here we were, half a
century down the road, back with the Purvis Commission's talk about
"employability"![5]

The consequences of this argument for income security programs were
clear enough: they were too costly and did not provide enough incentive
to work. They had to be replaced by programs that were less expensive and
more productive. Income security systems were accused of a passivity that

had to be supplanted by active programs with a bigger role for vocational training – even if this policy shift worked against the systems' original purpose of income protection. For UI, this meant, first, cutbacks and stronger disciplinary control. Government financial participation was singled out: its generosity would prejudice the labour supply.[6] All of this new talk came with the publication of research into the system's potential deterrent effects on the workforce.[7] In fact, these studies were updated versions of the old tales about UI "creating" unemployment.

Various writers held that the 1971 amendments had lengthened the average benefit period, swelled the workforce, encouraged worker turnover in businesses, and thus helped to raise the unemployment rate by a percentage point in 1975.[8] This version of the effects of UI came under fire. In particular, it was labelled as inconclusive inasmuch as it dealt only with the labour supply and failed to give enough consideration to the demand for labour in the form of job openings: "In 1978, the last year Statistics Canada published data on the number of jobless per vacant position, there were no fewer than 20 unemployed for each vacant position ... These data confirm that the major cause of our high jobless rate remains the shortage of jobs."[9] Voluntary unemployment was actually no more than a marginal phenomenon that, as the focus of attention, overshadowed the economic system's inability to provide jobs for people who wanted to work: "But as long as the government fails to maintain full employment, there will be many in our society who will have no choice between work and unemployment insurance benefits. These are the involuntarily unemployed, compared to whom the amount of insurance-induced unemployment appears insignificant."[10]

This neoliberal approach, in the best tradition of the actuarial ideology, shifted the responsibility for unemployment to its victims. It would certainly come in handy for a government that in 1975 wanted to cut its UI funding role. The result was a gradual realignment of Canada's economic policy. The government presence in labour markets became less decisive. The full employment objective was challenged and then dropped. Henceforth, job creation would increasingly be the business of the marketplace. From this standpoint, the jobless were now mere cogs in the labour machine. UI was cast not just as a heavy expense for the state but also as unproductive due to deterrent effects that jeopardized labour markets. This was why access had to be made harder, coverage reduced, and penalties for voluntary unemployment raised. Since this realignment helped to lower costs, governments would support the revival of actuarial thinking. The list of restrictions imposed from 1975 on stemmed from the coexistence of the two objectives of reducing the government's financial commitments and promoting the UI system's role as a labour market regulator. It would be the 1980s, however, before the neoliberal criticism of

UI won a majority audience and led, in a context of free trade with the United States, to the counterreforms of the 1990s.

The second half of the 1970s saw the passage of two bills that would substantially curtail the system's so-called generosity. To justify their litany of restrictions, attacks were mounted, first on the "bad" unemployed and then on people in McJobs until, finally, all UI recipients were in the assailants' sights. This wave of offensives slashed jobless rights and fostered an "antijobless" atmosphere later described by Bryce Mackasey, who as minister had masterminded the 1971 reform: "Either by coincidence or design, prior to every one of these amendments we had a well-orchestrated campaign based on the alleged abuse of the plan, thus preparing and conditioning people for the amendment and supposedly aimed at reducing the abuse or tightening up the regulations."[11]

The first wave of cuts came with the passage of Bill C-69 in late 1975.[12] The benefit rate was levelled at 66 2/3 percent – a move defended by references to an increase in family allowances, now indexed to the cost of living.[13] The maximum length of disqualification was doubled to six weeks. As it had when introducing Bill C-125 in 1973, the government justified this change as a deterrent to increasing benefit claims from the voluntarily unemployed. At the same time, the formula for calculating government financial contributions was amended. The 4 percent threshold, after which the government assumed the added costs associated with high unemployment, was replaced by a less stringent standard. Henceforth, the government's financial commitment would not kick in until the average annual unemployment rate exceeded the average rate for the eight-year period ended the previous 30 June.

Generally speaking, employers supported the bill, and unions were against it. For the Canadian Council on Social Development, Ottawa's reduced contribution reflected "a continuing abrogation of the responsibility of the federal government for establishing full employment conditions."[14]

The amendments in Bill C-27, passed in 1977,[15] extended the two components of the system's new thrust. The cuts continued, while the focus fell on UI's role in disciplining the labour market. The target this time was the entrance requirement. The standard eight weeks of insurable employment were replaced by a "variable entrance requirement" (VER) of ten to fourteen weeks, depending on the effective unemployment rate in the region where the insured person lived. This complex mechanism was the outcome of a compromise extracted by the union opposition, joined by MPs from peripheral regions that included the Atlantic provinces, over an initial plan for an across-the-board, twelve-week requirement. The employers wanted this requirement raised to twenty weeks. It was arranged, however, that the VER would remain in force for only thirty-six months unless the government renewed it by an order in council that had to be ratified by Parliament. Failing renewal within this time, a uniform fourteen-week standard would apply. This placed a real sword of Damocles above the heads of some of the most marginal unemployed. Also, by extending benefits to reflect the length of previous employment at the contributors' expense, the government achieved significant savings and increased people's incentive to keep their jobs.

Another innovation of Bill C-27 was the range of new, later to be known as "active," employment measures in the UI system.[16] These measures involved consolidating the existing vocational training program and new job-saving and job-creation programs within the UI environment.[17] Under the job-creation program, claimants could continue collecting benefits if they agreed to work in a community agency as referred by the commission. Their benefits would then be increased and extended, although their employment would not be insurable.[18] Meanwhile, under the work-sharing program to avoid business closings, the commission could authorize claimants to collect benefits for part of a week while they worked the other days. Finally, trainees referred to vocational training courses would be able to collect benefits not just in extension periods but also the whole time that they were training, for up to 104 weeks. One detail had meaning for claimants' rights: there would be no appeal from any commission decision approving or disapproving a job-creation project or work-sharing agreement.[19]

With these new provisions came a major shift in the use of the Unemployment Insurance Account. Up to then, the account had existed solely to compensate loss of employment; now it could be used for other purposes. The change drew barbs from the opposition: "This party rejects the idea of the Minister of Manpower and Immigration [Mr. Cullen] using unemployment insurance funds for these programs, not because we are against job creation per se but because we are against stealing funds from the unemployed for them."[20]

Incorporation of this new, "active" approach raised some fundamental problems. Could the UI system be used to fund job creation, job saving, or vocational training? Was there not a risk that this new role might jeopardize its primary function of income support? Should not the cost of vocational training be funded, as underscored by the Gill Report, from general tax revenue instead of the Unemployment Insurance Account? And how about the constitutionality of these measures in terms of federal jurisdiction over UI?

The new measures were fought by both unions and employers. The unions worried about the effect of the work-sharing program on working conditions, and the employers worried about inflating the cost of the system. Ottawa calmed these fears by arguing that training and job-creation programs were proliferating and that UI as a universal program had to be accessible to claimants involved in them. Since benefits would be paid to these jobless anyway, and the government was continuing to bear the cost of extended benefits, why not use benefits as "training allowances" or to keep people working?[21] Unemployment insurance soon became the main source of income support for claimants in federal training programs.[22] The UI system's new vocation enabled the federal government to play a major role in this area while cutting back on the proportion of training expenditures borne by the Consolidated Revenue Fund.

In terms of administrative organization, the bill provided for the creation of the Canada Employment Insurance Commission (CEIC), which now assumed responsibility for labour market, employment, and unemployment insurance programs under the new Department of Employment and Immigration. And when it came to remedies, the act dropped the requirement for prior authorization of appeals by the chair of the Board of Referees. Clearly, the expansion of the right of appeal benefited workers and employers in equal measure. However, appeals to the umpire were now limited to one of the following grounds: jurisdictional error, error in law, or noncompliance with the principles of natural justice by the Board of Referees or if the conclusions of the Board of Referees were so obviously unreasonable, unsubstantiated, or contrary to the evidence. Although the umpire continued to enjoy broad discretion in his power to act, the new definition of his authority was closer to judicial review than a genuine appeal *de novo,* as had formerly been the case.[23] The right of appeal was now more general, but its purpose was more circumscribed.

The special targets of Bill C-14, passed in late 1978,[24] were the marginal workers. The system already distinguished two categories of claimants by their work histories; this classification now became more complex with the introduction of tougher qualifying conditions for first-time claimants and those who, by contrast, called on the system "too" often. With this bill, the essentially economic and statistical concept of "labour force" entered the act. First, a higher standard would be required of the relatively marginal group of "new entrants or re-entrants to the labour force" (NERE). These were people who could not prove fourteen weeks of insurable employment in the year preceding their qualifying period or generally in the period between the 53rd and 104th weeks preceding their claim – "insurable employment" including, apart from paid work as such, collecting UI benefits or worker's compensation, attending a CEIC-approved course, and unemployment due to a labour dispute. They would now have to prove twenty weeks of such employment in their qualifying period. Whereas the 1971 reform had attempted to bring them into the labour force, the new idea was apparently to push them out! The same tougher VER would apply to "repeaters," led by seasonal workers. More weeks of employment were required if a claimant had collected more weeks of benefits in the qualifying period than the number of weeks of insurable employment required by the VER. However, the regular VER would continue to apply to repeaters where the regional unemployment rate was greater than 11.5 percent. Here again arguments for this measure included clear references to the actuarial ideology. The government was bent on reducing "UI dependency."[25]

It is important to note that the exception that kicked in when the unemployment rate rose above 11.5 percent, like the VER itself, was time-sensitive. Unless the government renewed it within eighteen months, a standard entrance requirement of fourteen weeks would apply. An already complex act was becoming more convoluted still.[26] Workers and jobless had trouble finding their way around it, as did many analysts. It will be revealed later how this complexity served political purposes.

Bill C-14 cut the benefit rate to 60 percent for all claimants. The extended benefits based on length of previous employment were now funded in the same way as initial benefits, with contributors bearing the cost up to a given level after which the federal treasury took up the slack. The government was well aware that this offloading of costs on contributors was worse for the not so rich, as admitted in an August 1978 finance department memo: "Also it must be recognized that a shift from [progressive income tax] financing of benefits to premium financing will mean a shift towards lower income persons."[27]

The bill passed against strong opposition outside Parliament, with the unions rejecting almost all of the amendments. In May 1979, Joe Clark's Conservatives gained power. There was no change in legislative timing, however, and provisions that had been deferred came into force as scheduled. In any case, the spring of 1980 saw the Liberals back in office as the proponents of the new economic order and new-style ideology. The war on unemployment and poverty had yielded to war on the unemployed!

The 1971 unemployment rate of 6.2 percent became the 7.5 percent of 1980. Ottawa, which in 1975 assumed "its responsibility for the jobless" by bearing 51 percent of the cost of the system, now bore only 22 percent of that cost. A number of the gains made by the jobless in the 1971 reform were no more. The people most affected by this policy shift included the marginal workers who, ironically, needed the system most.

Fortunately, the 1980s would see a respite, albeit temporary, in this backward movement: the few legislative changes in this decade sometimes even favoured the jobless. Ideologically, however, the drive for a system geared more to labour market management was maintained. The main reports and studies published in this period were all looking for a cheaper, "more productive" UI system that harkened to labour market imperatives. The major stakeholders, the unemployed, were spared little consideration.

The mandate handed to a 1980 departmental task force by Lloyd Axworthy, the Liberal employment minister of the day, reflected the policy shift that had been dogging the system since 1975. Recommendations would have to consider "factors likely to influence the operation of Canadian labour markets in the 1980s."[28] Here was a total about-face from the white paper proposals of 1970. Whereas the earlier document had emphasized the system's role in redistributing wealth, the Gershberg Task Force Report of 1981 favoured a more general strategy, with the primary aim of labour force adjustment to the new job market. Except for a few recommendations to correct inequities affecting specific groups, all proposed changes had this as their goal. The UI system stood accused of blocking labour's mobility and incentive to work.

The Gershberg Report's leading recommendation was to expand the VER to cover all claimants. The flexibility on benefit periods in regions of high unemployment was criticized as restricting labour mobility: "UI provisions now allow someone in Newfoundland to work 10 weeks to qualify for 42 weeks of benefits."[29] What became known as the "10/42 formula" would be used by neoliberals to denounce the system's generosity in those outlying regions. That formula, a distillation of the actuarial position on voluntary unemployment, turned out to be an ideological marketing success. By associating UI claims with lotteries (6/49) in the public mind, it managed to juxtapose the ideas of insurance, voluntary unemployment, and fast money to undermine the system's regional sensitivity. And the targets of choice in the neoliberally inspired studies of the 1980s were these very workers on the fringes of the labour market, led by the seasonal labour force in outlying regions.

The report argued that this new VER, ranging from fifteen to twenty weeks to reflect regional unemployment rates, would make UI less attractive by removing the complex rules of exception for recent labour force entrants and frequent claimants. Length of benefit would also be cut, especially for claimants with short-term employment. Thus amended, the system would be better attuned to work incentive and labour force mobility objectives while costing the government less.

On maternity benefits, the report recommended abolishing the "10 magic weeks" rule and section 46, according to which minor attachment claimants were unavailable for fifteen weeks surrounding their date of confinement. The task force also recommended extending these benefits to adoptive parents.

In line with its mandate to promote efficient labour market operation, the Gershberg Report paid special attention to the matter of disqualifying "claimants who have committed work-related infractions."[30] The task force commented pointedly on the increase in voluntary leavings in the wake of the 1971 reform that cut the maximum disqualification to three weeks and then the drop in these numbers when the maximum was returned to six weeks in 1976, but the task force shrank from making a direct connection between these two variables. A number of other factors likely played a role, for instance the system's increased accessibility and stricter controls. At any rate, the task force thought that tougher disqualifications for voluntary leaving would help to buttress job stability and cut the numbers of these cases. Two possibilities were bruited, the first being to raise the maximum disqualification to twelve weeks with a seven-week floor, and the second being the complete loss of benefit entitlement. In the latter case, a claimant would have to hold a new job long enough to regain the right to benefit. The task force chose the first approach as less radical: after all, it could be very hard to find a new job in a period of high unemployment.

The report also recommended keeping the benefit rate at 60 percent and the government contribution at a fixed 15 percent. Yet its philosophy did not escape detection: "The overall approach of the Task Force is based on the assumption that the unemployment insurance program can be redesigned to reduce unemployment itself. It implies that the unemployed are primarily responsible for their own joblessness."[31]

The recession of 1981-82, combined with resistance from the unions and people in outlying regions, would oblige Ottawa to put off giving effect to the Gershberg Report's main recommendations. In fact, with the outbreak of "the worst economic crisis since the Great Depression,"[32] talk of individual responsibility just did not stand up anymore: "The dramatic increase in the rate of unemployment in the 1980s has brought the program, and the groundlessness of the allegations of abuse, much closer to Canadians. It is difficult to sustain an argument that the unemployed are bums when claims rise to 3 million a year, and virtually everyone knows someone personally who has been touched by unemployment."[33] In these circumstances, there was no question of the government placing further restrictions on UI. Ottawa still wanted to use the system to curb the effects of unemployment by the generalized use of work-sharing and job-creation benefits,[34] but the 1980s saw only minor legislative and regulatory change.

In 1980 itself, for example, a regulation lowered the length of employment and weekly earnings requirements for insurability. Thereafter, all that was needed was fifteen hours or 20 percent of the maximum insurable weekly earnings. In 1983, the act's maternity benefit provisions were amended by the repeal of the "10 magic weeks" rule and section 46, which made minor attachment claimants unavailable during a fifteen-week period surrounding their date of confinement. At the same time, fifteen weeks of adoption benefits were provided for major attachment claimants.

In 1984, the newly elected Mulroney government proclaimed its intention of overhauling Canada's entire social security system.[35] The economic policy unveiled by Minister of Finance Michael Wilson in November of that year referred to a number of the Gershberg Report's recommendations. However, the opposition, stirred up by the Conservatives' plan to reform social security, for example by deindexing old-age pensions,[36] forced the Mulroney government to revise its strategy.[37] Postponing any major UI counterreforms, it would merely make cuts by the regulatory route for the time being.

In 1985, the regulatory provisions for deducting earnings from benefit payments were amended. For benefit calculation purposes, severance pay and retirement income were now included. Starting on 5 April 1987, however, retirement income would no longer be deducted from benefits when the weeks of insurable employment used to establish the benefit period were accumulated after pension payments began.[38] It will be noted that these new provisions departed from the insurance principles so dear to the actuarial ideologues.

Meanwhile, employers continued to call for harsher restrictions in cases of voluntary leaving that included loss of entitlement, even though some of them shrank from this penalty: "The Canadian Federation of Independent Businesses believes that no voluntary quitter should get any UI benefits at all. Wood, although a CFIB member, considers this 'pretty hard' because it would put an employee at the mercy of an unreasonable employer."[39]

Although the provisions affecting labour disputes saw no significant amendment, their legitimacy still came under fire. The very principle of state neutrality, supposedly the basis of the disentitlement rule, looked more and more open to challenge: "When the modern State has shown itself ready to intervene in so many aspects of life, it is difficult to accept that it is being neutral when it holds itself aloof from one aspect in particular ... The State is obviously not a neutral element in strikes and to claim that it is so, simply because access to one set of benefits is restricted to non-strikers, is an obvious nonsense."[40] Its refusal to consider the positions of the parties to the dispute – as did a number of US states, where benefits could be paid in lockouts caused solely by the employer,[41] and Ireland,[42] where disentitlement was ruled out if the loss of employment was due to unreasonable behaviour by the employer – made the Canadian government not only not neutral but also actively pro-boss: "By imposing across the board exclusions based solely on the employment situation of the claimant without regard to any subjective factors, the ... state assumes a very active role in labour disputes on the side of management."[43]

We should remember that disentitlement in labour disputes also applied to welfare. In Quebec, for example, anyone directly involved in a labour dispute lost the right to welfare benefits, a hardship that was visited on dependants as well.[44] This disentitlement was applied in most Canadian provinces, often stringently.[45] Using cold legal logic, the lawmaker denied the family of a person involved in a labour dispute the basic right to assistance that British judges had recognized in the Merthyr Tydfil affair of 1898.[46] Decidedly, progress was unstoppable!

With a potential free-trade agreement with the United States in the offing, the neoliberal UI review was soon back on the agenda. In 1985, a challenge to the Unemployment Insurance Act had been filed in connection with trade agreements between Canada and the United States. The complainants asked for compensation on the ground that Canada's UI provisions for independent fishers constituted an undue subsidy of the Atlantic fishing industry in violation of trade agreements between the two countries.[47] Noting that the provisions for fishers differed from those for other self-employed workers, the US Department of Commerce still had to rule that they did not represent preferential treatment for this group compared to the program as a whole.[48] Even so, this case revealed an American sensitivity to the system's provisions that departed from US practice, including its funding and regional bias.

The years leading up to the Canada-US Free Trade Agreement saw various attempts to prepare the Canadian economic ground. Created by a Liberal government in 1982, the Royal Commission on the Economic Union and Development Prospects for Canada was asked to write a new master plan for the economy. In spite of pressure from unions and grassroots organizations for a more active government role in the economy to boost employment, the report issued in 1985 called for disengagement: "In general ... governments should endeavour to facilitate the operation of the market mechanisms of our economy, rather than to seek occasions for further intervention."[49]

The perceived link between Canada's economic growth and the free-trade agreement with the United States meant that our economy and UI system had to become more flexible, more competitive, to survive under the new order. These concerns prompted a number of the Macdonald Commission's analyses and recommendations. While acknowledging that unemployment insurance had an income protection role for the jobless, the report held that it was not up to UI to "redistribute income and wealth in the Canadian economy," a function to be performed by other income security systems. Admittedly, UI contributed to the country's economic stability, but "certain provisions of unemployment insurance do not encourage the return to work and have a negative effect on the adjustment mechanism of our national labour market."[50]

The report revealed its debt to the private sector in references to themes, "moral risk" for example, that were dear to the hearts of the actuarial ideologues. Armed with this vision, the commissioners found the UI system working to increase length of unemployment and providing "too generous a subsidy to Canadians, whose labour force behaviour was characterized by repeated unstable employment."[51] Their proposals, though largely unsubstantiated, were Draconian: a uniform entrance requirement of twenty weeks, benefit rates cut to 50 percent, and regional distinctions abolished. This last recommendation affected not only entitlement to benefits but their length as well: two or three weeks of work would confer the right to a week of benefit. In practice, this meant an appreciable reduction in length, as two or three years of work would be needed to collect one year of benefits. Finally, the commissioners recommended a new funding formula with an experience-rating component. It was no surprise to see the influence of the US system in these proposals.[52] Like the Gershberg Report, this one was replete with references to US research and the US model.

The cold logic of the Macdonald Report's recommendations left virtually no room for the social and human aspects of unemployment and the real problems of the principal stakeholders, the jobless themselves. The main targets were the workers from outlying regions and specifically their seasonal labour forces. Advocating a system without regional bias to enhance labour mobility and end subsidies to industries providing unstable employment, the report took aim at a major facet of the Canadian program. The challenge involved not only the redistributive nature of the UI system but also its role in reducing regional disparities under federalism, a characteristic that differentiated this system from the US model. The Forget Report of the following year, which shared the objective of ending state financial support for the system, would attempt to view the process in a more social perspective.

At any rate, the Macdonald Commission's recommendations offered a candid reflection of what the neoliberal school wanted to see in the Canadian UI system of tomorrow. At that time, Ottawa's financial contribution to the UI account basically covered the extension of benefit periods based on the regional unemployment rate. Here was government playing a leading role in redistributing income and wealth to disadvantaged regions. But the system's regional sensitivities, reflecting this aspect of unemployment in Canada and the state's responsibility for it, were incompatible with the neoliberal concept of the government role in a UI program. The regional strategy was expensive for the government and no good for labour markets. Our economy and our taxation, it was argued, had to be more competitive, and UI must not weigh more heavily on our economy and our businesses than the US system did. The priorities dictated by this new economic vision would grow more urgent with the imminence of a free-trade agreement with the United States.

In July 1985, the Mulroney government convened a Commission of Inquiry on Unemployment Insurance. The system had seen various reviews in recent years, but this new inquiry reflected the political conjuncture. In November 1984, as has been noted, this government had announced its agenda of overhauling Canada's social security system only to be sent packing. It then played for time while looking for arguments that might win the public over to the need for sweeping counterreform. However, the political climate was not conducive to the radical surgery called for by the neoliberal school. The recession of the early 1980s had prompted many Canadians to acknowledge the need for effective protection against unemployment, while the animosity in the outlying regions to any new restrictions that might impinge on them was undimmed. In these circumstances, the restrictions proposed by the Macdonald Commission were politically unrealistic since the electoral consequences might be disastrous, especially in the Atlantic provinces. The axe would not fall in earnest until the Mulroney government's second term (1988-93).

In the meantime, the government strategized and prepared its ground. The Forget Commission was a part of this strategy. Under cover of a general social approach to unemployment problems, the majority report's chief recommendations would be intended to relieve the system of its regional baggage and make it self-financing, like the US schemes. This policy was promoted as necessary in a context of budget cuts and fairer to contributors in regions with lower unemployment.

The Forget Report's positive features owed much to the makeup of the commission. Of its six members, two came from the employer community, Guylaine Saucier and Roy F. Bennett; two came from the unions, Frances Soboda and Jack Munro; Moses O. Morgan was from the academic world; and Chair Claude Forget, a former Liberal minister in Quebec, was a lawyer and economist then working in the private sector. The union presence on the commission led to criticism of a dominant view of UI found in virtually all studies conducted since the 1971 reform and copiously referenced by the majority report. Since the commissioners were unable to agree on the general thrust of their proposals, the minority from the union movement wrote a separate report. Although this report did not get as much play as the majority document, it stood as one of the rare rejoinders to the neoliberal approach to UI. And although the two reports differed completely on the future focus of the system, they came together on specific points. The commissioners from the employer community, though members of the majority, insisted on adding their own supplementary comments on some issues.

The majority report began by emphasizing that the various briefs and hearings had convinced its authors that Canadians wanted UI reform. This change, however, should come with a policy of economic growth and full employment as part of a broader framework of social security reform. In essence, the UI system was accused of getting away from the concept of social insurance by paying benefits based on regional criteria. Instead of mere income replacement for unemployed workers, its regional features made it look more like an income supplement program. The Forget Report repeated the analysis seen in the Gill Report nearly twenty-five years earlier, stressing that the system had become overly complex. It was also inequitable. Was it fair to subject workers in a region of lower unemployment to a tougher system due simply to their place of residence, when they might be facing the same problems finding a job as anyone else? The ease with which claimants could collect benefits for fairly long periods was again underscored: ten weeks of premiums produced forty-two weeks of benefits. The Forget Report saw the end of these regional variations as essential: "If Unemployment Insurance is no longer used as an instrument of income supplementation, its role as a social insurance program can be strengthened."[53]

The report went on to recommend an annualized system with a single entrance requirement, single phase, and single maximum length of benefits. Annualization used a different method of accounting for earnings that reflected hours worked instead of weeks: the entrance requirement would be 350 hours over the past year. Whereas the existing system used the number of weeks actually worked (the last ten to twenty, depending on the entrance requirement) to determine average insurable weekly earnings, this number would now be fifty-two – all the weeks of the year preceding the claim, worked or not. This approach would be introduced by degrees until the current 60 percent benefit rate was replaced by a rate of 66 2/3 percent. And annualization would be accompanied by the introduction of a Cumulative Employment Account. Modelled on retirement plans, this account would build up at a rate of two weeks per year of work and could be used only after twenty-five years of service. When the annualization formula put claimants at a disadvantage due to low earnings in the year preceding their claim, this account could be used to increase or extend their benefits.

Reviewing the Macdonald Report's proposal for a single twenty-week entrance requirement in line with a number of US systems, the Forget Commission found this unfair[54] since it deprived many workers of all protection. Annualization would save just as much money, estimated at $2.5 billion;[55] it would operate on social insurance principles, it would be funded entirely by premiums, and it would be fairer, based on one rule for all workers. Clearly, there would be significant loss of income for the jobless. To cushion the impact of abolishing the regional provisions, Ottawa should work with the provinces to establish one or more income supplement systems and take measures to ensure economic growth.

The presentation was adept inasmuch as there was no suggestion of raising the entrance requirement or reducing the duration or rate of benefit. The result, however, was even more dramatic than earlier proposals. It was not hard to see that seasonal workers in a Gaspé fish-processing plant who earned the right to benefit after ten weeks of work a year would watch the earnings used to determine their weekly rate divided not by ten but by fifty-two. The heavily penalized seasonal workers would be joined by large numbers of people in marginal employment who were not fortunate enough to work full-time all year round. Not without reason did the report call for the gradual adjustment of the UI system in tandem with the creation of income supplement schemes. In fact, anyone would be penalized who worked fewer than fifty-two weeks full-time in a year.

The family resemblance between the Forget and Gill Reports was obvious. The proposed system would be self-financed and the "marginal" workforce left to the mercies of other schemes more akin to assistance. The Forget Report, like the Gill Report, was opposed to paying for vocational programs out of the UI account: "Employment training is a valuable activity, but it should not be funded directly from employer and employee premiums. The role of Unemployment Insurance should be more limited."[56] Waving the actuarial banner, the Forget Report made the interests of the private sector and the marketplace its own.[57]

Annualization was central to the disagreement that split the commissioners. The minority decried the plan in unequivocal terms: if given effect, it "would represent by far the biggest cut in benefits in the history of the program."[58] The resulting privation would affect most jobless Canadians, and provinces with high unemployment rates might see benefits cut to the 50 percent level. What is more, annualization would divide workers into two classes, radically cutting the benefits of the ones most at risk of becoming victims of unemployment while favouring those who were basking in job security.

The minority members saw this proposal as reflecting a view of unemployment as primarily a personal responsibility. They accused their colleagues of justifying annualization by a desire to correct certain abuses without taking a critical look at the myths surrounding them. The consultation process had persuaded minority members that, contrary to what was argued in the majority report, Canadians were generally satisfied with the system, and workers from regions with lower unemployment were prepared to bear the cost of helping their less fortunate counterparts. They called for maintaining the VER, extending the length of benefit to seventy-one weeks, and, above all, continuing the government's financial commitment to the UI system as part of a full employment policy: "Although the funding formula has been altered almost continuously since 1971, the basic principle of social responsibility for a share of the costs of unemployment has remained part of the program. Indeed, the link between public funding of UI benefits and unemployment rates is arguably the closest thing Canada has to a 'Full Employment Act.'"[59] They also thought that this system, contrary to what was argued in the majority report, was fully compatible with social insurance principles: "*Social* insurance is just that: *social* insurance. In our view, public funding of an element of the risk of unemployment that is a social and not an individual responsibility is not a departure from social insurance principles; it is the very essence of social insurance."[60]

The debate over annualization and funding featured two opposing concepts of UI and the government role. The majority report, drawing on the actuarial ideology, called for a self-financing system based on the private model that would deal with workers on the basis of their individual risks of unemployment. The system proposed by the minority members would recognize unemployment as a state responsibility and thus provide better protection to workers in regions more troubled by unemployment: on the one hand, a system and a government taking collective responsibility for unemployment and employment; on the other, a government and a system closer to the rule of "every person for himself or herself." And over this debate there was always the looming shadow of free trade: "Its coming into force would seriously disrupt our income security system and reduce its protection to a level more comparable to US standards."[61]

The Forget Report also contained recommendations on voluntary unemployment and labour disputes. Despite the classic controversies over these issues, they do not seem to have been major concerns for the commissioners: their conflicts in this regard were much less dramatic, and recommendations were often shared. On labour disputes, the report had this to say about the basis of the measure's legitimacy: "This provision is based on two considerations. The first is that a strike is voluntary ... The second consideration is neutrality, in that paying Unemployment Insurance benefits to strikers would make Unemployment Insurance, in effect, a strike fund."[62] Armed with these principles, the report went on to call for certain amendments to the act.[63] Disentitlement should not be used in lockouts, and people involved willy-nilly in labour disputes should have the right to benefit unless they could later profit from any gains arising from the strike. Similarly, maternity, sickness, and adoption benefits should be paid during labour disputes. To be abolished was the use of the jurisprudential threshold of 85 percent of previous staffing and production levels to define the end of a work stoppage. Disentitlements should be removed at the end of labour disputes even if full resumption of activity did not occur at once. Finally, anyone who was hired elsewhere while a dispute was going on and subsequently laid off should be entitled to benefits without any requirement for minimum length of employment in the new job.

The commissioners from the employer community could not be won over to certain recommendations. They believed that the 85 percent rule should be kept to determine the end of a work stoppage since a strike was a voluntary act for which strikers had to bear the short- and long-term consequences. As regards voluntary leaving, the report agreed to keep the maximum disqualification at six weeks since an overly harsh penalty might increase the risk of collusion between employers and employees not to report these separations. It also recommended a list of just causes for voluntary leaving to include sexual harassment, discrimination, threats to health and safety, separation to follow the spouse to a new job in another region, and a layoff in reverse order of seniority. Finally, the Forget recommendations included the introduction of parental benefits and financial assistance to community groups,[64] such as the Mouvement Action-chômage, that advised and assisted claimants appealing benefit rulings.[65]

The Forget Report had few immediate results. Opposition from unions and outlying regions forced Minister Benoît Bouchard to distance himself from the report's conclusions, which he duly referred to the House of Commons Standing Committee on Labour, Employment, and Immigration. On 19 March 1987, this committee used these words to reject annualization as advocated by the Forget Report: "'Annualization' would result in a reduction of benefits for large numbers of claimants; would create undue hardship and increase the costs of other social programs; would adversely affect both the long-term and short-term labour market objectives of Unemployment Insurance; and would be totally at variance with the concept of pooling risks within a social insurance program."[66]

Reacting, the House of Commons committee made a large number of recommendations to expand the protection afforded by the system, including a uniform entrance requirement of ten weeks of insurable employment for both regular benefits and maternity, sickness, and adoption benefits. Although the committee basically repeated the Forget Report's recommendations on voluntary leaving, it set out the rule that the CEIC had to give claimants a reasonable time to expand their job searches before declaring them ineligible due to nonavailability.[67] Finally, the committee reaffirmed the tripartite funding principle.

The parliamentary committee's report came under fierce attack, especially by employers. Since the debate was so polarized, the government elected to postpone its reform until after it had gone back to the polls. Even after the Conservative government was reelected, however, Minister Bouchard had to announce that there would be no reform of the system.

Although the UI system's growth up to 1975 had been positive in terms of the recognition and expansion of the rights of the jobless, things were very different thereafter. Influenced by neoliberal thinking, the federal government made cuts that impaired jobless rights. Although the economic recession of 1981-82 forced governments to postpone the reform process, the ideological offensive continued with the publication of studies that reflected a determination to adjust the system to the environment of free trade with the United States. Then, with the reelection of the Mulroney government and the advent of the Free Trade Agreement, the political scene changed: in April 1989, the great counterreform got under way.

7
Rights Enshrined in Case Law, 1940-90

Bit by bit, the case law built up. Umpires and, later on, the Federal Court were asked to define the scope of key provisions in decisions that accumulated slowly up to 1971. Their interpretations generally favoured the rights of the jobless. The decision in *Abrahams*, delivered by the Supreme Court in 1983, consolidated this jurisprudential trend. That court asserted the primacy of the act's social aim of paying benefits to the unemployed and admonished that the act should be liberally interpreted. *Abrahams* was followed by a wave of UI case law liberalization.

This development was mainly concerned with disentitlement in labour disputes, a rule that clearly revealed the founding compromise of the UI system. In *Hills*, a decision with clear political overtones, the Supreme Court went as far as to appropriate certain criticisms of the customary defence of disentitlement, including the alleged neutrality of the state.

Although this trend in case law enshrined the act's social aim, concerns about workforce regulation were not absent from judicial pronouncements. Just when case law on voluntary unemployment was vouchsafing some wins for the jobless, a noteworthy exception arose in *Tanguay*. Stemming from a British precedent, this decision echoed the actuarial ideology since it refused to lend a social purpose to the "just cause" required for voluntary leaving.

The first decisions rendered by umpires expressed more concern about equity than the meanings of the concepts used in the act. At that time, claimants were not appealing Boards of Referees decisions in large numbers. Not only did nonunionized claimants have a limited right of appeal, but also many of them did not even know what rights they did have. Moreover, though the appeal procedure was free, claimants desiring legal representation had to bear that cost.

The jurisprudence coalesced first at the umpire level. Unlike members of Boards of Referees, who did not have to be lawyers, umpires were actual judges appointed as *persona designata*. They came originally from the

Exchequer Court, and, when this court was abolished in 1970, they were chosen from the judges of the Federal Court or provincial high courts, with the latter serving as deputy umpires. The UI commission and Boards of Referees were bound by the umpires' decisions[1] and, obviously, by the decisions of the higher courts – after 1970, the Federal Court of Appeal and the Supreme Court of Canada.

Challenges to decisions affecting benefits were always handled by umpires, but challenges to decisions on insurability followed a more convoluted route. Under the 1940 act, these decisions could be appealed to the umpire. Starting in 1971, however, they were made by the minister of national revenue.[2] This change was made for pragmatic reasons: the department had solid expertise in taxation. The first appeal was to the umpire, whose judgment could then be appealed to the Pension Appeals Board. Since 1983, the sole appeal jurisdiction has been the Tax Court of Canada.[3] Obviously, a decision by this court, like a decision by an umpire, can be taken for review to the Federal Court of Appeal.

The first cases taken to the Supreme Court turned mainly on insurability of employment (and thus the collection of premiums) and labour disputes. Just as the development of case law on the first issue reflected employer challenges, as in the decisions in *Martin* and *Scheer*[4] on the insurability of the employment of nonowner taxi drivers, the jurisprudence on labour disputes was driven by union pressure. Unions have always had the right to appeal, and they have had the financial and professional resources to challenge administrative rulings in this area.

Starting in 1975, appeals to the umpire showed a sharp increase, as Table 1 shows. There were several reasons for this exponential explosion – first the various waves of cutbacks that shook the system after 1975, then the expansion of the right of appeal to all insured persons beginning in 1977, and above all the effect of larger numbers of advocacy groups defending jobless rights. The need for these groups was felt even more when the 1971 reform further muddied the act: "This statute is even more difficult than most modern complicated statutes, in my view, to comprehend. It is replete with special concepts created for the purpose of the statute. Its general scheme is almost completely obscured by being buried in detailed provisions."[5]

A number of jobless rights advocacy groups, such as the Mouvement Action-chômage in Quebec, were created in the 1970s and delivered advisory and litigation services in several regions. As well, low-income people could now avail themselves of the new legal aid services in various provinces. Facing an increasingly complex act, many jobless turned to these services.

They were especially effective in Quebec. A 1989 CEIC study showed their impact on the success rate of Board of Referees appeals.[6] Representation

Table 1

Appeals to Boards of Referees and umpires, 1943-88

Year	Appeals to Boards of Referees	Appeals to umpires	Initial and renewal benefit claims (000s)
1943	1,085	11	36.7
1945	10,838	37	296.4
1950	12,153	173	1,150.2
1958	n/d	115	2,780.5
1962	n/d	190	2,192.2
1966	16,494	111	1,547.7
1973	45,289	156	2,237.5
1976	51,022	438	2,678.2
1979	21,864	1,019	2,600.1
1982	15,718	1,130	3,919.2
1984	n/d	1,105	3,492.4
1988	20,203	1,746	3,230.8

Notes: UI commission publications do not provide information about the number of appeals taken to the Board of Referees for all the years in this period. The data on the Board of Referees and the umpire come from the following sources: Unemployment Insurance Commission, *Third Annual Report* (Ottawa: The Commission, 1944); *Fifth Annual Report* (Ottawa: The Commission, 1947); *Tenth Annual Report* (Ottawa: Unemployment Insurance Canada, 1951); *Nineteenth Annual Report* (Ottawa: Unemployment Insurance Canada, 1961); *Twenty-Second Annual Report* (Ottawa: Unemployment Insurance Canada, 1964); *Twenty-Sixth Annual Report* (Ottawa: Unemployment Insurance Canada, 1969); and Employment and Immigration Canada, *Annual Report 1988-1989* (Hull: Employment and Immigration Canada, 1989); Statistics Canada, *Unemployment Insurance Statistics,* January 1990, 10; Pierre Issalys and Gaylord Watkins, *Unemployment Insurance Benefits: A Study of Administrative Procedures in the Unemployment Insurance Commission* (Ottawa: Law Reform Commission of Canada, 1977), 144, 175; Pierre Issalys, *Rationalization of Social Benefit Appeals* (Ottawa: Department of Justice, 1986). Moreover, it is difficult to be precise about the number of active claimants during all these years since the statistical tools refer variously to the claimant or UI recipient – the claimant being the one who filed a claim and the recipient being the one who actually collected the benefits. I have therefore chosen to illustrate the course of the number of jobless using unemployment insurance by the number of initial or renewal claims filed within a particular benefit period on a monthly basis. This inventory has the advantage of providing a constant for the whole period, since this type of statistic has been compiled since the system began. In this connection, see Statistics Canada, *Social Security, National Programs (a Review for the Period 1946-1975)* (Ottawa: Statistics Canada, 1976), 106-07; Statistics Canada, *Statistical Report on the Operation of the Unemployment Insurance Act* (Ottawa: Statistics Canada, 1979), 71; Statistics Canada, *Unemployment Insurance Statistics,* January 1990, 10. Note, finally, that the statistics on appeals to the Board of Referees are for the fiscal year, whereas those for initial and renewal claims are for the calendar year. However, to provide a general view, I have spread all of these data over the dominant calendar year, with the fiscal year counting for nine months in this base year.

before the umpire was also important in Quebec. Whereas umpires' decisions in other Canadian provinces were generally made on the docket, with no claimant demand for hearings, the situation was the opposite in Quebec.[7] Advocacy groups played a major role there, and the Forget Report even recommended funding them publicly.[8] Judge Reed underscored the need for the jobless to have "an independent advice agency ... from which reliable information might be sought."[9] This more effective legal representation for the unemployed would also spur the emergence of case law on various concepts in the act, including those around voluntary unemployment.

Paradoxically, umpires' decisions speeded the development of a jurisprudence that, though not always exhaustively defining the concepts, still produced legal interpretations favouring the jobless. However, the 1977 changes in the appeal system considerably curtailed the power of umpires to overturn decisions by Boards of Referees. Umpires were powerless to act except in special circumstances, such as errors of jurisdiction or law or a board's failure to observe a principle of natural justice;[10] their power to intervene on matters of fact was very limited, as the Federal Court of Appeal pointed out: "The proper test under s. 95(c) is whether there was any evidence upon which the Board of Referees could have found as they did, or whether they made any mistake of principle."[11]

This new appeal system affected the jurisprudence. In a number of decisions, umpires proclaiming disagreement with the reasoning or findings of Boards of Referees still refused to intervene when none of the criteria provided by the act was present. Admittedly, the definition of concepts in the act was a matter of law, whereas the application of these concepts in individual situations was a matter of fact. Even so, "a complete judgment as to the application of the statute in a particular instance is a question of mixed law and fact."[12]

This made it imperative, since umpires could not act in many cases that then came down to matters of fact, to more narrowly define the various concepts in the act. Since errors of jurisdiction and obvious breaches of the principles of natural justice by Boards of Referees were actually not that frequent, and since few decisions could be described as unreasonable, the easiest way for the umpire to intervene was on errors of law. Ironically, the amendment limiting the claimant's right of appeal fuelled an accelerated development of case law – especially when UI law was enriched by a major influx from human rights legislation.

The right to equality provided in the Canadian Bill of Rights[13] was cited in *Bliss* to challenge the provision prohibiting the payment of regular benefits to a minor attachment claimant for the fifteen-week period around her confinement date.[14] The refusal of Stella Bliss was turned into a political triumph.[15] As court decisions had aroused fierce reactions in feminist circles, section 46 was repealed in 1983.[16] Moreover, women's rights organizations became actively involved in the drafting process for the 1982 Constitution Act to make sure that the right to equality, particularly where women were concerned, was more effectively shielded by unambiguous legal texts.[17] A few years later, this right, as protected by section 15 of the Canadian Charter of Rights and Freedoms and thus duly constitutionalized, was cited in two major cases, *Tétreault-Gadoury* and *Schachter*.[18]

Marcelle Tétreault-Gadoury challenged the constitutionality of section 31 of the Unemployment Insurance Act, prohibiting the payment of regular benefits to persons aged over sixty-five, on the ground that the provision was in violation of section 15 of the charter. The Federal Court of Appeal and then the Supreme Court of Canada had to agree, finding the provision discriminatory and thus incompatible with the right to equality. The Supreme Court ruled further that the umpire had authority to consider constitutional arguments. Here was a major gain for the jobless, who could now appear before an administrative tribunal with charter challenges to a provision's constitutionality. This option was all the more attractive inasmuch as justice at that level was free of charge. Ottawa, though arguing the act's constitutionality before the Supreme Court in this case, would amend it in the counterreform of 1990.[19] The offending provision was thereby repealed.

In the second case, claimant Schachter, the father of a newborn child, challenged the refusal of parental benefits to biological parents when adoptive parents could collect fifteen weeks to get a child settled in its new family. He maintained that this treatment discriminated against parents in his situation in contravention of section 15 of the charter. After winning in the Federal Court of Appeal, Schachter failed in the Supreme Court, although by that time the lawmaker had partially vindicated him in the counterreform of 1990. Adoption benefits were replaced by ten weeks of parental benefits available to all parents.

The accumulating case law followed a route of progressive recognition of rights that would gain momentum with the 1983 *Abrahams* decision. That judgment was the culmination of this jurisprudential process, upholding the general aim of the scheme as the dominant factor in its interpretation: "Since the overall purpose of the Act is to make benefits available to the unemployed, I would favour a liberal interpretation of the re-entitlement provisions. I think any doubt arising from the difficulties of the language should be resolved in favour of the claimant."[20]

At first glance, there is nothing revolutionary here. The goal of any UI system, as the name suggests, is to insure workers against the risk of unemployment and pay them benefits when the risk occurs. Similarly, the broad, liberal interpretation that the act should receive was consistent with the interpretive principle valid for all legislation and enshrined in the Interpretation Act.[21] However, the truly remarkable thing about this decision was its recognition of the act's overriding social aim at the precise time when the rise of neoliberal thinking was changing UI policy to give priority to market objectives at the expense of the interests and rights of the unemployed.

The interpretation issued by the Supreme Court in *Abrahams* had ramifications for the entire act. Thereafter, an obligation existed to interpret the act favourably to the jobless. A review of case law development around labour disputes and voluntary unemployment shows that it had not always been thus.

The disqualification linked to labour disputes introduced to our unemployment system in 1940 was an almost word-for-word replica of a British provision then in force.[22] It is therefore no surprise to detect the influence of British jurisprudence in a number of Canadian decisions. As the provision would see little major change until the counterreform of 1990, its application was decided in the courts. The act stated[23] that claimants involved in a labour dispute were not entitled to benefits unless they could prove that they were not participating in the dispute, were not financing it, were not directly interested in it, and did not belong to a group of workers directly involved in any of these three ways. The disentitlement would not end until the work stoppage ended, unless the claimant took a new job in the meantime that met certain conditions.

Both British and Canadian case law held that disentitlement could not apply unless the following four conditions were met: loss of employment, a work stoppage, a labour dispute, and a causal connection linking these first three elements. Here the burden of proof fell to the UI commission or the employer.[24] When the conditions were met, however, the burden of proof fell to claimants, who had to show that they were not directly involved in the labour dispute, that the work stoppage was over, or that a new job enabled them to lift the disentitlement. Until *Abrahams,* the concept of disentitlement and its conditions of application tended to be broadly interpreted, while exceptions were narrowly interpreted at the expense of the right of the jobless to their benefits.

Loss of employment would raise a number of questions, one being whether job loss for seasonal workers could be ascribed to a labour dispute when they were already unemployed and then prevented from resuming work after the dispute by the seasonal nature of their employment. For all the ambivalence of British jurisprudence on this point,[25] Canadian umpires had established that disentitlement should be applied to claimants from the time that a labour dispute prevented them from returning to their former employment.[26] The Federal Court of Appeal, in *Gionest,* overturned arbitral practice by ruling that the loss of employment described in section

44 of the act could not occur to persons who were already unemployed. In this case, the employer had delayed opening his fish-processing plant in early spring, preferring to wait until a new collective agreement was signed. Gionest and his workmates had been found disentitled to benefits from the time that they could have returned to work. Judge Pratte, speaking for the court, had this to say about the disentitlement of the already unemployed: "One cannot lose what one does not have. A person cannot lose *his* employment if he does not first have employment which he subsequently loses. It is true that someone who is unemployed and who misses a chance, an opportunity to be employed, in a sense loses that employment; but he does not lose *his* employment, since the employment never was his."[27] Judge Pratte's words are reminiscent of the argument in the Gill Report about the seasonal worker's lack of insurable interest.[28] It should also be emphasized that the court, in this decision, used a broad definition of "labour dispute" that encompassed the period when negotiations usually take place.

The decision in *Gionest* was followed by a number of similar rulings.[29] However, the Federal Court of Appeal, in *Morrison,* qualified the interpretation advanced in *Gionest.* Morrison, a logger who was unemployed when a strike broke out, was to return to work on a specific date but was found disentitled from that date.[30] To the court, Morrison's situation differed from Gionest's, in which there was no specific back-to-work date. However, the same court in the same year would refuse an application for a judicial review of an arbitral decision consistent with the jurisprudence in *Gionest:* this case involved a recall, though with no commitment by the employer.[31]

The text creating the disentitlement, drafted for one job, raised problems when a claimant held two jobs. It was a matter of knowing whether the loss of one of the two would cause complete disentitlement if the claimant was without any job. Like the appeal court decisions in Britain,[32] Canadian case law would reveal some confusion on this issue. The Federal Court of Appeal found that a worker who had held two jobs at a time and lost one of them due to a labour dispute could not be considered as having lost employment and thus avoided disentitlement.[33] However, most of the court's judgments found the contrary: the loss of a part-time job due to a labour dispute disentitled claimants even if they had already established their right to benefit through prior employment.[34] Acknowledging the inequity of this result, the judges still felt bound by the text on disentitlement. After *Abrahams,* at any rate, some arbitral rulings cast doubt on the use of disentitlement for the loss of a part-time job.[35]

Another situation criticized by a lot of umpires was the "injustice" arising from the disentitlement of people who were absent from work during labour disputes for personal reasons. For example, a claimant who was already disentitled due to a work stoppage in a labour dispute could not collect maternity benefits.[36] The same rationale was used for sick leave and absence from a training course.[37] However, some decisions tempered the use of disentitlement in cases where claimants had planned their leave before a work stoppage began.[38]

Claimants could be exempted from disentitlement by proving that neither they nor the group of workers to which they belonged were taking part in the dispute or its funding or had any direct interest in a potential settlement. The burden then fell to them to show that they met these conditions. It is worth remembering here that disentitlement was not reserved solely for workers who were members of the certification unit involved in the labour dispute: it applied to all workers laid off due to that dispute. For example, office workers, members of a certification unit other than the one for a firm's production workers but who were laid off due to a strike declared by those workers, were also affected by disentitlement. They then had to prove its various elements to claim the exception.

The interpretation of this provision aroused some fairly passionate debate, especially about participation. Did the refusal of workers who had no direct involvement in a dispute to cross picket lines for fear of physical reprisals constitute participation in the dispute itself? And, if not, what burden of proof did a claimant have to bear for such nonparticipation by members of the worker group to which that claimant belonged? Let us remember that the Gill Report was against paying benefits to workers who refused to cross a picket line for any reason.[39]

Canadian as well as British jurisprudence[40] held that workers had to show that reasonable fear of violence was preventing them from going to work. In *Valois*,[41] however, the Supreme Court decided in a representative case[42] that such proof of intimidation did not have to be produced by every worker named in an appeal. The proof given in the test case applied to every member of the appellant worker group.

Proof of nonfinancing, the second element of the exception, was also controversial due to the support that workers received in labour disputes from union contributions to strike funds. Despite differences in legal labour relations frameworks, Canadian case law[43] had followed the British interpretation[44] in disentitling any worker who paid dues to a union involved in a dispute. The Supreme Court, in *Hills*, reversed this trend by citing the differences in the two countries and, in particular, Canada's practice of mandatory payment of union dues. Referring to the interpretation in *Abrahams*, the court read the verb "finance" in the exception "as requiring active and voluntary participation by the claimant," thus excluding union dues. Yet there was nothing very revolutionary about requiring that contributions be "voluntary" before the exception could be applied. The Supreme Court seemed to overlook the fact that the British lawmaker in 1975, following the Donovan Commission's recommendations,[45] had removed all reference to funding in the text on disentitlement due to labour disputes, along with the claimant's affiliation with a group of workers of the same grade or rank.[46]

Although the UI commission had been empowered since 1955[47] to use regulation to define the circumstances of the beginning and termination of the work stoppage, it left this job to the tribunals. The interpretation of the provision was guided by different concepts, borrowed in part from British case law. In this way, Canadian jurisprudence would find that a work stoppage had to be substantial to involve disentitlement[48] and ended only when business activities had been substantially restored. The so-called 85 percent rule, which did not exist in British jurisprudence,[49] was developed by Canadian umpires[50] with the idea of "exceptional temporary means" to define the times when a work stoppage began and ended.[51] Sometimes out of pragmatic considerations, these concepts made for a strict use of the disentitlement provision that came under fire.[52] Unlike the end of a work stoppage, where the timing could be pinpointed by relatively fixed criteria, the measurement of substantiality defining the occurrence of the work stoppage would depend on the circumstances in each situation. Both production levels and employee numbers affected by the work stoppage could be considered for this purpose.

The Federal Court of Appeal, in *Caron*, reviewed "substantial resumption of operations" as the criterion defining the termination of the work stoppage. Caron and his workmates had lost their jobs in a lockout declared on 3 March 1986 by their employer, the Société Canadienne des Métaux Reynolds of Baie-Comeau, Quebec. On 29 March, the dispute was settled, and a back-to-work agreement was signed. The same day 970 of the 1,430 workers went back in. Using the criterion of substantial resumption of operations, the CEIC maintained the disentitlement until 17 May 1986, when production volumes reached 75 percent of the level prior to the dispute and the workforce stood at 90 percent of its earlier level. On appeal, the Board of Referees found that the work stoppage had ended on 26 April 1986, when aluminum production reached the substantial level of 71 percent with 90 percent of the workers back. The umpire confirmed this decision, finding the Board of Referees' review of the evidence not unreasonable in view of the state of the law on the issue. However, the majority judgment from the Federal Court of Appeal set aside the practice of continuing disentitlement until the substantial resumption of operations. According to Judges Hugessen and Desjardins, this interpretation was not consistent with the act:

How can it be said that there is still an *"arrêt de travail"* (the English word "stoppage" seems even stronger) when on the one hand, the employer has agreed to call its employees back to work, and on the other hand the latter have agreed to return and have in fact returned to work, at least in part? The facts of the case at bar are a striking illustration of this: if there was still a work stoppage at the Reynolds company's operations on March 29, 1986, then what were the 970 people who returned on that day doing?[53]

When a labour dispute ended, therefore, the resumption of operations did not need to be substantial or appreciable to terminate the work stoppage. Judge Hugessen underscored the court's thinking that continuing disentitlement after the dispute was "an act that causes the government to lose its neutrality."[54] Dissenting, Judge Marceau held that earlier jurisprudence was consistent with both the legislative provision's wording and its objectives: "Paying unemployment insurance benefits to employees who are waiting to return to work is, first, using the Unemployment Insurance Fund to compensate employees who are not unemployed without intending and accepting that result in advance, and second – even more seriously – it is releasing employees from part of the 'cost' of the strike or lockout without giving similar treatment to the employer in terms of its 'lost earnings' or the hardship it will suffer."[55] Although, in the meantime, the 85 percent rule had been enshrined in the regulations by the counterreform of 1990,[56] this judgment was appealed by the attorney general of Canada. In a majority decision written by Madam Justice L'Heureux-Dubé, the Supreme Court affirmed the judgment on the ground that the existing legislative provision did not authorize the use of criteria that placed such a limited definition on the expression "termination of the stoppage of work."[57]

Moreover, British case law had determined that a work stoppage could last even if the employer managed to regain its normal operating level through the use of exceptional and temporary means.[58] Canadian jurisprudence, drawing on British precedents,[59] would reach similar conclusions.[60] In 1990, the CEIC used these words to justify the use of this concept as developing in Canadian case law: "It would go against the very object of the provisions on labour disputes and create a serious inequity to authorize the payment of benefits to strikers on the sole ground that the employer managed to resume and maintain its operations by exceptional means."[61] In view of the limiting effect of this idea on claimants' rights, it is not surprising that the courts have sometimes tried to qualify its use. In CUB 13307, for example, Judge McNair allowed the claimant's appeal on the ground that the actions of the employer, in particular by hiring a large number of workers to regain its normal production level, could not constitute exceptional, temporary, or provisional means in the circumstances.

The concept of "exceptional and temporary means" as exceptions to the 85 percent rule revealed the government's bias. If the employer suffered no financial loss, how could it be argued that its workers had no right to benefit? An employer could call a lockout, replace its workers by new ones, and maintain operations at almost normal levels by enlisting its supervisors. Disentitlement would be maintained owing to the exceptional and temporary nature of the measures taken by the employer.[62] These new employees, although in unsuitable employment within the meaning of the Unemployment Insurance Act,[63] could become eligible for benefits if they stayed on the job long enough. Meanwhile, the former workers would not be entitled to benefits, thanks to state neutrality!

Like their British counterparts,[64] the umpires had established that disentitlement should be lifted from the time that claimants were able to show that, although there was no labour dispute, they could not go back to work.[65] Apart from the assumption of abandonment arising from a labour dispute, this situation could occur in seasonal industries with the coming of the off season.

The Federal Court of Appeal, however, would rule otherwise in its decision in *Imbeault*.[66] In this case, forest workers involved in a labour dispute were claiming benefits for the Christmas season on the basis that, even without the labour dispute, they would have been unemployed for that period. Overturning case law granting benefits in comparable situations, the court found that the text of the legislative provision could not bear this interpretation. Dissenting in *Ouellet*, Judge Marceau tried to temper the interpretation by imagining a middle way of determining the time when a work stoppage was terminated in these circumstances. He distinguished two phases in a work stoppage: the one where the stoppage was the direct product of a labour dispute, and the one where it could be ascribed to another cause, thus ending the disentitlement.[67] Here was yet another instance of how the basic inconsistency of the concept of disentitlement made its application problematic.

At that time, section 44 of the act provided two mechanisms for restoring benefit entitlement to people in new jobs taken after a work stoppage in a labour dispute. Workers could either hold a new, bona fide job in their usual occupation or be regularly hired in another occupation. The good-faith stipulation was intended to avoid fake hiring for the sole purpose of removing disentitlement.[68] The act did not prescribe a minimum duration for the new job, leaving it to the courts to define this hazy concept,[69] since no two cases were identical. Beginning in 1971, however, the regulations[70] required a minimum term of two weeks for a bona fide hiring. No term was prescribed for the other option of regular work in another occupation. As in Britain,[71] the jurisprudence considered the intent of claimants, who had to give up their former jobs to prove that they were regularly engaged elsewhere.[72] Like the 85 percent rule and the concept of "exceptional and temporary means," this obligation did not appear anywhere in the act or regulations.

Citing the act's objectives, the Supreme Court, in *Abrahams*, set this interpretation aside. Refusing to use the criteria for involvement in the dispute – subsection 44(2) – to determine whether a person was regularly engaged in another occupation,[73] the Supreme Court held that the issue was not whether someone did or did not intend to return to the former job but the characteristics of the new job. And here the decisive factor was not the duration of the new job but its regular work schedule. This decision was followed by a number of Federal Court of Appeal rulings on the issue.[74]

The Supreme Court, in *Hills*, would go on to deal with the alleged neutrality of the state. Let us remember that disentitlement in both Canada and Britain was unrelated to the parties' responsibility for the work stoppage, since the language of the provision made no distinction between strikes and lockouts. The influence of British justice was clear in early Canadian decisions on this point,[75] defended on the ground of the state's neutrality regarding the parties to a dispute. This so-called neutrality was criticized as serving the interests of the bosses.[76] In *Hills*, the Supreme Court went as far as to wonder about the merits of the provision and challenge the lawmaker. For Madam Justice L'Heureux-Dubé, the principle of state neutrality did not take account of the often lopsided power relationship between the opposing parties: by refusing to consider the parties' merits, the act could even become an "instrument of coercion."[77] Similarly, the Supreme Court rejected the argument that disentitlement was necessary to avoid the employer's financing a strike against itself. It concluded that, in any case, the employer could pass the strike's cost on to its employees or customers. Had Churchill and the Board of Trade team not sold their UI scheme to British employers by arguing that they could have others bear the cost of their financial participation?

The practice of disqualification for voluntary leaving, misconduct, or refusal of employment reflected the actuarial definition of voluntary unemployment and had proven its effectiveness as a labour market regulator. At the same time, the act ruled out loss of employment due to union membership or involvement in legal union activities as reasons for disqualification.[78] Since this protection extended to all benefit provisions, some claimants attempted to use it against disentitlement in labour disputes, though without success: the protection covered loss of individual employment only.[79]

Of all the reasons for disqualification, voluntary leaving was by far the most frequently used. In 1981, for example, it figured in over 84 percent of disqualifications.[80] The UI commission, Board of Referees, and umpires held an extraordinary discretionary power over length of disqualification, subject to a six-week ceiling set by law or three weeks in the years 1971-75.

Actually, misconduct and voluntary leaving without just cause were often two sides of the same coin. Someone leaving a job in an especially tense work environment could be penalized for that. If the same person elected to remain in the job and was later dismissed, he or she could be disqualified for misconduct.[81] Since the act did not define key terms such as "just cause" for voluntary termination, "misconduct," or "good cause" for refusing employment, case law was left to connect the dots.

Someone could have good reasons for leaving a job but not "just cause" within the meaning of the act. Tribunals limited the maximum length of disqualification to the most serious cases.[82] Umpires often ruled that refusal by the commission or a Board of Referees to recognize the existence of "extenuating circumstances" constituted an error in law.[83] This jurisprudence actually grew up in reaction to the commission's habit of automatically imposing the maximum disqualification. Yet, in fact, testifying in 1990 before a Senate committee studying Bill C-21,[84] Department of Employment and Immigration officials stated that the average length of disqualification was then about two weeks.[85]

The case law on disqualification would therefore be founded on two main premises: on the one hand, the lack of legal definitions of the ideas used to describe voluntary unemployment and, on the other, the discretionary decision on length of disqualification. Numerous decisions would hold that the explanations provided by the claimant, even if they did not add up to just cause within the meaning of the act, included extenuating circumstances for imposing a lesser disqualification than the six-week maximum. Umpires would make good use of this opportunity to cut a disqualification instead of narrowly defining its rationale. The jobless would seize on this approach since cases, as in all worldly matters, were never completely black or white. Discretionary appraisal would thus be an essential element of the disqualification system and a major current in the related jurisprudence.

Although this procedure was not always used, case law had established that the imposition of a disqualification for voluntary leaving should occur in two stages. First, the burden of proof as to the voluntary nature of the termination fell to the UI commission.[86] The claimant must have clearly taken the initiative in leaving. In cases where the claimant's decision stemmed from the employer's conduct or attitude, disqualification could not apply. For example, if the employer unilaterally changed the conditions of employment to the point of substantially altering their nature, this was viewed as "constructive dismissal" and thus involuntary termination.[87] The conduct of a boss who had egged an employee on to quit a job could also be considered as just cause for voluntary leaving.[88] Certain decisions held that the absence of this voluntary dimension called for a review about imposing a disqualification for dismissal due to the claimant's misconduct.[89] However, the jurisprudence of the day insisted that a Board of Referees lacked jurisdiction to rule on any issue other than the one before it. This meant that Boards of Referees could not rule on a disqualification for misconduct when the decision being appealed was for voluntary leaving.[90]

Coming to the second stage, when the voluntary nature of a termination had been established, it was up to the claimant to prove just cause.[91] The idea of just cause for abandoning a job gave rise to a succession of developments in case law. Initially, certain decisions tried to pin down the reasons that could be adduced as "just cause" for quitting a job by making a distinction between this idea and the concept of "good cause" for refusal of employment. For some, a review of the act brought out a distinction in the seriousness of reasons used. Although the concept of "just cause" could encompass more subjective and personal reasons, the criteria would be stricter.[92] This approach helped to define personal reasons inasmuch as society generally recognized them as just causes for quitting a job. A typical example was the wife who quit her job to follow her husband.[93]

Nonetheless, a number of umpires would use the less restrictive criteria for "good cause" to shape less restrictive definitions of "just cause." For example, a claimant would have just cause for quitting a job if that person behaved as a reasonable person would have in similar circumstances.[94] At the same time, a more conservative school of thought insisted on the presence of compelling factors to warrant the claimant's decision. The situation would have to be governed by prudence and justified by necessity, urgency, or constraint.[95] Generally speaking, however, the interpretation of the idea of just cause would be swayed by claimant viewpoints and thus likely to embrace a much wider range of reasons. In 1985, the parameters of just cause formed the subject of a significant decision by the Federal Court of Appeal in *Tanguay*.

As part of a workforce reduction, Maurice Tanguay and a number of older workers who had built up seniority opted for early retirement to avoid layoffs of younger workers. Their move fitted in with a restructuring plan as undergone by a number of businesses after the recession of the early 1980s. In accordance with the received jurisprudence of that time,[96] the CEIC imposed two-week disqualifications on this group for quitting their jobs without just cause. When Tanguay won his case before the Board of Referees, the commission appealed to the umpire, who ruled that his reason could not constitute just cause within the meaning of the act. The umpire's decision was upheld by the Federal Court of Appeal, which referred to a British decision based on insurance principles. Lord Denning saw the terms "good cause" and "just cause" as referring to two very separate concepts: "It is not sufficient for him to prove that he was quite reasonable in leaving his employment. Reasonableness may be 'good cause,' but it is not necessarily 'just cause.' 'Without just cause' means without any just cause for throwing on the unemployment fund the payment of unemployment benefit. If he voluntarily retires on pension, he is getting a substantial financial benefit for himself, and it is not fair or just to the unemployment fund that he should also get unemployment benefit for the six weeks."[97]

The Federal Court of Appeal borrowed the same reasoning to define "just cause" in terms of "the duty that ordinarily applies to any insured, not to deliberately cause the risk to occur." That court stressed the actuarial logic of the system: "He is only justified in acting in this way if, at the time he left, circumstances existed which excused him for thus taking the risk of causing others to bear the burden of his unemployment."[98] "Just cause" was thus interpreted in the light of an actuarial ideology that disregarded the system's social dimension. Note that the limiting effect of this interpretation was in contrast to the principles set out by the Supreme Court in *Abrahams*. This approach accommodated neither the social objectives of these retirees nor the many years during which Tanguay and his friends had paid into the system. Clearly, the Federal Court of Appeal's decision could only be detrimental to claimants.

Many reasons could be adduced in support of voluntary leaving, some of them connected with working conditions and others with personal circumstances. I will mention only a few of them here, emphasizing the ones that entered the act in the counterreforms of the 1990s. To begin with, immediate departure was acceptable only in intolerable or clearly unsatisfactory circumstances; in all other cases, the claimant had to make some attempt to correct the situation before quitting the job. Moreover, the jurisprudence often required the claimant to take steps to secure another job before leaving the current one; however, some decisions did not recognize this obligation, finding that it was not a formal requirement under the act.[99]

In terms of a claimant's working life, the tribunals acknowledged dangerous working conditions and significant changes in conditions of employment, such as a substantial wage cut, as constituting just cause. In the latter case, the jurisprudence held that leaving was justified even when the worker had no prospect of another job. Similarly, refusal to work excessive overtime also constituted just cause. Antagonism from a superior, provided that this behaviour was not basically due to the claimant's own behaviour, could be just cause for voluntary leaving. Harassment and discrimination could also constitute just cause. Finally, a claimant had just cause to quit a job when persuaded of the employer's involvement in unlawful activities. But job-related just cause required a high degree of urgency: the claimant had to show that the working conditions were truly unpleasant.[100]

As far as the claimant's personal life went, the tribunals accepted the need to accompany a spouse or take care of a child or close relative or deal with health problems as just cause. Serious transportation problems could also constitute just cause.[101] And even when these reasons were not recognized as a full defence for voluntary leaving, they could serve as extenuating circumstances for reducing the length of disqualification. For example, the initial disqualification was reduced from six weeks to two weeks in a case where the claimant had acted impulsively. An error in judgment in another case enabled the umpire to cut the length of disqualification to two weeks.[102]

Until the 1980s, there was little case law on misconduct, though it was established that it had to be personal and conclusively proven. Moreover, certain assumptions were ruled out: incompetence and personality conflict could not constitute misconduct, and acts had to be connected with work performance to qualify. For want of a more explicit definition, however, umpires had little control over the decisions of Boards of Referees.[103] The concept of misconduct began to take clearer shape in the 1980s by way of a debate over whether misconduct in labour law was the same as misconduct in the Unemployment Insurance Act. Was a reason justifying the dismissal of an employee the equivalent of misconduct within the meaning of the Unemployment Insurance Act?

One school of thought, led by Judges Mahoney and Dubinsky, supported a distinction between the misconduct that justified dismissal and the misconduct for which the act disqualified a claimant from collecting benefits.[104] According to this theory, the concept of misconduct was much more exigent in unemployment insurance.[105] However, Judge Cattanach held that just cause for firing an employee constituted misconduct within the meaning of the act. He saw no distinction between misconduct as just cause for dismissal and misconduct within the meaning of the act.[106]

This issue, however, was not dealt with definitively by the Federal Court of Appeal until its decisions in *Joseph* and *Tucker.* In *Joseph,* the court held that misconduct had to be gauged by the Board of Referees independently of the merits of the employer's decision to dismiss: "To prove misconduct by an employee it must be shown that he behaved in some way other than he should have. Accordingly, such an allegation is not proven simply by showing that the employer found his employee's conduct to be reprehensible, or charged him with misconduct in general terms. For a board of referees to conclude that there was misconduct by an employee, it must have before it sufficiently detailed evidence for it to be able, first, to know how the employee behaved, and second, to decide whether such behaviour was reprehensible."[107] The *Tucker* decision[108] was consistent with *Joseph* in finding the idea of misconduct unconnected with the merits of the employer's decision. In this case, the claimant, a stewardess, was suspended for four months for being intoxicated on a flight. The CEIC imposed a disqualification for misconduct. The claimant, while admitting her intox-ication, denied having deliberately neglected her work. The Federal Court of Appeal endorsed the position of the umpire, who had allowed the claimant's appeal and held that misconduct had to be voluntary. By requiring proof of the voluntary nature of the claimant's act, the decision made the idea of misconduct autonomous within the meaning of the Unemployment Insurance Act and dissociated it from any review of the merits of the employer's penalty.

It emerges from the body of case law on misconduct that the following factors need to exist to justify disqualification on this ground: the actions of which the claimant is accused have to constitute misconduct, whether by their description or penalty in labour law; such misconduct has to be prov-ably the claimant's; and it has to be the real cause of loss of employment.[109]

At the same time, the jurisprudence has clearly established that the bur-den of proof for misconduct falls to the commission or the employer. Detailed evidence[110] has to establish both the claimant's misconduct and the fact that it is the reason and not the pretext for dismissal.[111] Again on the burden of proof, older decisions held that the factors constituting mis-conduct had to be proved beyond reasonable doubt, as in criminal mat-ters.[112] In *McDonald,* however, the Federal Court of Appeal ruled in 1991 that the degree of proof to warrant an administrative penalty for false statements made knowingly by a claimant was the preponderance of evi-dence.[113] Accordingly, it is now recognized that the same degree of proof is required for misconduct.

Three factors have to exist to impose a disqualification for refusing suit-able employment. First is clear evidence that the claimant has refused a job offer. Although the act also cites the case of neglecting a job offer, this is quite rare and inconspicuous in the jurisprudence. Second is the suit-ability of the employment. And third is the absence of "good cause" for re-fusal. These last two factors can sometimes work together. For example, lack of transportation can make a job unsuitable for a claimant or constitute a good cause for refusing a job offer. The burden of proof of the existence of a good cause falls to the claimant. Finally, due to the idea of "extenuating circumstances," a reason used by a claimant that is not accepted as a truly "good" cause can still give rise to a less lengthy disqualification.[114]

Let us remember that, as the benefit period opens, a claimant cannot be forced to accept a job outside his or her usual occupation and with work and pay conditions inferior to those offered by the market for this type of occupation. However, after a reasonable time that is not defined by the act, the claimant will be obliged to accept a job outside his or her usual occupation that meets general market conditions. For example, a claimant who previously held a full-time job may, after a reasonable time, have to accept a part-time job.[115] The jurisprudence offers no specific criterion for determining the length of this reasonable time, which depends on the situation.

Essentially, the criterion for good cause refers to the duty of caution prescribed for any reasonable person in similar circumstances.[116] In *Moura*, the Federal Court of Appeal reversed an umpire's decision allowing the appeal of a claimant who had refused a part-time job because it did not pay enough to cover the expenses that she would have had to incur. The umpire believed that the claimant had acted in good faith. Reversing the decision, the court held that the legal criterion was the existence of good cause, not good faith.[117]

Here we can appropriately compare the requirements for "good cause" with those of availability. The latter remains the claimant's main obligation under the act. At the time, its penalty seemed potentially more severe than the one for refusing employment, since the disentitlement of a claimant found to be unavailable could encompass the entire benefit period. Disqualification for refusing suitable employment required a specific act by claimants, whereas availability had more to do with their attitude and behaviour regarding the labour market. Note that disentitlement and disqualification could be imposed for the same situation, refusing employment for example. Refusal of employment could be taken as proof of a person's unavailability. The two ideas functioned independently and cumulatively.[118] The disqualification period had to be served when the disentitlement period was done.

The availability for work required of claimants was active, meaning that they could be asked to produce evidence of their job searches. In the early 1970s, one claimant challenged the commission's authority to regulate active availability and force claimants to look for jobs.[119] Did the wording of the act's provision on availability ("capable of and available for work and unable to obtain suitable employment [on that day]") allow the commission to pass regulations to enforce active job searches?[120] The Federal Court of Appeal concluded that the commission was empowered to pass such regulations inasmuch as the process required of claimants was reasonable in the circumstances. In 1975, the lawmaker chose to build this active job-search requirement into the act itself: "The Commission may require this claimant to prove that he is taking the usual and reasonable steps to find suitable employment."[121]

Availability was often a matter of fact proven primarily by job searches. However, there were certain principles governing the process.[122] Since the provision dealing with availability covered suitable employment, the concept of "reasonable time" applied. After a reasonable time, the claimant had to expand the job-search perimeter. For a long time, claimants were not advised of this requirement and their resulting obligation. Some claimants unemployed for a number of months who, when called to the commission's offices, said that their job searches were limited to their usual occupations would see a disentitlement imposed for nonavailability. With reason, one writer saw this failure to advise claimants as scandalous and contrary to basic legal principles: "If such a practice existed in the field of say, taxation law, there would, rightly, be outcries invoking the principle of the rule of law. Strangely, however, we seem to accept this bizarre denial of the principle in unemployment insurance law."[123]

Criticisms of this kind would later be found in the report of the parliamentary committee studying the Forget Report's recommendations.[124] The tribunals would send the same messages.[125] It was now up to the CEIC to tell claimants if their job-search parameters were unreasonable as the benefit period began and later advise them of the reasonable time after which their job searches had to be widened.

The jurisprudence of the system's first half-century was marked by a gradual recognition of jobless rights. The decisions in *Abrahams* and *Hills* came as confirmation that the act should be interpreted in ways favourable to the unemployed. The language of the Supreme Court has indicated an awareness of social values somewhat distant from the lawmaker's language about the responsibility for unemployment. This jurisprudence upholding the priority of the act's social aim would obviously favour the unemployed. At the same time, the influence of the actuarial ideology was still present in the jurisprudence, as seen in *Tanguay*. Once again the private concept of insurance was called on to deny the relevance of social considerations in the interpretation and application of the Unemployment Insurance Act. Initially limited, the effects of this decision became significant in the jurisprudence of the 1990s.

8
The System Hijacked, 1989-96

The Conservatives swept back into office in 1988, and early 1989 brought the coming into force of the Free Trade Agreement with the United States.[1] In April of the latter year, the big counterreform planned and polished in the 1980s finally got under way. This was the initial phase of a pervasive campaign that would whittle away at the UI system through the 1990s to peak in 1996 with the passage of the Employment Insurance Act.

A crucial turning point came in 1990, when the government's exit as a financial participant signalled its retreat from social problems involving jobs and the jobless. After this, wave upon wave of cuts would harry every facet of the UI system. Entrance requirements were raised, benefit periods and rates reduced, provisions on labour disputes made more market friendly, and penalties for voluntary unemployment substantially strengthened. In the process, the government hijacked the system away from its priority social mission of compensating the jobless and its primary role as a social insurance plan. From now on, Ottawa would use the UI account for needs other than the payment of claimant benefits, diverting UI premiums from the specific purpose for which they were collected. All of this downgraded the protection that the jobless were entitled to expect.

The counterreform was heralded in a 1989 policy statement on the government's new "Labour Force Development Strategy." All the components of this counterstrike then turned up in Bill C-21, tabled in July of that year, which also contained a provision for the disappearance of the federal contribution on which the policy statement was silent but the budget speech was not.

Introduced by Minister of Employment and Immigration Barbara McDougall, the April 1989 policy statement[2] cited the need to upgrade the vocational training of the Canadian workforce in the new economic conjuncture and called for increased use of the UI system for "active" purposes. To streamline the system's performance, the policy also proposed to make it less open-handed as an incentive to keep people working. Although the policy statement was silent on this, the proposed changes were part of a new UI funding framework to offset the phaseout of the government contribution that would be announced in the budget speech a few days later.[3]

The policy statement proposed the diversion of increasing amounts to fund "active measures," chiefly for vocational training. The UI budget would have to be rearranged to reflect the new priorities. Since one of these was to increase incentives to work, a number of limits on the rights of the unemployed would free up the money needed to develop active measures. So the government had both bases covered: on the one hand, UI restrictions would create downward pressure on wages and promote worker versatility, thus making the workforce more flexible, while, on the other hand, the system's new proactive thrust would spare employers some of the added costs of vocational training.

The new priorities would be funded by more stringent qualifying conditions followed by generally shorter benefit periods. In addition, the maximum disqualification for voluntary leaving, dismissal for misconduct, and refusal of suitable employment went from six weeks to twelve weeks, with a minimum of seven. On top of this came a benefit rate reduction from 60 percent to 50 percent for the rest of the period. That these measures slashed the rights of the unemployed and left them in virtual pauperdom was largely a matter of unconcern to Ottawa. Introducing its policy, the government officially anticipated that "only" 30,000 new unemployed would be driven to welfare by its new rules.[4]

In the main, the Labour Force Development Strategy for Canada drew on[5] the labour market policy[6] of the Organisation for Economic Co-operation and Development (OECD).[7] For a number of years, the OECD had taken the neoliberal line on broad social policy thrusts[8] to help shape and harmonize these policies and employment practices in its member states. In terms of compensating the unemployed, for example, the OECD basically wanted to replace income replacement with "active" measures.[9] This strategy was summed up in 1993: "The new framework for labour market policies – approved by the labour ministers of the OECD countries in 1992 – proposes that resources be progressively diverted from passive income security measures to active measures with three objectives – to mobilize manpower resources, develop job-related skills and foster the effective operation of labour markets."[10]

The OECD's approach reflected a redefined government role in which controlling inflation was more important than combating unemployment. Neoliberal thinking saw unemployment as primarily an individual responsibility. To defend this strategy, talk of "dependency" resurfaced and now went beyond the damnation of welfare. The contributory UI system itself, supposed to mitigate the stigma of joblessness, stood accused of generating claimant dependency. The protection provided by all unemployment compensation plans should be slashed, as recommended by the OECD:

- Restrict UI benefit entitlements in countries where they are especially long to the period when job search is intense and rapid job-finding remains likely.
- Impose restrictive conditions on indefinite-duration assistance benefits for employable people.[11]

The approach of using UI to repair the workforce and break the dependency cycle of the long-term unemployed[12] would empty the system of thousands of jobless, many of whom, having become welfare recipients, then signed up for active measures to collect their full benefits.

This dependency agenda found strong echoes in Canada. The debate over active versus passive labour market management would be used to defend UI cuts. This involved a new, improved version of the actuarial homily: from now on, the responsibilities of the jobless were expanded from unemployment itself to include vocational training. Anyone who rose in defence of UI risked charges of encouraging the unemployed to sit at home waiting for their cheques to come through the door. "The best way of killing a man is to pay him for doing nothing." This catchphrase from a Félix Leclerc song[13] was quoted by Minister of Employment and Immigration Bernard Valcourt in defence of the 1993 cuts and later applied across the board.

Talk would get even tougher when it came to stricter curbs on voluntary unemployment. Who could defend anyone who left a job to bask in the blessings of UI? Valcourt, at a January 1992 Paris meeting of the OECD Committee on Employment, Labour and Social Affairs, used these words to describe the thrust of the system redesign begun in 1990:

This strategy basically called for a major shift in resources and funds, moving them from passive programs (Unemployment Insurance) into training and re-employment activities. It seemed obvious as the years went by that passive income support had the significant side effect of discouraging the job search. The resulting reform of the Unemployment Insurance System featured an increase in the qualifying number of weeks of employment, increased penalties for those quitting their jobs voluntarily and a reduced maximum benefit period. At the same time, we introduced a major increase in maternity and parental benefits ... The productive measures involved directing the savings achieved through more restrictive qualifying conditions for unemployment insurance to more effective and more complete training and re-employment programs for the jobless.[14]

The Canadian Labour Force Development Strategy was a major redesign of federal involvement in vocational training. To get a better idea of the issues here, let us recall the status of federal "active" measures when Minister of Employment and Immigration Barbara McDougall was introducing her policy. At that time, Ottawa's involvement in vocational training was primarily based on the spending power conferred by the Canadian Constitution and secondarily the special jurisdiction over unemployment insurance. The spending power enabled it to allocate budgets for training, while the Unemployment Insurance Act empowered the CEIC to refer claimants to training courses. In April 1989, most federal expenditures for vocational training went through the Jobs Strategy program set up in 1985. This program had a $1.8 billion budget in fiscal 1988-89, most of it spent under the National Training Act,[15] which authorized the payment of claimants' income replacement, transportation, child care allowances, and training expenses. Let us also remember that some other labour market management programs had been absorbed by the UI system since 1977 in the form of work-sharing, job-creation, and training benefits. In 1988, the amount spent on training benefits under section 26 of the act[16] was $255 million, or 2 percent of the total UI budget.[17] The Labour Force Development Strategy now proposed to spend ever larger amounts on vocational training, to be gleaned from a UI account now bereft of government support. Yet more expenses were added, such as the new "active" program to assist the self-employed.

The government refused to subject businesses to a special levy to fund these measures, thus tacitly rejecting the main recommendation of the Advisory Council on Adjustments (the de Grandpré Report).[18] The April 1989 policy statement came barely a month after the publication of that report recommending that Canada's vocational training system be fine-tuned to the new North American free-trade environment. The report saw training as a corporate responsibility and suggested a 1 percent payroll tax. It was a clarion call that failed to spark enthusiasm in the business community.[19]

Like the de Grandpré Report, the federal policy statement acknowledged the reluctance of Canadian businesses: "Overall, the private sector spends about $1.4 billion for this training, which, on a per-employee basis, represents less than half of what is spent by the American private sector."[20] Although paying homage to the de Grandpré Report, the Conservative government adopted a sunnier solution for employers: they would contribute to training through their payments to a UI account that was no longer sacred to jobless benefits. Worker premiums and cuts in the system would also help to pay for the training that the de Grandpré Report had seen as solely a corporate responsibility. Questioned about the extent of these cuts, a senior official confirmed that the system's regional resonance was fated to disappear.[21]

These remarks as the policy was being introduced prove the connection between the counterreform emerging in 1989 and the primary concern of the Macdonald and Forget Reports, both of which wanted to divest the system of its regional resonance. Cancelling the federal contribution would be the first stage in the process, since it was Ottawa that bore the cost of benefits tied to regional job markets. In 1988, for example, the federal contribution to the UI account was more than $2.6 billion, or nearly 23 percent of the system's total cost (Table 2): amounts for regional adjustments represented more than 85 percent of that total.[22] The disappearance of this funding would create a huge UI deficit that could be offset only by raising premiums and cutting benefits. Marginal employees, especially seasonal workers, would bear the brunt.

Although the UI account had an accumulated surplus of $356 million at that time, the minister of finance would use the shaky condition of the public treasury to defend the cancellation measure in the budget, tabled weeks later, as "necessary in view of the current financial situation and taking into account the fact that the government lacks the resources to contribute to funding the system as long as it is running a large and persistent deficit."[23] The measure was Draconian: the government had been making significant contributions to the system since its inception, as seen in Table 2. It is difficult to be satisfied with the minister's explanation and not see more than coincidence between this sudden radical measure and the suddenly real Free Trade Agreement. The government would reject any thought of compromise, ignoring the Senate's suggestion that the contribution simply be reduced without eliminating it altogether.[24]

Minister McDougall's Labour Force Development Strategy and the resulting Bill C-21[25] met with fierce resistance. Opposition parties rose in strong reaction to the scale of the proposed changes and their impacts on the jobless and high-unemployment regions. The Conservatives were accused of breaking their election promise to leave the social programs alone and wanting to "make the unemployed pay for their manpower training and free trade adjustment programs."[26] One of the bill's[27] rare supporters outside the Conservative government was Quebec Minister of Manpower, Income Security and Occupational Training André Bourbeau, who found the proposals consistent with the welfare counterreform that his own government had enacted a few months earlier.

The unions and grassroots organizations also accused the government of making the jobless bear the cost of training. Some of them also underscored the proposed government role in managing unemployment.[28] Other unionists stressed the measure's impact on the social fabric and its impoverishment of workers and jobless alike. A Canadian Labour Congress study[29] challenged the figure of 30,000 jobless who would be relegated to welfare, insisting that 130,000 would become disentitled, 44,000

Table 2

Historical overview of the Employment Insurance Account (UI fund)[a]

| Year[b] | Total cost of the system | | | | Cumulative balance in the account |
| | Private sector share[c] | | Government share[d] | | |
	($ millions)	(%)	($ millions)	(%)	($ millions)
1941	36	78	10	22	44
1942	57	78	16	22	114
1943	62	78	18	22	190
1944	62	77	19	23	268
1945	61	75	20	25	317
1946	68	69	31	31	373
1947	66	60	52	40	448
1948	84	61	54	39	530
1949	99	68	46	32	583
1950	126	71	51	29	665
1951	152	73	56	27	773
1952	153	73	58	27	852
1953	158	73	59	27	881
1954	157	72	62	28	841
1955	168	73	62	27	854
1956	187	74	67	26	875
1957	192	73	71	27	744
1958	185	72	72	28	500
1959	229	74	82	26	366
1960	275	74	97	26	185
1961	278	74	101	26	67
1962	286	73	105	27	10
1963	297	73	108	27	1
1964	311	73	116	27	40
1965	328	77	100	23	141
1966	344	75	113	25	258
1967	347	75	116	25	303
1968	433	76	134	24	382
1969	492	76	153	24	458
1970	495	75	164	25	324
1971	765	81	184	19	235
1972	1,111	56	880	44	-152
1973	1,243	58	917	42	-502
1974	1,430	62	875	38	-418
1975	1,627	49	1,707	51	-97
1976	2,173	62	1,356	38	204

▶

◄ *Table 2*

| | Total cost of the system | | | | Cumulative balance in the account |
| | Private sector share[c] | | Government share[d] | | |
Year[b]	($ millions)	(%)	($ millions)	(%)	($ millions)
1977	2,336	57	1,788	43	414
1978	2,507	53	2,255	47	741
1979	2,897	69	1,295	31	650
1980	3,774	78	1,037	22	-6
1981	4,369	81	1,001	19	331
1982	7,513	81	1,784	19	-2,397
1983	8,463	75	2,822	25	-3,854
1984	8,307	74	2,902	26	-4,546
1985	8,639	75	2,901	25	-4,445
1986	8,946	76	2,831	24	-3,792
1987	8,769	76	2,785	24	-2,368
1988	9,131	77	2,654	23	356
1989	9,595	78	2,765	22	1,113
1990	11,920	83	2,437	17	2,161
1991	18,966		-		-2,045
1992	20,516				-4,676
1993	19,677				-5,884
1994	17,044				-3,601
1995	14,913				666
1996	14,092				5,665
1997	13,085				11,960
1998	12,332				19,251
1999 (est.)	12,081				25,735*

a   This table is based on the following sources: Jonathan R. Kesselman, *Financing Canadian Unemployment Insurance* (Toronto: Canadian Tax Foundation, 1983), 41, 44, 62; *Report of the Committee of Inquiry into the Unemployment Insurance Act (Gill Report)* (Ottawa: Queen's Printer, 1962), 68, 102; Michel Bédard, *Report of the Chief Actuary on the Employment Insurance Contribution Rate for 2000* (Hull: HRDC, 1999), Annex IV, 4, and the Human Resources Development Canada Web site, <http://www.drhc-hrdc.gc.ca/insur/histui/hrdcf.html>.

b   The reference years are fiscal years up to 1971. Only from that year do the data correspond to calendar years. To provide a general view, however, I have rolled back all these data into the predominant calendar year, with the fiscal year counting for nine months in this reference year.

c   From the system's beginnings until 1971, employer and worker premiums were roughly equal. Beginning in 1971, the employer's contribution was 1.4 times that of the employee. *Unemployment Insurance Act, 1971*, S.C. 1970-71-72, c. 48, s. 64(1).

d   Until 1971, the government defrayed the administrative cost of the system in addition to some special contributions in the years 1943-60, for example on behalf of members of the Canadian Forces.

*   The Chief Actuary's report for 2001 established this amount at $25,682 million and estimated a cumulative balance of $33,586 million for the year 2000. Michel Bédard, *Report of the Chief Actuary on the Employment Insurance Contribution Rate for 2001* (Hull: HRDC, 2000), 2.

of them in Quebec. The same study reckoned that 133,000 claimants in Quebec alone would see their length of benefits cut. Moreover, an internal review by the Quebec Department of Manpower, which oversaw welfare in that province, estimated that 10,000 families would be driven to social assistance as qualifying conditions were tightened and benefit periods cut.[30]

Not only did the employers come out in favour of the counterreform, but they also criticized the government for not going far enough. Employer organizations were relieved to be rid of the "punitive" vocational training levy proposed by the Grandpré Report. Quebec's Conseil du Patronat, while voicing some reservations about the more "social" provisions in the counterreform – such as the parental benefit, which they thought should not come out of UI – voiced support for the Conservative plan: "The President of the Conseil du Patronat (CPQ), Mr. Ghislain Dufour, is pleased with the amounts provided for worker training, as 'with free trade, something had to be done.'"[31]

The Conservatives pushed the bill through against strong opposition in the House of Commons. The process was more laborious in the Senate, however, where the Liberal opposition commanded the majority. Senators railed against cutting benefits amid high unemployment and the actuarial reasoning behind the move: "The government would seem to believe that many of the unemployed are in a position of their own making, and that, with proper 'incentives,' they would find work or remain in their jobs longer. This, of course, fails to recognize that what is needed is jobs, not incentives to find jobs or training for jobs that simply do not exist."[32] The same logic was used to criticize the increased penalties for voluntary leaving. Senators took testimony by Employment and Immigration officials that the average disqualification was two weeks as proof that "most workers do have good reasons for leaving their employment." The bill's primary outcome would be to "tie workers to their jobs regardless of the circumstances and to induce them to accept poor working conditions."[33]

Senators also underscored the seriousness of cancelling government funding for the system. Referring to the policy paper on *Unemployment Insurance in the 70s*,[34] they pictured the government "abdicating its responsibility to build a stable economic future for all regions of the country."[35] Disputing the government arguments for reallocating UI funds for active measures, senators opposed their use to fund these programs, including assistance to the self-employed. It was unfair to ask the jobless to fund training. Programs to benefit society as a whole should continue to be paid out of general revenues.[36]

Finally, senators denounced the Conservative machinations to force Bill C-21 through, which did the Mulroney government no honour. It will be remembered that the VER and the exception for repeaters living in regions of high unemployment now had to be renewed by the CEIC and the government, subject to parliamentary confirmation; otherwise, the minimum entrance requirement reverted to fourteen weeks across the board.[37] This system had not been a problem as Parliament agreed several times to extend the more generous standard for high-unemployment areas. With the Senate stalling C-21, however, the Mulroney government refused to renew the VER. As of 6 January 1990, at least fourteen weeks of work would be needed in all regions, whatever the local unemployment rate happened to be.[38]

Since the minimum qualifying conditions in Bill C-21 were under fourteen weeks, Conservative MPs called on the jobless in outlying regions to bring pressure to get the legislation passed. Many of them were oblivious to the Machiavellianism of this manoeuvre,[39] which forced thousands of workers in the most vulnerable parts of the country to go on welfare. But no sleep would be lost in Westmount. The bill was shoved through in October 1990 with a few minor amendments.[40]

Except in high-unemployment regions, Canadians would now need more weeks of work to collect benefits for generally shorter periods. The VER of ten to fourteen weeks was raised to ten to twenty, repeaters included. The higher requirement for NERE would continue to apply. Length of benefit was now calculated in one phase instead of several – and here again the trend was downward, making the benefit period more a reflection of work history than the regional unemployment rate. This reduced the system's redistributive effect for all but claimants with long employment histories in regions of high unemployment. Major cities were hit especially hard. In the Montreal area, where unemployment stood at over 9 percent, at least sixteen weeks of work instead of ten were now needed to qualify for a maximum of twenty-seven weeks instead of thirty-two. A full year was needed to collect forty-nine weeks of benefits.

The bite of counterreform was softened by a few "social" measures stemming from recent case law on the right to equality.[41] The introduction of parental benefits was not unrelated to the Federal Court of Appeal decision in *Schachter*. Although the government challenged this ruling in the Supreme Court and ultimately won,[42] it was thought prudent and politically astute to combine the counterreform with ten weeks of benefits to be shared by fathers and mothers. The end of discrimination against workers aged sixty-five and over was a direct result of the Federal Court of Appeal decision in *Tétreault-Gadoury*, which would be upheld by the Supreme Court on the discriminatory effect of the provision challenged.[43] Workers aged sixty-five and over would again be admitted to the system and collect benefits.

Although the federal government was no longer a contributor to the UI system, it did remain responsible for paying benefits when the funds ran out, to be charged as advances and repaid from the UI account.[44] This financial disengagement by the state would be offset by cuts and higher premiums.[45] The active measures charged entirely to the account were expensive and more numerous. For example, the maximum extension of benefit periods for training was raised to 156 weeks. The system took over expenses formerly borne by the Consolidated Revenue Fund, such as transportation, child care, and tuition, plus new "active" programs such as assistance to the self-employed.[46] Indirectly, this reallocation of funds was used to finance the national deficit.

To cover the $800 million needed for active measures, the act earmarked a 15 percent share of the system's total outlay.[47] However, this reallocation of funds in an account now deprived of a state contribution made the issue of these measures' constitutionality all the more urgent. Was Parliament exceeding its constitutional jurisdiction? The policy statement also proposed major spending on private sector training.[48] Minister McDougall had some trouble proving constitutionality here: "The only obligation still limiting the options of the Minister of Finance is constitutional: the 1940 Act prohibits the use of the Fund for anything but unemployed benefits. Yesterday, the Minister of Employment and her officials had some difficulty justifying the $230 million to be paid out to help businesses recycle their work force."[49]

For the jobless, the cost of government withdrawal would mean a loss of rights – first as a result of all the eligibility and coverage restrictions and the more repressive provisions, especially for voluntary leaving and labour disputes, and then by the lack of a right to appeal CEIC decisions on active measures.

When they had to do with work-sharing and job-creation programs, these decisions were already exempted from the appeal process. This exemption was now extended to all active measures.[50] The UI system would also force employed and jobless workers to foot a major share of training costs, with no inherent right to benefit from them. Decisions about training, assistance to training, and reemployment involved the commission's discretionary powers and could not be appealed to the Board of Referees. This denial of the right to appeal affected a growing area of law, conditioning many decisions involving the jobless and revealing a change in the very nature of the system with active measures as the pretext. Assistance programs were introduced without the legal safeguards typical of social insurance. Considering the significance of the active measures, senators found the denial of the right of appeal unacceptable.[51]

In line with the 1989 policy statement, the act increased the penalties for voluntary leaving. On actuarial grounds, the government rejected the amendments moved by the Senate as weakening "individuals' attachment to work."[52] As the price of peace, however, it did agree to write into the act a list of situations already acknowledged in case law as just cause for voluntary leaving.[53] This concession brought little in the way of new rights for the jobless, since these reasons were already covered in the *Guide to Benefit Entitlement*.[54] And the list was prefaced by an introductory paragraph that limited the scope of "just cause" as heretofore understood by the courts. The criterion of the reasonable or prudent person yielded to a new and more restrictive test of "whether the claimant had no reasonable alternative to leaving immediately."[55] The lawmaker was not only making a break with the earlier interpretation, clearly seen as too lax, but also trying to reflect a more limiting interpretation, as illustrated by the decision in *Tanguay*.

Another example of the new severity was that unserved weeks of disqualification at the end of a benefit period would be carried over for the next two years unless the worker filed a new claim and proved that he or she had held insurable employment for at least twenty weeks since the last benefit period. However, weeks of disqualification could be deferred if a claimant became eligible for sickness, maternity, or parental benefits.

A number of changes were made to the criteria for disentitlement in labour disputes. Most of them reflected earlier court rulings, but they were also tinged with the counterreform ideology. Despite criticisms of its legitimacy, the principle of disentitlement was strengthened as the state sided with the bosses. Although its strict application in special situations was somewhat tempered, the collective aspect of disentitlement was entrenched. The Forget Report's suggestions that disentitlement end at the same time as labour disputes and benefits be paid in lockouts[56] were not accepted. Although these changes were made in a conjuncture favourable to free trade, there was no emulation of the US approach in which many states had made rules to reinforce their systems' impartiality in labour disputes.[57]

The reform expanded the scope of disentitlement, which now, to curb the precedent set by the decision in *Gionest*,[58] affected people who were unemployed at the time of a work stoppage and unable to return to work because of it. For example, disentitlement could be applied to laid-off workers waiting to be called back, especially in seasonal businesses. Given this change, it was no surprise to see new problems with the production of evidence. Although job loss is an easily verifiable fact, the likelihood of being called back to work is harder to prove. This is basically a virtual situation since the claimant is not actually back at work. Disentitlement to benefits may then hinge on a single party to the dispute: the employer. All the employer had to do was set some back-to-work dates when laying people off, or subsequently by letter, notice, et cetera,[59] to remove the unemployed workers' right to benefit in the event of a work stoppage. Certainly, the employer could use this approach to sway laid-off workers in anticipation of a strike vote, as Madam Justice L'Heureux-Dubé properly reminded us in *Hills*.[60]

Debate in this case might well turn on the employer's bona fide. The question would be whether the callback really met the employer's needs or was part of a negotiating strategy. The decisions rendered at this time by the Federal Court of Appeal were significant in terms of the types of issues that the courts would be dealing with – for example, whether or not the employer was really committed to a serious callback process.[61]

The determination to strengthen disentitlement was also seen when it came to deciding when a work stoppage ended. Here again the ideological bias was evident and showed how hypocritical the notion of state neutrality was. Changes took the regulatory route through a minor amendment to the enabling text that allowed the CEIC to define the circumstances that determined the end of a work stoppage and set aside the interpretation given in the *Lalonde* and *Caron* decisions.[62] This is how the Conservatives brought back the 85 percent rule. Although its merits had been contested by the tribunals, along with the concept of "substantial resumption of operations" on which it rested, the new regulation made it a mandatory test for both production and employee numbers.[63] To forestall court challenges, the government also elected to enshrine the idea of "exceptional and temporary means" in the regulations. Finally, to gain acceptance for the generalization of this rule, the new text provided an exception when an employer could not regain its former operating level for reasons unconnected with the labour dispute. For example, a company shutdown or permanent restructuring, force majeure, technological change, or new market situation became reasons for softening the rule.

The regulations thus differentiated two stages in the unemployment of someone who was disentitled due to a labour dispute: first, when that unemployment was the direct outcome of the dispute and, second, when it could be ascribed to another cause. By anticipating the likelihood of the work stoppage ending, even without a return to regular operations, the CEIC was apparently trying to mitigate the disentitlement. In any case, maintaining a rule based on a percentage resumption of operations became absurd when a business was closing for good. By refusing to remove disentitlement when a labour dispute was no longer causing the claimant's unemployment,[64] the government once again revealed the neutral state idea as spurious.

By ranking a regular work schedule before length of employment when strikers found new jobs, the decision in *Abrahams* had invalidated the minimum two-week requirement for strikers working elsewhere in their usual occupations.[65] The new act extended the principles in *Abrahams* to all workers, with disentitlement ending the day that a claimant "became regularly engaged elsewhere in insurable employment." For people holding two jobs, the Conservatives maintained the disentitlement in the face of "liberal" case law.[66] To soften the blow, however, a partial disentitlement system was set up to reflect the ratio between earnings in the lost job and all of the claimant's earnings in the qualifying weeks. In cases of authorized leave planned before a labour conflict, Judge Reed's reasoning in CUB 10623 was copied by the lawmaker. There was no question of removing the disentitlement in these circumstances: it was merely suspended until such time as claimants were prevented by the dispute from returning to their former jobs. This convoluted device illustrated the problem of applying a disentitlement rule from another era to contemporary circumstances. Finally, however, even the Conservative lawmakers had to bend before the decisions of the highest court in the land.[67] They repealed the provision requiring claimants who applied for an exemption from disentitlement to prove nonmembership in any grade or rank of workers involved in the labour dispute.

Despite its regressive nature and the number of restrictions that it placed on the rights of the jobless, the 1990 counterreform was only the first stage in a process. By 1993, a new phase was under way in an unprecedented antijobless environment. That year's Conservative budget visited new UI cuts on both "good" and "bad" unemployed. The benefit rate came down from 60 percent to 57 percent for all claimants, and the total suppression of rights would now apply to voluntary leaving without just cause and dismissal for misconduct. These Draconian curbs on voluntary unemployment were indicative of a massive resurgence of actuarial thinking. The new wave of counterreforms was announced by the budget speech of December 1992 with its new UI restrictions and continued with the tabling of Bill C-105, which ran into strong resistance from union and grassroots circles and was withdrawn, and, finally, Bill C-113, in which the same basic measures finally became law.

In his December 1992 economic and financial statement, Minister of Finance Don Mazankowski introduced a number of austerity measures that were argued as necessary to contain the UI account deficit. The government hoped to save $2.5 billion over 2.5 years.[68] The deficit created by the cancellation of state funding in 1990 was now enlisted to defend the new restrictions. However, in the next fiscal year, Ottawa would pick up the UI bill for new businesses started up during that year. It would also cover the supplementary premiums charged to some small businesses that created jobs during 1993.

The minister announced that spending on training and development programs would reach $2.21 billion in 1993, an increase of $300 million compared with the previous year, or 10.1 percent of the total UI budget. However, the Jobs Strategy budget covered by general revenue was only $1.6 billion.[69] This massive reallocation of money from the UI account to active measures drew steady criticism, and even the Canadian Labour Force Development Board (CLFDB)[70] voiced reservations: "The Board wishes to preface its formal recommendations by noting its concerns about several related matters: the recent cuts to general revenue financing of training and employment programs; the use of the UI program to finance things other than income support; and, the shifting balance in the source of funding for training and employment programs away from general revenues to UI Developmental Uses."[71]

The UI restrictions were part of Bill C-105 tabled in the House of Commons on 9 December 1992.[72] The government defended them by describing a forecast cumulative deficit of over $8 billion in the UI account.[73] Yet attention soon focused on the real scapegoats for this repression: "It's to stop people 'quitting their jobs to sit at home' or 'spend the winter in Florida collecting unemployment insurance' that they have decided to cut off the goodies for everybody who quits a job without sufficient reason."[74] Minister of Employment and Immigration Bernard Valcourt warmed to this subject in language that could only be described as earthy: "It's about time a government had the balls to face facts and realize that, at a time when jobs are so rare, no one should be rewarded for quitting a job for no reason but the mere goal of collecting unemployment insurance."[75] There was the old fraud theme again.[76] With its bill strongly opposed, the government brandished examples of fraudulent benefit claims. Rumours about the creation of "UI police" made the rounds.[77] The government bought full-page newspaper ads to sell its bill to the public. While the public was thus buttonholed, an amendment to cut the benefit rate went largely unnoticed. Yet this measure alone was expected to bring the Conservative regime more than $1.5 billion over the coming two years, straight from the pockets of the unemployed.[78]

For all these diversionary tactics, C-105 aroused fierce antagonism in both union circles and broad swaths of public opinion. Opponents dwelt on the harshness of penalties for voluntary leaving on grounds that were valid, but did not amount to "just cause" within the meaning of the act, and the fact that the disentitled were now forbidden to plead "extenuating circumstances." They stressed that the rules of evidence remained intact: even if the reason for leaving was recognized as "just cause," the claimant had to prove it, which was not always an easy matter. Voluntary leavings prompted by sexual harassment were examples.

The bill's opponents also dwelt on the use of attrition. Under the pressure of the economic recession that gripped Canada in the early 1980s, many older workers had been asked to take early retirement to avoid layoffs of wage earners with less seniority. Now these people would lose their right to benefit, since the Federal Court of Appeal had already ruled in *Tanguay* that this reason did not constitute just cause within the meaning of the act.[79] Minister Valcourt confirmed his intention to leave it at that.[80]

The opposition took to the streets, staging a number of demonstrations and sit-ins in MPs' and CEIC offices.[81] The movement peaked in a monster demonstration in Montreal on 7 February 1993 that attracted over 45,000 militants in temperatures of minus twenty-five degrees Celsius.[82] The government then chose to execute a strategic withdrawal. Bill C-105 was no more, but it would soon be replaced by its clone, Bill C-113.

Actually, Bill C-113,[83] tabled in the House of Commons on 17 February 1993, did contain some new elements to appease the critics. Further just causes for voluntary leaving were added to the ones already enumerated in the act.[84] The commission was authorized to pass regulations granting benefits to people who quit their jobs as part of a workforce reduction. The bill also provided special procedural rules for cases of sexual or other harassment to be used for initial decisions and appeal hearings before Boards of Referees.

Pilloried as a "snow job" and "window dressing" by a number of groups opposing the change,[85] Bill C-113 was as adamantly opposed as its predecessor. As in 1989-90, the Liberals in the House of Commons were not to be outdone, and a letter went out from Jean Chrétien, then leader of the opposition: "These measures are worrying Liberals. Cutting benefits and increasing penalties for those leaving employment voluntarily, the government is obviously indifferent to the victims of the economic crisis. Instead of attacking the basic problem, it is going after the unemployed."[86] Nonetheless, the government, now with both Commons and Senate majorities, soon passed amendments to the Unemployment Insurance Act[87] that came into force on 3 April 1993. This completed Part 2 of the Conservative counterreform.

The change in the 1993 act that hit the jobless the hardest was the total disqualification for voluntary leaving without just cause and dismissal due to misconduct.[88] This outrageous provision represented a substantial loss of their acknowledged rights. The discretionary power over length of disqualification that the act gave to the CEIC, Boards of Referees, and umpires had always played a crucial role in the use of this penalty. These tribunals were liable to lose sight of the fact that a claimant could have perfectly valid reasons for quitting a job but not just cause within the meaning of the act. Following the counterreform of 1990, for example, a minimum seven-week disqualification was upheld by an umpire against a mother who quit a part-time job that paid too little to cover her child care and transportation expenses.[89]

As the 1993 act came into force, however, this discretionary power was no more. As far as case law went, a trend favouring the claimant had emerged over the years, and there was general agreement that the maximum disqualification should be imposed only in the most serious cases. But now, stripped of any right to benefit unless their reasons corresponded to what the new act accepted as "just cause," claimants could not even plead "extenuating circumstances." The 1993 amendment was therefore repressive to the workers, especially to those still working, and a disavowal by the lawmaker of the umpires' jurisprudence.

The custodians of case law would now have to start dealing with the absolutism of this penalty. Either claimants had just cause in law for quitting a job, or they did not. By destroying a system that allowed the decision maker to adjust the penalty to reflect the specific circumstances of each case, the lawmaker prompted a review of the jurisprudence to define the relevant concepts in narrower terms. In any case, since 1990 the test for just cause had been the "only reasonable solution" available to the claimant.

In addition to disqualification for the whole benefit period, the act provided that the weeks of insurable employment accumulated by the claimant prior to resignation or dismissal, whether in the last job or in an earlier job, could not be used to establish a new benefit period. This would apply, for example, to people who, having held a job for several years, decided on a change: if they then quit their new job, they would not be able to count the time spent in that job or the one before it as insurable employment.

The act added eight additional reasons to justify voluntary leaving. Here were the Conservatives using the same strategy as in 1990 to minimize resistance to their bill. And, as in 1990, the concession was more symbolic than real, since most of these reasons were already recognized by the jurisprudence.[90] Questions also arose about the power granted to the CEIC to pass a regulation to define "reasonable circumstance." How were we to regulate what was reasonable? Would this responsibility not fall to the decision makers, especially the umpires? Moreover, the commission was now empowered to pass regulations to define "workforce reduction" and the circumstances in which a voluntary separation as part of this reduction could still give rise to benefits. The regulatory amendment later passed made it possible to accept as just cause for such separation what the Federal Court of Appeal in *Tanguay* had not. This gave the employer a decisive enforcement role. The explanatory notes supporting the regulation waxed eloquent on the system's new thrust, more concerned about the fate of companies than the jobless: "Recognizing that there are voluntary separations by individuals that result in someone else being able to remain in employment, it was decided that there should be an exemption from disqualification for voluntary quitting that would apply to these cases. It was considered that these voluntary separations, when they were part of an employer-initiated workforce reduction plan, could contribute positively to the competitiveness and economic viability of the particular firms."[91]

Beyond the added reasons for voluntary separation, the act contained new provisions of a procedural nature. The CEIC, before ordering a total disqualification, had to afford the claimant and employer a chance to produce their versions of the facts and take them into account when making the decision. In reality, however, this brought no change to existing jobless rights. It was already the commission's established practice in cases of dismissal or voluntary leaving[92] to collect the claimant's and employer's stories out of respect for procedural fairness.

Finally, new rules were provided for cases of sexual or other harassment in hearings by Boards of Referees. The commission was empowered to pass a regulation enabling a board's chair to exclude the claimant, the employer, their representatives, or any other person likely to testify from part of the hearing and then rule on disclosure in such cases.

The innovative nature of these provisions must not be overestimated. In fact, the Federal Court of Appeal had long held that hearsay evidence could be used by a Board of Referees.[93] Respect for the principles of natural justice by this tribunal, however, did not include the right to cross-examine.[94] And even the legality of a number of the details of this "exception" procedure was debatable. They included the power of exclusion granted to the chair of a Board of Referees. Admittedly, the claimant would still be able later on to read and dispute the evidence produced by the employer, but the claimant's right to an impartial hearing would be seriously impaired.[95] Some years earlier, when having to elucidate a similar provision in Quebec's Charte des droits et libertés de la personne,[96] Judge Deslongchamps of that province's Superior Court had ruled that the exclusion of a person accused of sexual harassment from part of the Human Rights Commission's investigation was in violation of his or her right to a public and impartial hearing.[97] Presumably, the right to an impartial hearing as guaranteed by the Canadian Bill of Rights could be raised in the same sense.[98]

In any event, the power that the act gave the chair of the Board of Referees to order an in-camera hearing and publication ban in harassment cases was unlikely to have real effects. These hearings were already held in CEIC offices, and the only people present were, beyond the members of the board, the parties, their representatives, and, in exceptional cases, a commission representative. The only public hearings of which I am aware have been held at claimants' requests.

It is noteworthy, in connection with the counterreform of 1993, that the act implementing the North American Free Trade Agreement was passed on 27 May of that year.[99] Just as they did with the changes made to the UI system by the Conservatives, the Liberals would attack NAFTA. These issues, joined by the controversy around the new Goods and Services Tax (GST), became important in the 1993 election campaign.[100] Having been fiercely antagonistic to these measures, the Liberals in power would soon forget their election promises and hoist the neoliberal banner of the fight against inflation and the deficit.

Any hopes that the Liberals would mitigate the recent repressive changes in the system were short-lived. Minister of Finance Paul Martin's 1994 budget speech announced major new UI cuts. The Liberal tone was very different from what it had been in opposition the year before. The Chrétien government would essentially maintain the restrictive, coercive Conservative measures and even speed the cutting process. This round saw sweeping transformation in both qualifying conditions and the length and rate of benefits. To address the national deficit, the government planned to reduce the deficit in the UI account, then $6 billion,[101] by $2.4 billion in fiscal 1994-95 alone.[102] Of course, this deficit was the result of the withdrawal of government funding and the cost of the active measures.

Entrance requirements for benefit entitlement were tightened, and the minimum weeks requirement rose from ten to twelve. Length of benefit was cut relative to both weeks of previous employment and the regional unemployment rate. As in 1990, the regional factor was reduced by making length of benefit more dependent on work history. Claimants would have to work longer for the same number of benefit weeks. For example, the 1990 entrance requirement in a region with 9 percent unemployment was sixteen weeks and the maximum length of benefit twenty-seven weeks; the latter figure had been thirty-two weeks before 1990, and now, with the Martin budget, it fell to twenty. Coming into 1994, a regional unemployment rate of over 12 percent, as in Montreal at the time of the Martin budget, brought a maximum of thirty-nine weeks of benefit for someone who had accumulated sixteen weeks of work. The same claimant would now be entitled to only twenty-eight weeks. This was a substantial drop. The counterreformers, by continuing to favour work history, continued to weaken the system's redistributive impact for both labour force segments and high-unemployment regions.

The benefit rate was cut from 57 percent to 55 percent for most claimants, about 85 percent of them:[103] only those with family responsibilities who earned less than half of the maximum insurable weekly wage ($390 in 1994) saw their benefit rate go up to 60 percent. Despite this nod to the economically weakest subscribers, the measures affecting eligibility and all benefit components would impoverish the jobless. The Liberals' three-year target was no less than $5.5 billion out of their pockets. At almost twice the 1993 figure, this levy was keenly felt by the workforce segment already hardest hit by the recession, people in marginal, short-term employment. The act containing the measures announced in the February budget came into force on 15 June 1994.[104] Never had a piece of legislation that made such sweeping changes to the UI system been exposed to so little consultation with the Canadian public.

The provisions for voluntary separation and misconduct that had sparked so much debate in 1993 saw minor amendments in this new act.

Aware of the harshness of the penalty but reluctant to lessen its deterrent effect, the government elected to tinker with the rules of evidence and rectify the most flagrant injustices. For example, when termination followed a suspension or authorized leave, or when voluntary separation occurred shortly before a planned layoff, disqualification now became disentitlement. Since 1993, anyone suspended by an employer for over a week had been considered as dismissed for UI purposes and received a total disqualification for misconduct: if this person returned to work and was later laid off, the workweeks prior to his or her suspension could not be used to establish a benefit period. Now these weeks could be counted and the suspension treated as a period of disentitlement. The same applied to employees taking authorized leave. If, after returning to work, they lost their job for a reason that had nothing to do with the leave, they could use the workweeks prior to that leave to establish a benefit period. Finally, the same exception would apply to persons whose jobs were shortly to end anyway but were lost through voluntary leaving or dismissal for misconduct. If the termination was foreseeable and would occur less than three weeks after the event causing the disqualification, the worker would be eligible for benefits from the time that the former job was slated to disappear.

For evidence of voluntary leaving, the lawmaker again chose to amend the rules instead of reviewing the principle of total disqualification. Thus, when there was a balance of proof of circumstances justifying a separation, the claimant would be granted the benefit of the doubt. Since most of these matters boiled down to fact finding, which was the job of the Board of Referees, the true impact of this measure was unknowable until tried by time and practice. In any case, the tough message sent by disqualification for voluntary leaving was addressed primarily to the employed. Its content was unaffected by changes in the rules of evidence for these situations. And the penalty was unchanged for nearly all workers affected by the measure: they would still not be able to collect benefits. A little like the 1990 tinkering with disentitlement in labour disputes, minor mitigations were added for the most flagrant injustices caused by the measure without questioning the merits of either the measure or its severity. The Liberals were picking up the Tories' ideological touch.

With the passage of these "liberal" measures, the legal framework affecting voluntary leaving and labour disputes was in step with the system's new thrust in favour of a free labour market. These provisions would survive intact in the new employment insurance (EI) system of 1996.

The 1994 act empowered the CEIC to pass regulations setting up pilot projects. These regulations included federal-provincial employability initiatives such as the "New Brunswick Works" program for welfare recipients.[105] The act's definition of pilot project was compatible with these programs and covered initiatives involving former as well as current claimants.[106] Moreover, the new provisions authorized benefit payments on a basis other than insurable weekly earnings. This approach would help to reduce direct government investment in these programs.

The pilot projects reflected the same reasoning as the increased 60 percent benefit rate for low-income claimants with family responsibilities.[107] Targeting benefits for the most vulnerable to cut the costs of social programs was a classical neoliberal move.[108] Its use in the Canadian context, however, calls for comment. Actually, what Ottawa was aiming at with these measures was to have the UI account take over expenses that it had borne directly, in large part through the Canada Assistance Plan.[109] Somewhat higher benefits were made available to clients who would likely need welfare without them, while the active measures funded by the UI system were made accessible to people who were often on welfare already. In either case, these measures would alleviate provincial welfare budgets, to which Ottawa contributed through the CAP. Since the federal outlay reflected the amounts paid out by provinces, it was correspondingly reduced.

Behind the active measures smokescreen could be seen the hijack that made the system a growing source of funds for the federal state. Vocational training was increasingly covered by the system: as the budget for UI-funded active measures grew, the outlay from general revenue went down.[110] And if the UI account could be used to pay for these active measures, why not use it for welfare as well? This was why, after expanding the active measures under UI, the government expanded the pool of people who could access them even if they were not insured. From now on, a portion of welfare spending was borne by UI contributors through reduced benefits. It was an absurd situation: welfare recipients involved in these active measures might have already funded them by being prevented from collecting UI benefits.

This refocusing of the UI system on the needy was part of an overall strategy that the federal government was introducing to the Canadian social security system as a whole. A social-insurance-based system with universal benefits was being made over into a welfare-based system. This strategy was compatible with the social security reform that Lloyd Axworthy would embark on in 1994.

The various changes made to the system from 1990 on were much more radical than the ones made in the 1970s. These were not just restrictions but also new thrusts. The primary aim of the system now was not so much to "provide benefits to the unemployed" as to enlist in the new "all-market" focus of the Canadian federal state. As these changes fell into place, the counterreform preached by the Macdonald and Forget reports was fully launched.

Not satisfied with cutting UI coverage, Ottawa hijacked the system's objectives. In addition to cancelling its financial contribution, the government would now use UI premiums to fund expenses other than income support for the jobless to the detriment of their rights. This process reached its culmination with the passage of the Employment Insurance Act.

9
Onward to EI

The overhaul of social security inaugurated by Minister of Human Resources Lloyd Axworthy in 1994 was driven by imperatives from the new economic environment of free trade and market globalization.

As the centrepiece of this reform, the Employment Insurance Act strengthened the pro-market bias at work since 1990. The cuts went deeper, and the hijackers became bolder. Now that the new employment benefit budget and jobless compensation functioned separately, the government could earmark increased amounts for "active measures" while continuing to significantly curtail social protection. At the same time, new criteria for establishing the benefit rate legitimized the use of the EI account surplus to reduce the federal deficit. The "leaner" system that came with this hijack looked like the US model, and the manipulation of the account raised serious questions – for one thing, about its constitutionality.

In 1994, amid a hail of publicity, the Chrétien government embarked on public consultations about its plan to reform the country's social security system. The plan covered a range of labour-related programs: unemployment insurance, welfare, vocational training, family allowances, and other matters such as Ottawa's contribution to funding postsecondary education. As its justification, the government pointed to the new economic environment. The "computer revolution" and "economic globalization" had created a conjuncture that narrowed the leeway of national governments. Meanwhile, the labour market was in upheaval: a shift of unskilled jobs to the Third World was coupled with growing demand for highly paid technological workers in the northern hemisphere, yet economic growth was no longer synonymous with job creation. The structural unemployment generated by these phenomena was reaching heights unequalled in industrialized nations since the 1930s. And the chronic unemployment and job insecurity hit harder at more vulnerable groups such as Aboriginals and youth.

If the diagnosis was realistic, the solutions advanced were largely, if not solely, products of the neoliberal ideology. They could come only from the private sector, and the government role should be limited to supporting market operations. This went for income security systems as well as other state entanglements. Moreover, the overhaul would have to accommodate federal budget cuts. The immediate result was the removal of government as the guarantor of a social contract that was now in the hands of social partners and individuals. Social risks were to be managed primarily by the latter. Government involvement in social matters had to be better targeted: did the deficit crisis not require more effective management of limited budgets? In short, Ottawa's Keynesian postwar strategy had to be reviewed and rectified. The government's redistributive role must be limited to the needy. This redefinition first became clear when universality was abandoned as the basic philosophy. Henceforth, Canadian social security was not universal but selective: "Social security is society's commitment to take care of its most vulnerable citizens – people without work, lone parents with limited means struggling to raise a family, children in poverty, and people who face barriers to employment due to disability or chronic illness."[1] The middle class would be left to its own devices as the government's social largesse went to the disadvantaged. Programs would be more tight-fisted and targeted, and incentives to work would be strengthened.

In fact, the process was more geared to persuading people of a need for downsizing than genuinely discussing the future shape of social security. Reform proposals all bore the same ideological bias,[2] and legislative initiatives in recent years had shown the process already under way. Family allowances, for example, which had lost their universality in 1993,[3] now included an employment bonus for low-income parents. Since 1994, in fact, the Unemployment Insurance Act had contained tougher general conditions but a more generous benefit rate for low-income people with dependent children.

The same general thrust conditioned proposals for UI reform. Collective responsibility dissolved in the presence of renewed actuarial dogma: the solution rested primarily with the individual. The system did not provide enough incentive to rejoin the workforce. A number of provisions were too generous: "Unemployment insurance creates unemployment." Even Prime Minister Jean Chrétien had no problem using demagoguery to defend the new policy shift, which he characterized as doing away with the "guy who sits at home drinking his beer" instead of being socially productive.[4] The system had to become more competitive, more efficient, and thus less open-handed to provide more incentive to work and achieve real savings. These savings would be redirected toward more market-friendly objectives – active measures or reduced premiums that, to go by the neoliberal orthodoxy, would create jobs. The system's universal protection had to give way to more targeted coverage that reflected the condition of the public purse: *"Canada needs a financially sustainable UI program, and a program that recognizes individual responsibility to work towards self-sufficiency.* While the federal government is committed to providing income support to those who truly need it, Canadians want to ensure that limited resources are used to achieve the best possible results ... People using the UI program are not to blame for these problems. It is often the system which is at fault."[5]

Subtly, these arguments were aimed less at the unemployed, as in earlier counterreforms, than at the system itself. But let us not be deceived: the responsibility for unemployment would soon be shifted to the shoulders of the jobless because the system created dependency. They were not lazy, of course: the system made them lazy. The language dear to the OECD was here again: "The UI program has ... faced increasing pressures for change to address the steady growth of structural unemployment and dependency on UI."[6]

Nowhere was there mention of job-creation policies: after all, they would have called for active government involvement. The solutions to unemployment and lack of work began with fresh UI cutbacks. In fact, the workers hardest hit by the cutbacks were the same ones whom the Macdonald, Forget, and Gill reports had already bracketed in their sights: "Almost 40% of the people on unemployment insurance had claimed UI benefits at least three times in the previous five years – and the number is rising."[7] Many of these people ended up in a vicious circle and needed help to break free of it. This was the basic fate in store for the "marginally" active workforce of casual and seasonal labourers featured in the proposals as having to rely on systems other than UI. Two proposed adjustment scenarios were cynically described as "prospects." Some prospects, since both ended in the pauperization of the jobless.

In the first scenario, claimants were divided into two categories to reflect the number of benefit claims made in the preceding five years. Those who had filed three or more claims were described as "frequent claimants"; the rest were "occasional claimants." This distinction was defended by the need to reduce the dependency affecting the most marginal workers and especially the seasonal ones. Several of the Forget Report's ideas resurfaced here. For frequent claimants, UI had become "an annual income supplement system, not an insurance system."[8] At the same time, there was an emphasis on the significant shift of resources from central and western Canada to Quebec and the Maritimes. With economic globalization, the interregional common front, a favourite theme of the Canadian welfare state, had lost its currency.

For occasional claimants, basic insurance was maintained on the same basis as before, and they would be the only claimants to collect special benefits. Frequent claimants were to get an adjustment benefit program. Their rate might be lower and depend on other criteria such as family income, including spousal income. Payment of this type of benefit might also be conditional on the claimant's willingness to participate in employment programs or community work. What better way could there be of impoverishing an already marginalized workforce? The federal green paper put it bluntly: "Frequent claimants – people who experience recurring unemployment and reliance on UI – would receive lower benefits, combined with more active assistance in finding a job. Income support could be conditional on their willingness to participate in programs that make them more employable."[9]

The word *employability* had been absent from the language of federal social policy since the late 1930s.[10] Used in the United States for various workfare programs, the concept reentered Quebec's welfare vocabulary in the 1980s. Employability was more a matter of personal adjustment to the labour market than actual vocational training.[11] The Axworthy reform project now brought employability into the UI environment. The difference was not merely semantic: the whole outlook was different. For example, adjustment benefits could take the form of unwanted work. The active measures would not be purely voluntary anymore: they might become mandatory.

The second proposed scenario to achieve the savings needed for reallocating funds was a new wave of cuts that would still maintain the UI system in its existing form. Various approaches were then considered: increasing the minimum entrance requirement to fourteen weeks, or twenty-six weeks over two years, and reducing the benefit rate to 50 percent. As for length of benefit, the regional variations in the system might be cut back or completely eliminated.[12]

Finally, there was a proposal to do away with the minimum level of insurability that removed any job involving fewer than fifteen hours a week from the system. Premiums would be paid on all hours worked, subject to minimum annual earnings. The proposal would attempt to be fairer to part-time workers, given the proliferation of this type of employment: in 1993, 60 percent of all jobs created were part-time.[13] What the paper did not say, however, was just how lucrative this operation, with its greatly expanded contributor base, could be for the government.

Although the green paper abounded in theories tending to support the notion that the system's generosity would create dependency and unemployment, we have very little data on the actual social consequences of the recent counterreforms. The following comment on the potential effects of a higher entrance requirement seems to be revealing: "Increasing entrance requirements will inevitably push some out-of-work individuals onto welfare (though there is no empirical evidence as to how large an effect this might be)."[14] There is something indecent about this remark when we know how many studies Ottawa and the provinces commissioned on the impact of UI changes on welfare coffers.

The counterreforms of the 1990s pushed hundreds of thousands of jobless out of the UI system. Many of them were forced to go on welfare. The impact on their rights was felt in both UI and welfare. And the bloodletting is seen in the statistics. Average monthly claims for regular benefits, from over 1.1 million in 1991, fell to under 900,000 in 1994 and 736,000 in 1995. The total number of benefit weeks paid during the same period met a similar fate, dropping from over 60 million in 1991 to 38 million in 1995.[15] In November 1995, the amount of benefits paid over the first three months had fallen to its lowest level since 1990[16] – from $19.3 billion in 1992 to only $13.7 billion in 1995.[17]

Admittedly, not everyone who lost the right to benefit was suddenly eligible for welfare. Yet the general effect of these cutbacks in the system was to impoverish the jobless and send more people to claim the assistance of last resort. UI's poverty prevention role was indeed a thing of the past.[18]

It will be remembered that, when the Labour Force Development Strategy was introduced in 1989, the government of Canada put the number of jobless who would be forced to turn to welfare at 30,000, with 10,000 of them in Quebec. A 1994 update by the Quebec government confirmed that bleak prognosis, estimating that "the federal reforms of unemployment insurance had brought some 30,000 new households to welfare from 1990 to 1994."[19] A study on the impact of the 1994 counterreforms, this time by the federal government, came to the same conclusion: "The general effect of these changes will be an increase of 19,000 new welfare cases across Canada. This figure includes the 4,400 people who will no longer be entitled to unemployment insurance because they could not meet the requirement of 12 weeks of work and the 14,500 who will have exhausted their unemployment insurance benefits ... There is also talk of 52,500 people who will have to claim welfare benefits for two additional months."[20] And a report released in October 1997 confirmed the major impact of these counterreforms on the welfare intake in Quebec: "The results of the statistical analysis based on the macroeconomic data of the last two decades and the simulations that can be drawn from them indicate that the three major amendments made to the Canadian unemployment insurance system in 1990, 1994 and 1996 will ultimately have caused a cumulative increase of about 194,000 people on Quebec's welfare rolls (using a constant 1997 population)."[21]

As well, 1993 research on the consequences of cancelling rights in cases of voluntary leaving found that UI claims by this group had strikingly declined, while their use of welfare had increased in equal if not greater proportions.[22] There could now be a double penalty for people forced to ask for welfare after a voluntary separation. For example, under Quebec's

Act Respecting Income Security, they could see their benefits cut by $100 for twelve months if they quit their jobs for no serious reason.[23]

Although the employment insurance bill tabled in the House of Commons in December 1995[24] contained a number of the proposals put forward in Lloyd Axworthy's reform package, other things happened in 1995 that can help us to delineate the government's strategy more clearly.

Unlike its two immediate predecessors, the budget brought down early that year contained no major changes in UI itself. However, slated for the following year was a significant change that would downsize the system by at least 10 percent. Ottawa also announced the 1996 launch of the Canada Health and Social Transfer (CHST) to replace most of the funding going to provinces under CAP, and Established Programs Financing (EPF) for health care and postsecondary education.[25] The envelope for this block transfer, however, would shrink appreciably from $29.6 billion in fiscal 1995-96 to less than $25.1 billion for 1997-98.[26] This meant radical cuts in federal funding for provincial jobless assistance programs. In addition, several requirements that provinces had to meet to collect the federal funds, which guaranteed certain rights to welfare recipients, were now cancelled.[27] The only one kept was a prohibition on provincial residence requirements as a precondition for collecting welfare.[28] The new transfer did nothing to stop provinces from setting up "workfare" programs that forced recipients to do volunteer labour in exchange for their benefits.

In late summer 1995, a document making the rounds in Ottawa threw a little more light on the government's intentions. Entitled *The Human Resources Investment Fund* (HRIF) and marked "Secret," this paper outlined the federal labour market strategy with an emphasis on vocational training. Noting the reduced amounts in the new CHST, the paper suggested that almost all federal labour market activities be handled by the UI system. The ground for this move seemed to be solid enough: "HRIF refocusses federal labour market activities on a clear constitutional basis – UI."[29]

The active measures would not now be aimed solely at UI claimants, which would open the way for the system to fund employability measures that had formerly come under welfare and been funded by the CAP. The future clientele was defined by the same criteria as for pilot projects: current claimants and people who had collected benefits over the past three years. The document defended its choice of clients in these words:

- they are a clear federal responsibility
- programs of passive income support are not sufficient to get some of them back to work – they need active measures
- would include social assistance recipients that exhausted UI benefits – reduces offloading onto provinces.[30]

The basic funding for the new program would come from the UI account up to the $1.98 billion level already earmarked for active measures plus an influx of $800 million released by new cuts in the system. At the same time, general tax revenue spent on active measures would be cut from $1.4 billion in fiscal 1994-95[31] to $850 million in 1996-97. In essence, this amount would now go only to specifically targeted client groups: "Almost all this budget will be used in 1996-97 to support carry-over from 1995-96, aboriginal programming, support to literacy, Vocational Rehabilitation of Disabled Persons (VRDP) and youth programming."[32] By refocusing its strategy on UI, Ottawa was killing two birds with one stone. It was able to maintain an active role in vocational training while reducing the overall cost of its activities.

The first version of the employment insurance bill that reached the House of Commons in late 1995 would make its way crabwise under the grand old strategy tested in 1990 and 1993. The Chrétien government reacted to the outcry against its bill from union and grassroots circles and regions of high unemployment by withdrawing this version and replacing it with a slightly reworked bill[33] aimed at soothing antagonists. With a few minor amendments by the Parliamentary Committee on Human Resources Development, the bill received the royal assent on 20 June 1996.[34] In recognition of the substantial impact that the new measures would have, the act would be monitored for its effects on individuals and communities in the years 1997-2001 and the resulting report studied by a House of Commons committee formed for the purpose.

There was something cynical about the system's new name. The consolidation of almost all of Ottawa's active measures for insured persons and other clients served as a pretext for a social marketing campaign that echoed the labour market policies of the OECD. The passive UI system made way for the active EI system, as "employment" apparently struck a more optimistic note than "unemployment." Let us make no mistake, however: behind these words, what the unemployed, the most marginal workers, and people in outlying regions were actually getting was even more cutbacks and impoverishment. The new cuts in the system would produce savings in excess of $2 billion, $800 million of which would be reinvested in the active measures now known as "employment benefits."[35]

The Employment Insurance Act involved a complete overhaul of the system, which was now divided into two parts: unemployment benefits and employment benefits.[36] The latter included the National Employment Service. The Unemployment Insurance Act and the National Training Act were replaced. The new unemployment benefit system was designed to further reduce the level of protection for marginal workers, including seasonal ones. However, instead of raising the general entrance requirement to twenty weeks, which would have come as a cruel blow to workers in outlying regions, the lawmaker chose a more sophisticated approach that affected both the entrance requirement and the benefit calculation process. Out of this came a formula reminiscent of the annualization that Forget had called for.[37] The new requirement would be calculated in hours, and the new denominator for establishing the amount of benefit would no longer solely reflect the last weeks worked.

The general UI entrance requirement of twelve to twenty weeks was converted to hours in line with a full-time work schedule of thirty-five hours a week and so varied from 420 to 700 hours. Maximum insurable earnings were reduced to $39,000, while people who earned less than $2,000 a year could get their premiums refunded by producing their tax returns. Noble motives were cited to legitimize the new formula, for instance the desire to include part-time jobs in the system. People failing to meet the minimal insurable weekly standard (fifteen hours or 20 percent of maximum insurable earnings) would now be covered, which made benefits available to those holding several jobs of this kind.

The government reaped a clear advantage from the new formula since all hours worked up to the maximum annual earnings became contributory. This approach enabled Ottawa to tap a workforce that would have a lot of problems qualifying for unemployment benefits, mainly due to the increased entrance requirement. Thus, the minimum number of hours required to collect benefits went from 180 (twelve weeks at a minimum of fifteen hours a week) to 420. Many people with employment earnings of more than $2,000 would still be unable to accumulate these hours.

Moreover, the amendments affecting NERE showed the government's indifference to their fate. The applicable requirement of twenty weeks (minimum of 300 hours) went to 910 hours, or the equivalent of twenty-six full-time weeks. As well, the shift from weeks to hours for calculation purposes and the use of a full-time workweek of thirty-five hours raised the entrance requirement for special benefits from 300 to 700 hours.[38] Since most part-time and casual employees were women,[39] they were doubly penalized.

The system became extremely harsh on claimants making false statements.[40] Not only did they have to refund benefits paid in error with a penalty, but they were also subject to a punitive entrance requirement reflecting various criteria that included the amount obtained by the fraud or repeat offence. The minimum requirement of 420 hours could be doubled for a repeat offender within five years. These were outrageous penalties for offences that in so many cases stemmed from the survival instinct. As in the glory days of classical liberalism, pauperization and repression went hand in hand.[41]

Another feature picked up from the Forget Report was the way in which benefits were calculated. Previously, they had been based on the average of the last weeks worked up to a maximum of twenty weeks. Henceforth, benefits would be calculated by dividing the number of weeks worked in a base period not to exceed twenty-six weeks by a denominator that ranged from fourteen to twenty-two to reflect the regional unemployment rate. The initial bill (C-111) anticipated a gradual move to a standard denominator of twenty. Given the strong opposition from the outlying regions, there was agreement on a denominator calculated by converting the VER into weeks and adding two. A qualified claimant with a number of hours equivalent to fourteen weeks of work would thus have total earnings from those fourteen weeks divided by a denominator of sixteen.[42]

This change in the way that benefits were calculated, though subtler than raising the entrance requirement to twenty weeks, still had the same outcome for the jobless. Admittedly, compared to the alternative considered at the outset, more people were able to qualify for benefits, but those benefits were now appreciably smaller. Moreover, by severing this amount from the real number of weeks worked, the lawmaker was introducing a mechanism that would later be easy to shift upward.

The marginal workforce, especially its seasonal contingent, was also targeted by the "intensity" rule. Claimants who had collected more than twenty weeks of benefits over the past five years saw their basic rate of 55 percent cut by 1 percent for each additional twenty-week period until a minimum 50 percent rate was reached. However, this system would not apply to low-income claimants with dependants at home, for whom a family supplement replaced the old program that had raised their rate to 60 percent. A number of the criteria for claiming this supplement were found not in the Employment Insurance Act but in the Income Tax Act. This fiscalization of the family supplement made it a complex mechanism[43] that destabilized remedies in this area of the law. Consistently with the neoliberal approach,[44] the family supplement also helped to lessen the impact of the spate of EI restrictions on provincial welfare budgets.

Converting weeks into hours in a full-time schedule also affected the length of benefits. For example, someone who had worked part-time at twenty-five hours a week for twenty-six weeks used to be entitled to twenty-three weeks of benefits. Now the entitlement was cut back to nineteen weeks. Before 1990, the same claimant had been entitled to forty-five weeks.

All these new measures breathed the actuarial tradition of the Gill and Forget reports. They were designed so that only people able to prove a real labour force attachment – that is, a permanent full-time job – could collect decent unemployment benefits with the blessing of the private insurance rule book.

Although the labour dispute provisions were unchanged, new rules for voluntary leaving highlighted the repressive quality of this feature. Certain situations were now categorized as voluntary separations in which all rights were removed: for example, refusal of a job offer as a solution to potential job loss, refusal to return to work, or refusal to stay in a job when functions were being transferred to another employer. These provisions reflected the lawmaker's concern with corporate interests over those of the unemployed. Moreover, to thwart a case law trend favouring the jobless,[45] the act stated that disqualification would now apply to loss of employment occurring when a period had been established, not just to the voluntary leaving that prompted the claim.

Even for employment benefits, new repressive provisions emerged. For example, a six-week disqualification could be imposed on a claimant expelled from a course, thus empowering a third party to rule on eligibility for benefits. And an unprecedented penalty three times the benefit amount could be imposed on someone who, without good cause, abandoned, failed to attend, or was expelled from a course.[46] With a criminal penalty attached to this obligation, EI emerged as a genuine instrument of social control through which participants would gain access to training ... made mandatory!

As the unemployment benefit component drew nearer to the private insurance model, the employment benefit component moved away from it. The act now referred not to "insured persons" but to "insured participants."[47] Access to this type of benefit was expanded to people who had collected benefits for three years – five years in the case of parental and maternity claimants. These employability programs, formerly part of the welfare system, were now funded by reduced access to unemployment benefits.

Clearly subject to "market imperatives," employment benefits included the old active measures plus new programs of wage subsidies or employment income supplements for low-income workers. These programs would sometimes be accessible by the employed, thus minimizing employer liability for vocational training. Training purchases could be made with vouchers for use in educational institutions. The unemployed could be tapped too, since the support that they received might take the form of loans.[48] Subsidies would also be available to agencies providing employment assistance services to the jobless.

Under the act, most of these benefits were designed for provincial oversight. Provinces looking for this federal funding had to follow certain loose guidelines of obvious ideological lineage. They had to try to reduce dependency on unemployment benefits.[49] The unemployed themselves had no rights other than to participate in certain programs in the official language of their choice "where there is significant demand for that assistance in that language."[50] More flexible than the CAP, this new system still resembled its ancestor, though with one major difference: the money now came from the EI account and not the Consolidated Revenue Fund.

On 21 April 1997, an agreement between Ottawa and Quebec joined similar agreements already concluded with Alberta, New Brunswick, New-foundland, and Manitoba.[51] The Canada-Quebec agreement put the province in charge of active measures, including assistance programs,[52] financed by the EI account. However, Ottawa would continue to pay unemployment benefits to "active" EI claimants. The National Employment Service in Quebec would be run by Quebec, and the agreement included a transfer of federal public servants to the provincial bureaucracy. Finally, management agreements for employment benefits could also be reached directly with private sector organizations, thus helping to privatize this system component.

CEIC decisions on employment benefits could be appealed to a Board of Referees[53] only when they involved a penalty for a false statement or failure to attend a course. This came as a severe blow to the unemployed on provincial assistance programs. The CAP standards obliging provinces to guarantee certain rights to the jobless had been largely obliterated in the new CHST. The new employment benefits system confirmed this truncation of their rights.

The new contributory formula also highlighted the ideological wellspring of the new system. Whereas the more marginal workers were obliged to contribute to the system from the first hour worked, the top earners saw their premiums go down. The maximum insurable earnings that reached $43,940 in early 1996 were frozen at $39,000 for the years 1997-2000. This double amendment increased the degressive character of the funding while reducing its redistributive effect.

The arguments defending this lowered contributory ceiling in Axworthy's EI manifesto gave off an unmistakable whiff of the actuarial ideology. The neoliberal planners had made the private vision of insurance their own: "Lower premium rates occur because workers at higher earning levels are less likely to become unemployed and claim benefits than those with lower earnings. They are, therefore, net contributors to the UI program ... Approximately 70 per cent of UI claimants, but only 52 per cent of the labour force, have individual incomes of less than $25,000. Meanwhile, workers with individual incomes over $50,000 represent about 12 per cent of the labour force and account for less than three per cent of total UI claimants."[54] What is more, by using premiums for purposes other than paying insurance benefits, the new act made them into a degressive tax. A droll system for the distribution of wealth in which the poorest workers helped to fund the cost of assistance programs made possible by cutting insurance coverage!

Another factor was at work in this transformation of the system's contributory mechanism into a degressive tax: the disappearance of the ratio, expressed as a percentage (15 percent), of the employment benefit budget to total system spending.[55] From now on, 0.8 percent of all insurable earnings subject to premiums could be spent on employment benefits.[56] This jiggery-pokery allowed the government to spend more money on its active measures while continuing to cut the funds available for unemployment benefits. Moreover, by taking all insurable earnings in Canada as its reference,[57] the EI system acquired an independence that helped to separate it from social insurance to compensate unemployment.

One of the Axworthy reform recommendations was to create a surplus in the EI account to avoid raising premiums in periods of economic slowdown.[58] This seemingly Keynesian move was actually a neoliberal one. With a self-financing system, the stabilizer role in recessions would be played by the contributors, not the government. Clearly, this surplus could not be created without major cuts in coverage. We were in the presence of a historical reversal. The Keynesian jobless who had been among the main beneficiaries of the stimulation of economic activity were now its victims. The money stored up against future recessions was generated by their current impoverishment.

To accumulate this surplus while maintaining coverage at a low level, the act's funding rules were radically changed. Under the old Unemployment Insurance Act, the premium rate had reflected benefits actually paid over the last three years.[59] From now on, premiums would reflect vague criteria designed to ensure the system's performance and a stable rate determined by the government alone:

Annual premium rate setting – The Commission shall, with the approval of the Governor in Council on the recommendation of the Minister and the Minister of Finance, set the premium rate for each year at a rate that the Commission considers will, to the extent possible,

a)   ensure that there will be enough revenue over a business cycle to pay the amounts authorized to be charged to the Employment Insurance Account; and
b)   maintain relatively stable rate levels throughout the business cycle.[60]

In this way, the provision broke with a principle in force since the system's inception and the essence of social insurance: a direct connection between the account's premium rate and benefit payout.

This policy breathed the neoliberal vision of UI: it was also nicely timed for a government short of cash. The idea of creating a cushion of stability suggested the potential for using that cushion to absorb the national deficit. The auditor general had recommended in 1985 that the government incorporate the system's budget into its general fund.[61] As the government was then funding UI, and the account was in the red, this recommendation

was sound and understandable. Beginning in 1986, the system's accounting was taken over by the state, with premiums treated as receipts and
benefits as expenditures.[62] By 1994, UI premiums were "the largest source
of federal revenue next to personal income taxes."[63] UI cutbacks would
create a surplus that later, as a government asset, reduced the deficit correspondingly. The government's 1997 estimates put the UI account's cumulative surplus at $6.5 billion, and it was $12.2 billion by 31 March 1998.[64]
The president of the Treasury Board was clear on his government's position: "Mr. Massé had no trouble seeing the surplus as a source of revenue
for the federal government. 'If you cut a source of income and want to
keep cutting the deficit, you are obliged to find another source.' ... The
solution to offset this shortfall, continued Mr. Massé, would be to increase
income tax, which his government refuses to do ... If the surplus was
recorded separately, the federal deficit would be $25 billion this year and
not $19 billion, as Minister Martin announced when tabling his budget."[65]

By approving a premium rate that had ceased to reflect benefits, the new
approach legitimized the existence of a massive surplus while thousands
of jobless watched the protection that the system should have provided
decline significantly, with the number of jobless actually compensated by
the system still in free fall: "The number of people applying for employment insurance benefits in August reached the lowest level in 15 years ...
The national agency partly ascribes the drop in claims to the new legislation in force since July 1."[66]

The 1990s changes that culminated in employment insurance formed a
continuum. This hijack of the system, always at the expense of jobless
rights, raises a number of basic questions about the legitimacy and legality
of the process. The counterreforms reflected the new federal revelation:
government must remain at arm's length from market forces, channelling
rather than meddling. Employment and unemployment were private sector and, more specifically, personal matters. Full employment was axio-
matic: all that was needed was to provide an optimal environment that
let the market release its job potential. When the government ended its
financial support for the system in 1990, it relinquished effective control.

Nevertheless, the principle that the state as the manager of the national
economy had a responsibility for unemployment was solidly entrenched
in Canada as in almost all industrialized countries. A 1955 ILO publication[67] had put forth the arguments in favour of government involvement
in funding UI systems: beyond the state's social liability for unemployed
workers and their families, the concern to spread the financial burden as
progressively and fairly as possible across the whole population justified
the systems' access to general revenues.

The discontinuation of government funding made the system's downsizing inevitable. At some more or less distant day, it would have to lose its

most redistributive features, including the regional variations that had basically been covered by federal funding. Moreover, the recommendations in the Macdonald and Forget Reports clearly show how these two issues were interlocked. Genuinely redistributive arrangements for marginal workers, including regional resonance, would be hard to maintain if the system had to be self-financing.

Abolishing the regionalisms was a long-term process. The string of amendments passed in 1990-94, followed by the EI system, tied length of benefits closely to work history, sidelining the regional unemployment factor. And contrary to the general impression, the marginal workforce in the big cities was also hit hard by the loss of regional resonance. The blow really fell on all marginal workers, not just on the ones in the outlying regions.

A basic tenet of social insurance is recognition of the right to benefit. When the system was hijacked in the 1990s, denial of the right to unemployment insurance was coupled with denial of the right to training. Groupthink had done its work, and the word was that, in the new environment created by advanced technology and planetary competition, the active measures were not only needed but also beneficial for the unemployed. After all, there was no point paying them to sit at home doing nothing!

The jobless were the victims of this hijack of the UI system to pay for active measures. They could not be denied an opportunity to upgrade their vocational training in a period of involuntary inactivity: the seed had been planted in the act of 1940. But there needed to be a genuine training scheme with a recognized right to its use. And since training benefited society as a whole, with business in the lead, society and business had to pay for it. In no case could training be legitimately funded at the expense of income support, the system's primary purpose: "In terms of the needs of unemployed workers, it is clear that training can improve an individual's chances of obtaining a decent job. However, this is no justification for cutting back on so-called 'passive' spending on UI which is essential to the income security of workers and to income support during layoffs and periods of job search."[68] In 1992, the co-chairs of the CLFDB had voiced their concern about this use of the UI account. Even the Forget Report, like the Gill Report before it, had been opposed to vocational training at the expense of unemployment insurance.

And what of the right to this new basic benefit? The active measures did not come with the same legal guarantees as social insurance, and some of the new employment benefits were handled as social assistance. Granted on a purely discretionary basis with no appeal process, they were the antithesis of a genuine training entitlement: individuals could not challenge decisions to grant or deny access to a measure or to one measure rather than another. With EI, this denial of the right to training went much farther. Failure to attend a course without a valid reason brought disqualification and a penalty to boot.

The Axworthy manifesto's reference to the concepts of employability and community work tells us something about the type of training or, rather, pseudo-training that might be delivered by some of these measures earmarked for the jobless at the bottom of the totem pole. Swallowed up with the labours of the 1930s Purvis Commission,[69] the concept of employability now resurfaced in the lingo of federal training policy. This was no accident. The development of employability, with its ideological bias, could live with some minimally effective training programs.

Genuine vocational training involves recognition of an individual's right to choose a particular type of training and the freedom to set about it.[70] Instead, these active measures for developing employability were typified by lack of choice, as access to training now reflected government policies and directives. Indeed, training "choices" were often enforced, since programs were associated with the US practice of "workfare" or welfare employment. As a rule, welfare recipients participated to get more benefits or avoid getting less or even none. So beleaguered an environment could hardly acknowledge a right of appeal or even a remedy against these measures.[71] The lack of rights and the limiting factors in these programs made them measures of social control that had little to do with any real vocational training policy.[72]

The law should include criteria such as the ones for determining suitability of employment. Does this training cater to the person's needs and abilities? Does it reflect his or her educational history, previous work experience, or professional aspirations? People have to feel involved in the training process to put their utmost into it. Moreover, decisions affecting all of the active measures, including the type of training offered, should be subject to an appeal process like any other decisions affecting claimants' rights.

Finally, let us not forget the ideological significance of the idea of employability as rehabilitated by the rise of neoliberalism. This was the flip side of full employment, supply-side economics in the workforce: rather than supporting demand for work by a policy of full employment, the government should get involved in the work supply, that is, worker qualification. The focus of activity was shifting toward the individual, who had to be moulded to market specifications with the market left to do the rest. The government could then claim to be doing something for the jobless by "developing their employability" while concealing its own poor job-creation record. The aim now was, rather than providing jobs for the jobless, making them employable.

The result of this new thrust was an across-the-board attack on the right to unemployment insurance. The system became less accessible, less open-handed, and more repressive. Eligible population numbers plummeted.

The early changes affecting disentitlement in labour disputes were reflective of the policy shift. This barometer for the government's UI role and social power relationships came out of the process stronger than ever. Despite the Supreme Court's criticisms of the old provision's strictness and rationality, especially when it came to the allegedly neutral state, the lawmaker substituted even more restrictive measures that revealed an obvious bias. A few minor corrections were made to the system to avoid certain flagrant instances of individual suffering, of course, but the overall effects of disentitlement were toughened.

An example was the use of disentitlement for people who were already unemployed in an attempt to overturn the *Gionest* precedent.[73] How could anyone claim to be protecting state neutrality while challenging the right to benefit of people who were already jobless? The actuarial reasoning that assumed the existence of an insurable interest – "you can't lose what you don't have" – evidently yielded here to the harsh truism that "might is right." The regulatory reinstatement of the 85 percent rule obeyed the same imperative. For Judge Hugessen, maintaining disentitlement after a labour dispute was resolved was "an act that causes the government to lose its neutrality."[74] This is exactly what the lawmaker did in 1990.

The ideological bias that informed this tinkering with disentitlement would have the UI system and government itself work actively for free markets and even, if needed, gut provisions in social laws that might limit or infringe on the freedom of business executives to act. This bias was clear in the 1993 elimination of the right to benefit in cases of voluntary separation. Its effect was especially severe on people in marginal employment, often under tough conditions and at low wages. A 1992 survey by Statistics Canada revealed higher resignation rates among low-income workers.[75] This segment of the workforce was especially targeted by the measure. And the message was understood, as many of these people thereafter abstained from filing benefit claims after voluntary separations.[76]

Although Canada has often boasted of having one of the most generous UI systems, we have to admit that such is no longer the case. The abolition of rights in cases of voluntary leaving and misconduct has made Canada's one of the most repressive systems in the industrialized world: with some US states, Canada is alone in imposing such severe penalties.[77] Under the Thatcher government in the United Kingdom, the maximum length of disqualification for voluntary leaving was increased from six weeks to twelve weeks and then, less than eighteen months later, twenty-six weeks.[78] This British process bore a strange resemblance to what happened here. Yet the "iron lady" herself did not dare to completely eliminate benefits in these cases!

The downsizing of the system dictated by this market-based job strategy echoed the harmonization process associated with the Canada-US Free Trade

Agreement. It will be remembered that one of the most hotly debated topics when the FTA was being negotiated was its potential negative impact on our social programs. Many analysts and politicians argued that it was only a trade agreement and therefore no threat to these programs. However, other observers predicted a negative impact on social security as the new framework of globalization minimized or denied its economic stimulator role.[79]

Payroll taxes, including UI premiums, had to come down to make Canadian companies more competitive in the new North American economic environment. There was a total convergence of views between the neoliberal ideology nationally and the free-trade doctrine internationally. And in the adjustment process, the UI system gradually edged closer to the US model. The following changes reflect this process: withdrawal of government funding, successive hikes in the entrance requirement, reduced rates and length of benefits, and, finally, the new penalties for voluntary leaving. The effect of all these measures has been to cut the percentage of jobless Canadians able to collect unemployment insurance almost to the US level.

Let us remember that US governments do not fund unemployment insurance[80]: apart from a few exceptions, UI premiums are borne wholly by the employers.[81] The federal statute imposes a 6.2 percent contribution on earnings up to US$7,000 that can earn a tax credit of 5.4 percent if the employer contributes to the state scheme. This leaves the government with only 0.8 percent to fund extended benefits and ensure the scheme's liquidity. The minimum entrance requirement, which may reflect earnings, length of employment, or both, is generally the equivalent of twenty weeks, and the benefit rate is 50 percent. In most states, the basic program lasts for twenty-six weeks. When unemployment reaches a certain level, an extended benefit program kicks in that is funded jointly by the federal and state governments and may last for a further thirteen weeks. In 1988, the average maximum benefit was US$188, the equivalent of Cdn$275.[82]

The Reagan-Bush years were disastrous for jobless Americans. The policies of the Reagan administration in the early 1980s forced US states, despite rising unemployment, to raise entrance requirements, and a lot of workers lost coverage. In 1975, more than 75 percent of Americans without work qualified for the system; the 1985 figure was only 32.9 percent. In 1994, one out of three unemployed Americans still qualified for the system, but in fourteen states the percentage was only 25 percent.[83]

Successive counterreforms would gradually harmonize the Canadian and US systems. The benefit rate, slipping to 57 percent and then 55 percent, grew closer to the American 50 percent, not to mention that the new EI benefit calculation method cut payouts even more for many marginal workers. Similarly, the counterreforms of 1990 and 1994 substantially reduced the average benefit period, which stood at only twenty-six weeks in the latter year.[84] Later the maximum length of the new EI benefits was cut from fifty weeks to forty-five weeks.

The measures dealing with voluntary leaving and labour disputes, often more repressive than the ones in the United States, clearly revealed the ideological underpinnings of the 1990 counterreforms. Admittedly, the elimination of rights for voluntary leavers applied in nearly all US states.[85] Yet some states provided different penalties for misconduct cases.[86] Vermont, for example, used a disqualification of six to twelve weeks for less serious cases.[87] When it came to labour disputes, a number of states did not use disentitlement for lockouts, at least not when the lockout was solely the employer's responsibility.[88]

In 1989, 85 percent of jobless Canadians qualified for benefits. The figure was only 41 percent by early 1997.[89] The proportion of jobless protected by unemployment insurance was thus getting closer to the US average. At the same time, a UI system that was less generous to the jobless while bringing as much if not more money into the federal coffers was good business in Ottawa's financial predicament. Instead of reducing premiums in line with neoliberal free-trade thinking, the government chose to use the surpluses rung up by the cuts,[90] albeit temporarily, to bring down its deficit.

There has not been much discussion recently of the constitutional aspect of this hijack of the UI account. Can premiums really be used for purposes other than compensation? Can Ottawa's use of UI funds for active measures be viewed constitutionally on the same basis as its use of the federal spending power? The "secret" paper of summertime 1995 seemed to claim that all management of the jobless came under the federal jurisdiction over unemployment insurance.[91] Open to challenge though this claim may be, it seems to be essential to the federal strategy. In this sense, the expansion of active measures to include former claimants in the pilot projects of 1994 had to be a trial balloon: given the paucity of reaction to this, Ottawa thought that it had a free rein for its EI scheme.

Nevertheless, I do not think that the jurisdiction granted to Parliament by the constitutional amendment of 1940 authorized the use of UI premiums for purposes other than the payment of benefits. The decisions in the court challenge to the 1935 Employment and Social Insurance Act[92] are instructive in this regard. The Supreme Court of the day likened "social insurance" to "commercial insurance," and the Privy Council, without making any explicit pronouncement on this issue, stressed the analogy between the two types of insurance.

And the system set up as a result of the 1940 constitutional amendment was essentially identical to the one described in the 1935 act. That system's affinity to other forms of insurance would later be highlighted in a number of decisions, including *Hills:* "The Act's insurance feature prevailed all along through the national pooling of both the risks and the costs of unemployment."[93] Called on to define the nature of another social insurance scheme, the Canada Pension Plan, the Supreme Court concluded that it was a form of insurance similar to commercial insurance.[94] UI differs from commercial insurance in various respects, but it does share its insurance "feature" that ties premiums and benefits intrinsically together: despite the federal spending power, these premiums could be used only for a specific purpose, namely to compensate the insured unemployed.

Some might claim that Parliament is empowered to train the jobless by its jurisdiction over unemployment insurance. The "active measures" or "employment benefits" components would thus be integral to the UI system. Remember that the cost of extending these "active measures" in 1977 was borne by Ottawa. However, the Supreme Court, ruling in 1989 on a dispute over the application of labour legislation to claimants enrolled in a job-creation program, decided that the funding basis for these programs was the spending power of Parliament and not the jurisdiction over unemployment insurance.[95] With the disappearance of state financial support in 1990, these "active measures" ceased to be funded from the general spending power of Parliament: the money now came from the UI account, then the EI account, to the detriment of the system's insurance function. The funding of these measures by the EI account with no government contribution therefore does not meet the requirements of subsection 91(2A) of the BNA Act.

Finally, this whole restructuring took place with no actual debate on the social issues linked to the changes. It must be said that a number of provinces shared the federal neoliberal beliefs and, in any event, seemed to be more interested, amid a crisis in public finances, in reaping a potential federal windfall than in questioning its constitutional orthodoxy or social implications. Besides, like the lawmaker, the tribunals themselves were not indifferent to the neoliberal wave of the 1990s, as seen in some of their interpretations of the provisions for voluntary leaving.

10
Case Law in the Neoliberal Riptide of the 1990s

The neoliberal wave that propelled counterreform was also felt in the courts, though to a much lesser extent. Beginning in 1990, a number of decisions parted company with *Abrahams*, especially on voluntary unemployment, and placed limits on previously acknowledged claimant rights. Before moving on to look at the most significant decisions of the 1990s involving labour disputes and voluntary leaving, however, it is important to realize the impact that legislative changes had on the jobless and their rights.

The 1993 move to total disqualification for voluntary leaving had the effect of lowering the number of disqualifications imposed for this reason. The 169,000 disqualifications of this type in 1992 became the 98,400 of 1993.[1] The deterrent effect was unquestionably successful: many people decided not to file benefit claims in the belief that they had lost their UI entitlement. A 1995 study confirmed the existence of this "discouragement effect."[2] The message was effective: keep your job at any cost, or you may not collect UI.

Another outcome more generally connected to all these restrictions was an increase in appeals to Boards of Referees and umpires in the years 1989-95 (see Table 3).

Disentitlements due to labour disputes dropped appreciably from 24,940 in 1990 to 9,450 in 1991 and 5,010 in 1995.[3] There were various explanations for this decline – less frequent disputes in this period[4] and the clarification of the act by the 1990 amendments. For example, the law was more specific about restoring entitlement to claimants with new jobs after *Abrahams* and the changes that resulted from that decision.[5] The same went for the new provisions for sick leave during labour disputes and loss of part-time employment. This clarification was coupled with stability in the jurisprudence. Most decisions supported the principles set out in earlier case law. Where some tended to interpret the act liberally, others reaffirmed the severity of disentitlement and the unambiguousness of the 1990 counterreform.

Since 1990, disentitlement could be imposed for a working person's loss of employment and an unemployed person's recall to work. The principles in *Gionest* against disentitling the jobless had been watered down in subsequent rulings.[6] This whole issue would be raised again in *Pelletier*,[7] a Federal Court of Appeal decision that clearly stated the applicable principle: a callback had to be bona fide, not bogus. Did it indicate a genuine need for manpower on the employer's part, or was it merely an employer ploy to embroil unionized workers in a dispute when they were unemployed? In the latter case, disentitlement could not be used. Although that decision was rendered under the old statute, it would guide the interpretation of "callback" in the Employment Insurance Act.

It is interesting to watch this interpretation, requiring good faith from the employer in the callback process, temper the rule that the merits of the disputing parties' positions were not to be questioned. The Canadian act, like the British one, refused to take these positions into account. The definition of "labour dispute," which had not really changed since the system's inception, applied to both strikes and lockouts. The courts might use this liberal, textually sound reading to find some relief from the repressive effects of this amendment, which ran counter to the stated objective of government neutrality and even exposed this neutrality as spurious.

The principles in *Gionest* also applied in cases involving layoffs prior to work stoppages, even when the employer had been manoeuvring in anticipation of a dispute. The Federal Court of Appeal reasserted these principles by a reference to the meaning that should be given to the law and disentitlement: "Courts are urged by the Supreme Court of Canada to

Table 3

Board of Referees and umpire decisions, 1989-97

Year	Board of Referees decisions	Umpire decisions	Umpire appeals
1989-90	20,820	1,860	1,742
1990-91	24,348	1,965	1,690
1991-92	31,927	2,602	1,967
1992-93	35,245	3,708	1,692
1993-94	37,010	4,648	1,901
1994-95	39,288	5,182	3,514
1995-96	36,443	4,233	6,615
1996-97	33,948	3,675	4,822

Note: Since commission publications do not always give the number of appeals to the umpire, I obtained the figures for these appeals, starting in 1989, from Georges Goulet of HRDC's Appeal Division on 3 April 1998. The same applies to the number of appeals to the Board of Referees. The difference between numbers of appeals and umpires' decisions mainly reflects abandonments.

support the claims of workers to benefits where the language permits a choice."[8] However, the same court quashed the decision of an umpire and Board of Referees that disentitlement could not be imposed on a trainee starting work. There could be no loss of employment since there had been no contract of employment because, while training, no services were provided and the trainee had no guarantee of a job at the end of his training period. Holding that these people were still bound to the employer by a service contract, the court concluded that disentitlement was indicated because "the marginal and irregular nature of a job could not affect the very existence of the job."[9]

An important decision was handed down in *Thomas* on determining the existence of a work stoppage. At that time, the idea of "exceptional and temporary means" was used to identify the circumstances surrounding the inception as well as the termination of a work stoppage.[10] Thus, a work stoppage could be found to exist if the employer used exceptional and temporary means to maintain its production and workforce at their usual levels.

The circumstances of this case were as follows. Carole Thomas was a unionized flight attendant with Nationair. In anticipation of a labour dispute with its workers, the employer had recruited and trained "replacement personnel." On 19 November 1991, Nationair locked out its unionized employees and immediately called in these replacements, which meant that company operations were unaffected by the lockout and flights continued as usual. The CEIC imposed a disentitlement on Nationair staff that was upheld by a Board of Referees: the employer's use of exceptional and temporary means to keep its airplanes flying could not prevent the finding that a work stoppage existed. The umpire overturned this decision: the jurisprudence dealing with exceptional and temporary means could not be applied to "a situation where the manager had prepared replacement people before ordering a lockout" – not to mention the fact that the employer's activities had continued as usual. Referring to the decision in *Hills,* Judge Rouleau found that maintaining the disentitlement in these circumstances would be against the principle of neutrality behind the legislative provision. This decision was upheld by the Federal Court of Appeal.[11]

It should also be recalled that, as a result of the 1990 counterreform, the CEIC used the regulatory route to bring back the 85 percent rule for determining when a work stoppage ended: the purpose here was to defuse the interpretation advanced in *Caron.*[12] The legality of the new regulation was challenged in *Oakes-Pépin,* in which the appellant argued that it was arbitrary, ignoring the wording, spirit, and impact of the enabling legislation and disregarding the established interpretive principles for unemployment insurance. Moreover, she held, it belied the act's stated objective in labour disputes to affirm the neutrality of the state. Like the umpire, the

Federal Court of Appeal rejected these claims, believing that the content of the regulation was clearly authorized by the amendments to the enabling legislation describing the circumstances in which a work stoppage ended.[13]

In *Dallaire,* finally, the Federal Court of Appeal had to rule on the concept of "labour dispute," which had rarely seen clarification by case law apart from *Gionest.* In this case, amid the renewal of the decrees governing Quebec's construction industry, some workers had walked out in protest against Bill 142 to deregulate certain parts of that industry. These walkouts were actually aimed at the government, not the employers. Disentitled during the walkouts, the workers argued that their loss of employment had nothing to do with the negotiations about renewing the decree with their employers; rather, it stemmed from a political conflict between them and the government. The Board of Referees found that their loss of employment was not due to a labour dispute within the meaning of the act, only to be overturned by the umpire. This last position was validated by the Federal Court of Appeal, which had this to say about its reasoning: "[The umpire] considered the Minister's legislative intervention to be incidental to the dispute, a way to break the deadlock and a step in the resolution of the employer-employee dispute. He disagreed that because the bill had triggered the work stoppage it could be considered independent of or external to the dispute."[14]

If the interpretation of the provisions on labour disputes found a mixed verdict, the provisions on voluntary unemployment reflected an actuarial bias that worked against jobless rights. The liberal reading on this issue represented by *Abrahams* was often demolished on both the basic concepts in the provision and the jurisdictional issues around its application. A number of decisions on voluntary leaving and misconduct reflected the neoliberal context, and some of them contained actuarial references.

Beginning in 1990, umpires were commenting on the harshness of the new disqualification rules. Some Federal Court of Appeal decisions on misconduct reflected the same concern. The serious consequences of the new provisions, these judges held, required special delicacy with the concepts and how they were applied. More importance should be attached to determining the facts in cases of voluntary leaving now that claimants could be stripped of their rights.[15] Apart from these scattered comments, however, reported cases involving voluntary separation in the wake of these counterreforms do not show a more relaxed interpretive approach, with *Tanguay* still a primary reference.

Moreover, the influence of *Tanguay* was implicit in the interpretation of the new criterion of the "only reasonable solution"[16] in the circumstances. This criterion implied that the claimant should take steps to find another job before quitting the current one or try to correct the poor working conditions causing the separation. The tribunals were not unanimous, of course, but these two preconditions for just cause seem to have been generally accepted.

The majority jurisprudence required prior job searches. Only in exceptional, intolerable situations could the claimant quit a job without making sure of having work elsewhere. Decisions calling for corrective action prior to leaving exhibited the same severity. A number of decisions made this a requirement. The same reasoning was seen in various decisions in which claimants cited working conditions dangerous to health.[17] However, the Federal Court of Appeal, in a sexual harassment case, would hold that the tests of "urgency or necessity" were not prerequisites for just cause in voluntary leaving: "These tests are more exigent than the language of the Act which requires only that 'in all the circumstances ... the claimant had no reasonable alternative.'"[18]

References to *Tanguay* were more explicit in the Federal Court of Appeal. Although some decisions on claims procedure went in favour of the jobless, the ones reviewing just cause based on working conditions were particularly unfavourable in a context of continuously marginalized employment. In *Jenkins*, for example, the claimant had filed a benefit claim after losing his full-time job as an accountant. He subsequently worked part-time as a taxi driver and then quit. A disqualification was imposed. Relying on the interpretation in *Abrahams*, the Federal Court of Appeal found that disqualification could be used only for the initial benefit claim and not a later claim in the same period. According to that court, the CEIC's position would discourage part-time work.[19]

In any case, the rules in the Employment Insurance Act worked against this movement in favour of claimants.[20] Here the lawmaker's pro-market bias was clear, sidestepping common-sense solutions when they were even slightly favourable to claimants. Nor did this bias spare the jurisprudence. In *Tremblay*, for example, the umpire had quashed a Board of Referees decision and allowed a claimant's just cause for quitting his job due to inadequate wages: "A prudent individual may leave an employment that produces earnings below the minimum wage without suffering harmful consequences." But the Federal Court of Appeal invalidated the umpire's ruling. Referring to the actuarial principle set out in *Tanguay*, the court held, "The fact that in the claimant's view an employment is not sufficiently well paid certainly cannot as such justify him in abandoning it and compelling others to support him through unemployment insurance benefits (see *Maurice Tanguay* [CUB 9653], A-1458-84, October 2, 1985)."[21] This decision clearly shows how far the actuarial ideology could be used to support arguments for controlling the workforce: in a context in which employment is being marginalized, the system must not be used to protect workers from a market that forces them to take ill-paid jobs. The decision obviously made no reference to the claimant's premiums or the broad social insurance objectives of unity and redistribution. It led one to wonder whether the point of the system was still to pay benefits to the unemployed or if it was now to "preconvict" workers losing their jobs.

The decision in *Dietrich* suggested that judicial tribunals showed little consideration for situations that were hard on claimants emotionally. An umpire had thrown out a Board of Referees decision that stress-related headaches, cited by a claimant at the last minute to justify quitting her job, could not constitute just cause within the meaning of the act. Yet the disqualification had been cut from ten weeks to seven weeks, and the umpire accepted the claimant's version despite the lack of medical evidence. The Federal Court of Appeal quashed this decision, holding that the umpire had substituted his appraisal of the facts for that of the Board of Referees and drawn "a conclusion favourable to the respondent in the absence of any objective evidence."[22]

On misconduct, although the broad principles of the jurisprudence were maintained, some decisions did tend to whittle away at the open-endedness of earlier ones. For example, did reprehensible conduct outside the workplace but incompatible with job requirements constitute misconduct within the meaning of the act? This issue would be debated in several Federal Court of Appeal hearings. In *Nolet,* for example, a disqualification was imposed on a school bus driver who was dismissed when his employer learned of a prior conviction as a child molester. To the court, however, these acts prior to hiring were not misconduct within the meaning of the act: misconduct had to "constitute a breach of a duty that is express or implied in the contract of employment."[23]

In *Brissette,* the court tempered the limiting definition of misconduct used in *Tucker*[24] and *Nolet* with particular reference to *Tanguay.* Brissette, a trucker by trade, had lost his licence after a conviction for impaired driving. Although the offence had occurred outside working hours, he was still fired since he no longer had the driver's licence needed to perform his duties. Finding misconduct in this case, the court disregarded the copious case law refusing to accept such offences committed outside the workplace and working hours as misconduct.[25] Not only did the court rule that misconduct could include acts committed away from work, but it also thought that drunk driving met the requirements in *Tucker:* the decision to drive was voluntary. Here the court cited the actuarial principles in *Tanguay:* "The respondent was risking the loss of his driver's licence and thus his job by driving after consuming a quantity of alcohol that exceeded the allowable limit: he knowingly and deliberately caused the risk to occur." Also rejected was the argument that loss of employment had to result from the misconduct and no other fact, in this case the claimant's loss of his driver's licence. Repeating the logic in *Nolet,* the court concluded that the claimant, by wilfully losing his licence, "breached an express duty in the contract of employment."[26]

The decision in *Jewell* further reflected this broad concept. This case revived the debate between Judges Dubinsky and Cattanach:[27] could dismissal without just cause in labour law still be used to impose a disqualification for misconduct under the act? Jewell, a teacher, had been dismissed for using extreme language to a student. The umpire allowed the claimant's appeal, remarking that this was not sufficient cause for dismissal though at the same time failing to determine whether it constituted misconduct within the meaning of the act. The Federal Court of Appeal quashed this decision since the umpire had not ruled on the key issue, which was whether the claimant had lost his job due to his own misconduct, and restored the decision of the Board of Referees that misconduct could exist even if a dismissal was unjustified in labour law: "Thus, as the law stands today, section 28 is applicable so long as the employer was satisfied that the misconduct complained of warranted dismissal, even if that subjective assessment could not be sustained as a defence in a wrongful dismissal action."[28]

This judgment represented a substantial setback compared to the earlier jurisprudence and even Judge Cattanach's position. A dismissal, however wrongful in labour law, could constitute misconduct within the meaning of the act. The application of the concept of misconduct thus depended entirely on how an employee's conduct was subjectively perceived by the employer. In *Eppel,* however, Judge Marceau mitigated the impact of this new jurisprudence,[29] and the same judge in *Choinière* refuted the principle advanced in *Jewell.* In that case, a note written by a CEIC agent stipulating that the claimant had been dismissed for taking a day of unauthorized leave was produced in evidence but did not move the court to find misconduct: "We do not think so, in light of the decisions of this Court, which has gone to great lengths on many recent occasions to repeat that it was a mistake to think for one moment that the employer's opinion concerning the existence of misconduct that would warrant dismissal might suffice to trigger the penalty, now so arduous, of section 28 and that on the contrary an objective assessment was needed sufficient to say that misconduct was in fact the cause of the loss of employment."[30]

Notable in this commentary, which provided a balance with *Jewell,* was its reference to the seriousness of the penalty that could now be meted out for misconduct – the complete elimination of the right to benefit. The decision in *Meunier* would also show this concern. A Montreal newspaper photographer, Meunier had been suspended without pay after being charged with sexual assaults on young girls. The claimant had used his press photographer's credentials to further his wrongdoing. The Federal Court of

Appeal would rule that unproven allegations by the employer were not enough to prove misconduct by the claimant.[31] Here again we find the concern to temper the impact of the *Jewell* decision and require more solid evidence in view of the severity of this new penalty for misconduct.

On availability, the decision in *Stolniuk* marked a major setback for the rule obliging the CEIC to advise claimants that they were breaching their duty to be available before imposing a disentitlement. The claimant in this case, a teacher, had said that she was available for part-time work since she was busy in the summer on the farm that she and her husband owned. The commission found her unavailable since she was not prepared to take a part-time job. The umpire agreed with the Board of Referees that she was unavailable but allowed her appeal nonetheless on the ground that the commission had failed in its duty to advise her that her limited availability failed to meet the requirements of the act. Quashing this decision, the Federal Court of Appeal ruled that the duty of availability created by the act was clear. Cases of evident nonavailability released the commission from its obligation to apply its own early warning policy.[32] The court held that the commission's failure to follow its policy in a particular case might give that claimant a cause of action in administrative law for a remedy based on administrative liability but could not be used as a defence against a breach of the duty of availability. It concluded that, in this case, the claimant had limited her availability as her benefit period began and was therefore clearly not available for work.

This decision undermined the existing jurisprudence on this warning requirement, which was used indiscriminately as to whether limits were stated at the outset or during the benefit period. Moreover, for Judge Marceau, the commission's duty to warn the claimant did not stem from the theory of procedural fairness[33] but simply from an internal policy. It was up to the commission to decide what fairness required in any specific case.

Forcing claimants in these cases to seek guidance from the tribunals in disputes about procedures for applying the act deprived them of an opportunity to exercise certain rights and totally denied the lawmaker's intent to make a simple and effective remedy available to claimants, as Chief Justice Thurlow emphasized in *Findenigg:* "Parliament, in providing for appeals to such a Board, must be taken to have intended to confer an effective right of appeal and implicitly to have authorized the Board to give any decision that in the circumstances of the case before it is necessary to ensure that the result is in accordance with the law."[34] According to the appeal court's new position, neither the Board of Referees nor the umpire was empowered as an administrative tribunal to review the fairness of the commission's actions in these cases. Furthermore, by basing the commission's duty to advise claimants of their nonavailability on a nonbinding internal policy, the appeal court left them at the mercy of a discretionary power. The arbitrary nature of these situations had drawn harsh criticism in the past.[35]

Although this decision expanded the CEIC's discretionary power in administering the act, the same power would lead in the 1990s to decisions that were less than compelling in terms of both their reasoning and their reflection of the values of social law.

A number of decisions had confirmed that the CEIC could not alter the reasons for a notice of disqualification or disentitlement once the claimant had gone to appeal. This rule, first set out in *Findenigg*, was repeated in other decisions.[36] The Board of Referees' jurisdiction was thus limited to the reason given in the commission's decision. In *Easson*, the Federal Court of Appeal broke with this rule. Easson had been given a ten-week disqualification for being fired due to his own misconduct. The Board of Referees found that the claimant had not been fired but quit his job voluntarily and reduced the disqualification to eight weeks. The umpire found that the Board of Referees had exceeded its jurisdiction by ruling on a reason other than the one referred to it. To quash the umpire's decision, which was consistent with case law, the Court of Appeal maintained that the claimant had been disqualified under section 28 of the act, a section that covered both voluntary leaving and misconduct. According to the court, the two reasons were connected. The lawmaker had chosen to deal with them in one provision for logical and practical reasons: both notions stemmed from the assumption that loss of employment was the result of a deliberate act by the employee. The Board of Referees' finding stood because the commission's decision was based on that section: the decision in *Hamilton* could be used to support this,[37] and other decisions would follow.[38]

By changing an issue involving the appeal instance's jurisdiction into a problem with interpreting section 28, the court avoided the debate raised in *Findenigg*. In fact, the decision that a claimant receives tells him or her what the commission's position is. If the claimant appeals, he or she will build the case accordingly. Thus, the claimant's burden of proof is not the same for voluntary leaving and misconduct. Since the Board of Referees could now use the other reason for disqualification, not cited in the challenged decision, the hearing might turn into a fishing expedition at the expense of the claimant's rights. This notion is not consistent with the principles of natural justice and goes against the liberal interpretation that the act should be given.

The issue of appeal instance jurisdiction also arose around the discretionary power to determine the effects of a disqualification. In the counterreform of 1990, the maximum length of certain disqualifications, including the one for voluntary leaving, became twelve weeks, with a minimum of seven, while the benefit rate was cut to 50 percent. The CEIC determined the number of weeks of disqualification and the number of benefit weeks to which the reduced rate should apply.[39]

Prior to these amendments, claimants had always been able to appeal the length of their disqualifications and argue extenuating circumstances. In the 1990s, however, the commission took a hard line and kept challenging the claimant's right to appeal decisions arising from the use of these discretionary powers. The same strategy was used with other provisions in the act that conferred discretionary powers, for example to extend the deadline for appeals to the Board of Referees in unusual circumstances or to fix the amount of the penalty for making a false statement. In cases of voluntary separation and misconduct, the commission would automatically, and without any possibility of appeal from its discretion, slash the claimant's benefits to 50 percent for the whole benefit period after the weeks of disqualification.

In *Archambault*, the Federal Court of Appeal followed the umpire in ruling that the commission had to use its discretionary power judicially and reach a genuine determination in each case of the number of weeks when the reduced rate was to apply.[40] Yet this court had already decided in *Kolish*, a case dealing with a comparable situation, that it was not up to the umpire to exercise this discretion on the CEIC's behalf.[41] The court therefore sent the case back to the umpire so that he would send it back to the Board of Referees, which in turn would refer it to the commission's discretion. If the claimant thought that the commission had not used its discretion judicially, he or she could appeal to the Board of Referees again.

Two decisions would use the same logic to determine the length of a disqualification.[42] Again the CEIC was to exercise its discretion judicially and reserve the longest period of disqualification for the most serious cases. Yet by holding that these decisions were exclusive to the commission, the Federal Court of Appeal substantially reduced claimants' rights, not to mention putting an end to a system that had worked well for fifty years and allowed the Board of Referees and the umpire to use discretion concerning the existence of extenuating circumstances. The role of these tribunals would now be limited to reviewing whether the commission had used its discretion judicially.

These Court of Appeal positions came in for some serious criticism.[43] In particular, umpires voiced their own and claimants' frustration at the appeal system's inability to handle a growing number of disputes.[44] The claimant's right of appeal was diminished by these decisions, while more and more CEIC rulings, including many that involved active measures, could now not be appealed at all. A decision by Judge Reed provided a real indictment of the Kafkaesque universe engulfing UI claimants.[45]

Acknowledging the merits of the criticisms hurled by umpires, the Federal Court of Appeal made a complete about-face in *Morin*. When Boards of Referees or umpires had jurisdiction to rule, they had "the power to make the decision that the commission should have made, regardless of whether the decision is characterized as discretionary."[46] However, one can but remark, in spite of the court's about-face, that this jurisprudential trend had a highly negative outcome for the jobless. In fact, the employment insurance system still uses disqualifications of varying lengths, particularly for cases where suitable employment is refused.[47] The Board of Referees and umpire cannot act unless the commission has failed to exercise its discretion judicially. These tribunals' latitude to decide the length of disqualification is greatly reduced compared to the situation that prevailed before 1990. The earlier jurisprudence had recognized wide latitude for Boards of Referees or umpires to take extenuating circumstances into account: this would clearly not be happening anymore.

Like the legislation itself, the jurisprudence registered a negative performance for the period, especially on issues involving voluntary unemployment. Admittedly, this was not unanimous: some judges ventured to criticize the severity of the act or its overly restrictive interpretation by the commission. However, the rigid application of actuarial logic to unemployment insurance, to the point where even the most marginal workers were paying more for less, was unrealistic or at least revealed a remarkable misunderstanding of how the system had been hijacked in recent years.

In defence of the courts, it might be pointed out that, when judges did give the act a liberal interpretation, they were sometimes called to order by the lawmaker, as happened after the *Jenkins* decision. Beyond question, the lawmaker of the 1990s did not share the vision of UI expressed by the Supreme Court in *Abrahams*.

Conclusion

What will our verdict be on the Canadian UI system from the jobless rights standpoint as this new century gets under way? Has social insurance been, and is it still, an effective vehicle for these rights? More specifically, has the contributory funding of UI tended to entrench them? How will they be affected by the new impetus given to the system since 1990, assuming that this change of direction is found to be constitutional? And considering the new configuration of work, is there a future for UI at all?

The UI story suggests that the biggest factor in answering these questions is, and has always been, the prominence and type of role that the government sees for itself in dealing with the economic and social problems associated with jobs and joblessness. Canada's "case" over the years seems to fully validate my starting assumption in this book that acceptance of genuine jobless rights depends on the level of state commitment to a UI system.

The advent of unemployment insurance in Britain early in the past century created a conceptual frame of reference. Even today our defence and understanding of unemployment compensation are conditioned by the use of social insurance and its built-in compromise: by agreeing to underwrite part of the compensation, the government admitted a responsibility for unemployment. Moreover, if the acknowledgment of jobless rights was the social purpose of this law, the responsibilities that came with it were concessions to the bosses on workforce regulation. The debates between Winston Churchill and Llewellyn Smith highlighted the implacable tension within UI between the system's compensatory wellspring and its objective of worker control.

Canada did not see unemployment insurance until 1940. There were various reasons for the delay. The face-off between employers and workers over the government role in employment was exacerbated by that hardy perennial, the constitutional question. The sense of urgency arising from the Depression of the 1930s was needed to gain final acceptance of a level of state involvement that would enshrine jobless rights in a system of social insurance.

The system's evolution from the 1970s to the late 1980s was basically the story of the expansion of this involvement and thus the entrenchment of jobless rights. The signs of backlash seen by the end of this period denoted the persistence of a conflict that had lurked behind earlier hesitation – a conflict between a genuinely social concept and one that reflected actuarial concerns implying deep misgivings that went as far as hostility toward this government role. The changes to the system during the 1990s showed a strong resurgence of the latter concept accompanied, predictably, by an erosion of the rights of the jobless. Without the state commitment that was its logical outcome, the conceptual framework of a century ago seems to be off balance: the responsibilities of the unemployed have generally taken precedence over their rights.

The 1990s wound up with jobless rights in a highly negative position, especially in the law but also, in some respects, in the courts. If the jurisprudence still accepts the system's social purpose of paying benefits to the unemployed, the lawmaker has evidently ceased to see this purpose as significant.

When unemployment insurance was launched in Britain and then in Canada, there was much talk of the superiority of a contributory system as guaranteeing real jobless rights. Was contributory UI not, as its proponents claimed, the best compensation system, with rights "purchased" by the payment of premiums?

During the 1990s in both countries, counterreforms demonstrated the weakness of this contributory model. Debate on a British bill of 1995 saw a meaningful exchange between MPs on the limits of the guarantee built into the contributory philosophy. This bill[1] had much in common with the Canadian counterreforms: it proposed to increase premiums while reducing the maximum length of benefit from twelve months to six months. One MP objected that such sweeping changes would constitute a breach of the implicit insurance contract between the government and its citizens: "If this were a private contract, people would be able to enforce their rights in the courts. The courts would say that breaking the contract was improper behaviour. But we have a sovereign body here in the Chamber, the Government controls the Chamber and can therefore break their word."[2] The responsible minister merely retorted that the government was empowered by law to make the necessary arrangements to manage the money.

So what now remains of this contributory model? Canadians are left with a degressive funding process that admits very few rights, especially for the low-income group, even though its members contribute more than their share. With EI, have the "insured persons" not become the victims of a system that takes their premiums and puts them to uses other than compensation for unemployment? As evidenced by what has happened to the Canadian system, only a government acknowledging a liability for general unemployment and individual joblessness can guarantee effective protection. Its courts, having bravely enshrined the social objective of this legislation, are now busy interpreting provisions that clearly reduce claimant rights. Yet they have not been asked a very important preliminary question: does Parliament's jurisdiction in unemployment insurance empower it to allocate premiums collected under this system to fund activities other than unemployment compensation – especially if, in so doing, it prejudices the right of claimants to this protection against unemployment?

Subsection 91(2A) of the 1867 BNA Act as amended in 1940 mentions "unemployment insurance," thereby implying that Parliament can collect premiums and pay benefits under a system so described. The current provisions seem to go beyond this framework for both premiums and benefits. The following questions arise: is it constitutional to use UI premiums to fund "active measures" at the expense of the income guarantee that the system exists to offer? And is it constitutional to use UI premiums for purposes other than compensating the insured?

Considering the system's deterioration in recent years, the jobless have every reason to want these issues decided by the courts. The court debate would shed some light on the basic issues involved in changing the system that have all too often gone unnoticed in the past decade.[3]

Moreover, this deterioration in Canada's UI system has coincided with a more general deterioration in the overall job picture. Given this new employment configuration, does UI as jobless compensation have a future, and where does it stand in the Canadian context?

Since the 1980s, under the impact of economic globalization and technological development, we have been seeing "imperatives" of competitiveness and downsizing being used to cast doubt on the model of permanent, full-time, wage-earning employment. Governments have been under strong pressure to "relax" employment and social protection systems as barriers to corporate competitiveness and job creation. We have seen a dramatic increase in nonstandard employment (part-time, casual, self-employment, etc.) combined with labour market polarization. Some people have been able to hang on to relatively well-paid, often unionized jobs, while thousands of others are unlikely to see stable employment again. This trend came with massive waves of layoffs as part of a general downsizing process.

This new job market has left many doubting the very future of regular wage-earning employment, which is apparently becoming rare, if not extinct. Clearly, such sweeping transformations of the salary framework raise questions about the purpose of maintaining UI as a jobless compensation system. However, I do not think that regular work is slated to disappear. It is therefore essential to continue our existing protections for employment and social security. Our response to the endlessly repeated demands from dominant market forces for more deregulation of employment and weaker unemployment compensation systems must be heightened vigilance. Special care is needed to distinguish the issues. Some of them result from the profound changes that the new technologies have wrought in the human relationship with work. These are not to be confused with the issues conjured up by triumphant capitalism as it uses the new context to impose fresh variants of worker exploitation. We must beware of concluding that regular work and unemployment insurance are outmoded, thus playing into the hands of the proponents of labour market deregulation: "A bird in the hand is worth two in the bush."

The UI story tells us that no fair solution can be found for the problem of unemployment, whether ascribed to economic globalization, changes in work organization, or the very evolution of the concept of work, without a play of forces obliging the state, the repository of everyone's interests, to regulate the change. I see any plan of action or cast of thought that overlooks this preliminary as doomed to fail and aggravate a sense of powerlessness in the present situation.

Accordingly, until the play of political forces can accommodate more general solutions to current employment and unemployment problems, I believe that an adequately state-funded UI system can provide appropriate protection for the whole workforce and be a useful device for distributing wealth. This approach clearly works for Canadians.

The Canadian system could also easily expand the protection that it affords the marginal workforce. With the hourly calculation of length of insurable employment introduced by EI, these workers are being tapped more than ever: they should be given protection that takes both their marginal employment status and their financial contribution into account. The system could also protect self-employed workers: such extended coverage has already been introduced in Denmark and California.[4]

At a time when the workings of dominant market forces are tending to further erode employment relationships, it is more necessary than ever to reassert a collective responsibility for the employed and the unemployed.

Epilogue
Bill C-2, February 2001

On 2 February 2001, the Chrétien government tabled Bill C-2 in the House of Commons.[1] With a few minor variants, this was a replica of a bill introduced in the fall of 2000[2] that had died on the order paper when the prime minister called an election. Bill C-2 would pass without appreciable amendment.[3]

Although it contained some improvements in coverage that were trifling compared to the wholesale cuts of earlier years, Bill C-2 continued downsizing EI by cutting back on the system and sanctioned the government hijack of the account's immense surplus.

The intensity rule affecting the benefit rate and the clawback provision were both gone.[4] The benefit rate was restored to 55 percent for all claimants, and the benefit repayment rate would not depend on the frequency of earlier claims. In fact, benefit repayment would no longer apply at all if no claim had been filed during the ten preceding years or for special maternity, parental, and sickness benefits.

Although marginal and especially seasonal workers were the first to benefit from these amendments, they were still hit hard by the other changes that came with the counterreforms of the 1990s, particularly in qualifying conditions and length of benefit. For example, many jobless were faced with the "black hole" phenomenon: their benefits did not last until they could get back to work, and so, left without incomes, they were forced to apply for welfare.

In this bill, the entrance requirement for NEREs[5] no longer applied to parents who left for a year or more to raise their children and collected special benefits. This move had to be applauded, but why not do away with the restrictive entrance requirement altogether[6] rather than exempt just one claimant group? Would the NERE provisions not continue to hit the jobless on the fringe of the labour market, where women and youth were overrepresented? The news release accompanying the bill used these words to defend the move: "This rule was put in place to discourage dependency cycles and increase workforce attachment, particularly for youth."[7]

The bill contained a major change in the way that maximum insurable earnings (MIE) were calculated. Let us recall that the 1996 maximum of $43,940 was cut and frozen by the Employment Insurance Act at $39,000 for the period 1997-2000.[8] This $39,000 ceiling will be maintained until the average industrial wage reaches the same level. Only then will the insurable maximum be indexed again. In June 2000, average earnings in all Canadian industries amounted to $32,500.[9] Given the increase in the average industrial wage (AIW) over the past decade,[10] another ten years could go by before the AIW gets to $39,000. By way of comparison, the maximum annual insurable income under Quebec's workmen's compensation program was $51,500 in 2001.[11]

This MIE amendment affects the overall size of the system in terms of both premiums and benefits. It will have the effect of further reducing its redistributive function by limiting the responsibility of higher-paid workers for those with low incomes and make its funding more degressive as medium- and low-wage earners are asked to contribute more. At the same time, public support for EI will decline because fewer workers will be assured of adequate replacement income when unemployed. As the freeze came with reduced premiums for the year 2001,[12] the system's downsizing was further accentuated.

The way in which the premium rate is set will change, at least temporarily. With the mechanism in the act set aside,[13] this rate will be determined for the next two years not by the CEIC but solely by the government, which need not consider either the costs to be borne by the EI account or the surplus required to keep rates stable. Although the account in 2000 had a substantial surplus that, according to the chief EI actuary, greatly exceeded the reserve needed to cover the cost of a potential recession without raising the premium rate,[14] the government need not take this into account when setting the rate. Actually, this surplus is only virtual, since the account is part of general revenue and has been tapped to wipe out the national deficit, as recently confirmed by the auditor general.[15] It is interesting to note that the following passage from the news release that accompanied the fall 2000 bill did not appear in the one issued when the current bill was tabled: "Last fall, the House of Commons Finance Committee concluded that the rate setting process as currently set out in the EI Act is flawed. It requires looking back to take into consideration the level of past surpluses of revenues relative to program cost, when in fact there are no past surpluses sitting in a separate account."[16] The account's surplus is therefore theoretical.[17] In fact, it does not exist. Now we can understand why the Bloc Québécois[18] withheld its consent to rapid passage of the first bill before the election call, arguing that it legalized "the diversion of the EI Fund."[19]

The sequel is predictable. Having used the account to eliminate its deficit, the government will begin by gradually reducing the premium rate to meet the criteria in the act. A thorough review of the rate-setting mechanism has already been announced.[20] The rate will be set with an eye to the reduced protection available, thus placing a kind of clamp on the cut in the system. This will make it very difficult to return to a more generous approach.

The system's cumulative surplus will become a thing of the past. Who would want to get a government into debt that has fought its deficit with such bravura? Who cares if the deed was largely done on the backs of the jobless and at the cost of impoverishing broad swaths of the workforce? Canadians, including the richest ones, got a tax cut in 2001[21] as a thank-you for their part in combating the deficit. The gesture merely confirmed the antisocial bias of the counterreforms.

Notes

Chapter 1: Why UI?

1 Anthony I. Ogus, "Great Britain," in P0.A. Köhler, H.F. Zacher, and P.J. Hesse, eds., *The Evolution of Social Insurance, 1881-1981* (London: F. Pinter, 1982), 156.
2 On working-class poverty in the late nineteenth century, see the accounts of Charles Booth's investigations of various London neighbourhoods: Charles Booth, ed., *Labour and Life of the People,* 3 vols. (London: Williams and Norgate, 1889-91).
3 *Poor Relief Act 1662*, 14 Car. II, c. 12.
4 *Poor Relief Act 1795*, 36 Geo. III, c. 23.
5 Pierre Rosanvallon, *La crise de l'état-providence* (Paris: Seuil, 1981), 143-44 (our translation).
6 Karl Polanyi, *The Great Transformation: The Political and Economic Origins of Our Time* (1944; Boston: Beacon Press, 2001).
7 From the Report of the Royal Commission on the Poor Laws, 1834, in S.G. Checkland and E.O.A. Checkland, eds., *The Poor Law Report of 1834* (Harmondsworth: Pelican Books, 1974), 335.
8 *Poor Law Amendment Act 1834*, 4 and 5 Will. IV, c. 76.
9 On the Canadian version of the system, see Allan Irving, "'The Master Principle of Administering Relief': Jeremy Bentham, Sir Francis Bond Head, and the Establishment of the Principle of Less Eligibility in Upper Canada," *Canadian Review of Social Policy* 23 (1989): 13-18.
10 *Representation of the People Act, 1884*, 48 Victoria, c. 3.
11 Bentley B. Gilbert, "Winston Churchill versus the Webbs: The Origins of British Unemployment Insurance" *American Historical Review* 71 (1966): 847.
12 *National Insurance Act, 1911*, 1 and 2 Geo. V, c. 55.
13 Edw. VII, c. 18.
14 Quoted in Rosanvallon, *La crise*, 149 (our translation).
15 Ogus, "Great Britain," 174.
16 Robert Castel, *Les métamorphoses de lu question sociale: Une chronique du salariat* (Paris: Fayard, 1995), 200 (our translation).
17 Dominique Méda, *Le travail, une valeur en voie de disparition* (Paris: Aubier, 1995), 331 (our translation).
18 François Ewald, *L'état providence* (Paris: Grasset, 1986), 24 (our translation).
19 *Ibid.,* 181.
20 F. Netter, *La sécurité sociale et ses principes* (Paris: Sirey, 1959), 189 (our translation).
21 Ewald, *L'état providence*, 373 (our translation).
22 *Ibid.,* 538 (our translation).

23 Castel, *Les métamorphoses*, 297 (our translation).
24 Christian Topalov, *La naissance du chômeur 1880-1910* (Paris: Albin Michel, 1994), 410.
25 William Henry Beveridge, *Insurance for All and Everything* (London: Daily News, 1924), 6-7.
26 Leonard C. Marsh, *Report on Social Security for Canada* (Ottawa: King's Printer, 1943), 10. Marsh, whose 1943 report would mark the emergence of the Canadian social state, was a member of the team that drafted Canada's unemployment insurance system. See Chapter 3, 35ff.
27 Detlev Zöllner, "The Federal Republic of Germany," in Köhler et al., eds., *The Evolution of Social Insurance*, 49.
28 Katherine Lippel, *Le droit des accidentés du travail à une indemnité: Une analyse historique et critique* (Montreal: Thémis, 1986), 63-64 (our translation).
29 Hans F. Zacher and Francis Kessler, "Rôle respectif du service public et de l'initiative privée dans la politique de sécurité sociale," *Revue internationale de droit comparé* 42 (1990): 235.
30 On the actuarial ideology, see Chapter 4, 67ff.
31 Zacher and Kessler, "Rôle respectif," 215.
32 Ewald, *L'état providence*, 209, 221.
33 Gaston V. Rimlinger, "The Emergence of Social Insurance: European Experience before 1914," in Köhler et al., eds., *The Evolution of Social Insurance*, 114.
34 This interpretation of workmen's compensation would emerge later in Canada: "Workmen's compensation may be an exception to this general statement. It seems to derive from employer's liability legislation which, progressively, placed upon the employer responsibility for the injury and disease of workers as a consequence of employment ... Thus, in historical origins, the employer is the insured rather than the employee." A.D. Watson, *The Principles Which Should Govern the Structure and Provisions of a Scheme of Unemployment Insurance* (Ottawa: Unemployment Insurance Commission, 1948), 3.
35 See Eveline M. Burns, *Social Security and Public Policy* (New York: McGraw-Hill, 1956), 160.
36 By 1955, in addition to Canada, a number of industrialized countries that had built compulsory systems had opted for tripartite funding. These included Belgium, Japan, Norway, the Netherlands, Ireland, and the United Kingdom; others, including Germany and Austria, had chosen bipartite funding; and, finally, other countries, Italy included, had chosen the American model of funding wholly by employer contributions. See ILO, *Unemployment Insurance Schemes* (Geneva: ILO, 1955), 200-1. The funding status of these systems was appreciably the same in 1987: in Germany and Austria, however, the government was now responsible for covering potential deficits in the unemployment insurance fund, while in Italy the government defrayed certain costs involving the system's administration. France, which had created a compulsory system in 1958, later opted for a bipartite funding formula. See ILO, *Employment Promotion and Social Security*, Report IV (1), 73rd session 1987, International Labour Conference, Geneva, 154-59.
37 Robert Pinker, *Social Theory and Social Policy* (London: Heinemann, 1971), 90; Peter Baldwin, "Beveridge in the *longue durée*," *International Social Security Review* 45 (1992): 53.
38 On this subject, see J. Smits *(rapporteur)*, "Le concept de droits acquis en matière de sécurité sociale face à l'évolution de la situation économique," Report VI, International Social Security Association, General Meeting 1986, Montreal, 50.
39 Ross Cranston, *Legal Foundations of the Welfare State* (London: Weidenfeld and Nicolson, 1985), 180-81.
40 Zacher and Kessler, "Rôle respectif," 215.
41 United Kingdom, 21 *H.C. Deb.*, 5th series, 586 (10 February 1911).
42 Méda, *Le travail*, 122 (our translation).
43 William Henry Beveridge, *Full Employment in a Free Society* (London: Allen and Unwin, 1944).
44 See article 1.1 of Convention no. C122 (1964), which Canada would ratify. ILO, *Convention (no. C122) Concerning Employment Policy*, in ILO, *International Labour Conventions and Recommendations*, vol. 1 (Geneva: ILO, 1985), 71-72.
45 Georges Gurvitch, *La déclaration des droits sociaux* (New York: Maison Française, 1944), 133-34.
46 *Universal Declaration of Human Rights*, United Nations General Assembly, 3rd Session, Part I, Resolution 217 A (III), 71, UN Doc A/810 (1948).

47 The Constitution of the International Labour Organization forms Part XIII of the Treaty of Versailles. *Peace Treaty between the Allied Powers and Associates and Germany, and Protocol, Signed at Versailles, June 28, 1919* (Ottawa: King's Printer, 1935).

48 The information about British trade union unemployment insurance schemes comes from the following sources: William Henry Beveridge, "Memorandum on Scheme, Draft Head of Bill, Criticisms, and Amendments 1908-1909," Board of Trade, Beveridge Papers, no. 37, A-1; Beveridge, "Memoranda on Specific Aspects of Scheme 1907-1909," Board of Trade, Beveridge Papers, no. 39, C-11; Beveridge, "Memoranda on UI for Poor Law Commission 1907," Board of Trade, Beveridge Papers, no. 41, D-3; Beveridge, *Unemployment: A Problem of Industry*, 2nd ed. (New York: AMS Press, 1930), 223-29; Humphrey Southall, "Neither State nor Market: Early Welfare Benefits in Britain," *Genèses* 18 (1995): 6; and Noël Whiteside, "Définir le chômage: Traditions syndicales et politique nationale en Grande-Bretagne avant la Première Guerre Mondiale," in M. Mansfield, R. Salais, and N. Whiteside, eds., *Aux sources du chômage, 1880-1914* (Paris: Belin, 1994), 381.

49 Beveridge, "Memoranda on UI," 4.

50 Southall, "Neither State," 12.

51 ILO, *Unemployment Insurance Schemes*.

52 On the St. Gallen experiment, see R. Jay, "L'assurance obligatoire contre le chômage dans le canton de Saint-Gall," *Revue politique et parlementaire* 1, 1 (1894): 267; and David F. Schloss, *Insurance against Unemployment* (London: P.S. King and Son, 1909), 8-19. For a critical analysis of the St. Gallen experiment, see Beveridge, "Memoranda on Specific Aspects," 14-15.

53 Louis Varlez, *Les formes nouvelles de l'assurance contre le chômage* (Paris: Rousseau, 1903), 92-93.

54 P. Pic, *Traité de législation industrielle: Les lois ouvrières*, 3rd ed. (Paris: Rousseau, 1909), 1090.

55 Leslie A. Pal, *State, Class, and Bureaucracy* (Kingston: McGill-Queen's University Press, 1988), 22.

56 Beveridge, "Memoranda on Specific Aspects," 16.

57 E.P. Hennock, *British Social Reform and German Precedents: The Case of Social Insurance 1880-1914* (Oxford: Clarendon Press, 1987), 161, 162, 169.

Chapter 2: The British Act of 1911

1 Anthony I. Ogus, "Great Britain," in P.A. Köhler, H.F. Zacher, and P.J. Hesse, eds., *The Evolution of Social Insurance, 1881-1981* (London: F. Pinter, 1982), 169.

2 William Henry Beveridge, *Unemployment: A Problem of Industry*, 2nd ed. (New York: AMS Press, 1930), 208-9.

3 Christian Topalov, *La naissance du chômeur 1880-1910* (Paris: Albin Michel, 1994), 357 (our translation).

4 José Harris, *Unemployment and Politics* (Oxford: Clarendon Press, 1972), 309.

5 *A Bill to Promote Work through Public Authorities for Unemployed Persons*, 7 Edw. VII, c. 3.

6 On this question, see K.D. Brown, *Labour and Unemployment 1900-1914* (Totowa, NJ: Rowman and Littlefield, 1971), 68-130.

7 William Henry Beveridge, *Power and Influence* (New York: Beechhurst, 1955), 87.

8 Derek Fraser, *The Evolution of the British Welfare State* (New York: Harper and Row, 1973), 44.

9 Ogus, "Great Britain," 169.

10 *Labour Exchanges Act 1909*, 9 Edw. VII, c. 7.

11 Bentley B. Gilbert, "The British National Insurance Act of 1911 and the Commercial Insurance Lobby," *Journal of British Studies* 4 (1965): 129.

12 William Henry Beveridge, *The Past and Present of Unemployment Insurance* (London: Oxford University Press, 1930), 11.

13 *National Insurance Act, 1911*, 1 and 2 Geo. V, c. 55.

14 William Henry Beveridge, "Memorandum on Scheme, Draft Head of Bill, Criticisms, and Amendments 1908-1909," Board of Trade, Beveridge Papers, no. 37, A-1, 14-15.

15 *Ibid.*, 5.

16 *Ibid.*, no. 37, A-2, 3.
17 *Ibid.*
18 *Ibid.*, no. 37, A-4, 3 (criticism by Mr. Barstow).
19 William Henry Beveridge, "Memoranda on Specific Aspects of Scheme 1907-1909," Board of Trade, Beveridge Papers, no. 39, C-11, "Notes on Malingering (the President)," 3. The Supreme Court of Canada would later express a similar opinion in *Hills* v. *A.G. Canada,* [1988] 1 S.C.R. 513, 538.
20 Beatrice Webb, *Our Partnership* (London: Longmans, Green, 1948), 430.
21 Beveridge, "Notes on Malingering," 2.
22 *Ibid.*, 3-4.
23 Beveridge, "Memoranda on Specific Aspects," 3.
24 *Ibid.*, no. 37, A-1, 7.
25 Bentley B. Gilbert, *The Evolution of National Insurance in Great Britain* (London: Michael Joseph, 1966), 270, 271.
26 Beveridge, "Notes on Malingering," 3.
27 In insurance theory, "moral hazard" denotes the possibility that the mere existence of the insurance may prompt the insured to cause the occurrence of the event insured against in order to collect benefits. This thinking would be taken up in spades by the neoliberal school. In unemployment insurance, the notion of voluntary unemployment stems largely from the same thinking. See Chapter 4, 67ff., esp. 71.
28 William Henry Beveridge, "Memoranda on Specific Aspects," Board of Trade, Beveridge Papers, no. 39, C-9, "Control of Unemployment," 3.
29 F. Pennings, *Benefits of Doubt: A Comparative Study of the Legal Aspects of Employment and Unemployment Schemes in Great Britain, Germany, France, and the Netherlands* (Boston: Kluwer Law and Taxation Publishers, 1990), 5.
30 According to Ogus, "Great Britain," 187, the concessions to employers went far beyond mere penalties for voluntary separation or misconduct.
31 *A.G.* v. *Guardians of the Poor of Merthyr Tydfil Union,* [1900] 1 Ch. 516 (C.A.).
32 For a review of this decision, see W. Ivor Jennings, "Poor Relief in Industrial Disputes," *Law Quarterly Review* 46 (1926): 225.
33 Noël Whiteside, "Définir le chômage: Traditions syndicales et politique nationale en Grande-Bretagne avant la Première Guerre Mondiale," in M. Mansfield, R. Salais, and N. Whiteside, eds., *Aux sources du chômage, 1880-1914* (Paris: Belin, 1994), 405-6.
34 *Social Security Act 1975,* c. 14, s. 4.
35 *National Insurance Act, 1911,* s. 84.
36 *Ibid.*, s. 88-91, and *Unemployment Insurance Regulations 1912,* s. 20-21, in A.S. Comyns Carr, W.H. Stuart Garnett, and J.H. Taylor, *National Insurance,* 3rd ed. (London: Macmillan, 1912), 658-60.
37 Beveridge, *Unemployment,* 268.
38 *Unemployment Insurance Regulations 1912,* s. 13.
39 Carr, Garnett, and Taylor, *National Insurance,* 439.
40 *Unemployment Insurance Regulations 1912,* s. 12.
41 *Unemployment Insurance Act, 1927,* 17 and 18 Geo. V, c. 30, s. 5(2)(ii).
42 *Unemployment Insurance Act, 1930,* 20 and 21 Geo. V, c. 16, s. 4.
43 *Unemployment Insurance Act, 1920,* 10 and 11 Geo. V, c. 30, s. 8(2).
44 Nick Wikeley, "Unemployment Benefit, the State, and the Labour Market," *Journal of Law and Society* 16 (1989): 308.
45 *Jobseekers Act 1995,* c. 18, s. 19.
46 United Kingdom, 31 *H.C. Deb.*, 5th series, col. 1728 (7 November 1911).
47 *Ibid.*, col. 1744.
48 This definition of "labour dispute" is taken from the *Trade Disputes Act 1906,* 6 Edw. VII, c. 47.
49 Carr, Garnett, and Taylor, *National Insurance,* 430.
50 *Ibid.*
51 *Unemployment Insurance (No. 2) Act, 1924,* 14 and 15 Geo. V, c. 30, s. 4(1).
52 On this episode, see K.D. Ewing, *The Right to Strike* (Oxford: Clarendon Press, 1991), 70-73.

53 *Unemployment Insurance Act, 1927,* s. 6.
54 On arguments for the idea of disqualification for labour disputes, see *Caron* v. *Canada,* [1989] 1 F.C., 628, 635 (Judge Marceau's minority opinion). For a critical perspective on this arrangement, see *Hills* v. *A.G.,* 538.
55 See Chapter 3 generally.
56 *Unemployment Insurance Act, 1935,* 25 Geo. V, c. 8.
57 ILO, *Unemployment Insurance Schemes* (Geneva: ILO, 1955), 31-41.
58 ILO, *Convention (no. 2) Concerning Unemployment (1919),* in ILO, *International Labour Conventions and Recommendations,* vol. 1 (Geneva: ILO, 1985), 69-70.
59 ILO, *Recommendation (no. 1) Concerning Unemployment,* passed by the International Labour Conference in its 1st session, Washington, 28 November 1919, in ILO, *International Labour Organization 1919-1966* (Geneva: ILO, 1966), 11.
60 ILO, *Convention (no. 44) Ensuring Benefits or Allowances to the Involuntarily Unemployed,* 1934, in ILO, *International Labour Conventions and Recommendations,* vol. 1 (Geneva: ILO, 1985), 803-7. Note that Canada, although often participating actively in developing ILO conventions setting out minimum standards for unemployment insurance systems, never actually ratified these conventions. On the ILO conventions setting out these standards, see ILO, *Employment Promotion and Social Security,* Report IV (1), 73rd Session, 1987, International Labour Conference, Geneva, 3-7, and ILO, *Convention (no. 168) Concerning Employment Promotion and Protection against Unemployment,* International Labour Conference, B.O., vol. LXXI, 1988, series A, no. 2, 91. On Canadian nonratification of these conventions, see ILO, *List of Ratifications by Convention and Country,* Report III (Part 5), 79th Session, 1992, International Labour Conference, Geneva, 213; Lucie Lamarche, "Le droit au travail et à la formation: Les enjeux et les doutes du droit international," in Lucie Lamarche, ed., *Emploi précaire et non-emploi: Droits recherchés,* Actes de la 5e journée de droit social et du travail (Cowansville: Yvon Blais, 1994), 83; and Department of Labour, *Canadian Position with Respect to Conventions and Recommendations Adopted at the 74th (Maritime) and 75th Sessions of the International Labour Conference, Geneva, October 1987 and June 1988* (Ottawa: Labour Canada, 1988).
61 Guy Perrin, "L'assurance sociale – ses particularités – son rôle dans le passé, le présent et l'avenir," in P.A. Köhler and H.F. Zacher, eds., *Beiträge zu Geschichte und aktueller Situation der Sozialversicherung* (Berlin: Duncker u. Humbolt, 1983).
62 *House of Commons Debates,* 29 January 1935, 301.

Chapter 3: Developing a Canadian System
1 Judith Fingard, "The Winter's Tale: The Seasonal Contours of Pre-Industrial Poverty in British North America, 1815-1860," *Canadian Historical Review* 65 (1974): 94.
2 On these issues, see Hugh H. Wolfenden, *The Real Meaning of Social Insurance: Its Present Status and Tendencies* (Toronto: Macmillan, 1932), 107-10; Employment and Immigration Canada, *Commission of Inquiry on Unemployment Insurance* (Forget Report) (Ottawa: Employment and Immigration Canada, 1986), 48-50, 63, 71.
3 William Henry Beveridge, *Unemployment: A Problem of Industry,* 2nd ed. (New York: AMS Press, 1930), 208-9.
4 L. Richter, W.J. Couper, and B.M. Stewart, "The Employment and Social Insurance Bill," *Canadian Journal of Economics and Political Science* 1 (1935): 458.
5 HRDC, *From Unemployment Insurance to Employment Insurance* (Improving Social Security in Canada series) (Hull: HRDC, 1994), 37 ff.
6 James Struthers, *No Fault of Their Own: Unemployment and the Canadian Welfare State, 1914-1941* (Toronto: University of Toronto Press, 1983), 13.
7 Elisabeth Wallace, "The Origin of the Social Welfare State in Canada, 1867-1900," *Canadian Journal of Economics and Political Science* 16 (1950): 387.
8 Ontario, *Report of the Ontario Commission on Unemployment* (Toronto: A.T. Wilgress, 1916).
9 *Ibid.,* 80.
10 H. Blair Neatby, *Politics of Chaos: Canada in the Thirties* (Toronto: Macmillan, 1972), 47.
11 *Employment Offices Co-ordination Act,* S.C. 1918, c. 21.
12 Struthers, *No Fault of Their Own,* 22.

13 ILO, *Recommendation (no. 1) Concerning Unemployment*, passed by the International Labour Conference in its 1st session, Washington, 28 November 1919; *Peace Treaty between the Allied Powers and Associates and Germany, and Protocol, Signed at Versailles, June 28, 1919* (Ottawa: King's Printer, 1935).
14 D.C. Masters, *The Winnipeg General Strike* (Toronto: University of Toronto Press, 1950), 93.
15 *Commission Appointed under Order-in-Council (P.C. 670) to Enquire into Industrial Relations in Canada, Report* (Ottawa: Royal Commission on Industrial Relations, 1919), 8, para 36.
16 To curb union inroads, King favoured setting up "boutique" unions using a system that would be prohibited in the United States with the 1935 passage of the Wagner Act under Roosevelt. See Bernard St-Aubin, *King et son époque* (Montreal: La Presse, 1982), 63. Note also that the 1935 Social Security Act prohibited American states from refusing to pay unemployment benefits when employment was refused that involved compulsory membership in an employer-dominated union. See note 86.
17 William Lyon Mackenzie King, *Industry and Humanity* (Toronto: Thomas Allen, 1918), 346.
18 Bryce M. Stewart, "Canadian Opinion on Unemployment Insurance," *Social Welfare* 3 (1921): 272.
19 House of Commons, *Select Standing Committee on Industrial and International Relations,* 1928, 199.
20 *House of Commons Debates,* 23 May 1929, 2789.
21 Recipients tended to view unemployment assistance dimly as a stigmatized handout. English Canadians called it the "dole," a term used in Britain to describe this type of assistance.
22 W.L. Morton, *The Progressive Party in Canada* (Toronto: University of Toronto Press, 1967), 304.
23 Alvin Finkel, "Origins of the Welfare State in Canada," in Leo Panitch, ed., *The Canadian State: Political Economy and Political Power* (Toronto: University of Toronto Press, 1977), 344-70.
24 Daniel Nelson, *Unemployment Insurance: The American Experience 1915-1935* (Madison: University of Wisconsin Press, 1969), 26.
25 La Confédération des Travailleurs Catholiques du Canada, predecessor of the Confédération des Syndicats Nationaux (CSN). Founded in 1921, it flourished mainly in Quebec.
26 House of Commons, *Select Standing Committee,* 110.
27 Trades and Labour Congress of Canada, predecessor of the Canadian Labour Congress (CLC).
28 House of Commons, *Select Standing Committee,* 137-38.
29 The unemployment rate went from 10.8 percent in 1922 to 7.5 percent in 1926 and 8.3 percent in 1929. *House of Commons Debates,* 18 February 1935, table on 934.
30 I. Brecher, *Monetary and Fiscal Thought and Policy in Canada, 1929-1939* (Toronto: University of Toronto Press, 1957), 11.
31 *Report of the Royal Commission on Dominion-Provincial Relations* (Rowell-Sirois Report), Book I (Ottawa: King's Printer, 1940), 160.
32 A.E. Grauer, "Public Assistance and Social Insurance," *Report of the Royal Commission on Dominion-Provincial Relations* (Ottawa: King's Printer, 1939), Appendix 6, Table 1.
33 Frances Fox Piven and Richard A. Cloward, *Regulating the Poor: The Functions of Public Welfare,* 2nd ed. (New York: Vintage Books, 1993), 61-65.
34 On the connections of Bennett and his government with the business community, his company directorships, and his personal fortune, see Alvin Finkel, *Business and Social Reform in the Thirties* (Toronto: James Lorimer, 1979), 177.
35 Wolfenden, *The Real Meaning,* 33.
36 *Unemployment Relief Act,* S.C. 1930, c. 1.
37 On the impact of these expenditures on provincial budgets, see the Rowell-Sirois Report, Book I, 19.
38 Michel Pelletier and Yves Vaillancourt, *Les politiques sociales et les travailleurs, cahier II: Les années 30* (Montreal: self-published, 1978), 233.
39 Rowell-Sirois Report, Book I, 18.
40 On the matter of the work camps and the fights there, see Lorne Brown, *When Freedom Was Lost: The Unemployed, the Agitator, and the State* (Montreal: Black Rose Books, 1987).
41 Pelletier and Vaillancourt, *Les politiques sociales,* 88 (our translation).

42 A. Lawton, "Relief Administration in Saskatoon during the Depression," *Saskatchewan History* 22, 1 (1969): 59.

43 Andrée Lévesque, *Virage à gauche interdit: Les communistes, les socialistes, et leurs ennemis au Québec, 1929-1939* (Montreal: Boréal Express, 1984), 64-68.

44 The Co-operative Commonwealth Federation, predecessor of the NDP, founded in 1932.

45 The Communist Party of Canada, founded in 1921.

46 Carl J. Cuneo, "State Mediation of Class Contradictions in Canadian Unemployment Insurance, 1930-1935," *Studies in Political Economy* 3 (1980): 39-40.

47 Lévesque, *Virage à gauche interdit,* 91.

48 See *Rapport de la Commission des assurances sociales de Québec* (6e rapport) (Quebec City: Editeur officiel du Québec, 1933), 258.

49 See Wolfenden, *The Real Meaning,* 33.

50 Finkel, "Origins of the Welfare State," 355-56.

51 Sir Thomas White was Borden's old finance minister and a prominent Conservative Party stalwart; see Finkel, *Business and Social Reform in the Thirties,* 13.

52 R.B. Bennett Papers, Library and Archives Canada, Bennett to Sir Thomas White, 30 August 1934, 503202.

53 Leonard C. Marsh, Beveridge's research assistant, had come to Canada at the request of the principal of McGill University. See Yves Vaillancourt, *L'évolution des politiques sociales au Québec: 1940-1960* (Montreal: Presses de l'Université de Montréal, 1988), 92-93.

54 Leslie A. Pal, *State, Class, and Bureaucracy* (Kingston: McGill-Queen's University Press, 1988), 105.

55 Letter of 31 August 1934, reported in Brooke Claxton, "Social Reform and the Constitution," *Canadian Journal of Economics and Political Science* 1 (1935): 410.

56 A.M. Schlesinger, *The Coming of the New Deal,* vol. 2 of *The Age of Roosevelt* (New York: Houghton Mifflin, 1957), 3.

57 *Social Security Act,* U.S. 1935, c. 531.

58 R.B. Bennett Papers, Library and Archives Canada, "The Premier Speaks to the People (The First Address)," Ottawa, 2 January 1935, 440321.

59 *House of Commons Debates,* 17 January 1935, 3.

60 Brown, *When Freedom Was Lost,* 59-60.

61 R.B. Bennett Papers, Library and Archives Canada, Bennett to Howard Robinson, 11 June 1935, 439984.

62 A.E. Grauer, *Labour Legislation,* study prepared for the Royal Commission on Dominion-Provincial Relations (Ottawa: King's Printer, 1939), 6.

63 *Minimum Wage Act,* S.C. 1935, c. 44; *Limitation of the Hours of Work Act,* S.C. 1935, c. 63; and *Weekly Day of Rest Act,* S.C. 1935, c. 14.

64 *House of Commons Debates,* 12 March 1935, 1638-39.

65 James M. Rosbrow, *Fifty Years of Unemployment Insurance: A Legislative History 1935-1985* (Washington, DC: U.S. Department of Labor, Employment and Training Administration, Unemployment Insurance Service, 1986), 3.

66 Massachusetts, *Unemployment Insurance Bill, House Documents,* 1916, no. 825. For a description of the system proposed by this bill, see Alexander Keyssar, *Out of Work: The First Century of Unemployment in Massachusetts* (Cambridge, UK: Cambridge University Press, 1986), 276.

67 Christian Topalov, *Indemnisation du chômage et construction de la catégorie de chômeur: Étude comparative France, Grande Bretagne, Etats Unis* (Paris: Ministère des Affaires sociales et de l'Emploi, 1990), 103 (our translation).

68 I. Yellowitz, "The Origins of Unemployment Reform in the United States," *Labor History* 9 (1968): 356.

69 Charles Lipton, *The Trade Union Movement in Canada, 1827-1959* (Toronto: NC Press, 1973), 388.

70 Wisconsin *Unemployment Compensation Act of 1932,* Wisc. Laws Spec. Sess. 1931, c. 20.

71 For a description of the 1932 Wisconsin law, see Rosbrow, *Fifty Years,* 4.

72 Ohio, *Report of the Commission on Unemployment Insurance* (Columbus: F.J. Heer Printing Co., 1932).

73 Topalov, *Indemnisation du chômage,* 132 (our translation).
74 Piven and Cloward, *Regulating the Poor,* 64.
75 Kenneth M. Casebeer, "Unemployment Insurance: American Social Wage, Labor Organi-
    zation, and Legal Ideology," *Boston College Law Review* 35 (1994): 274-75.
76 *Ibid.,* 295.
77 *Worker's Unemployment and Social Insurance Act,* H.R. 7598, 73d Cong., 2d Sess. (1934).
78 *Unemployment Insurance: Hearings on H.R. 7598 before the House Comm. on Labor,* 73rd
    Cong., 2d Sess. 9 (1934).
79 Casebeer, "Unemployment Insurance," 294.
80 On this issue, see J.S. Quadagno, "Welfare Capitalism and the Social Security Act of 1935,"
    American Sociological Review 49 (1984): 641-43.
81 *Railroad Retirement Board* v. *Alton Railroad Co.,* 295 U.S. 330 (Railroad Retirement Act of
    1934); *Schechter Poultry Corp.* v. *United States,* 295 U.S. 495 (National Industrial Recovery
    Act of 1933); *Carter* v. *Carter Coal Co.,* 298 U.S. 238 (Bituminous Coal Conservation Act of
    1935); *United States* v. *Butler,* 297 U.S. 1 (Agricultural Adjustment Act of 1933).
82 Nelson, *Unemployment Insurance,* 206-7.
83 *Social Security Act,* U.S. 1935, c. 531, paras 303 (a) 2 and 903 (a) 1.
84 For a description of the various solutions offered to American states, see Rosbrow, *Fifty
    Years,* 8-10.
85 As of 1936, employee contributions were unusual and found in only two of the thirty-
    four laws passed by states after 30 November of that year.
86 *Social Security Act,* s. 903(a)5.
87 *Carmichael* v. *Southern Coal and Coke Co.,* 301 U.S. 495, 57 S.Ct. 868 (Alabama legislation);
    Steward Machine Co. v. *Davis,* 301 U.S. 548, 57 S.Ct. 883 (on the unemployment insurance
    provisions of the Social Security Act); and, finally, *Associated Industries of New York State* v.
    The Department of Labor of the State of New York, 301 U.S. 714, 57 S.Ct. 926 (on the consti-
    tutionality of the state law).
88 I would emphasize that the US Supreme Court modified its policy substantially after a
    confrontation with the Roosevelt administration. Criticizing the court for lack of respect
    for the decisions of legislative bodies, the president had tabled a bill to alter the court's
    makeup. However, when the court changed its tack on the New Deal legislation, the bill
    was dropped. On the whole business of court challenges to the New Deal legislation, see
    Eduard A. Lopez, "Constitutional Background to the Social Security Act of 1935," *Social
    Security Bulletin* 50, 1 (1987): 5.
89 For a more exhaustive description of the Social Security Act, see Rosbrow, *Fifty Years,* 8-10,
    and the Rowell-Sirois Report, Book II, 38. On the similarities and differences in the Cana-
    dian and American unemployment insurance systems passed in 1935, see Richter,
    Couper, and Stewart, "The Employment and Social Insurance Bill," 452-56.
90 Quadagno, "Welfare Capitalism," 646.
91 Richter, Couper, and Stewart, "The Employment and Social Insurance Bill," 454.
92 In this regard, see the comments of Madam Justice L'Heureux-Dubé in *Hills* v. *A.G.
    Canada,* [1988] 1 S.C.R. 513.
93 Richter, Couper, and Stewart, "The Employment and Social Insurance Bill," 455.
94 On developments in the British system during this period, see *House of Commons Debates,*
    29 January 1935, 298-302. For a critical view, see J.L. Cohen, *The Canadian Unemployment
    Insurance Act: Its Relation to Social Security* (Toronto: Thomas Nelson and Sons, 1935), 56-
    72. On the legal aspects of this development, see F. Tillyard, *Unemployment Insurance in
    Great Britain 1911-48* (Leigh-on-Sea: Thames Bank Publishing, 1949).
95 Cuneo, "State Mediation," 52-53.
96 *Employment and Social Insurance Act,* S.C. 1935, c. 38, s. 19-20 and 30.
97 W.H. McConnell, "The Judicial Review of Prime Minister Bennett's New Deal," *Osgoode
    Hall Law Journal* 6 (1968): 46-47.
98 Pelletier and Vaillancourt, *Les politiques sociales,* 316.
99 See s. 132 of the *British North America Act, 1867,* 30 and 31 Victoria, c. 3.
100 *Employment and Social Insurance Act,* S.C. 1935, c. 38, Preamble.
101 I emphasize the incongruous position of this province since the Maritimes would be the

main beneficiaries of the system. See Thomas Michael Cane, *A Test-Case for Canadian Federalism: The Unemployment Insurance Issue 1919-1940* (MA thesis, University of Western Ontario, 1971), 69.
102 *Reference re The Employment and Social Insurance Act*, [1936] S.C.R. 427, 452.
103 *Ibid.*, 454.
104 *A.G. Canada* v. *A.G. Ontario*, [1937] C.A. 355, 366.
105 F.R. Scott, "The Privy Council and Mr. Bennett's New Deal," *Canadian Journal of Economics and Political Science* 3 (1937): 239.

Chapter 4: The UI Act of 1940

1 *National Employment Commission Act, 1936*, S.C. 1936, c. 7.
2 Andrée Lévesque, *Virage à gauche interdit: Les communistes, les socialistes, et leurs ennemis au Québec, 1929-1939* (Montreal: Boréal Express, 1984), 72.
3 For a description of Purvis's ties to the business community, see James Struthers, *No Fault of Their Own: Unemployment and the Canadian Welfare State: 1914-1941* (Toronto: University of Toronto Press, 1983), 144.
4 *Ibid.*, 155.
5 A.E. Grauer, "Public Assistance and Social Insurance," *Report of the Royal Commission on Dominion-Provincial Relations* (Ottawa: King's Printer, 1939), Appendix 6, Table 1, 12.
6 In addition to the 1935 Employment and Social Insurance Act, the three other pieces of legislation regulating labour were also found to be unconstitutional. *A.G. Canada* v. *A.G. Ontario*, [1937] C.A. 326.
7 *House of Commons Debates*, 20 May 1938, 3094.
8 National Employment Commission, *Interim Report of the National Employment Commission* (Ottawa: King's Printer, 1937).
9 James Struthers, "The 30's: The 80's," *Canadian Forum* 64 (1984): 11.
10 National Employment Commission, *Final Report of the National Employment Commission* (Ottawa: King's Printer, 1938).
11 *Report of the Royal Commission on Dominion-Provincial Relations* (Rowell-Sirois Report), Book II (Recommendations) (Ottawa: King's Printer, 1940), 23.
12 *Act to Promote Unemployment Insurance*, S.Q. 1939, c. 2.
13 On the position endorsed by this political faction, see Esdras Minville, "Labour Legislation and Social Services in the Province of Quebec," Appendix 5 to the Rowell-Sirois Report.
14 Confédération des Travailleurs Catholiques du Canada (CTCC), *Mémoire de la Confédération des Travailleurs Catholiques du Canada au Cabinet Fédéral*, 20 January 1938.
15 Leslie A. Pal, *State, Class, and Bureaucracy* (Kingston: McGill-Queen's University Press, 1988), 150.
16 On this issue, see Jean-Guy Genest, *Godbout* (Quebec City: Septentrion, 1996), 158-61.
17 *House of Commons Debates*, 23 May 1929, 2782-83.
18 On this argument, see the Rowell-Sirois Report, Book II (Recommendations), 36-37, and Quebec City, *Rapport de la Commission des assurances sociales de Québec* (6e rapport) (Quebec City: Editeur officiel du Québec, 1933), 203.
19 House of Commons, *Report of the Debates of June 27, 1940*, 10 (letter from Adélard Godbout to Mackenzie King, 13 May 1940).
20 House of Commons, Special Committee on Bill no. 98 Respecting Unemployment Insurance, *Minutes of Proceedings and Evidence* (Ottawa, 1940, 137-38).
21 See the depositions of Tom Moore of the TLCC and Alfred Charpentier of the CTCC, *ibid.*, 205-7.
22 Rowell-Sirois Report, Book II, 24-26.
23 *British North America Act, 1867*, 30 and 31 Victoria, c. 3. Section 91 of the BNA Act was amended by the insertion of paragraph "2A. Unemployment Insurance."
24 *House of Commons Debates*, 25 June 1940, 1118.
25 *Unemployment Insurance Act, 1940*, S.C. 1940, c. 44.
26 *Unemployment Insurance Act, 1935*, 25 Geo. V, c. 8.
27 On this issue, see L. Richter, W.J. Couper, and B.M. Stewart, "The Employment and Social Insurance Bill," *Canadian Journal of Economics and Political Science* 1 (1935): 454.

28 House of Commons, Special Committee, *Minutes*, 26-27.
29 J.A. Garraty, *Unemployment in History: Economic Thought and Public Policy* (New York: Harper and Row, 1978), 5.
30 Gary Dingledine, *A Chronology of Response: The Evolution of Unemployment Insurance from 1940 to 1980* (Ottawa: Employment and Immigration Canada, 1981), 11.
31 See the references in the *Unemployment Insurance Act, 1940*, s. 17(4), 35, and Schedule 3, s. 2.
32 *Unemployment Insurance Benefit Regulations* (1942) 76 *Can. Gaz.* 3428, s. 6.
33 *Unemployment Insurance Act, 1940*, s. 28(iv).
34 *Unemployment Insurance Act, 1935*, s. 24(2).
35 *Ibid.*, s. 28.
36 *Social Security Act*, U.S. 1935, c. 531, s. 903(a)5.
37 *Unemployment Insurance Act, 1940*, s. 32.
38 On comparisons and contrasts between the US and Canadian legislation, see Chapter 3, 45ff., esp. 49-50, and notes 88 and 89.
39 *Unemployment Insurance Act, 1940*, s. 44.
40 *Ibid.*, s. 43(a).
41 House of Commons, Special Committee, *Minutes*, 115-16.
42 *Ibid.*, 116.
43 *Ibid.*, 206.
44 *House of Commons Debates*, 26 July 1940, 2031, 2033.
45 *Ibid.*, 2034 (M. Gillis, CCF MP for Cape Breton South).
46 *Unemployment Insurance Act, 1940*, s. 56(1)(a)(b)(d).
47 House of Commons, Special Committee, *Minutes*, 236-37.
48 *Unemployment Insurance Act, 1935*, s. 31(6), 35(1).
49 Leonard C. Marsh, *Report on Social Security in Canada* (Ottawa: King's Printer, 1943), 45.
50 *Unemployment Insurance Act, 1940*, s. 77(2).
51 *Ibid.*, s. 11.
52 *Employment and Social Insurance Act*, S.C. 1935, c. 38, s. 35(3).
53 The Gill Report would make this comment on the provision in 1962: "Withdrawals from the Fund could be made only for the purpose of payment of benefits and refund of contributions." Canada, *Committee of Inquiry into the Unemployment Insurance Act* (Gill Report) (Ottawa: Queen's Printer, 1962), 23.
54 *Unemployment Insurance Act, 1940*, s. 84. The 1935 act provided for a similar system. *Employment and Social Insurance Act*, ss. 36 and 37.
55 *Unemployment Insurance Act, 1940*, s. 17(2) and Schedule 2.
56 Yves Vaillancourt, *L'évolution des politiques sociales au Québec: 1940-1960* (Montreal: Presses de l'Université de Montréal, 1988), 320.
57 Gill Report, Table 52.
58 *Ibid.*, 20.
59 Montreal lawyer close to the Canadian Communist Party and involved in defending its members.
60 J.L. Cohen, *The Canadian Unemployment Insurance Act: Its Relation to Social Security* (Toronto: Thomas Nelson and Sons, 1935).
61 *Ibid.*, 139.
62 William Henry Beveridge, *Insurance for All and Everything* (London: Daily News, 1924), quoted in Cohen, *The Canadian Unemployment Insurance Act*, 147.
63 See Chapter 3, 40, and note 46; Carl J. Cuneo, "State Mediation of Class Contradictions in Canadian Unemployment Insurance, 1930-1935," *Studies in Political Economy* 3 (1980): 37.
64 Pal, *State, Class, and Bureaucracy*, 104.
65 R.B. Bennett Papers, Library and Archives Canada, Bryce Stewart to Finance Minister W.C. Clark, 16 January 1933, 501799.
66 Hugh H. Wolfenden, *The Real Meaning of Social Insurance: Its Present Status and Tendencies* (Toronto: Macmillan, 1932), 171.
67 *Ibid.*, 174.
68 J. Rueff, "L'assurance-chômage, cause du chômage permanent," *Revue d'économie politique* 45 (1931): 210.

69 For a contemporary critique of Rueff's position, see F. Maurette, "L'assurance-chômage, prétendue cause d'un chômage permanent," *International Labour Review* 24, 6 (1931): 663-84.

70 A.D. Watson, "Actuarial Report of the Contributions Required to Provide the Unemployment Insurance Benefits within the Scheme of the Draft of an Act Entitled The Employment and Social Insurance Act," 2 November 1934, quoted by Pal, *State, Class, and Bureaucracy*, 106.

71 Cohen, *Canadian Unemployment Insurance Act*, 76-77.

72 Dingledine, *Chronology of Response*, 15.

73 Marsh, *Report*, 13, quoting US Social Security Board Chairman A.J. Altmeyer.

74 Canada, *Income Security and Social Services*, Working Paper on the Constitution (Ottawa: Queen's Printer, 1969), 75.

75 Marsh, *Report*, 30.

Chapter 5: UI Expansion, 1940-75

1 *Committee of Inquiry into the Unemployment Insurance Act* (Gill Report) (Ottawa: Queen's Printer, 1962).

2 Department of Labour, *Unemployment Insurance in the 70s* (Ottawa: Queen's Printer, 1970).

3 Unemployment Insurance Commission, *First Report (1942)* (Ottawa: King's Printer, 1943), 7.

4 Department of Reconstruction, *Travail et revenus en ce qui a trait tout particulièrement à la première phase de la reconstruction* (Ottawa: King's Printer, 1945), 2 (our translation).

5 *Act to Amend the Unemployment Insurance Act, 1940*, S.C. 1946, c. 68, s. 34; *Act to Amend the Unemployment Insurance Act, 1940*, S.C. 1950, c. 1, s. 23.

6 J. Boivin and B. Solasse, *L'assurance-chômage et les services aux travailleurs*, Annex 21 to the *Rapport de la Commission d'enquête sur la santé et le bien-être social* (Castonguay-Nepveu Report) (Quebec City: Commission d'enquête sur la santé et le bien-être social, 1970), Table XXII, 249. On the expansion of the system's coverage during this period, see the Gill Report, 73-75.

7 *Act to Amend the Unemployment Insurance Act, 1940*, S.C. 1952-53, c. 51, ss. 1, 3.

8 *Unemployment Insurance Act*, S.C. 1955, c. 50.

9 Statistics Canada, *Annual Unemployment Insurance Statistics, 1995*, Table 16, 23 (contains statistics on unemployment insurance benefits and average weekly earnings in constant dollars and 1986 dollars for the period 1943-95). Boivin and Solasse, *L'assurance-chômage*, Table XIV, 236 (figures in parentheses indicate values in constant 1986 dollars).

10 Starting in 1941, the responsibility for unemployment statistics was handed to the Dominion Bureau of Statistics, now Statistics Canada, which in 1945 did a labour force survey. In 1960, this survey became the source of official unemployment figures.
    The unemployment rate is not defined in terms of numbers of unemployment insurance claimants but reflects the unemployed enumerated by the survey. Although the survey approach has varied somewhat over the years, the definition of unemployed has remained substantially the same. In 1989, the Labour Force Survey defined the unemployed as "Persons who, during the reference week, were without work, had looked for work over the past four weeks and were ready to work. As well, persons laid off temporarily or waiting for new jobs to start within the next four weeks are classified as unemployed even if they had not looked for work." Jean Marc Lévesque, "The Unemployed and Unemployment Insurance," *Perspectives on Labour and Income* 1 (1989): 54-55 (Statistics Canada no. 3).
    Anyone without a job who does not meet these criteria is excluded from the labour force. Thus, the real unemployment rate will almost always be higher than the one identified by the Labour Force Survey.

11 Gill Report, 1.

12 *Unemployment Insurance Act*, S.C. 1955, c. 50, s. 67(3)(c).

13 *Unemployment Insurance Regulations, 1946* (1946) 80 *Can. Gaz.* (No. 39, suppl.) 31. The regulations were passed under s. 42 of the *Unemployment Insurance Act, 1940*, S.C. 1940, c. 44.

14 Gary Dingledine, *A Chronology of Response: The Evolution of Unemployment Insurance from 1940 to 1980* (Ottawa: Employment and Immigration Canada, 1981), 25.

15 Gill Report, 96 (Table 21).
16 *Unemployment Insurance Commission Regulations,* CRC c. 1949, amended by SOR/50-515 (1950) 84 *Can. Gaz. II* 1582. Approved under the *Act to Amend the Unemployment Insurance Act, 1940,* S.C. 1950, c. 1, s. 11.
17 *Unemployment Insurance Commission Regulations,* CRC c. 1949, amended by SOR/50-515 (1950) *Can. Gaz. II* 1582, and by SOR/51-272 (1951) *Can. Gaz. II* 738, and by SOR/52-360 (1952) *Can. Gaz. II* 896. The supplementary condition was reduced to sixty days, the normal workweek being six days at that time.
18 Unemployment Insurance Commission, *Tenth Annual Report* (Ottawa: King's Printer, 1951), 38.
19 Confédération des Travailleurs Catholiques du Canada (CTCC), *Mémoire soumis au Comité des relations industrielles de la Chambre des Communes, Ottawa, en marge du bill no. 328 (refonte de la Loi sur l'assurance-chômage),* 31 May 1955, 4. Canadian Labour Congress, *Proceedings of the Annual Convention* (1951), 98; (1952), 71; (1953), 87; and (1954), 94. Trades and Labour Congress of Canada, *Trades and Labour Congress Journal* (November 1954): 8, (January 1956): 9-10. *Labour Gazette* (March 1957): 267 [National Council of Women of Canada (NCW)]. *House of Commons Standing Committee on Industrial Relations,* 6 June 1955, 472-73 [Canadian Federation of Business and Professional Women's Clubs (BPW)].
20 Dingledine, *A Chronology of Response,* 38. On the matter of the additional eligibility requirement for married women, see Ann Porter, "Women and Income Security in the Postwar Period: The Case of Unemployment Insurance, 1945-1962," *Labour* 31 (1993): 111.
21 The number of women employed in Canadian manufacturing industries rose from 25,300 in 1938 to more than 62,000 in 1945. F.H. Leacy, ed., *Historical Statistics of Canada,* 2nd ed. (Ottawa: Statistics Canada, 1983), E-41-48.
22 *Unemployment Assistance Act,* S.C. 1956, c. 26.
23 Despite its name, the program was also intended for needy people unprotected by other programs. See Yves Vaillancourt, *L'évolution des politiques sociales au Québec: 1940-1960* (Montréal: Presses de l'Université de Montréal, 1988), 456, 457.
24 *Canada Assistance Plan Act,* S.C. 1966-67, c. 45.
25 Allan Moscovitch, "Canada Health and Social Transfer: What Was Lost?" *Canadian Review of Social Policy* 37 (1996): 70-71.
26 *Social Aid Act,* S.Q. 1969, c. 63.
27 Boivin and Solasse, *L'assurance-chômage,* Table XI, 236.
28 Gill Report, 1.
29 *Ibid.,* 20.
30 *House of Commons Standing Committee on Industrial Relations,* Minutes, no. 2, 17 May 1955, 96-98.
31 See, in particular, Boivin and Solasse, *L'assurance-chômage,* 98-99, and Jean-Michel Cousineau, "Objectifs et modalités de l'assurance-chômage au Canada 1940-1986," *Relations industrielles* 41 (1986): 451.
32 Nonetheless, the Co-ordinating Committee of Unemployed Organizations (Toronto) and the Communist Party of Canada submitted briefs. Gill Report, 205.
33 Vaillancourt, *L'évolution,* 76-77.
34 Confédération des Syndicats Nationaux (CSN), *Mémoire de la Confédération des Syndicats nationaux au gouvernement fédéral concernant le Comité d'enquête relatif à la Loi sur l'assurance-chômage (Comité Gill),* Montreal, September 1963, 1.
35 Gill Report, 1.
36 *Ibid.,* 103.
37 This theme would be taken up and developed twenty-five years later in the Forget Report. Employment and Immigration Canada, *Commission of Inquiry on Unemployment Insurance* (Ottawa: Employment and Immigration Canada, 1986), 77.
38 Gill Report, 122.
39 *Ibid.,* 143.
40 *Ibid.,* 148-49.
41 *Ibid.,* 1-2.

42 *Ibid.,* 41.
43 *Ibid.,* 104.
44 *Ibid.,* 141.
45 Leslie A. Pal, "Maternity Benefits and U.I.: A Question of Policy Design," *Canadian Public Policy* 11 (1985): 552-53.
46 Gill Report, 135.
47 *Ibid.,* 159.
48 *Ibid.,* 146.
49 *Ibid.,* 149.
50 *Unemployment Insurance Regulations,* SOR/66-174, (1966) 100 *Can. Gaz.* 453.
51 *Adult Occupational Training Act,* S.C. 1966-67, c. 94.
52 Laurence A. Kelly, *Unemployment Insurance in Canada* (PhD dissertation, Queen's University, 1967), 398-99.
53 Jules Duchastel, "Chômage, politique sociale, et crise," *Cahiers du socialisme* 3 (1979): 107.
54 Andrew F. Johnson, "A Minister as an Agent of Policy Change: The Case of Unemployment Insurance in the 70s," *Canadian Public Administration* 24 (1981): 620.
55 These events prompted a number of analyses. See, in particular, Dennis Guest, *The Emergence of Social Security in Canada* (Vancouver: UBC Press, 1985), 178-85.
56 *Income Security and Social Services,* Working Paper on the Constitution, Ottawa, 1969, 109.
57 Department of National Health and Welfare, *Income Security for Canadians* (Ottawa: Queen's Printer, 1970), 36.
58 Department of Labour, *Unemployment Insurance in the 70s,* 3.
59 *Ibid.,* 6.
60 *Ibid.,* 5.
61 *Ibid.,* 7.
62 Minister of Finance (Paul Martin), *A New Framework for Economic Policy* (Ottawa: Department of Finance, 1994). See also the Forget Report, 115.
63 Department of Labour, *Unemployment Insurance in the 70s,* 23.
64 Gill Report, 100.
65 Department of Labour, *Unemployment Insurance in the 70s,* 19.
66 Only a simplistic concept of social insurance would exclude seasonal workers. See Vaillancourt, *L'évolution,* 338, and Yves Vaillancourt and Benoît Lévesque, "Les origines de l'Etat-providence au Canada: Retour sur la lecture du Rapport Macdonald," *Canadian Review of Social Policy* 18 (1987): 135-36.
67 *Unemployment Insurance Act, 1971,* S.C. 1970-71-72, c. 48.
68 Statistics Canada, *Annual Unemployment Insurance Statistics, 1995,* Table 16, 23.
69 *Unemployment Insurance Act, 1971,* s. 62, 63.
70 Pal, *State, Class, and Bureaucracy,* 30.
71 The Supreme Court had to acknowledge the discriminatory nature of these rules twenty years later in its decision in *Tétreault-Gadoury* v. *Canada* (1991) 2 S.C.R. 22.
72 Pal, "Maternity Benefits," 555.
73 *Ibid.,* and Jacques Frémont, "Assurance-chômage, maternité, et adoption: Les récentes modifications et leur validité," *Revue Juridique Thémis* 17 (1982-83): 497.
74 Frémont, "Assurance-chômage," and Simon Ledoux, *L'influence du droit constitutionnel dans l'émergence et l'évolution du droit aux prestations de maternité, d'adoption, et parentales au sein de la Loi sur l'assurance-chômage* (MA thesis, Université de Montréal, 1991).
75 *Unemployment Insurance Act, 1971,* s. 2(v), 30(3), 58(x), 64(5).
76 Ministère de la Famille et de l'Enfance, *Les enfants au coeur de nos choix: Livre Blanc sur les nouvelles dispositions de la politique familiale* (Sainte-Foy: Publications du Québec, 1997), 26. Coincidentally with the creation of the Quebec parental benefit plan, Quebec opened talks with the federal government about the transfer to that province of amounts representing the cost of pregnancy and parental benefits paid as part of unemployment insurance. Following a disagreement about the amount of this transfer, the Quebec government decided to challenge the constitutionality of these provisions of the Employment Insurance Act through a reference to the Quebec Court of Appeal. On 27 January 2004, that Court found unanimously that these provisions of the act exceeded Parliament's

jurisdiction over unemployment insurance, instead falling within provincial legislative competence and, more particularly, provincial legislative competence over property and civil rights and matters of a merely local or private nature under ss. 92(13) and 92(16) of the Constitution Act, 1867. The Court favoured a restrictive interpretation of federal jurisdiction over unemployment insurance, with benefits to be paid after loss of employment for economic reasons and not after a break in employment due to a personal inability to work. The Attorney General of Canada appealed this decision to the Supreme Court. Let us recall, however, the agreement in principle on this matter of 2 May 2004 between the government of Canada and Quebec ("Government of Canada concludes an Agreement in Principle on Quebec's Parental Insurance Plan," <http://www.hrsdc.gc.ca/en/cs/comm/hrsd/news/2004/040521.shtml>); *Act Respecting Parental Insurance*, S.Q. 2001, c. 9; *Renvoi à la Cour d'appel relatif à certaines dispositions de la Loi sur l'assurance-emploi*, C.A.Q. 200-09-003962-021: *Attorney General of Canada* v. *Attorney General of Quebec*, S.C. 30187.

77   *Bliss* v. *A.G. of Canada*, [1979] 1 S.C.R. 183. Like the federal Court of Appeal, the Supreme Court would rule that the provision was not discriminatory since it applied only to pregnant women, not all women. As well, the protection of the Canadian Bill of Rights could not apply to benefits conferred by a law, in this case unemployment insurance benefits. The Supreme Court would later reverse this view on discrimination against pregnant women. *Brooks* v. *Canada Safeway*, [1989] 1 S.C.R. 1219.

78   *Unemployment Insurance Act, 1971*, s. 16(1)(a).

79   *Ibid.*, ss. 41(3) and 58(4), and *Unemployment Insurance Regulations*, SOR/71-324 (1971) 105 *Can. Gaz.* 1130.

80   D.F. Potter, "Unemployment Insurance: Policies and Principles of Disqualification and Disentitlement for Benefits," *Dalhousie Law Journal* 3 (1976): 185.

81   See Chapter 2, 23ff.

82   See CUB 8107.

83   *Unemployment Insurance Act, 1971*, s. 58(f).

84   Compare *Unemployment Insurance Act, 1971*, s. 95(c), and *Unemployment Insurance Act*, S.C. 1955, c. 50, s. 72. See Chapter 7, 119.

85   Diane Bellemare, *La sécurité du revenu au Canada: Une analyse économique de l'avènement de l'Etat-providence* (PhD dissertation, McGill University, 1981), 577.

86   *Duties of the Minister of Labour under the Unemployment Insurance Act, 1971, transferred to the Minister of Manpower and Immigration*, SR/72-6 (1972) 106 *Can. Gaz.* II 200.

87   Employment and Immigration Canada, *Unemployment Insurance in the 80s* (Gershberg Report) (Ottawa: Employment and Immigration Canada, 1981), 6.

88   *Ibid.*, 70.

89   Unemployment Insurance Commission, *General Study of the Unemployment Insurance System in Canada* (Ottawa: Unemployment Insurance Commission, 1977), C-6.

90   See Johnson, "A Minister," 630.

91   Bill C-125, *Act to Amend the Unemployment Insurance Act, 1971 (no. 2)*, 1st Session, 29th Legislature, 1973.

Chapter 6: Vision under Siege, 1975-88

1   Michel Beaud and Gilles Dostaler, *La pensée économique depuis Keynes: Historique et dictionnaire des principaux auteurs* (Paris: Seuil, 1993).

2   See Milton Friedman and Rose Friedman, *Capitalism and Freedom* (Chicago: University of Chicago Press, 1962), and *Free to Choose* (New York: Harcourt Brace Jovanovich, 1980).

3   In 1994, the core unemployment rate in Canada was at least 8 percent. See Department of Finance, *A New Framework for Economic Policy* (Ottawa: Department of Finance, 1994), 20.

4   Employment and Immigration Canada, *Labour Market Development in the 1980s* (Dodge Report) (Ottawa: Employment and Immigration Canada, 1981), 18.

5   National Employment Commission, *Interim Report of the National Employment Commission* (Ottawa: King's Printer, 1937).

6   See Kevin Kerr, *Canada's Recent Unemployment Experience* (Ottawa: Library of Parliament, Research Branch, 1982), 12.

7 For a summary of arguments for and against the deterrent view of unemployment insurance developed in these various studies, see Derek P.J. Hum, *Unemployment Insurance and Work Effort: Issues, Evidence, and Policy Directions* (Toronto: Ontario Economic Council, 1981), 7-18; Dodge Report, 12; and HRDC, *From Unemployment Insurance to Employment Insurance* (Improving Social Security in Canada series) (Hull: HRDC, 1994), Chapter 2.

8 Dodge Report, 12.

9 Richard Langlois, "Le rapport Forget et l'assurance-chômage: CAP sur le workfare," *Canadian Review of Social Policy* 18 (1987): 144.

10 Hum, *Unemployment Insurance*, 25.

11 *House of Commons Debates*, 19 June 1980, 2290-91.

12 *An Act to Amend the Unemployment Insurance Act, 1971*, S.C. 1974-75-76, c. 80.

13 *Family Allowances Act*, S.C. 1973-74, c. 44, s. 13; *House of Commons Debates*, 27 October 1975, 8567.

14 House of Commons, Standing Committee on Labour, Manpower and Immigration, *Minutes of Proceedings and Evidence*, 20 November 1975, 2025.

15 *Employment and Immigration Reorganization Act*, S.C. 1976-77, c. 54.

16 The expression "active measures" entered the vocabulary of the Organisation for Economic Co-operation and Development (OECD) in the late 1970s to describe labour market policies. Income security systems were described as "passive" measures that should be supplanted by so-called "active" measures intended to integrate the jobless more with a market perspective, especially through vocational training. Expressing the neoliberal concept of supply, these measures put the interests of a smoothly operating free market ahead of those of the jobless insofar as their introduction worked against compensation for unemployment. See OECD, *Labour Market Policies for the 1990s* (Paris: OECD, 1990).

17 *House of Commons Debates*, 1 February 1977, 2592 (Hon. Jack Cullen).

18 On the effect of labour legislation on these projects, see *YMHA Jewish Community Centre of Winnipeg Inc.* v. *Brown*, [1989] 1 S.C.R. 1532.

19 *Employment and Immigration Reorganization Act*, S.C. 1976-77, c. 54, s. 41 amending ss. 37(2) and 38(11).

20 *House of Commons Debates*, 23 June 1977, 7070 (Mr. Cyril Symes).

21 On the introduction of these new measures to the unemployment insurance system, see Leslie A. Pal, "The Fall and Rise of Developmental Uses of UI Funds," *Canadian Public Policy* 9 (1983): 81-93.

22 Jonathan R. Kesselman, *Financing Canadian Unemployment Insurance* (Toronto: Canadian Tax Foundation, 1983), 79.

23 Compare the *Employment and Immigration Reorganization Act*, S.C. 1976-77, c. 54, s. 56, repealing ss. 95 to 97 and replacing them with the new s. 95, with the *Unemployment Insurance Act*, S.C. 1955, c. 50, ss. 72 to 81.

24 *An Act to Amend the Unemployment Insurance Act, 1971*, S.C. 1978-79, c. 7.

25 *House of Commons Debates*, 9 November 1978, 983.

26 *An Act to Amend the Unemployment Insurance Act, 1971*, S.C. 1978-79, c. 7, s. 4 amending s. 17.

27 Leslie A. Pal, "The Finance View: The Case of Unemployment Insurance 1970-1978," *Canadian Tax Journal* 33 (1985): 794. See also, in this connection, Canada, National Council of Welfare, *Bearing the Burden, Sharing the Benefits: A Report on Taxation and the Distribution of Income* (Ottawa: National Council of Welfare, 1978), 10-13.

28 Employment and Immigration Canada, *Unemployment Insurance in the 1980s* (Gershberg Report) (Ottawa: Employment and Immigration Canada, 1981), Foreword iii.

29 *Ibid.*, 40.

30 *Ibid.*, 69.

31 Marjorie Cohen, "Unemployment Insurance: The High Price of Equality," *Canadian Woman Studies* 3, 4 (1982): 36.

32 Employment and Immigration Canada, *Commission of Inquiry on Unemployment Insurance* (Forget Report) (Ottawa: Employment and Immigration Canada, 1986), 29.

33 *Ibid.*, 445-46 (minority report).

34 Kesselman, *Financing Canadian Unemployment Insurance*, 77.

35   Department of Finance, *A New Direction for Canada: An Agenda for Economic Renewal* (Ottawa: Department of Finance, 1984).
36   There was the famous incident on Parliament Hill when Prime Minister Mulroney was caught by a militant senior who chided him as "Charlie Brown" for breaking his election promise to maintain the social programs. The video of this exchange was broadcast Canada-wide.
37   Leslie A. Pal, "Sense and Sensibility: Comments on Forget," *Canadian Public Policy* 14 (1988): 8.
38   The effective date of the severance pay provision was 31 March 1985: *Unemployment Insurance Regulations,* SOR/85 (1985) 119 *Can. Gaz.* 1692. The effective date for retirement income was 5 January 1986: *Unemployment Insurance Regulations,* SOR/86 (1986) 120 *Can. Gaz.* 287. Regulatory change of 5 April 1987: *Unemployment Insurance Regulations,* SOR/87 (1987) 121 *Can. Gaz.* 1449.
39   Daniel Stoffman, "The Real UI Bill," *Canadian Business* 57, 3 (1984): 47.
40   J. Gennard, *Financing Strikers* (New York: Wiley, 1977), 12.
41   See, for example, the *Vermont Unemployment Compensation Law,* Vermont Statutes annotated, c. 17, s. 1344(a)(4) B); the *Pennsylvania Unemployment Compensation Act,* Pennsylvania Statutes, c. 14, art. 802(d); and the *Connecticut Unemployment Compensation Act,* General Statutes of Connecticut, c. 567, s. 236(3) c).
42   See R. Clark, "Towards the 'Just' Strike? Social Welfare Payments for Persons Affected by a Trade Dispute in the Republic of Ireland," *Modern Law Review* 48 (1985): 659-78.
43   Susan H. Ephron, "Redefining Neutrality: Alternative Interpretations of the Labour Dispute Disqualification in Unemployment Compensation," *Comparative Labor Law Journal* 8 (1986): 101.
44   See, in this connection, *An Act to Amend the Social Aid Act,* S.Q. 1978, c. 71, s. 2.
45   See Reuben Hasson, "The Cruel War: Social Security Abuse in Canada," *Canadian Taxation* 3 (1981): 142-43, and John R. Kilcoyne, "Developments in Employment Law: The 1987-88 Term," *Supreme Court Law Review* 11 (1989): 271-72.
46   *A.G. v. Guardians of the Poor of Merthyr Tydfil Union,* [1990] 1 Ch. 516. See Chapter 2, 26.
47   External Affairs and International Trade Canada, Canada-US Trade Relations Division, *A Ten-Year Experience* (Ottawa: Canada-US Trade Relations Division, 1993), 19.
48   United States Department of Commerce, *Final Affirmative Countervailing Duty Determination: Certain Fresh Atlantic Groundfish from Canada* (International Trade Administration)(C-122-507), 1986, 93.
49   *Report of the Royal Commission on the Economic Union and Development Prospects for Canada* (Macdonald Report) (Ottawa: Supply and Services, 1985), vol. II, part III.
50   *Ibid.,* ch. 15, "Work and Pay: The Functioning of Labour Markets," 602.
51   *Ibid.,* 610.
52   See Chapter 9, 163-64.
53   Forget Report, 296.
54   *Ibid.,* 208 ff.
55   Jean-Michel Cousineau, "Le rapport Forget et l'économie politique de l'assurance-chômage," *Canadian Public Policy* 14 (1988): 5.
56   Forget Report, 143.
57   Leslie A. Pal, *State, Class, and Bureaucracy: Canadian Unemployment Insurance and Public Policy* (Kingston: McGill-Queen's University Press, 1988), 90.
58   Forget Report, 439.
59   *Ibid.*
60   *Ibid.,* 441.
61   Langlois, "Le rapport Forget et l'assurance-chômage," 148.
62   Forget Report, 229.
63   *Ibid.,* 231 (Recommendations 29.1 to 29.5).
64   On these organizations, see Pierre Issalys and Gaylord Watkins, *Unemployment Insurance Benefits: A Study of Administrative Procedures in the Unemployment Insurance Commission* (Ottawa: Law Reform Commission of Canada, 1977), 225-29, and Claude Girard, "Le Mouvement action-chômage de Montréal: 20 ans de pratique sociale," *Nouvelles pratiques sociales* 2 (1989): 37.
65   Forget Report, 289.

66 House of Commons, Standing Committee on Labour, Employment and Immigration, *Minutes of Proceedings and Evidence,* 17 March 1987, 28:4.

67 *Ibid.,* 28:11 and 28:13.

Chapter 7: Rights Enshrined in Case Law, 1940-90

1 M.A. Hickling, *Labour Disputes and Unemployment Insurance Benefits in Canada and England* (Don Mills: CCH, 1974), 10.

2 *Unemployment Insurance Act, 1971,* S.C. 1970-71-72, c. 48, ss. 67, 75.

3 *Tax Court of Canada Act,* S.C. 1980-81-82-83, c. 158, s. 53.

4 *Martin Service Station* v. *Minister of National Revenue,* [1977] 2 S.C.R. 996; *R.* v. *Scheer,* [1974] S.C.R. 1046.

5 *Petts* v. *The Umpire (Unemployment Insurance),* [1974] 2 F.C. 225 (FCA), 233 (Judge Jackett: CUB 3538).

6 Thus, for fiscal 1986-87 and 1989-90, the success rate in Quebec was, respectively, 37.5 percent and 34 percent, whereas it was only 22.5 percent and 19.5 percent in the same periods for the rest of Canada. Moreover, the study shows that the number of claimants seeking representation in their Board of Referees appeals is higher in Quebec (34.4 percent) than in the other provinces (e.g., Alberta with 10.8 percent). Decisions by Boards of Referees also reflect the impact of this representation. In Quebec during 1989-90, some 46.7 percent of claimants with representation won their cases, while this percentage was only 27.4 percent for those who were not represented: Employment and Immigration Canada, *Study on Appeals to the Board of Referees* (unpublished, 1990).

7 In this connection, see Umpire Denault's comments in a speech delivered to the 1992 annual seminar of the Quebec Société de droit administratif in Johanne Renaud, "Les décisions des autorités administratives," *Journal du Barreau* 24, 20 (1992): 16.

8 Employment and Immigration Canada, *Commission of Inquiry on Unemployment Insurance* (Forget Report) (Ottawa: Employment and Immigration Canada, 1986), 269.

9 CUB 10510.

10 *Employment and Immigration Reorganization Act,* S.C. 1976-77, c. 54, s. 56 repealing ss. 95 and 97 and replacing them with the new s. 95.

11 *A.G. of Canada* v. *Roberts,* (1985) 60 N.R. 349, 352 (FCA).

12 *Canada (Attorney General)* v. *Tucker,* [1986] 2 F.C. 329 (FCA), 341.

13 *Canadian Bill of Rights,* R.S.C. (1985), Schedule C.

14 On availability during pregnancy, see Chapter 5, 87, and note 77.

15 Leslie A. Pal and F.L. Morton, "Bliss v. A.G. Canada: From Legal Defeat to Political Victory," *Osgoode Hall Law Journal* 24 (1986): 141.

16 *Act to Amend the Unemployment Insurance Act (No. 3),* S.C. 1980-81-82-83, c. 150.

17 See ss. 15(1) and 28 of the *Canadian Charter of Rights and Freedoms,* Part I of the *Constitution Act, 1982,* R.S.C. (1985), Schedule II, no. 44.

18 *Tétreault-Gadoury* v. *Canada,* [1989] 2 F.C. 245 (FCA) and [1991] 2 S.C.R. 22; *Schachter* v. *Canada,* [1990] 2 F.C. 129 (FCA) and [1992] 2 S.C.R. 679.

19 See Chapter 8, 135-36.

20 *Abrahams* v. *Canada (A.G.),* [1983] 1 S.C.R. 2, 10.

21 *Interpretation Act,* R.S.C. 1985, c. I-21, s. 12. See E.A. Driedger, *Construction of Statutes* (Toronto: Butterworth, 1983), 72-79.

22 *Unemployment Act, 1940,* S.C. 1940, c. 44, s. 43; *Unemployment Insurance Act, 1935,* c. 8, s. 26.

23 To make this easier to understand, I reprint the text of the provision as it appeared after the reform of 1971:

> 44(1) A claimant who has lost his employment by reason of a stoppage of work attributable to a labour dispute at the factory, workshop or other premises which he was employed is not entitled to receive benefit until
> (a) the termination of the stoppage of work,
> (b) he becomes *bona fide* employed elsewhere in the occupation that he usually follows, or

    (c)   he has become regularly engaged in some other occupation.
  (2) Subsection (1) is not applicable if a claimant proves that
    (a)   he is not participating in or financing or directly interested in the labour dispute that caused the stoppage of work; and
    (b)   he does not belong to a grade or class of workers that, immediately before the commencement of the stoppage, included members who were employed at the premises which the stoppage is taking place and are participating in, financing or directly interested in the dispute.
  (3) Where separate branches of work that are commonly carried on as separate businesses in separate premises are carried on in separate departments on the same premises, each department shall, for the purpose of this section, be deemed to be a separate factory or workshop.
  (4) In this Act, "labour dispute" means any dispute between employers and employees, or between employees and employees, that is connected with the employment or non-employment, or the terms or conditions of employment, of any persons.

24 Canadian jurisprudence: CUB 1136, CUB 5506; British jurisprudence: U.D. 17993/31; R.U. 17/52.
25 Hickling, *Labour Disputes*, 114.
26 See, for example, CUB 3051, 3052, and 3052A.
27 *Gionest v. UIC*, [1983] 1 F.C. 832 (FCA), 835.
28 *Committee of Inquiry into the Unemployment Insurance Act* (Gill Report) (Ottawa: Queen's Printer, 1962), 105.
29 *A.G. of Canada v. Carpentier et al.*, unpublished decision of 12 July 1983 (FCA, A-801-82) (CUB 7464); *A.G. of Canada v. Wataja et al.*, unpublished decision of 31 May 1983 (FCA, A-1036-82) (CUB 7833); *A.G. of Canada v. McKellar*, unpublished decision of 30 July 1982 (FCA, A-833-82) (CUB 7584); and CUB 9139, CUB 9830A, and CUB 15560.
30 *Morrison v. Canada Employment and Immigration Commission*, [1990] 2 F.C. 57 (FCA).
31 *A.G. of Canada v. Aubin*, unpublished decision of 13 September 1990 (FCA, A-44-90) (CUB 17664).
32 Hickling, *Labour Disputes*, 109-10.
33 *A.G. of Canada v. Giguère*, [1984] 2 F.C. 52 (FCA).
34 *Giroux v. A.G. of Canada*, unpublished decision of 1 May 1980 (FCA, A-6-80) (CUB 5207); *A.G. of Canada v. Schoen*, [1982] 2 F.C. 141 (FCA) (CUB 6384); *Boldt v. A.G. of Canada*, [1986] 2 F.C. 1 (FCA) (CUB 10338) and CUB 11300.
35 CUB 11475, CUB 12753, and CUB 14704.
36 CUB 9944, CUB 4872, and CUB 5335.
37 CUB 8124, CUB 10819, and CUB 11242.
38 CUB 8046 and CUB 10623.
39 Gill Report, 149; see also 103.
40 U.D. 1677/25, U.D. 1765/25, R.U. 3/69.
41 *Canada (Attorney General) v. Valois*, [1986] 2 S.C.R. 439.
42 Procedure often used in appeals brought by several claimants on the same issue. The parties agree to argue only one case, the decision in which shall be applied to all of the appellants. In this connection, see *Lemieux et al. v. Unemployment Insurance Commission and A.G. of Canada*, [1977] 2 F.C. 246 (DPI).
43 *McKinnon v. Honourable Judge Dubé*, [1977] 2 F.C. 569 (FCA).
44 See *Hills v. A.G. of Canada*, [1988] 1 S.C.R. 513, 542; Pierre Issalys, "Le recours au droit comparé en droit social canadien et québécois," *Bulletin de droit comparé du travail et de la sécurité sociale* 1 (1994): 76-95.
45 United Kingdom, *Report of the Royal Commission on Trade Unions and Employers Associations 1945-68* (Donovan Commission) (London: Her Majesty's Stationery Office, 1968, Cmnd. 3623, paras 980, 991.
46 *Employment Protection Act, 1975*, c. 71, s. 111(1).
47 *Unemployment Insurance Act*, S.C. 1955, c. 50, s. 67(3)(c).

48 U.D. 1953, U.D. 2575, CUB 1136, CUB 2287, and CUB 5506.
49 Hickling, *Labour Disputes,* 143.
50 CUB 827, CUB 2141, and CUB 6432.
51 CUB 10311, CUB 10447, and CUB 11456.
52 *A.G. of Canada* v. *Lalonde,* [1983] 2 F.C. 957 (FCA) (Res.) (CUB 8153).
53 *Caron* v. *Canada,* [1989] 1 F.C. 628, 638 (FCA).
54 *Ibid.,* 642.
55 *Ibid.,* 635-36.
56 See Chapter 8, 137ff.
57 *Caron* v. *Canada,* [1991] 1 S.C.R. 48.
58 U.D. 2575, U.D. 2706.
59 See CUB 2659.
60 CUB 2953, CUB 3602, and *A.G. of Canada* v. *Simoneau,* [1982] 1 F.C. 469 (FCA). Note that the idea of "exceptional and temporary means" also figures in the determination of the very existence of a work stoppage: *A.G. of Canada* v. *Daigneault,* [1980] 1 F.C. 53 (FCA).
61 Employment and Immigration Canada, *Digest of Benefit Entitlement Principles,* Bulletin No. 90-1 (Hull: Employment and Immigration Canada, 1990), 8-35.
62 CUB 6800.
63 *Unemployment Insurance Act, 1971,* S.C. 1970-71-72, c. 48, s. 40(2)(a).
64 U.D. 4850/26, R.U. 17/52.
65 CUB 1364, CUB 3102, and CUB 3265.
66 *Imbeault* v. *UIC,* [1984] 1 F.C. 1217 (FCA). The Supreme Court refused leave to appeal from the decision of the Federal Court of Appeal (*Imbeault* v. *UIC,* [FCA] 18801, 26.7.84 [1984] 2 S.C.R. viii).
67 *Ouellet* v. *UIC,* unpublished decision of 29 November 1984 (FCA, A-257-84); Judge Marceau would use this argument in the decision in *Caron* v. *Canada,* [1989] 1 F.C. 628, 632 (FCA).
68 On the background of this idea of "bona fide," see Hickling, *Labour Disputes,* 16.
69 CUB 1148, CUB 1589, and CUB 2208.
70 *Unemployment Insurance Regulations,* SOR/71-324, (1971) 105 *Can. Gaz.* 1130, s. 162.
71 U.D. 4234/26, U.D. 416/39.
72 CUB 4404 and CUB 4750.
73 *Abrahams* v. *Canada (A.G.),* [1983] 1 S.C.R. 2, 10-11.
74 See *CEIC* v. *Roy, CEIC* v. *Cournoyer,* and *CEIC* v. *Jacques,* [1986] 1 F.C. 193 (FCA).
75 See *Re: McKay* (1946), 53 Man. R. 364, 372-73. This is one of the rare published decisions of a Board of Referees. The references to British jurisprudence on the concepts applying to labour disputes are explicit.
76 See Chapter 6, 99.
77 *Hills* v. *A.G. of Canada,* [1988] 1 S.C.R. 513, 538.
78 *Davlut* v. *A.G. of Canada,* [1988] 1 S.C.R. 513, 538.
79 See *Re: McKay* (1946), 53 Man R. 364, and CUB 19620, where Judge Reed studies the issue in depth.
80 Statistics Canada, *Annual Unemployment Insurance Statistics 1995,* Table 4, 3.
81 Reuben Hasson, "Discipline and Punishment in the Law of Unemployment Insurance: A Critical View of Disqualification and Disentitlement," *Osgoode Hall Law Journal* 25 (1987): 623.
82 CUB 7110, CUB 8910, and CUB 15680.
83 CUB 6193 and CUB 7863.
84 Bill C-21, *An Act to Amend the Unemployment Insurance Act and the Employment and Immigration Department and Commission Act,* 2nd Session, 34th Parliament, 1989.
85 Senate, *Special Committee on Bill C-21, 4th Report,* 20 March 1990, 26:10-26:11. See Chapter 8, 130ff.
86 CUB 3305 and CUB 9653.
87 CUB 7074, CUB 9300, and CUB 12518.
88 CUB 3319.
89 CUB 1292 and CUB 6195.
90 *A.G. Canada* v. *Findenigg,* [1984] 1 F.C. 65 (FCA); *Hamilton* v. *Canada (A.G.),* (1988) 91 N.R. 145 (FCA).

91 CUB 6683 and CUB 8025.
92 Murray Rankin and Kip Wiese, "Unemployment Insurance: A Policy Dilemma," *Queen's Law Journal* 10 (1984): 88.
93 CUB 4652.
94 CUB 5762, CUB 7110, and CUB 11287.
95 CUB 8132 and CUB 8134.
96 CUB 2810 and CUB 2369.
97 *Crewe and Others* v. *Social Security Commissioner*, [1982] 2 All E.R. 745 (CA), quoted in *Tanguay* v. *UIC* (1985), 68 N.R. 154, 175 (FCA).
98 *Ibid.*, 156.
99 On procedures prior to departure, see CUB 2056, CUB 12078, CUB 4607, CUB 8007, CUB 6329, CUB 6497, CUB 7127, and CUB 10632.
100 On "just cause" as related to the insured person's professional life, see CUB 8097, CUB 4352, CUB 4882, CUB 5812, CUB 2037, CUB 378, CUB 4212, CUB 6348, CUB 12078, CUB 8892, CUB 11412, CUB 12125, and CUB 2030.
101 On "just cause" as related to the insured person's personal life, see CUB 3284, CUB 3298, CUB 5830, CUB 3097, CUB 7127, CUB 8853, CUB 7056, and CUB 8308.
102 On recognition of extenuating circumstances, see CUB 9763 and CUB 10798.
103 On the interpretation of the concept of misconduct during this period, the text refers to the following decisions: CUB 963, CUB 702, CUB 4906, CUB 5023, CUB 7007, CUB 8112, and *Canada* v. *Bedell*, (1984) 60 N.R. 115, (FCA) 117.
104 See CUB 4503.
105 CUB 5775.
106 CUB 6666.
107 *Joseph* v. *CEIC*, [1986] 2 F.C. F-10 (FCA), (FCA, A-636-85, 11 March 1986, 2).
108 *Canada (Attorney General)* v. *Tucker*, [1986] 2 F.C. 329 (FCA).
109 CUB 16547 and CUB 17649, where Judge Denault summarizes the jurisprudence on misconduct.
110 *Joseph* v. *CEIC*, [1986] 2 F.C. F-10 (FCA).
111 *Davlut* v. *A.G. of Canada*, [1983] 1 F.C. 398 (FCA).
112 CUB 4538, CUB 4861, and CUB 8183.
113 *McDonald* v. *CEIC*, (1991) 131 N.R. 389 (FCA).
114 On this type of disqualification, see CUB 1269, CUB 5464, CUB 8234, and especially CUB 10113, where Judge Denault summarizes his enforcement activity.
115 CUB 4036A, CUB 5639, and CUB 7239.
116 CUB 5464.
117 *Attorney General of Canada* v. *Moura*, [1982] 2 F.C. 93 (FCA).
118 *Rondeau* v. *Simard*, [1977] 1 F.C. 519 (FCA), and *Bertrand* v. *Attorney General of Canada*, (1983) 46 N.R. 527 (FCA).
119 *Ricard* v. *UIC*, [1976] 1 F.C. 228 (FCA).
120 Issalys and Watkins, *Unemployment Insurance Benefits*, 49-50.
121 *An Act to Amend the Unemployment Insurance Act, 1971*, S.C. 1974-75-76, c. 80, s. 19, enacting new s. 55.
122 The principles for enforcing the obligation of availability were summarized by Judge Joyal in CUB 17524. On this issue, also see *Ricard* v. *UIC*, [1976] 1 F.C. 228 (FCA).
123 Reuben Hasson, "The Cruel War: Social Security Abuse in Canada," *Canadian Taxation* 3 (1981): 121.
124 House of Commons, Standing Committee on Labour, Employment and Immigration, *Minutes of Proceedings and Evidence*, 17 March 1987, 28:13. See Chapter 6, 107, and note 66.
125 CUB 17524.

Chapter 8: The System Hijacked, 1989-96

1 *Canada-United States Free Trade Agreement Implementation Act*, S.C. 1988, c. 65.
2 Employment and Immigration Canada, *Success in the Works: A Labour Force Development Strategy for Canada* (Ottawa: Employment and Immigration Canada, 1989).
3 Department of Finance, *Estimates*, 27 April 1989, 29-30.

4 Michel Vastel, "Moins d'argent, mais plus de formation aux chômeurs," *Le Devoir* 12 April 1989: 1, 10.
5 HRDC, *From Unemployment Insurance to Employment Insurance* (Improving Social Security in Canada series) (Hull: HRDC, 1994), 8.
6 OECD, *Labour Market Policies for the 1990s* (Paris: OECD, 1990).
7 Unlike the International Monetary Fund or the World Bank, the OECD is not part of the UN system. Founded in 1960, it encompasses some twenty countries, most of them, like Canada, industrialized. The OECD's objectives include promoting policies for growth in the economy and employment and raising living standards in member countries while maintaining financial stability. In this way, the OECD also wants to boost the growth of international trade on a multilateral basis.
8 OECD, *New Directions in Social Policy (Memo from the General Secretary)*, Meeting of the Employment, Labour and Social Affairs Committee to discuss social policy at the ministerial level, Paris, 8 and 9 December 1992.
9 "Active" and "passive" measures are so called after postwar Swedish experiments in "active labour market policies." See OECD, *Labour Market Policies*, 13. I lack the space here to go over the major differences between the Swedish active labour market policy experiment and the use later found for it by the OECD's neoliberal philosophy. But let me mention the major state involvement in promoting employment in the Swedish experiment as opposed to the OECD's view that job creation is primarily a market activity. On jobless training, see OECD, *Labour Market Policies*, 39, and on the funding of the UI system, see F. Calcoen, L. Eeckhoudt, and D. Greiner, "Unemployment Insurance, Social Protection, and Employment Policy: An International Comparison," *International Social Security Review* 2 (1988): 119.
10 OECD, "Croissance et emploi: Un rôle clef pour la valorisation des ressources humaines," OECD *Observer* 184 (1993): 2 of the insert between 22 and 23 (our translation).
11 OECD, *The OECD Jobs Study: Facts, Analysis, Strategies* (Paris: OECD, 1994), 48.
12 OECD, *Labour Market Policies*, 8.
13 A popular Quebec singer. The original line is "La meilleure façon de tuer un homme, c'est de le payer à ne rien faire." The song is called "Les 100,000 façons de tuer un homme," Félix Leclerc, *Tout Félix en chanson* (Montreal: Nuit Blanche, 1996), 44. We may doubt that Félix Leclerc, whose songs describe the lives of ordinary people, would have savoured an association with a process that ultimately pauperized thousands of his compatriots.
14 Department of Employment and Immigration, *Notes for a Speech by Mr. Bernard Valcourt, Minister of Employment and Immigration, to the Meeting of the Employment, Labour and Social Affairs Committee, Organisation for Economic Co-operation and Development (OECD)*, Paris, 14-15 January 1992 (our translation).
15 *National Training Act*, R.S.C. 1985, c. N-19.
16 Note that the Unemployment Insurance Act was renumbered in 1985 for the consolidation of federal statutes. S. 39 of the *Unemployment Insurance Act, 1971*, became s. 26 of the *Unemployment Insurance Act*, R.S.C. 1985, c. U-1.
17 Employment and Immigration Canada, *Success in the Works*, 3.
18 Advisory Council on Adjustment, *Adjusting to Win: Report of the Advisory Council on Adjustment* (the de Grandpré Report, named for its chair, former Bell Canada president Jean de Grandpré) (Hull: Supply and Services Canada, 1989).
19 Vastel, "Moins d'argent," 1. See also the later comments by Jean de Grandpré in Miville Tremblay, "La taxe pour la formation de la main-d'oeuvre: De Grandpré n'y compte plus," *La Presse* 2 November 1989: D3.
20 Employment and Immigration Canada, *Success in the Works*, 2.
21 Michel Vastel, "Ottawa se retire de l'assurance-chômage," *Le Devoir* 14 April 1989: 1.
22 Employment and Immigration Canada, *Annual Report 1988-1989* (report of the auditor general of Canada) (Hull: Employment and Immigration Canada, 1989), 27 and appendix.
23 Department of Finance, *Estimates*, 1989, 30.
24 Senate, *Special Committee on Bill C-21: Third and Final Report*, 12-13 February 1990, 25:10.
25 Bill C-21, *An Act to Amend the Unemployment Insurance Act and the Employment and Immigration Department and Commission Act*, 2nd Session, 34th Parliament, 1989-90.

26 Canadian Press, "La réforme de l'assurance-chômage, tempête à Ottawa, accueil positif à Québec," *Le Devoir* 12 April 1989: 2.
27 *Income Security Act,* S.Q. 1988, c. 51.
28 Paule Des Rivières, "Le monde du travail accuse Ottawa de faire payer le recyclage aux chômeurs," *Le Devoir* 12 April 1989: 1.
29 Canadian Labour Congress (CLC), *Submission ... to the Legislative Committee on Bill C-21,* Ottawa, 1989.
30 Jean Bernier and Michel Martin, "L'impact de la réforme de l'assurance-chômage sur le programme d'aide sociale," Quebec City, Ministère de la Main-d'œuvre et de la Sécurité du revenu, Direction des programmes de sécurité du revenu, April 1989, unpublished discussion paper, 7.
31 Des Rivières, "Le monde du travail," 1.
32 Senate, *Special Committee on Bill C-21: Third and Final Report,* 12-13 February 1990, 25:19.
33 Senate, *Special Committee on Bill C-21: Fourth Report,* 20 March 1990, 26:11 and 26:10.
34 Department of Labour, *Unemployment Insurance in the 70s* (Ottawa: Queen's Printer, 1970).
35 Senate, *Special Committee on Bill C-21: Third and Final Report,* 25:30.
36 *Ibid.,* 25:31.
37 *Employment and Immigration Reorganization Act,* S.C. 1976-77, c. 54, s. 30. See Chapter 6, 91ff., and notes 15, 19, and 23.
38 Senate, *Special Committee on Bill C-21: Third and Final Report,* 25:16.
39 During this period, when the entrance requirement was raised, many workers who usually filed claims with the minimum number of weeks of employment required still managed to work the fourteen weeks needed to collect benefits. This period was later studied to show that the opportunity to collect benefits encouraged the filing of claims as soon as the required number of weeks had been worked. The old thesis of unemployment insurance creating unemployment was thus backed by an actual example. These studies clearly underestimated the extent to which the phenomenon was due, for many jobless, to a survival reaction. See HRDC, *From Unemployment Insurance,* 64.
40 *Act to Amend the Unemployment Insurance Act and the Employment and Immigration Department and Commission Act,* S.C. 1989-90, c. 40.
41 In *Success in the Works: A Labour Force Development Strategy for Canada,* these changes were defended by a desire to make the law more equitable and consistent with the Canadian Charter of Rights and Freedoms. The Federal Court of Appeal had found the provisions limiting access by those over sixty-five (*Tétreault-Gadoury* v. *Canada,* [1989] 2 F.C. 245) and reserving parental benefits to adoptive parents (*Schachter* v. *Canada,* [1990] 2 F.C. 129) unconstitutional.
42 *Schachter* v. *Canada,* [1992] 2 S.C.R. 679.
43 *Tétreault-Gadoury* v. *Canada,* [1991] 2 S.C.R. 22.
44 *Unemployment Insurance Act,* R.S.C. 1985, c. U-1, s. 119.
45 Premiums would see substantial increases. The employee premium of $1.95 per $100 of insurable employment in 1989 rose to $2.25 in 1990 and reached $3.07 in 1994; the employer premium went up as well, tied to 1.4 times the employee rate.
46 The integration of this program with the system can only be seen as an exception to the rules that had thus far governed entitlement to benefit, since self-employed workers had always been excluded on the ground that they were not liable to unemployment. (On the reasons for their exclusion, see Department of Labour, *Unemployment Insurance in the 70s,* 18. On the practical application of the idea of the self-employed worker, see CUB 5454). Yet provisions of this kind persist in our employment insurance legislation (*Employment Insurance Act,* S.C. 1996, c. 23, ss. 12(1) and 54(c), and *Employment Insurance Regulations,* SOR/96-332 (1996) 130 *Can. Gaz.* 2192, s. 30). Note, however, that assistance to the self-employed, like all active measures, was extended on a purely discretionary basis.
47 *Act to Amend the Unemployment Insurance Act and the Employment and Immigration Department and Commission Act,* s. 20 adding s. 26.2.
48 Employment and Immigration Canada, *Success in the Works,* 17.
49 Vastel, "Moins d'argent," 10.

50 *Act to Amend the Unemployment Insurance Act and the Employment and Immigration Depart-ment and Commission Act,* s. 19 enacting the new s. 26(8) and s. 20 enacting s. 26.1(2).
51 Senate, *Special Committee on Bill C-21: Third and Final Report,* 25:34.
52 Senate, *Special Committee on Bill C-21: Fourth Report,* 26:10.
53

> 28(4) For the purposes of this section, "just cause" for voluntarily leaving an employment exists where, having regard to all the circumstances, including any of the following circumstances, the claimant had no reasonable alterna-tive to leaving the employment:
> (a) sexual or other harassment;
> (b) obligation to accompany a spouse or dependent child to another residence;
> (c) discrimination on a prohibited ground of discrimination within the meaning of the Canadian Human Rights Act;
> (d) working conditions that constitute a danger to health or safety;
> (e) obligation to care for a child.

Bill C-21 as amended and passed by the House of Commons on 6 November 1989, s. 21 amending s. 28 of the *Unemployment Insurance Act.*
54 Employment and Immigration Canada, *Digest of Benefit Entitlement Principles,* Bulletin No. 89-1 (Hull: Employment and Immigration Canada, 1989).
55 *A.G. Canada* v. *Landry,* unpublished decision of 24 November 1993 (FCA, A-1210-92).
56 Employment and Immigration Canada, *Commission of Inquiry on Unemployment Insurance* (Forget Report) (Ottawa: Employment and Immigration Canada, 1986), 229.
57 See Chapter 6, 102ff.
58 *Gionest* v. *U.I.C.,* [1983] 1 F.C. 832 (FCA). See Chapter 7, 113-14.
59 Employment and Immigration Canada, *Digest of Benefit Entitlement Principles,* Bulletin No. 90-1 (Hull: Employment and Immigration Canada, 1990), 8-50.
60 *Hills* v. *A.G. Canada,* [1988] 1 S.C.R. 513, 538. See Chapter 7, 115, 119.
61 *Morrison* v. *Canada Employment and Immigration Commission,* [1990] 2 F.C. 57 (FCA); *A.G. of Canada* v. *Aubin,* unpublished decision of 13 September 1990 (FCA, A-44-90) (CUB 17664).
62 *A.G. Canada* v. *Lalonde,* [1983] 2 F.C. 957 (FCA) (Res.); *Caron* v. *Canada,* [1989] 1 F.C. 628, and [1991] 1 S.C.R. 48.
63

> 49(1) For the purposes of section 31 of the Act and subject to subsection (2), a stop-page of work at a factory, workshop or other premises is terminated when
> (a) the work-force at the factory, workshop or other premises attains at least 85 per cent of its normal level; and
> (b) the level of activities in respect of the production of goods or services at the factory, workshop or other premises attains at least 85 per cent of its normal level.

Unemployment Insurance Regulations, SOR/90-756, (1990) 124 *Can. Gaz.* 4941 s. 13.
64 The Forget Report recommended (29.1) that "a dispute should be considered over on the date that the collective agreement is signed, except in cases where a date for return to work is identified in a subsidiary agreement or protocol."
65 On the idea of "bona fide," see Chapter 7, 118.
66 See CUB 12753 and Chapter 7, 114.
67 *Hills* v. *A.G. Canada,* [1988] 1 S.C.R. 513, and *Canada (Attorney General)* v. *Valois,* [1986] 2 S.C.R. 439.
68 Department of Finance, *Economic and Fiscal Statement,* 2 December 1992, Table 2, 17.
69 Employment and Immigration Canada, "Les modifications proposées à l'assurance-chômage: Projet de loi C-105," advertisement in *La Presse* 6 February 1993: A-16.
70 Created in 1991, the CLFDB was mainly intended to make recommendations to the gov-ernment concerning vocational training policies and programs and the funding levels for

these purposes in the unemployment insurance system. See Employment and Immigration Canada, *Unemployment Insurance Developmental Uses Programs in 1993* (Ottawa: HRDC, 1992), 3. Note that in 1992 this role devolved to Quebec and the Société québécoise de développement de la main-d'oeuvre (SQDM) brought into being by the *Loi sur la société québécoise de développement de la main-d'oeuvre*, S.Q. 1992, c. 44. In 1997, the SQDM was replaced by Emploi-Québec and its local employment centres as brought into being by the *Loi sur le ministère de l'Emploi et de la Solidarité et instituant la Commission des partenaires du marché du travail*, S.Q. 1997, c. 63.

71 Employment and Immigration Canada, *Unemployment Insurance Developmental Uses Programs in 1993*, v.

72 Bill C-105, *Government Expenditures Restraint Act, 1993*, 3rd Session, 34th Parliament, 1991-92. Unlike the 1989 statute, this bill was not restricted to the Unemployment Insurance Act but included an array of provisions united by the spending reduction theme.

73 Minister of Employment and Immigration, *News Release 92-39*, 3 December 1992.

74 Jean Dion, "Un assaut contre les démunis," *Le Devoir* 4 December 1992: A-1.

75 Marie-Claude Lortie, "Chômage: Valcourt se fait grivois dans sa défense des compressions," *La Presse* 4 December 1992: A-1.

76 See Reuben Hasson, "The Cruel War: Social Security Abuse in Canada," *Canadian Taxation* 3 (1981): 114-17.

77 Michel Vastel, "Ottawa part à la chasse des fraudeurs: Une police du chômage," *Le Soleil* 10 February 1993: A-1.

78 Department of Finance, *Economic and Fiscal Statement*, Table 2, 17.

79 *Tanguay* v. *UIC*, (1985) 68 N.R. 154 (FCA). See Chapter 7, 120-23.

80 Chantal Hébert, "Les travailleurs qui quittent par attrition n'auront plus droit aux prestations," *Le Devoir* 12 February 1993: A3.

81 Jean Dion, "Des chômeurs mécontents manifestent à Longueuil," *Le Devoir* 26 January 1993: A4.

82 Gilles Paquin and Raymond Gervais, "Un non retentissant au projet de loi d'Ottawa," *La Presse* 8 February 1993: A-1.

83 Bill C-113, *Government Expenditures Restraint Act*, 3rd Session, 34th Parliament, 1991-92.

84

    28(4) ...

        (e)   obligation to care for ... a member of the immediate family;

        (f)   reasonable assurance of another employment in the immediate future;

        (g)   significant modification of terms and conditions respecting wages or salary;

        (h)   excessive overtime work or refusal to pay for overtime work;

        (i)   significant changes in work duties;

        (j)   antagonistic relations between an employee and a supervisor for which the employee is not primarily responsible;

        (k)   practices of an employer that are contrary to law;

        (l)   discrimination with regard to employment because of membership in any association, organization or union of workers;

        (m) undue pressure by an employer on employees to leave their employment; and

        (n)   such other reasonable circumstances as are prescribed.

Bill C-113, *Government Expenditures Restraint Act*, s. 19 to replace s. 28(4).

85 Confédération des Syndicats Nationaux (CSN), Guy Martin, Pierre Paquette, "De la poudre aux yeux des chômeurs," *Le Devoir* 15 March 1993: A7.

86 Jean Chrétien, letter to Bill C-113 opponents, 26 March 1993 (our translation).

87 *Government Expenditures Restraint Act, 1993, No. 2*, S.C. 1993, c. 13.

88 A similar viewpoint was expressed by a lawyer in an article for employers: Michael A. Braden, "Changes to the Unemployment Insurance Act," *Business and the Law* 10, 9 (1993): 65.

89 CUB 22555.

90 The reasons set out in section 28 draw on earlier jurisprudence: see Employment and Immigration Canada, *Digest of Benefit Entitlement Principles,* Bulletin no. 93-1 (Hull: Employment and Immigration Canada, 1993), para 6.2.1, 9. On the inclusion of a new reason in paragraph (e) of subsection 28(4) (the obligation to care for a member of the immediate family), see CUB 20781.
91 *Unemployment Insurance Regulations,* SOR/93-177, (1993) 127 *Can. Gaz.* 1749, 1750.
92 Pierre Issalys and Gaylord Watkins, *Unemployment Insurance Benefits: A Study of Administrative Procedure in the Unemployment Insurance Commission* (Ottawa: Law Reform Commission of Canada, 1977), 47, 59.
93 *A.G. Canada* v. *Mills,* (1984) 60 N.R. 4 (FCA).
94 CUB 12281.
95

2. Every law of Canada shall, unless it is expressly declared by an Act of the Parliament of Canada that it shall operate notwithstanding the *Canadian Bill of Rights,* be so construed and applied as not to abrogate, abridge or infringe or to authorize the abrogation, abridgment or infringement of any of the rights or freedoms herein recognized and declared, and in particular, no law of Canada shall be construed or applied so as to

...

   (e)   deprive a person of the right to a fair hearing in accordance with the principles of fundamental justice for the determination of his rights and obligations.

Canadian Bill of Rights, R.S.C. 1970, Schedule III(c).
96 *Charte des droits et libertés de la personne,* R.S.Q. c. C-12, s. 23.
97 *Commission scolaire St-Hyacinthe and Jacques Turgeon* v. *Commission des droits de la personne and Rachel Dionne and Lucille Day-Godin,* [1983] 4 C.H.R.R., Decision 256.
98 On the application of the Canadian Bill of Rights in the hearing procedure of the Board of Referees, see CUB 3805.
99 *Canada-United States Free Trade Agreement Implementation Act,* S.C. 1993, c. 44.
100 The Liberals promised to replace the GST with a fairer tax and renegotiate the NAFTA: Liberal Party of Canada, *Job Creation and Economic Recovery, Liberal Action Plan for Canada* (Ottawa: Public Works and Government Services Canada, 1993), 18, 20.
101 Department of Finance, *Budget 1994 (Proposed Changes to the Unemployment Insurance Program: Backgrounder)* (Ottawa: Department of Finance and HRDC, 1994), 15.
102 HRDC, *Improving Social Security in Canada: Discussion Paper* (Hull: HRDC, 1994), 24.
103 Fifteen percent of claimants would be entitled to the increased rate of 60 percent: Minister of Finance, *Budget 1994,* 9.
104 *Budget Implementation Act, 1994,* S.C. 1994, c. 18.
105 New Brunswick, Departments of Advanced Education and Labour and Income Assistance, *NB Works* (Fredericton: Department of Advanced Education and Labour, 1992). For a program outline and review, see Joan McFarland and Robert Mullaly, "NB Works: Image vs. Reality," in Jane Pulkingham and Gordon Ternowetsky, eds., *Remaking Canadian Social Policy: Social Security in the Late 1990s* (Halifax: Fernwood Publishing, 1996), 202.
106 *Budget Implementation Act, 1994,* s. 27 adding paragraph 75(1)(c).
107 The same reasoning was used for work income supplements. See HRDC, *Improving Social Security in Canada,* 42.
108 On the British experience, see Nick Wikeley, "Training, Targetting, and Tidying Up: The Social Security Act – 1988," *Journal of Social Welfare Law* (1989): 277.
109 *Canada Assistance Plan,* S.C. 1966-67, c. 45.
110 In 1994, support for active measures out of general revenue was only $1.4 billion, whereas the UI fund paid out $1.9 billion. See HRDC, *From Unemployment Insurance to Employment Insurance,* 89.

Chapter 9: Onward to EI
1 HRDC, *Improving Social Security in Canada: Discussion Paper* (Hull: HRDC, 1994), 69.
2 See "Guiding Principles for Reform," in HRDC, *Improving Social Security,* 25.

3 The abandonment of universality in the family allowance program begun in the 1970s would be complete with the 1993 introduction of the Integrated Child Tax Benefit. See the *Family Allowances Act*, S.C. 1973-74, c. 44; *An Act to Amend the Income Tax Act, to Enact the Children's Special Allowances Act, to Amend Certain Other Acts in Consequence Thereof, and to Repeal the Family Allowances Act*, S.C. 1992, c. 48.

4 *Le Devoir* and Canadian Press, "Réforme des programmes sociaux, Chrétien ira de l'avant coûte que coûte," *Le Devoir* 21 April 1994: A-1, A-10.

5 HRDC, *Improving Social Security*, 43.

6 HRDC, *From Unemployment Insurance to Employment Insurance* (Improving Social Security in Canada series) (Hull: HRDC, 1994), 9.

7 HRDC, *Improving Social Security*, 18.

8 HRDC, *From Unemployment Insurance*, 16.

9 *Ibid.*, 44.

10 In this connection, see the article by James Struthers that locates and explains "employability" in its Canadian historical perspective: James Struthers, "The 30's: The 80's," *Canadian Forum* 64 (1984): 8.

11 See Bernard Normand, "Le projet québécois de l'employabilité et les organismes sans but lucratif: Enjeux et interpellations," in Lucie Lamarche, ed., *Emploi précaire et non-emploi: Droits recherchés*, Actes de la 5e Journée de droit social et du travail (Cowansville: Yvon Blais, 1994), 109.

12 HRDC, *Improving Social Security*, 49.

13 *Ibid.*

14 HRDC, *From Unemployment Insurance to Employment Insurance*, 61.

15 Statistics Canada, *Annual Unemployment Insurance Statistics 1995*, Table 6, 4; Table 13, 20.

16 Canadian Press, "Assurance-chômage: La somme des prestations tombe à son plus bas niveau depuis 1990," *Le Devoir* 30 November 1995: B3.

17 Statistics Canada, *Unemployment Insurance Statistics* 54, 12 (1995): 5.

18 See Gerard Docquier, Hugh Mackenzie, and Richard Shellington, *Victimizing the Unemployed: How U.I. Cuts Will Promote Poverty in Canada* (Ottawa: Canadian Centre for Policy Alternatives, 1989).

19 National Council of Welfare, *Another Look at Welfare Reform* (Ottawa: National Council of Welfare, 1997), 8.

20 Huguette Young, "819,000 personnes iront à l'aide sociale et 44,000 seront privées de l'assurance-chômage," *La Presse* 15 April 1994: A-10.

21 Pierre Fortin, "L'impact des lois sur l'assurance-chômage de 1990, 1994, et 1996 sur l'aide sociale du Québec," École des sciences de la gestion, UQAM, October 1997. See also Ministère de la sécurité du revenu (Quebec), *Un parcours vers l'insertion, la formation, et l'emploi* (green paper), 1996, 27.

22 Martin Browning, Stephen Jones, and Peter Kuhn, *Studies of the Interaction of UI and Welfare Using the COEP Dataset* (Ottawa: HRDC, 1995).

23 *Income Security Regulations*, D. 922-89, (1989) 121 G.O.Q. II 3304, s. 83. In 1996, this would be increased to $150. D. 202-96, (1996) 128 G.O.Q. II 1500, s. 5.

24 Bill C-111, *Employment Insurance Act*, 1st Session, 35th Parliament, 1994-95.

25 *Federal-Provincial Fiscal Arrangements Act*, R.S.C. (1985), c. F-8 and Amendments, Part V.

26 Minister of Finance, *Budget in Brief*, Ottawa, 27 February 1995, 13.

27 Adherence to these standards formed the subject of a major decision: *Finlay v. Canada (Minister of Finance)*, [1993] S.C.R. 1080. See Chapter 5, 77-78.

28 *Budget Implementation Act*, S.C. 1995, c. 17: s. 32 repealed the *Canada Assistance Plan*, and s. 50 to amend the *Federal-Provincial Fiscal Arrangements Act* upheld the ban on a minimum residence requirement.

29 HRDC, The Honourable Lloyd Axworthy, Minister of Human Resources Development, *The Human Resources Investment Fund: A Presentation to the Program Review Committee*, August 1995 (Secret). This paper was leaked to the opposition parties in Parliament.

30 *Ibid.*, 7.

31 In 1994, the cost of active measures to the CRF was only $1.4 billion, while the share borne by the UI account was $1.9 billion. HRDC, *From Unemployment Insurance to Employment Insurance*, 89.

32 Axworthy, *The Human Resources Investment Fund,* 13.
33 Bill C-12, *Employment Insurance Act,* 2nd Session, 35th Parliament, 1996.
34 *Employment Insurance Act,* S.C. 1996, c. 23.
35 HRDC, *A 21st Century Employment System for Canada* (Hull: HRDC, 1995), 2.
36 This study is limited to the features of the Employment Insurance Act most relevant for my purposes.
37 On annualization, see Employment and Immigration Canada, *Commission of Inquiry on Unemployment Insurance* (Forget Report) (Ottawa: Employment and Immigration Canada, 1986), 143.
38 On 31 December 2000, the entrance requirement for this type of benefit was reduced to 600 hours and the maximum length of parental benefits raised to thirty-five weeks. *Budget Implementation Act, 2000,* S.C. 2000, c. 14. Then, in March 2002, the cumulative number of weeks that could be claimed when benefits were paid as maternity, sickness, or parental benefits in one benefit period, then limited to fifty, was raised to sixty-five. *Budget Implementation Act, 2001,* S.C. 2002, c. 9.
39 Diane Gabrielle Tremblay, "L'évolution du chômage et de l'emploi au Québec," *Interventions économiques* 25 (1994): 54.
40 See Jean-Guy Ouellet, "Les dispositions pénales de la Loi sur l'assurance-emploi: La pénalisation du chômage," in Pierre Robert, ed., *La gestion sociale par le droit pénal,* Actes de la 8e Journée de droit social et du travail (Cowansville: Yvon Blais, 1998), 97.
41 See Ross Cranston, *Legal Foundations of the Welfare State* (London: Weidenfeld and Nicolson, 1985), 29-45, and Christophe Guitton, "Le chômage entre question sociale et question pénale en France au tournant du siècle," in M. Mansfield, R. Salais, and N. Whiteside, eds., *Aux sources du chômage 1880-1914* (Paris: Belin, 1994), 63.
42 For a full understanding of this compromise standard, see the tables in ss. 7(2) and 14(2) of the Employment Insurance Act.
43 *Employment Insurance Regulations,* SOR/96-332, (1996) 130 *Can. Gaz.* II 2192, s. 34. The regulations were amended in January 1999 with the amount of this supplement to reflect the parents' income and number of children. *Regulation to Amend the Employment Insurance Regulations,* SOR/99-290, (1999) 133 *Can. Gaz.* II 1840.
44 On the neoliberal thrust of this fiscalization of social policies, see Georges Campeau, "La fiscalisation, instrument de la reconfiguration néolibérale de la politique sociale canadienne," in Diane Demers, Georges Lebel, and Ginette Valois, eds., *La gestion du social par la fiscalité,* Actes de la 9ième Journée en droit social et du travail (Cowansville: Yvon Blais, 1999), 3.
45 *Canada (A.G.) v. Jenkins,* (1995) 123 D.L.R. (4th) 639 (FCA).
46 *Employment Insurance Act,* s. 65, 1.
47 Some expressions were shared with the Quebec Income Security Act that classified welfare recipients by their ability or willingness to participate in employability programs. Job-ready recipients classified as participants collected the highest benefits (R.S.Q., c. S-3.1.1, ss. 6-24).
48 *Employment Insurance Act,* s. 61(1).
49 *Ibid.,* s. 57(1)(b).
50 *Ibid.,* s. 57(1)(d.1).
51 Government of Canada, *News Release 97-28,* 21 April 1997. Since that time, the federal authorities have concluded the same type of agreement with all Canadian provinces except Ontario, <www.hrsdc.gc.ca/en/gateways/nav/top_nav/program/ei.shtml>.
52 *Canada-Quebec Labour Market Agreement in Principle,* 21 April 1997, s. 3.1.3(a).
53 *Employment Insurance Act,* ss. 25(2), 64.
54 HRDC, *From Unemployment Insurance to Employment Insurance,* 83.
55 See Chapter 8, 135-36.
56 *Employment Insurance Act,* s. 78.
57 In 1994, this figure was reckoned at $267.7 billion. Statistics Canada, *Unemployment Insurance Statistics* 54, 12 (1995): 27.
58 HRDC, *Improving Social Security,* 51.
59 See Chapter 5, 85ff.

60 *Employment Insurance Act*, s. 66.
61 Receiver General, *Public Accounts for Canada 1985* (Ottawa: Supply and Services Canada, 1985), 3-3.
62 Receiver General, *Public Accounts for Canada 1986* (Ottawa: Supply and Services Canada, 1986), 2-6.
63 HRDC, *Improving Social Security*, 50.
64 These forecasts were to be confirmed in spades, as shown in Table 2.
65 Canadian Press, "Massé admet candidement que le surplus de l'assurance-emploi sert à diminuer le déficit," *La Presse* 22 February 1997: B8.
66 Canadian Press, "Assurance-emploi: De moins en moins de prestataires," *La Presse* 31 October 1996: E2.
67 ILO, *Unemployment Insurance Schemes* (Geneva: ILO, 1955), 186-92.
68 Canadian Labour Market and Productivity Centre, *Report of the CLMPC Task Forces on the Labour Force Development Strategy* (Ottawa: Canadian Labour Market and Productivity Centre, 1990), 263.
69 See Chapter 4, 56ff.
70 See Canadian Labour Market and Productivity Centre, *Report of the CLMPC Task Forces*, 265.
71 See the *Income Security Act*, R.S.Q., c. S-3.1.1, ss. 22, 23, and 76.
72 On the matter of workfare or social action on unemployment, see the review by Guy Standing, "The Road to Workfare: Alternative to Welfare or Threat to Occupation?" *International Labour Review* 129 (1990): 677.
73 *Gionest v. UIC*, [1983] 1 F.C. 832 (FCA). See Chapter 7, 113-14.
74 *Caron v. Canada*, [1989] 1 F.C. 628, 642. See Chapter 7, 116-17.
75 René Morrissette, Garnett Picot, and Wendy Pyper, "Workers on the Move: Quits," *Perspectives on Labour and Income* (Statistics Canada) 4, 3 (1992): 9.
76 See Chapter 10, 167.
77 HRDC, *From Unemployment Insurance to Employment Insurance*, 116. See also *OECD Employment Outlook* (Paris: OECD, 1991), 229.
78 Nick Wikeley, "Unemployment Benefit, the State, and the Labour Market," *Journal of Law and Society* 16 (1989): 301.
79 Yves Vaillancourt and Benoît Lévesque, "Le social dans le Rapport Macdonald, les politiques sociales à l'heure du libre-échange," *Canadian Review of Social Policy* 14-15 (1986): 64.
80 The cost of temporary extended benefits could be funded in part from the general revenues of the federal government. But these programs virtually disappeared with the changes of the Reagan years. Christopher J. O'Leary and S.A. Wandner, eds., *Unemployment Insurance in the United States: Analysis of Policy Issues* (Kalamazoo, MI: W.E. Upjohn Institute for Employment Research, 1997), 257, 357.
81 *OECD Employment Outlook*, 129; *Federal Unemployment Tax Act*, 26 USCA, c. 23, s. 3301 et seq. and, e.g., *Unemployment Insurance Law*, Consol. Laws of N.Y., Book 30, s. 18, para 550 (1).
82 Emmanuel Nyahoho, "Éléments de comparaison des régimes d'assurance-chômage canadien et américain," *L'actualité économique, Revue d'analyse économique* 67, 2 (1991): 251.
83 The national average in 1994 was 36.1 percent. Marion Nichols and Isaac Shapiro, *Unemployment Insurance Protection in 1994* (Washington: Center of Budget and Policy Priorities, 1995), 1, 2, 7.
84 HRDC, *From Unemployment Insurance to Employment Insurance*, 100.
85 *Ibid.*, 104.
86 On the recent evolution of US case law on "voluntary unemployment," see Deborah Maranville, "Changing Economy, Changing Lives: Unemployment Insurance and the Contingent Workforce," *Public Interest Law Journal* 4 (1995): 291.
87 *Vermont Unemployment Compensation Law*, Annotated Vermont Statutes, c. 17, s. 1344.
88 See Chapter 6, 99ff.
89 Michel Bédard, *Chief Actuary's Report on Employment Insurance Contribution Rates for 1998* (Hull: HRDC, 1997), 17.
90 The cumulative surplus for the EI account was over $25 billion in 1999 (Table 2).
91 Axworthy, *The Human Resources*, 4.

92 See Chapter 3, 51ff.
93 *Hills* v. *A.G. Canada*, [1988] 1 S.C.R. 513, 535. See also *Martin Service Station* v. *Minister of National Revenue*, [1977] 2 S.C.R. 996, 1004; *Bliss* v. *A.G. Canada*, [1979] 1 S.C.R. 183, 186; *Canadian Pacific Ltd.* v. *A.G. Canada*, [1986] 1 S.C.R. 678, 680.
94 *Canadian Pacific Ltd.* v. *Gill*, [1973] S.C.R. 654.
95 *YMHA Jewish Community Centre of Winnipeg Inc.* v. *Brown*, [1989] 1 S.C.R. 1532, 1548.

Chapter 10: Case Law in the Neoliberal Riptide of the 1990s

1 Statistics Canada, *Unemployment Insurance Statistics, Annual Supplement 1995*, Table 4, 3.
2 Peter Kuhn, *Effects of Bill C-113 on UI Take-Up Rates* (Ottawa: HRDC, 1995), 7.
3 Statistics Canada, *UI Statistics*, Table 4, 3.
4 The number of labour disputes in Canada dropped significantly in the early 1990s, as seen in the following figures: 1987: 668; 1989: 627; 1991: 463; 1993: 381; 1995: 328. Canada, HRDC, Labour Branch, Workplace Information Directorate, *Chronological Perspective on Work Stoppages* <http://labour-travail.hrdc-drhc.gc.ca/doc/wid-dimt/>.
5 See *CEIC* v. *Roy*, [1986] 1 F.C. 193 (FCA). See also Chapter 7, 118.
6 See Chapter 7, 113-14.
7 *Pelletier* v. *CEIC*, unpublished decision of 1 April 1993 (FCA, A-109-92), (CUB 18287A).
8 *White* v. *R.*, [1994] 2 F.C. 233 (FCA), 241.
9 *A.G. Canada* v. *Bouillon*, (1996) 203 N.R. 224, 226 (CUB 23625).
10 See Chapter 7, 116-18.
11 *Canada (A.G.)* v. *Thomas et al.*, (FCA, A-39-98, unpublished decision of 3 December 1998) (CUB 39841).
12 *Caron* v. *Canada*, [1989] 1 F.C. 628 (FCA), and [1991] 1 S.C.R. 48. See Chapter 7, 116-18.
13 *Oakes-Pépin et al.* v. *CEIC et al.*, (1996) 207 N.R. 305 (1996) (FCA) (CUB 31276). The Supreme Court refused leave to appeal from the Federal Court of Appeal decision: *Oakes-Pépin* v. *CEIC* (F.C.A.) (Que.) 25647, 20.3.97 [1997] 1 S.C.R. (Tables), x.
14 *Dallaire et al.* v. *CEIC et al.*, (1996) 207 N.R. 240 (FCA), unpublished French version (FCA, A-825-95, 17 September 1996), 3. The Supreme Court refused leave to appeal from this decision: *Dallaire* v. *CEIC* (F.C.A.) (Que.) 25667, 24.4.97 [1997] 2 S.C.R., viii.
15 CUB 24965 and CUB 21276.
16 See Chapter 8, 136-37.
17 On the application of the "only reasonable solution" test, see CUB 21817, CUB 21818, CUB 22341, CUB 22347, CUB 23299, CUB 24365A, CUB 25483, CUB 26602, CUB 27363, CUB 27806, and CUB 28567.
18 *Bell* v. *A.G. of Canada*, [1996] 2 F.C. D-46 (FCA) 2.
19 *Canada (Attorney General)* v. *Jenkins* (1995) 123 D.L.R. (4th), 639 (FCA) (CUB 24074).
20 *Employment Insurance Act*, S.C. 1996, c. 23, s. 29(a).
21 *A.G. Canada* v. *Tremblay*, (1995) 172 N.R. 305, 306 (FCA).
22 *Canada (A.G.)* v. *Dietrich*, unpublished French version (CAF, A-640-93, 16 December 1994), 2 (CUB 23101).
23 *A.G. Canada* v. *Nolet*, unpublished decision of 19 March 1992 (FCA, A-517-91), 2.
24 *Canada (Attorney General)* v. *Tucker*, [1986] 2 F.C. 329 (FCA). See Chapter 7, 123-24.
25 See CUB 7007 and CUB 8112.
26 *Canada* v. *Brissette*, [1994] 1 F.C. 684 (FCA), 689.
27 See Chapter 7, 123-24.
28 *Canada (A.G.)* v. *Jewell*, (1995) 175 N.R. 350, 352 [1995] 1 F.C. F-43 (FCA, A-236-94, 24 October 1994, 3-4).
29 *A.G. Canada* v. *Eppel*, [1996] 1 F.C. F-21.
30 *Choinière* v. *CEIC*, unpublished decision of 28 May 1996 (FCA, A-471-95), 2.
31 *Meunier* v. *Canada*, (1996) 208 N.R. 377 (FCA).
32 *Canada (A.G.)* v. *Stolniuk*, (1994) 174 N.R. 229 (FCA).
33 However, Judge Joyal maintained that this practice of warning the claimant about restrictions on availability for work was not founded on a text but on the requirements of procedural fairness (CUB 17524), 3. See also CUB 22889.

34 *A.G. Canada v. Findenigg,* [1995] 1 F.C. 65 (FCA), 71-72.
35 See House of Commons, Standing Committee on Labour, Employment and Immigration Canada, 17 March 1987, 28:11, 28:13.
36 *Hamilton v. Canada (A.G.),* (1988) 91 N.R. 145; *A.G. Canada v. Poulin,* unpublished decision of 2 April 1992 (FCA, A-518-91) (CUB 19688).
37 *Canada (A.G.) v. Easson,* (1994) 167 N.R. 232. The decision in *Hamilton* centred on the commission's refusal to antedate a benefit claim. The Board of Referees had disallowed the claimant's appeal on the ground that he had not been available for work. The Federal Court of Appeal found that the jurisdiction of the Board of Referees should be limited to the commission's decision taken on appeal, namely the refusal to grant the application to antedate (*Hamilton v. Canada [A.G.],* [1988] 91 N.R. 145).
38 *Canada (A.G.) v. Dufour,* (1993) 168 N.R. 69; *A.G. Canada v. Eppel,* [1996] 1 F.C. F-21.
39 *Unemployment Insurance Act,* R.S.C. 1985, c. U-1, ss. 30(1) and (7).
40 *Archambault v. Canada (A.G.),* (1993) 166 N.R. 299.
41 *Canada (A.G.) v. Kolish,* (1994) 167 N.R. 107.
42 *Canada (A.G.) v. Phung,* (1994) 178 N.R. 8, and *A.G. Canada v. Ruppel,* [1996] 1 F.C. F-2 (FCA).
43 Paul Stuart Rapsey, "Contempt of Court – A New Definition: An Examination of Trends in Recent Federal Court of Appeal Jurisprudence under the Unemployment Insurance Act," *Windsor Yearbook of Access to Justice* 14 (1994): 326.
44 See the decisions in CUB 28736 (Judge Reed) and CUB 29211 (Judge Rouleau).
45 CUB 28736.
46 *Morin v. A.G. Canada,* (1996) 196 N.R. 309 (FCA), 318.
47 *Employment Insurance Act,* ss. 27(1) and 28(1).

Conclusion

1 *Jobseekers Act 1995,* 1995, c. 18.
2 Frank Field, MP, House of Commons, vol. 271, col. 783, 17 January 1996, quoted in Trevor Buck, "Jobseeker's Allowance: Policy Perspectives," *Journal of Social Security Law* 3 (1996): 149-54, note 28.
3 Quebec unions have launched suits, arguing the unconstitutionality of the provisions in the *Employment Insurance Act* that allow this use of EI premiums. In a decision of 5 November 2003, the Superior Court of that province rejected these arguments to find that employment benefits came under federal jurisdiction over employment insurance, including the way premium rates are set (section 66), which makes it possible to build up major surpluses. However, the judge held that the government cannot do what it wants with these surpluses: the Act requires that these amounts be used solely for the purposes stated. This decision is being appealed. *Syndicat national des employés de l'Aluminium d'Arvida Inc. et al. v. Canada (Attorney General)* and *Confédération des syndicats nationaux v. Attorney General of Canada,* Superior Court no. 150-05-001538-984, 500-05-048333-999; Quebec Court of Appeal no. 500-09-014014-039.
4 HRDC, *From Unemployment Insurance to Employment Insurance* (Improving Social Security in Canada series) (Hull: HRDC, 1994), 78.

Epilogue: Bill C-2, February 2001

1 Bill C-2, *Act to Amend the Employment Insurance Act and Employment Insurance Regulations (Fishing),* 1st Session, 37th Parliament, 2002, tabled in the House of Commons on 2 February 2001.
2 Bill C-44, *Act to Amend the Employment Insurance Act,* 2nd Session, 36th Parliament, 1999-2000.
3 *Act to Amend the Employment Insurance Act and Employment Insurance Regulations (Fishing),* S.C. 2001, c. 5.
4 Since 1978, the Unemployment Insurance Act had contained a provision for partial benefit repayment. When total income for the year exceeded the maximum insurable earnings by 150 percent, the person had to repay 30 percent of benefits or surplus income, whichever was the lesser, with the annual tax return. This "clawback" provision

was sharpened in the Employment Insurance Act to reduce the annual income based on which repayment was required to 125 percent of maximum insurable earnings, thus slashing the clawback threshold from $63,750 to $48,750. Moreover, the intensity rule still applied: the clawback threshold was then cut to maximum insurable earnings or $39,000, and the benefit repayment percentage was increased if the claimant had collected more than twenty weeks of benefits during the past five years. A claimant who had collected more than 120 weeks of benefits during this period might have to repay all of them. *Act to Amend the Unemployment Insurance Act, 1971,* S.C. 1978-79, c. 7, s. 14, enacting s. 142, and *Employment Insurance Act,* S.C. 1996, c. 23, s. 145.

5 See Chapter 6, 96-97, and Chapter 9, 155.
6 In 1981, the Gershberg Report recommended that, for the sake of fairness, the special entrance requirements be removed. Employment and Immigration Canada, *Unemployment Insurance in the 1980s* (Ottawa: Employment and Immigration Canada, 1981).
7 HRDC, *News Release 01-05,* 2 February 2001.
8 See Chapter 9, 158.
9 Statistics Canada, *Employment, Earnings, and Working Hours,* vol. 78, no. 6, 2000 (Catalogue no. 72-002-XPB), 20.
10 Statistics Canada, *Annual Estimates of Employment, Earnings, and Working Hours, 1985-1997,* 1998 (Catalogue no. 72F0002XDB), 48.
11 *Loi sur les accidents du travail et les maladies professionnelles,* R.S.Q., c. A-3.001, s. 66, *Règlement sur la table des indemnités de remplacement du revenu,* (2000) 132 G.O.Q. II 7040.
12 On 1 January 2001, the employee premium rate was cut from $2.40 to $2.25 per $100 of insurable earnings, and the employer rate was cut from $3.36 to $3.15, <www.hrsdc.gc.ca/en/cs/comm/news/2000/001201_e.shtml>.
13 *Employment Insurance Act,* s. 66; see Chapter 9, 154-57.
14 Although the estimated cumulative surplus in the fund for 2000 was $33.6 billion, the chief actuary estimated that a reserve of $10 billion to $15 billion would be enough to meet these objectives. Michel Bédard, *Report of the Chief Actuary on the Employment Insurance Contribution Rate for 2001* (Hull: HRDC, 2000), 2, 11. In 2001, the accumulated surplus was $40.1 billion; see Actuarial Services Insurance (Outlook for EI Premium Rates in 2002), 2, <www.rhdcc.gc.ca/en/ei/images/pr2002.pdf>.
15 In the absence of the annual and accumulated surplus in the account, the government's annual budget surplus would have been under $7.2 billion and its net deficit greater than $28.2 billion. *Report of the Auditor General of Canada of February 6, 2001* <http://www.oag-bvg.gc.ca/domino/reports.nsf/html/00menu_e.html>, para 34.55.
16 HRDC, *News Release 00-66,* 28 September 2000.
17 *Report of the Auditor General.*
18 Political party founded in 1990 that advocates Quebec sovereignty.
19 *House of Commons Debates,* 20 October 2000, 9324.
20 HRDC, *News Release 01-05,* 2 February 2001.
21 Minister of Finance, *News Release 2000-101,* 21 December 2000 <http://www.fin.gc.ca/news00/00-101e.html>.

Selected Bibliography

Baldwin, Peter. 1992. "Beveridge in the *longue durée.*" *International Social Security Review* 45.

Bauriedl, Ulrich. 1981. "Cent ans d'assurance sociale allemande." *International Social Security Review* 34.

Beaud, Michel, and Gilles Dostaler. 1993. *La pensée économique depuis Keynes: Historique et dictionnaire des principaux auteurs.* Paris: Seuil.

Bédard, Michel. 1997. *Chief Actuary's Report on Employment Insurance Contribution Rates for 1998.* Hull: HRDC.

–. 1999. *Chief Actuary's Report on Employment Insurance Contribution Rates for 2000.* Hull: HRDC.

–. 2000. *Chief Actuary's Report on Employment Insurance Contribution Rates for 2001.* Hull: HRDC.

Bellemare, Diane. 1981. *La sécurité du revenu au Canada: Une analyse économique de l'avènement de l'État-providence.* PhD dissertation, McGill University.

Bennett, Richard Bedford. *R.B. Bennett Papers.* Collection available in the National Archives of Canada, Ottawa.

Bernier, Jean, and Michel Martin. 1989. "L'impact de la réforme de l'assurance-chômage sur le programme d'aide sociale." Quebec City, Ministère de la Main-d'œuvre et de la Sécurité du revenu, Direction des programmes de sécurité du revenu, April, unpublished discussion paper.

Beveridge, William Henry. 1924. *Insurance for All and Everything.* London: Daily News.

–. 1930. *The Past and Present of Unemployment Insurance.* London: Oxford University Press.

–. 1930. *Unemployment: A Problem of Industry,* 2nd ed. New York: AMS Press.

–. 1944. *Full Employment in a Free Society.* London: Allen and Unwin.

–. 1955. *Power and Influence.* New York: Beechhurst.

–. *Beveridge Papers.* collection available in the BLEPS (British Library of Economic and Political Science), London.

–. "Memorandum on Scheme, Draft Head of Bill, Criticisms, and Amendments 1908-1909." Board of Trade, *Beveridge Papers* no. 37, A-1.

–. "Memoranda on Specific Aspects of Scheme 1907-1909." Board of Trade, *Beveridge Papers* no. 39, C-1.

–. "Memoranda on Specific Aspects of Scheme 1908-1909." Board of Trade, *Beveridge Papers* no. 39, C-11, Notes on Malingering (The President).

–. "Memoranda on Specific Aspects of Scheme 1907-1909." Board of Trade, *Beveridge Papers* no. 39, C-12.

–. "Memoranda on UI for Poor Law Commission 1907." Board of Trade, *Beveridge Papers* no. 41, D-3.

–. "Explanatory Memorandum on Unemployment Insurance," (National Insurance Act, 1911), Part II (second edition, 1913), *Beveridge Papers* no. 43.

Booth, Charles, ed. 1889-91. *Labour and Life of the People,* 3 vols. London: Williams and Norgate.

Braden, Michael A. 1993. "Changes to the Unemployment Insurance Act." *Business and the Law* 10, 9.

Brecher, I. 1957. *Monetary and Fiscal Thought and Policy in Canada, 1929-1939.* Toronto: University of Toronto Press.

Brière, Jean-Yves. 1994. "Le Big Bang de l'emploi ou la confrontation de la Loi sur les normes et des emplois atypiques." In *Emploi précaire et non-emploi: Droits recherchés,* edited by Lucie Lamarche, Actes de la 5e Journée de droit social et du travail. Cowansville: Yvon Blais.

Brown, K.D. 1971. *Labour and Unemployment 1900-1914.* Totowa, NJ: Rowman and Littlefield.

Brown, Lorne. 1987. *When Freedom Was Lost: The Unemployed, the Agitator, and the State.* Montreal: Black Rose Books.

Browning, Martin, Stephen Jones, and Peter Kuhn. 1995. *Studies of the Interaction of UI and Welfare Using the COEP Dataset.* Ottawa: HRDC.

Buck, Trevor. 1996. "Jobseeker's Allowance: Policy Perspectives." *Journal of Social Security Law* 3.

Burns, Eveline M. 1956. *Social Security and Public Policy.* New York: McGraw-Hill.

Calcoen, F., L. Eeckhoudt, and D. Greiner. 1988. "Unemployment Insurance, Social Protection, and Employment Policy: An International Comparison." *International Social Security Review* 2.

Campeau, Georges. 1999. "La fiscalisation, instrument de la reconfiguration néolibérale de la politique sociale canadienne." In *La gestion du social par la fiscalité,* Actes de la 9e Journée en droit social et du travail, edited by Diane Demers, Georges Lebel, and Ginette Valois. Cowansville: Yvon Blais.

Cane, Thomas Michael. 1971. *A Test Case for Canadian Federalism: The Unemployment Insurance Issue 1919-1940.* MA thesis, University of Western Ontario.

Carr, A.S.C., W.H. Stuart Gamett, and J.H. Taylor. 1912. *National Insurance,* 3rd ed. London: Macmillan.

Casebeer, Kenneth M. 1994. "Unemployment Insurance: American Social Wage, Labor Organization, and Legal Ideology." *Boston College Law Review* 35.

Castel, Robert. 1995. *Les métamorphoses de la question sociale: Une chronique du salariat.* Paris: Fayard.

Clark, R. 1985. "Towards the 'Just' Strike? Social Welfare Payments for Persons Affected by a Trade Dispute in the Republic of Ireland." *Modern Law Review* 48.

Claxton, Brooke. 1935. "Social Reform and the Constitution." *Canadian Journal of Economics and Political Science* 1.

Cohen, J.L. 1935. *The Canadian Unemployment Insurance Act: Its Relation to Social Security.* Toronto: Thomas Nelson and Sons.

Cohen, Marjorie. 1982. "Unemployment Insurance: The High Price of Equality." *Canadian Woman Studies* 3, 4.

Cohen, Neil, and Jennifer McKenna. 1987. "Forget's Moral Hazard." *Canadian Dimension* 21.

Cranston, Ross. 1985. *Legal Foundations of the Welfare State.* London: Weidenfeld and Nicolson.

Cousineau, Jean-Michel. 1988. "Le rapport Forget et l'économie politique de l'assurance-chômage." *Canadian Public Policy* 14.

Cuneo, Carl J. 1979. "State, Class and Reserve Labour: The Case of the 1941 Canadian Unemployment Insurance Act." *Canadian Review of Sociology and Anthropology* 16.

–. 1980. "State Mediation of Class Contradictions in Canadian Unemployment Insurance, 1930-1935." *Studies in Political Economy* 3.

Dingledine, Gary. 1981. *A Chronology of Response: The Evolution of Unemployment Insurance from 1940 to 1980.* Ottawa: Employment and Immigration Canada.

Docquier, Gerard, Hugh Mackenzie, and Richard Shellington. 1989. *Victimizing the Unemployed: How U.I. Cuts Will Promote Poverty in Canada.* Ottawa: Canadian Centre for Policy Alternatives.

Driedger, E.A. 1983. *Construction of Statutes.* Toronto: Butterworth.

Duchastel, Jules. 1979. "Chômage, politique sociale, et crise." *Cahiers du socialisme* 3.

Ephron, Susan H. 1986. "Redefining Neutrality: Alternative Interpretations of the Labour Dispute Disqualification in Unemployment Compensation." *Comparative Labor Law Journal* 8.

Ewald, François. 1986. *L'état providence*. Paris: Grasset.

Ewing, K.D. 1991. *The Right to Strike*. Oxford: Clarendon Press.

Fingard, Judith. 1974. "The Winter's Tale: The Seasonal Contours of Pre-Industrial Poverty in British North America, 1815-1860." *Canadian Historical Review* 65.

Finkel, Alvin. 1977. "Origins of the Welfare State in Canada." In *The Canadian State: Political Economy and Political Power*, edited by Leo Panitch. Toronto: University of Toronto Press.

–. 1979. *Business and Social Reform in the Thirties*. Toronto: James Lorimer.

Fortin, Pierre. 1997. *L'impact des lois sur l'assurance-chômage de 1990, 1994, et 1996 sur l'aide sociale du Québec*. Montreal, UQAM, École des sciences de la gestion, October.

Fraser, Derek. 1973. *The Evolution of the British Welfare State*. New York: Harper and Row.

Frémont, Jacques. 1982-83. "Assurance-chômage, maternité, et adoption: Les récentes modifications et leur validité." *Revue Juridique Thémis* 17.

Friedman, Milton and Rose. 1962. *Capitalism and Freedom*. Chicago: University of Chicago Press.

–. 1980. *Free to Choose*. New York: Harcourt Brace Jovanovich.

Fulla, G.A., ed. 1981. *A Catalogue of the Papers of William Henry Beveridge*. London: British Library of Economic and Political Science (BLEPS).

Garraty, J.A. 1978. *Unemployment in History: Economic Thought and Public Policy*. New York: Harper and Row.

Genest, Jean-Guy. 1996. *Godbout*. Quebec City: Septentrion.

Gennard, J. 1977. *Financing Strikers*. New York: Wiley.

Gilbert, Bentley B. 1965. "The British National Insurance Act of 1911 and the Commercial Insurance Lobby." *Journal of British Studies* 4.

–. 1966. *The Evolution of National Insurance in Great Britain*. London: Michael Joseph.

–. 1966. "Winston Churchill versus the Webbs: The Origins of British Unemployment Insurance." *American Historical Review* 71.

Girard, Claude. 1989. "Le Mouvement action-chômage de Montréal: 20 ans de pratique sociale." *Nouvelles pratiques sociales* 2.

Grauer, A.E. 1939. *Labour Legislation,* study prepared for the Royal Commission on Dominion-Provincial Relations. Ottawa: King's Printer.

–. 1939. "Public Assistance and Social Insurance." Appendix 6 to the *Report of the Royal Commission on Dominion-Provincial Relations*. Ottawa: King's Printer.

Guest, Dennis. 1985. *The Emergence of Social Security in Canada*. Vancouver: UBC Press.

Guitton, Christophe. 1994. "Le chômage entre question sociale et question pénale en France au tournant du siècle." In *Aux sources du chômage 1880-1914*, edited by M. Mansfield, R. Salais, and N. Whiteside. Paris: Belin.

Gurvitch, Georges. 1944. *La déclaration des droits sociaux*. New York: Maison Française.

Harris, José. 1972. *Unemployment and Politics*. Oxford: Clarendon Press.

Hasson, Reuben. 1981. "The Cruel War: Social Security Abuse in Canada." *Canadian Taxation* 3.

–. 1987. "Discipline and Punishment in the Law of Unemployment Insurance: A Critical View of Disqualification and Disentitlement." *Osgoode Hall Law Journal* 25.

Heclo, Hugh. 1974. *Modern Social Politics in Britain and Sweden*. New Haven and London: Yale University Press.

Hennock, E.P. 1987. *British Social Reform and German Precedents: The Case of Social Insurance 1880-1914*. Oxford: Clarendon Press.

Hickling, M.A. 1974. *Labour Disputes and Unemployment Insurance Benefits in Canada and England*. Don Mills: CCH.

Hum, Derek P.J. 1981. *Unemployment Insurance and Work Effort: Issues, Evidence, and Policy Directions*. Toronto: Ontario Economic Council.

Irving, Allan. 1989. "'The Master Principle of Administering Relief': Jeremy Bentham, Sir Francis Bond Head, and the Establishment of the Principle of Less Eligibility in Upper Canada." *Canadian Review of Social Policy* 23.

Issalys, Pierre. 1991. "L'harmonisation du droit dans le système canadien et québécois de sécurité sociale." *Cahiers de droit* 32.

–. 1994. "Le recours au droit comparé en droit social canadien et québécois," *Bulletin de droit comparé du travail et de la sécurité sociale* 1.

Issalys, Pierre, and Gaylord Watkins. 1977. *Unemployment Insurance Benefits: A Study of Administrative Procedures in the Unemployment Insurance Commission.* Ottawa: Law Reform Commission of Canada.

–. 1979. *The Pension Appeals Board: A Study of Administrative Procedures in the Area of Social Security.* Ottawa: Law Reform Commission of Canada.

Jay, R. 1894. "L'assurance obligatoire contre le chômage dans le canton de Saint-Gall." *Revue politique et parlementaire* 1.

Jennings, W. Ivor. 1926. "Poor Relief in Industrial Disputes." *Law Quarterly Review* 46.

Johnson, Andrew F. 1981. "A Minister as an Agent of Policy Change: The Case of Unemployment Insurance in the 70s." *Canadian Public Administration* 24.

Kelly, Laurence A. 1967. *Unemployment Insurance in Canada.* PhD dissertation, Queen's University.

Kerr, Kevin. 1982. *Canada's Recent Unemployment Experience.* Ottawa: Library of Parliament, Research Branch.

–. 2001. *Summary and Analysis of Bill C-2.* Ottawa: Library of Parliament, Research Branch, February 5. <http://www.parl.gc.ca/commons>.

Kesselman, Jonathan R. 1983. *Financing Canadian Unemployment Insurance.* Toronto: Canadian Tax Foundation.

Keynes, John Maynard. 1936. *The General Theory of Employment, Interest and Money.* London: Macmillan.

Keyssar, Alexander. 1986. *Out of Work: The First Century of Unemployment in Massachusetts.* Cambridge and New York: Cambridge University Press.

Kilcoyne, John R. 1989. "Developments in Employment Law: the 1987-1988 Term." *Supreme Court Law Review* 11.

King, William Lyon Mackenzie. 1918. *Industry and Humanity.* New York: Houghton Mifflin.

Kuhn, Peter. 1995. "Effects of Bill C-113 on UI Take-Up Rates." Ottawa: HRDC.

Lamarche, Lucie. 1994. "Le droit au travail et à la formation: Les enjeux et les doutes du droit international." In *Emploi précaire et non-emploi: Droits recherchés,* edited by Lucie Lamarche, Actes de la 5e Journée de droit social et du travail. Cowansville: Yvon Blais.

Langlois, Richard. 1987. "Le rapport Forget et l'assurance-chômage: CAP sur le workfare." *Canadian Review of Social Policy* 18.

Lawton, A. 1969. "Relief Administration in Saskatoon during the Depression." *Saskatchewan History* 22.

Leacy, F.H., ed. 1983. *Historical Statistics of Canada,* 2nd ed. Ottawa: Statistics Canada.

Ledoux, Simon. 1991. *L'influence du droit constitutionnel dans l'émergence et l'évolution du droit aux prestations de maternité, d'adoption, et parentales au sein de la Loi sur l'assurance-chômage.* MA thesis, Université de Montréal.

Lévesque, Andrée. 1984. *Virage à gauche interdit. Les communistes, les socialistes et leurs ennemis au Québec, 1929-1939.* Montreal: Boréal.

Lévesque, Jean-Marc. 1989. "Unemployment and Unemployment Insurance: A Tale of Two Sources." *Perspectives on Labour and Income* (Statistics Canada) 1, 3.

Lin, Zhengxi. 1998. "Employment Insurance in Canada: Policy Changes." *Perspectives on Labour and Income* (Statistics Canada) 10, 2.

Lippel, Katherine. 1986. *Le droit des accidentés du travail à une indemnité: Une analyse historique et critique.* Montreal: Thémis.

Lipton, Charles. 1973. The Trade Union Movement of Canada, 1827-1959. Toronto: NC Press.

Lopez, Eduard A. 1987. "Constitutional Background to the Social Security Act of 1935." *Social Security Bulletin* 50, 1.

Luelles, Didier. 1986. *Droit des assurances, aspects contractuels,* 2nd ed. Montreal: Thémis.

Macklem, Patrick. 1992. "Developments in Employment Law: the 1990-1991 Term." *Supreme Court Law Review* 2.

Maranville, Deborah. 1995. "Changing Economy, Changing Lives: Unemployment Insurance and the Contingent Workforce." *Public Interest Law Journal* 4.

Marsh, Leonard C. 1943. *Report on Social Security for Canada*. Ottawa: King's Printer.

Masters. D.C. 1950. *The Winnipeg General Strike*. Toronto: University of Toronto Press.

Maurette, F. 1931. "L'assurance-chômage, prétendue cause d'un chômage permanent." *International Labour Review* 24, 6.

McConnell, W.H. 1968. "The Judicial Review of Prime Minister Bennett's New Deal." *Osgoode Hall Law Journal* 6.

–. 1971. "Some Comparisons of the Roosevelt and Bennett New Deals." *Osgoode Hall Law Journal* 9.

McFarland, Joan, and Robert Mullaly. 1996. "NB Works: Image vs. Reality." In *Remaking Canadian Social Policy: Social Security in the Late 1990s*, edited by Jane Pulkingham and Gordon Ternowetsky. Halifax: Fernwood Publishing.

Méda, Dominique. 1995. *Le Travail, une valeur on voie de disparition*. Paris: Aubier.

Mérrien, François-Xavier. 1990. "Le développement des États-providence en Europe." *Revue française des affaires sociales* 44.

Minville, Esdras. 1939. "Labour Legislation and Social Services in the Province of Quebec." Appendix 5 to the *Report of the Royal Commission on Dominion-Provincial Relations*. Ottawa: King's Printer.

Morrissette, René, Garnett Picot, and Wendy Pyper. 1992. "Workers on the Move: Quits." *Perspectives on Labour and Income* (Statistics Canada) 4, 3.

Morton, W.H. 1967. *The Progressive Party in Canada*. Toronto: University of Toronto Press.

Neatby, H. Blair. 1972. *Politics of Chaos: Canada in the Thirties*. Toronto: Macmillan.

Nelson, Daniel. 1969. *Unemployment Insurance: The American Experience 1915-1935*. Madison: University of Wisconsin Press.

Netter, Francis. 1959. *La Sécurité sociale et ses principes*. Paris: Sirey.

Nichols, Marion, and Isaac Shapiro. 1995. *Unemployment Insurance Protection in 1994*. Washington: Center of Budget and Policy Priorities.

Normand, Bernard. 1994. "Le projet québécois de l'employabilité et les organismes sans but lucratif: Enjeux et interpellations." In *Emploi précaire et non-emploi: Droits recherchés*, edited by Lucie Lamarche, Actes de la 5e Journée de droit social et du travail. Cowansville: Yvon Blais.

Nyahoho, Emmanuel. 1991. "Éléments de comparaison des régimes d'assurance-chômage canadien et américain." *L'actualité économique, Revue d'analyse économique* 67, 2.

Ogus, Anthony I. 1979. "Conditions in the Formation and Development of Social Insurance: Legal Development and Legal History." In *Bedingungen für die Entstehung und Entwicklung von Sozialversicherung*, edited by Hans F. Zacher. Berlin: Duncker & Humbolt.

–. 1982. "Great Britain." In *The Evolution of Social Insurance, 1881-1981*, edited by P.A. Köhler, H.F. Zacher, and P.J. Hesse. London: F. Pinter.

–, ed. 1995. E.M Barendt, and N.J. Wikeley. *The Law of Social Security*, 4th ed. London: Butterworth.

Ouellet, Jean-Guy. 1998. "Les dispositions pénales de la Loi sur l'assurance-emploi: La pénalisation du chômage." In *La gestion sociale par le droit pénal*, edited by Pierre Robert, Actes de la 8e Journée de droit social et du travail. Cowansville: Yvon Blais.

Pal, Leslie A. 1983. "The Fall and Rise of Developmental Uses of UI Funds," *Canadian Public Policy* 9.

–. 1985. "The Finance View: The Case of Unemployment Insurance 1970-1978," *Canadian Tax Journal* 33.

–. 1985. "Maternity Benefits and U.I.: A Question of Policy Design." *Canadian Public Policy* 11.

–. 1988. "Sense and Sensibility: Comments on Forget." *Canadian Public Policy* 14.

–. 1988. *State, Class, and Bureaucracy: Canadian Unemployment Insurance and Public Policy*. Montreal and Kingston: McGill-Queen's University Press.

Pal, Leslie A., and F.L. Morton. 1986. "*Bliss* v. *A.G. Canada*: From Legal Defeat to Political Victory." *Osgoode Hall Law Journal* 24.

Pelletier, Michel, and Yves Vaillancourt. 1978. *Les Politiques sociales et les travailleurs, cahier II: Les années 30*. Montreal: self-published.

Pennings, F. 1990. *Benefits of Doubt: A Comparative Study of the Legal Aspects of Employment and Unemployment Schemes in Great Britain, Germany, France, and the Netherlands.* Boston and Deventer: Kluwer Law and Taxation Publishers.

Perrin, Guy. 1983. "L'assurance sociale – ses particularités – son rôle dans le passé, le présent et l'avenir." In *Beiträge zu Geschichte und aktueller Situation der Sozialversicherung,* edited by P.A. Köhler and H.F. Zacher. Berlin: Duncker & Humbolt.

Pic, P. 1909. *Traité de législation industrielle: Les lois ouvrières,* 3rd ed. Paris: Rousseau.

Pinker, Robert. 1971. *Social Theory and Social Policy.* London: Heinemann.

Piven, Frances Fox, and Richard A. Cloward. 1993. *Regulating the Poor: The Functions of Public Welfare,* 2nd ed. New York: Vintage Books.

Polanyi, Karl. 2001 [1944]. *The Great Transformation: The Political and Economic Origins of Our Time.* Boston: Beacon Press.

Porter, Ann. 1993. "Women and Income Security in the Postwar Period: The Case of Unemployment Insurance, 1945-1962." *Labour* 31.

Potter, D.F. 1976. "Unemployment Insurance: Policies and Principles of Disqualification and Disentitlement for Benefits." *Dalhousie Law Journal* 3.

Quadagno, J.S. 1984. "Welfare Capitalism and the Social Security Act of 1935." *American Sociological Review* 49.

Rankin, Murray, and Kip Wiese. 1984. "Unemployment Insurance: A Policy Dilemma." *Queen's Law Journal* 10.

Rapsey, Paul Stuart. 1994. "Contempt of Court – A New Definition: An Examination of Trends in Recent Federal Court of Appeal Jurisprudence under the Unemployment Insurance Act." *Windsor Yearbook of Access to Justice* 14.

Richter, L., W.J. Couper, and B.M. Stewart. 1935. "The Employment and Social Insurance Bill." *Canadian Journal of Economics and Political Science* 1.

Rimlinger, Gaston V. 1982. "The Emergence of Social Insurance: European Experience before 1914." In *The Evolution of Social Insurance, 1881-1981,* edited by P.A. Köhler et al. London: F. Pinter.

Rosanvallon, Pierre. 1981. *La Crise de l'état-providence.* Paris: Seuil.

Rueff, J. 1931. "L'assurance-chômage, cause du chômage permanent." *Revue d'économie politique* 45.

St-Aubin, Bernard. 1982. *King et son époque.* Montreal: La Presse.

Schlesinger, A.M. 1957. *The Coming of the New Deal,* vol. 2 of *The Age of Roosevelt.* New York: Houghton Mifflin.

Schloss, David F. 1909. *Insurance against Unemployment.* London: P.S. King and Son.

Scott, F.R. 1937. "The Privy Council and Mr. Bennett's New Deal." *Canadian Journal of Economics and Political Science* 3.

Smits, J. (rapporteur). 1986. "Le concept de droits acquis en matière de sécurité sociale face à l'évolution de la situation économique." Report VI, International Social Security Association 1986 General Meeting, Montreal.

Southall, Humphrey. 1995. "Neither State nor Market: Early Welfare Benefits in Britain." *Genèses* 18.

Standing, Guy. 1990. "The Road to Workfare: Alternative to Welfare or Threat to Occupation." *International Labour Review* 129.

Stewart, Bryce M. 1921. "Canadian Opinion on Unemployment Insurance." *Social Welfare* 3.

Stoffman, Daniel. 1984. "The Real UI Bill." *Canadian Business* 57, 3.

Stoljar, Samuel. 1984. *An Analysis of Rights.* New York: St. Martin's Press.

Struthers, James. 1983. *No Fault of Their Own: Unemployment and the Canadian Welfare State: 1914-1941.* Toronto: University of Toronto Press.

–. 1984. "The 30's: The 80's." *Canadian Forum* 64.

Tillyard, F. 1949. *Unemployment Insurance in Great Britain 1911-48.* Leigh-on-Sea: Thames Bank Publishing.

Topalov, Christian. 1990. *Indemnisation du chômage et construction de la catégorie de chômeur: Étude comparative France, Grande Bretagne, États-Unis.* Paris: Ministère des Affaires sociales et de l'Emploi.

Topalov, Christian. 1994. *La naissance du chômeur 1880-1910.* Paris: Albin Michel.

Tremblay, Diane Gabrielle. 1994. "L'évolution du chômage et de l'emploi au Québec." *Interventions économiques* 25.

Vaillancourt, Yves. 1988. *L'évolution des politiques sociales au Québec: 1940-1960*. Montreal: Presses de l'Université de Montréal.

Vaillancourt, Yves, and Benoît Lévesque. 1986. "Le social dans le Rapport Macdonald – Les politiques sociales à l'heure du libre-échange." *Canadian Review of Social Policy* 14-15.

Varlez, Louis. 1903. *Les formes nouvelles de l'assurance contre le chômage*. Paris: Rousseau.

Wallace, Elizabeth. 1950. "The Origins of the Social Welfare State in Canada, 1867-1914." *Canadian Journal of Economics and Political Science* 16.

Watson, A.D. 1948. *The Principles Which Should Govern the Structure and Provisions of a Scheme of Unemployment Insurance*. Ottawa: Unemployment Insurance Commission.

Webb, Beatrice. 1948. *Our Partnership*. London: Longmans, Green.

Whiteside, Noel. 1994. "Définir le chômage: Traditions syndicales et politique nationale en Grande-Bretagne avant la Première Guerre Mondiale." In *Aux sources du chômage, 1880-1914*, edited by M. Mansfield, R. Salais, and N. Whiteside. Paris: Belin.

Wiggins, Cindy. 1996. "Dismantling Unemployment Insurance: The Changes, the Impacts, the Reasons." *Canadian Review of Social Policy* 37.

Wikeley, Nick. 1989. "Training, Targetting, and Tidying Up: The Social Security Act – 1988." *Journal of Social Welfare Law*.

–. 1989. "Unemployment Benefit, the State, and the Labour Market." *Journal of Law and Society* 16.

Wolfenden, Hugh H. 1932. *The Real Meaning of Social Insurance: Its Present Status and Tendencies*. Toronto: Macmillan.

Yellowitz, I. 1968. "The Origins of Unemployment Reform in the United States." *Labor History* 9.

Zacher, Hans F., and Francis Kessler. 1990. "Rôle respectif du service public et de l'initiative privée dans la politique de sécurité sociale." *Revue internationale de droit comparé* 42.

Zöllner, Detlev. 1982. "The Federal Republic of Germany." In *The Evolution of Social Insurance, 1881-1981*, edited by P.A. Köhler et al. London: F. Pinter.

Jurisprudence

Abrahams v. *Canada (A.G.)*, [1983] 1 S.C.R. 2.

A.G. Canada v. *Eppel*, [1996] 1 F.C. F-21.

A.G. Canada v. *Findenigg*, [1984] 1 F.C. 65 (FCA).

A.G. Canada v. *Lalonde*, [1983] 2 F.C. 957 (FCA).

A.G. Canada v. *Nolet*, unpublished decision of 19 March 1992 (FCA, A-517-91).

A.G. Canada v. *Tremblay* (1994) 172 N.R. 305 (FCA).

Archambault v. *Canada (A.G.)*, [1993] 166 N.R. 299 (FCA).

Attorney General of Canada v. *Moura*, [1982] 2 F.C. 93 (FCA).

Bliss v. *A.G. of Canada*, [1979] 1 S.C.R. 183.

Canada (A.G.) v. *Dietrich* (1994) 178 N.R. 375 (FCA).

Canada (A.G.) v. *Easson* (1994) 167 N.R. 232 (FCA).

Canada (A.G.) v. *Jewell* (1994) 175 N.R. 350 (FCA); [1995] 1 F.C. F-43 (FCA).

Canada (A.G.) v. *Kolish* (1994) 167 N.R. 107 (FCA).

Canada (A.G.) v. *Stolniuk* (1994) 174 N.R. 229 (FCA).

Canada (A.G.) v. *Thomas et al.*, unpublished decision of 3 December 1998 (FCA, A-39-98).

Canada (Attorney General) v. *Jenkins*, (1995) 123 D.L.R. (4th), 639 (FCA).

Canada (Attorney General) v. *Tucker*, [1986] 2 F.C. 329 (FCA).

Canada (Attorney General) v. *Valois*, [1986] 2 S.C.R. 439.

Canada v. *Brissette*, [1994] 1 F.C. 684 (FCA).

Caron v. *Canada*, [1989] 1 F.C. 628 (FCA) and [1991] 1 S.C.R. 48.

Choinière v. *CEIC*, unpublished decision of 28 May 1996 (FCA, A-471-95).

Dallaire et al. v. *CEIC* (1996) 215 N.R. 240 (FCA).

Gionest v. *UIC*, [1983] 1 F.C. 832 (FCA).

Hamilton v. *Canada (A.G.)* (1988) 91 N.R. 145 (FCA).

Hills v. *A.G. Canada*, [1988] 1 S.C.R. 513.

Imbeault v. *UIC*, [1984] 1 F.C. 1217; (1984) 68 N.R. 74 (FCA).

Joseph v. *CEIC*, [1986] 2 F.C. F-10 (FCA).

McDonald v. *CEIC* (1991) 131 N.R. 389 (FCA).

Martin Service Station v. *Minister of National Revenue*, [1977] 2 S.C.R. 996.

Meunier v. *Canada*, [1997] 1 F.C. F-30 (FCA).

Morin v. *A.G. Canada* (1996) 196 N.R. 309 (FCA).

Morrison v. *Canada Employment and Immigration Commission*, [1990] 2 F.C. 57 (FCA).

Oakes-Pépin et al. v. *CEIC* (1996) 207 N.R. 305 (FCA).

Ouellet v. *UIC*, unpublished decision of 20 November 1984 (FCA, A-257-84).

Pelletier v. *CEIC*, unpublished decision of 1 April 1993 (FCA, A-102-92), (CUB 18287A).

R. v. *Scheer*, [1974] S.C.R. 1046.

Schachter v. *Canada*, [1990] 2 F.C. 129 (FCA) and [1992] 2 S.C.R. 679.

Tanguay v. *UIC* (1985) 68 N.R. 154 (FCA).

Tétreault-Gadoury v. *Canada*, [1989] 2 F.C. 245 (FCA) and [1991] 2 S.C.R. 22.

Index

Note: t indicates a table

Act Respecting Income Security (Quebec), 152-53
active measures: and assistance for the self-employed, 136, 206n46; and employability measures, 153, 162; as employment benefits, 157; and employment insurance system, 95, 148; funding for, 154, 166, 209n110; and job creation, 149; and labour market policies, 199n16, 205n9; as mandatory, 151; and Quebec, 158; and the Senate, 134; and unemployment insurance system hijack, 146, 159, 161, 165, 180; and vocational training, 127-28, 130
actuarial ideology, 69-71, 158, 171-72; Bill C-21, 131; and the Employment Insurance Act, 156; and the Gill Report, 78-79, 80, 84-85; and individual responsibility, 70-71; moral hazard, 25, 71; and neoliberalism, 93, 158; privatizing view of unemployment, 71; and vocational training, 129; and voluntary unemployment, 80, 84-85
actuarial logic: and 1970 white paper, 84; and Canadian unemployment insurance scheme, 45, 54, 69-71, 79; and concept of social insurance, x; and disentitlement, 163; and Forget Report, 105, 106; and Gill Report, 78, 80; and individual responsibility, 149; and jurisprudence, 126; and just cause, 122; and marginal workers, 177; and moral risk, 101; and neoliberalism, 93; public and private insurance, 71-72; and qualification for insurance, 24; and rationale for insurance, 7; and

responsibilities of the jobless, 129; and self-financing system, 106; and state involvement in unemployment insurance, 10, 179; and variable entrance requirement, 97; and voluntary leaving, 108; and voluntary unemployment, 25, 98, 139
administrative tribunals: and constitutional arguments, 112; and disentitlement for nonavailability, 126; and disqualification, 120, 141; and just cause to quit, 122; legal challenge mechanism of, 24; limits to role of, 176-77; new criterion of the "only reasonable solution," 170-74; and right to benefit, 27; and work stoppage, 116. *See also* Board of Referees; Canada Employment Insurance Commission (CEIC)
adoption benefits, 99, 106-7, 112
Adult Occupational Training Act, 1967, 82
Advisory Council on Adjustments (the de Grandpré Report). *See* de Grandpré Report
A.G. v. Guardians of the Poor of Merthyr Tydfil Union, 100
Alberta, 59, 158, 201n6
Amalgamated Society of Engineers, 14
American Association for Labor Legislation (AALL), 45
American Communist Party, 46
American Federation of Labor, 45
Amsterdam (Netherlands), 16
annualization, 104-7, 155
Asquith, Herbert Henry, 19
Atkin, Lord, 53

Atlantic provinces, 94, 101, 103, 150, 192n101
Australia, 41
availability for work: and disentitlement, 88, 125; lack of information about, 126, 174, 214n37; and laws affecting workforce, 2; obligations of, 27, 65, 107; principles of, 204n122; women and, 77, 81, 87
Axworthy, Lloyd, 97, 146, 148, 151, 158, 162

Basel (Switzerland), 15
Beaulé, Pierre, 37
Bédard, Michel, 133*t*
Belgium, 15, 186n36
benefit disentitlement: and availability for work, 126, 174; and Canada Employment Insurance Commission, 175; due to labour disputes, 100, 106, 108, 116, 137-38, 169-70; and exceptional and temporary means, 118; exemption from, 115; of the jobless, 114, 168; and misconduct, 144-45; partial system of, 138-39; as penalty, 88; and refusal of suitable employment, 125; and self-employed workers, 206n46; and work stoppage, 113, 119, 165
benefit entitlement: and actuarial process, 10; and Canadian unemployment insurance scheme, 63, 65, 72, 75; and disqualification, 145, 167; and eligibility, vii, 49, 51, 62, 68, 95, 157; and entrance requirements, 144, 206n39, 211n38; and liberalization of benefit access, 86; and Macdonald Report, 102; and payment of premiums, xi, 12, 25, 76, 85, 166; and right to benefit, 14, 161; and voluntary leaving, x, 99; and voluntary unemployment, 24; and work stoppage, 118
Bennett, R.B., 31, 38-40, 42-45, 49, 51, 55, 57, 70, 190n34
Bennett, Roy F., 103
Bern (Switzerland), 15
Beveridge, William Henry, 9, 13, 17, 20-21, 24, 32, 34, 68, 191n53
Bill 142 (Quebec), 170
Bill C-2, *Act to Amend the Employment Insurance Act and Employment Insurance Regulations (Fishing)*, xii, 182
Bill C-14, *An Act to Amend the Unemployment Insurance Act, 1971*, 96-97
Bill C-21, *An Act to Amend the Unemployment Insurance Act and the Employment and Immigration Department and Commission Act*, 120, 127, 131, 134-35, 207n53

Bill C-27, *Employment and Immigration Reorganization Act*, 94-95
Bill C-69, *An Act to Amend the Unemployment Insurance Act, 1971*, 94
Bill C-105, *Government Expenditures Restraint Act, 1993*, 139-41
Bill C-111, *Employment Insurance Act*, 156
Bill C-113, *Government Expenditures Restraint Act*, 139, 141, 208n84
Bill C-125, *Act to Amend the Unemployment Insurance Act, 1971 (no. 2)*, 89, 94
bipartite funding, 186n36
Bismarck, Otto von, 4, 16, 38, 41
Bliss, Stella, 111
Bloc Québécois, 184
Board of Referees: appeals to, 108, 110*t*, 167, 201n6; and availability, 174, 214n37; and Canada Employment Insurance Commission, 158, 170, 175; and decisions of umpires, 109, 111, 123, 168*t*, 172; discretionary power of, 176-77; and disentitlement, 169; and extenuating circumstances, 120; and harassment, 141; and labour disputes, 203n75; and length of disqualification, 119, 143; and misconduct, 136, 173; and right of appeal, 96; and voluntary leaving, 121, 144-45; and work stoppage, 116
Board of Trade (UK), 14, 16, 19-20, 27, 30, 119
bona fide hiring, 88, 118, 138, 201n23, 203n68, 207n65
Borden, Robert, 33-35, 191n51
Bouchard, Benoît, 107
Bourassa, Henri, 60
Bourbeau, André, 131
British Columbia, 39, 43
British North America Act (BNA Act), 1867, 52, 61, 166, 180
Buck, Tim, 44
Budget Implementation Act, 210n28
Bulgaria, 29
Bush, George, 164

California (US), 181
Canada, unemployment insurance/employment insurance system: and British unemployment insurance legislation, 50, 62; cancellation of federal contribution, 131, 135, 147; and capitalist system, 43; counterreforms of 1990s, 148, 152-53; and creation of employment benefits, 154; development of unemployment insurance scheme, 30-31, 36, 92-93; as dominion of the British empire, 35, 52; federal

jurisdiction, 57, 59-61, 67, 89, 96-97, 183-84, 198n76; and financial crisis in the system, 79; and maternity benefit plan, 87; and neoliberalism, 100, 107, 159; provincial jurisdiction, 39, 53, 55, 104, 158, 190n37, 197n76; and provincial welfare budgets, 156; and social security system, 99-100, 103, 146, 148; and state responsibility for unemployment, 33, 56, 77, 84, 102, 126, 160; and tripartite funding formula, 66; and vocational training, 130; and war on poverty, 82-83

Canada Assistance Plan (CAP), 77, 146, 153, 157-58, 210n28

Canada Employment Insurance Commission (CEIC): and Board of Referees appeals, 109; discretionary power, 142, 175-76; and disentitlement, 116, 169, 174; and employment benefits, 158; and job-search parameters, 126; and jurisprudence, 117, 121, 123-24, 173; and part-time work, 171; and premium rate, 183; responsibility for labour market, 96; and resumption of operations, 138, 141; and right to appeal, 136; and variable entrance requirement, 135; and vocational training, 130; and voluntary leaving, 107, 142-43, 144-45, 176

Canada Health and Social Transfer (CHST), 153, 158

Canada Life Insurance Company, 78

Canada Pension Plan, 86, 166

Canada Temperance Act, 1878, 54

Canada-US Free Trade Agreement, 101, 107, 127, 163-64. *See also* free trade; North American Free Trade Agreement (NAFTA)

Canadian Bank of Commerce, 41

Canadian Bill of Rights, 112, 143, 198n77, 209n95

Canadian Chamber of Commerce, 61, 179

Canadian Charter of Rights and Freedoms, 112, 206n41

Canadian Constitution, 130

Canadian Council on Social Development, 94

Canadian federalism, 35, 55, 83, 102

Canadian Federation of Independent Businesses, 100

Canadian Forces, 133*t*

Canadian Human Rights Act, 207n53

Canadian Labour Congress, 131

Canadian Labour Force Development Board (CLFDB), 139-40, 161, 207n70

Canadian Labour Force Development Strategy, 130

Canadian Life Underwriters Association, 70

Canadian Manufacturers' Association, 41

capitalism, 1-7, 38, 43-44, 181

Cassidy, Harry, 57

casual employment. *See* nonstandard employment

Cattanach, Judge, 123, 173

Charpentier, Alfred, 64

Charte des droits et libertés de la personne (Quebec), 143

Chicago School, 91

Chrétien, Jean, 141, 144, 148-49, 154, 182

Churchill, Winston, 19-20, 22-25, 119, 178

civil liability, 5-7, 10-12

civil rights, 35, 53, 198

Clark, Joe, 97

Clark, W.C., 59

Cohen, Lawrence Jacob, 68-69, 71

collective bargaining, 6

collective responsibility, vii, 11, 64, 149, 181

commercial insurance, x, xi, 8-10, 23, 54-55, 68, 70, 165-66

Commission of Inquiry on Unemployment Insurance (Canada). *See* Forget Commission

Committee of Inquiry into the Unemployment Insurance Act (Canada), 78

Communist Party of Canada, 38-40, 43-44, 58, 69. *See also* American Communist Party

Confédération des Travailleurs Catholiques du Canada (CTCC), 37, 40, 60, 64

Congress (US), 48

conjunctural unemployment, 32

Conseil du Patronat du Québec (CPQ), 134

Conservative Party (UK), 28

Conservative Party of Canada, 38, 78, 97, 127, 130-31, 134-35, 138-42, 144-45, 191n51

Consolidated Revenue and Audit Act, 1931, 66

Consolidated Revenue Fund (CRF), 66, 136, 157, 210n31

Constitution Act, 1982, 112

contributory system: and basic eligibility, 51; and claimant dependency, 128; compulsory, 10, 21-22, 46-47, 52, 66, 70, 186n36; and individual responsibility, 12; and maximum annual earnings, 155; and payment of premiums, xi, 46, 133*t*, 159, 192n85; and right to benefit,

27; and rights of the jobless, viii, x, 56, 67-68, 179; and risk, 8; of social insurance, 54-55; state-run system of, 49; as taxation, 53, 158; voluntary, 115. *See also* noncontributory scheme

Co-operative Commonwealth Federation (CCF), 40, 43, 57, 60

Couper, Walter James, 49

Court of Appeal (Quebec), 197n76

Court of Appeal (UK), 26

Court of Referees, 27, 65

Crevier, Étienne, 78

Cullen, Bud, 95

cyclical employment. *See* nonstandard employment

de Grandpré Report, 130, 134

Denault, Judge, 201n7, 204n109

Denmark, 16, 181

Denning, Lord, 121

Department of Commerce (US), 101

Department of Employment and Immigration (Canada), 96, 120

Department of Justice (Canada), 37, 52

Department of Labour (Canada), 34-35, 58, 62

Department of Manpower (Quebec), 134

Department of Manpower and Immigration (Canada), 82

Department of National Defence (Canada), 39

Department of National Health and Welfare (Canada), 83

Department of National Revenue (Canada), 85

Depression, the, vii, 13, 38, 41, 45, 52, 57-58, 99, 178

Desjardins, Judge, 116

Deslongchamps, Judge, 143

Deutsch, John J., 78

Diefenbaker, John, 78

Dingledine, Gary, 72

discrimination, 107, 122, 198n77, 208n84

disentitlement. *See* benefit disentitlement

dismissal. *See* misconduct, dismissal for

dole, 39, 190n21

Dominion Bureau of Statistics, 195n10

Donovan Commission, 116

Dubinsky, Judge, 123, 173

Dufour, Ghislain, 134

Duplessis, Maurice, 58-60

Ecker, Frederick H., 78

economic globalization, 148, 150, 164, 180-81

economic unemployment, 25

Edwards, Deputy Minister, 35

eligibility. *See* benefit disentitlement; benefit entitlement

employability, 57, 92, 145, 151, 153, 157, 162, 210n10, 211n47

employer liability, 10, 28, 157, 186n36

Employment Insurance Account (Canada), 132*t*, 166, 183, 215nn14, 15; Cumulative Employment Account, 104. *See also* Unemployment Insurance Fund (Canada)

Employment Insurance Act, 1996, 127, 147-48, 154, 156, 168, 171, 183, 197n76, 211n36, 214-15n3

employment insurance system. *See* Canada, unemployment insurance/ employment insurance system

Employment, Labour and Social Affairs Committee, 205n8

Employment Service (Canada), 37

Employment and Social Insurance Act, 1935, 42, 44, 47-52, 54-55, 58, 69, 71, 165, 193n6

entitlement. *See* benefit entitlement

Established Programs Financing (EPF), 153

Ewald, François, 7

exceptional and temporary means, 116-18, 138, 169, 203n60

Exchequer, the (UK), 19-20

Exchequer Court (Canada), 65, 109

extended benefits system, 50, 79-80, 164, 212n80

extenuating circumstances, 120, 123-24, 140, 142, 176

Fabian movement, 17, 19

family allowance program, 94, 148-49, 156, 210, 210n3

Farmer-Labour Party of Minnesota, 46

Federal Court of Appeal, 108-9, 111, 119, 122, 143

Federal Court of Appeal, cases: *Archambault* v. *Canada (A.G.)*, 176; *Brissette (Canada* v.*)*, 172; *Caron* v. *Canada*, 116, 138, 169, 203n67; *Choinière* v. *CEIC*, 173; *Dallaire* v. *CEIC*, 170; *Dietrich (Canada [A.G.]* v.*)*, 172; *Easson (Canada [A.G.]* v.*)*, 175; *Eppel (A.G. Canada* v.*)*, 173; *Findenigg (A.G. Canada* v.*)*, 174-75; *Gionest* v. *UIC*, 113-14, 137, 163, 168, 170; *Hamilton* v. *Canada (A.G.)*, 175, 214n37; *Imbeault* v. *UIC*, 118; *Jenkins (Canada [A.G.]* v.*)*, 171, 177; *Jewell (Canada [A.G.]* v.*)*, 173-74; *Joseph* v. *CEIC*, 123; *Kolish (Canada [A.G.]* v.*)*, 176; *Lalonde (A.G. of Canada* v.*)*, 138;

McDonald v. *CEIC*, 124; *Meunier* v. *Canada*, 173; *Morin* v. *A.G. Canada*, 176; *Morrison* v. *Canada Employment and Immigration Commission*, 114; *Moura (Attorney General of Canada* v.*)*, 125; *Nolet (A.G. Canada* v.*)*, 172-73; *Oakes-Pépin et al.* v. *CEIC et al.*, 169-70; *Ouellet* v. *UIC*, 118, 203n67; *Pelletier* v. *CEIC*, 168; *Schachter* v. *Canada*, 112, 135, 206n41; *Stolniuk (Canada [A.G.]* v.*)*, 174; *Tanguay* v. *UIC*, 108, 121, 126, 137, 140, 142, 170; *Tétreault-Gadoury* v. *Canada*, 112, 135, 197n71, 206n41; *Thomas et al. (Canada [A.G.]* v.*)*, 169; *Tremblay (A.G. Canada* v.*)*, 171; *Tucker (Canada [Attorney General]* v.*)*, 123, 172

Federal-Provincial Fiscal Arrangements Act, 210n28

Finlayson, R.K., 41

First World War, 33-34, 54

Forget, Claude, 103, 155

Forget Commission, 102; report, 102-7, 111, 126, 131, 137, 146, 150, 155-56, 161, 196n37, 207n64

France, 11, 16, 71

fraud, 80, 140, 155

free employment contract, 5-6

free trade, 91, 94, 101-2, 106, 134, 148, 164. *See also* Canada-US Free Trade Agreement; North American Free Trade Agreement (NAFTA)

frictional unemployment, 32, 79

Friedman, Milton, 91

full employment, viii, 13, 57, 60, 74-75, 92-93, 105, 160, 162

George, Lloyd, 19

Germany, 4, 8, 10-11, 15-16, 19, 29, 41, 186n36

Gershberg Task Force Report, 98-99, 102, 215n6

Ghent model, 15-16, 18, 33-34

Gill, Ernest C., 78

Gill Report, 67, 74, 78, 80-85, 87, 95, 103, 105, 114-15, 133*t*, 150, 156, 161, 194n53

Godbout, Adélard, 60-61

Gompers, Samuel, 45

good cause. *See* refusal of suitable employment

Goods and Services Tax (GST), 143, 209n100

Goulet, Georges, 168*t*

Great War. *See* First World War

Gregory Commission (UK), 50

Guide to Benefit Entitlement, 137

Guthrie, Hugh, 43

harassment, 107, 122, 140-41, 143, 171, 207n53

Herridge, W.D., 42

Hoover, J. Edgar, 38

House of Commons (Canada), xii, 35, 40, 60-61, 64, 89, 134, 141, 153-54, 182, 207n53

House of Commons (UK), 20, 28

House of Commons Committee on Industrial and International Relations (Canada), 35, 37

House of Commons Finance Committee (Canada), 183

House of Commons Standing Committee on Labour, Employment, and Immigration (Canada), 107

House of Representatives (US), 42

House of Representatives Labor Committee (US), 47

Hugessen, Judge, 116-17, 163

Human Resources Development Canada's Appeal Division, 168*t*

Human Resources Investment Fund (HRIF), 153

Human Rights Commission, 143

Imperial Economic Conference, 41

Income Security for Canadians, 83

income security programs, 44, 72, 82-83, 92, 101, 149, 199n16

Income Security and Social Services, 83

income supplementation, 79, 103-5, 150, 157, 209, 209n107

Income Tax Act, 156

individual responsibility: liberal belief in, 5, 71; and poverty, 33; and risk spreading, 7; and social insurance law, 11; unemployment as, 1, 3, 6, 46, 67, 71, 92, 99, 105, 150. *See also* liberalism; neoliberalism

industrial unemployment, 33, 36

industrialization, viii, 1-2, 4-7, 10, 23, 29, 32, 34

insurable employment: and actuarial ideology, 72, 79; background to, 62; for benefit calculation, 100; criterion of, 96; as defined in law, 86; and disentitlement, 138-39; hourly calculation of length of, 181; and job-creation programs, 95; restrictions on, 142; as a right, 24; and voluntary unemployment, 89

Integrated Child Tax Benefit, 210n3

intensity rule, 156, 182, 215

International Labour Organization (ILO), 13, 34, 160, 187n47, 189n60

International Labour Organization (ILO) Convention: (no. 2) on Unemployment

(1919), 29, 52; (no. 44) on Unemployment (1934), 29
International Labour Organization (ILO) Recommendation (no. 1) Concerning Unemployment, 29, 52
International Monetary Fund, 205n7
Interpretation Act, 113
involuntary unemployment, 23, 70, 93, 120
Ireland, 100, 186n36

Japan, 186n36
job-creation programs, 95, 99, 130, 150, 166, 205n9
jobless winter fund, 36
Jobs Strategy Program, 130, 139
Johnson, Lyndon B., 82
Joyal, Judge, 204n122, 213n33
just cause. *See* voluntary leaving
just society, 82-83

Keynes, John Maynard, 44, 92
Keynesianism: and Canadian UI system, vii, xi, 51, 56, 59-60, 72, 90-91, 149, 159; and emergence of Canadian welfare state, 74; and UK unemployment insurance system, 13
King, Mackenzie, 31, 35-38, 44-45, 51-52, 56, 58-61, 190n16
Korea, 76
Korean War, 74

labour disputes: and benefit entitlement, 14, 26, 115, 136, 201-2n23; and British act of 1911, 30; and British jurisprudence, 203n75; and Canada Employment Insurance Commission, 169; definition of, 114, 168, 170, 188n48, 207n64; and disentitlement, 88, 116, 118, 137, 145, 163, 167; and disqualification, 29, 76, 113, 189n54; and Forget Report, 106; liability for, 29; provisions for, 127, 156, 165; and resumption of operations, 117; state involvement in, x, 28, 100; statistics, 213n4; and vacant jobs, 24, 27, 64
labour exchange, 13-14, 17-18, 22-23, 27, 33
Labour Force Development Strategy for Canada, 127-28, 152
Labour Force Survey, 195n10
labour market: and annualization, 107; and availability for work, 125; Canadian, 31, 98, 101; deregulation of, 181; exclusions from, 195n10; free, 145; and industrialization, 5; management of, 24, 97, 130; and married women, 77;

and neoliberalism, 91; polarization of, 180; policies, 199n16, 205n9; state involvement in, ix, 69, 81, 93, 96, 153; and the unemployed, 3, 18, 20, 63, 92, 182; and voluntary unemployment, 8
labour market attachment, 80, 84-87, 156, 183
labour movement, 67, 72
Labour Party (UK), 12, 17-18, 28
labour relations, 9, 51
laissez-faire economics, 31, 38, 42-43, 92
Laurier, Wilfrid, 33
League for Social Reconstruction, 57
Leclerc, Félix, 129, 205n13
less eligibility principle, 2
Lévesque, Jean Marc, 195n10
L'Heureux-Dubé, Madam Justice, 117, 119, 137
Liberal Party (UK), 17, 19
Liberal Party of Canada, 35-36, 60, 82, 89, 97-98, 101, 103, 134, 141, 143-45, 209n100
liberalism: and British legislation, 2-3; and Canadian unemployment insurance system, 76; and individual responsibility, viii, ix, 21, 67, 71; and risk technology, 8; and social insurance, 1, 10; and social reform, 4; and unemployment compensation, 69, 92. *See also* individual responsibility; neoliberalism
living conditions, 2, 5
London (UK), 3, 185n2
London Central Unemployed Committee, 17
Lundeen Bill (US), 46

Macdonald Commission Report, 101-4, 131, 146, 150, 161
McDougall, Barbara, 127, 130, 136
McGill University (Montreal), 41, 191n53
Mackasey, Bryce, 82, 94
Mackintosh, W.A., 57-59
McNair, Judge, 117
Mahoney, Judge, 123
Manitoba, 158
Marceau, Judge, 117, 173-74, 203n67
marginal workers: and 1970 white paper, 84-85; and Bill C-14, 96; and disentitlement, 169; and employment insurance benefit system, 154, 164, 181; and income supplementation, 105; and intensity rule, 156; and self-financing system, 161; and unemployment insurance dependency, 150; and unemployment insurance expansion, 88, 90; and unemployment insurance system

hijack, 131, 144, 177; and variable entrance requirement, 95. *See also* seasonal workers

Maritimes. *See* Atlantic provinces

market imperatives, x, 97, 157

Marsh, Leonard, 9, 41, 66, 72, 186n26, 191n53

Marshall Plan, 74

Martin, Paul, 144, 160

Massachusetts, 45

Massé, Marcel, 160

maternity benefits: accessibility of, 86-87, 211n38; and benefit repayment, 182; as contrary to insurance logic, 81; and disentitlement, 115; in the Forget Report, 106; in the Gershberg Report, 98; increase in, 129; and weeks of disqualification, 137. *See also* parental benefits; women

maximum insurable earnings (MIE), 85, 155, 158, 183, 214-15n4

Mazankowski, Don, 139

means test, 39, 50, 68

Meighen, Arthur, 35-37

Merthyr Tydfil, 26, 100

Metropolitan Life Insurance Company, 78

Milan (Italy), 16

Ministry of Labour (UK), 18, 41

Minnesota, 46

misconduct, dismissal for: disqualification for, 25-26, 28-29, 63, 87, 119-21, 128, 141, 175-76; and insurable employment, 65, 89; jurisprudence for, 172, 204n109; and labour law, 123-24; and "last employment," 88; penalties for, viii, 188n30; provisions for, 144-45; and rights of the jobless, 139, 163, 170; without just cause, 173

mobility of the workforce, 2-3, 98, 102

Montpetit, Édouard, 40

Montpetit Commission, 40, 60

Montreal (Quebec), 57, 144, 173

Moore, Tom, 37, 64

moral hazard theory, 25, 71, 80, 101, 188n27

Morgan, Moses O., 103

Mouvement Action-Chômage, 107, 109

Mulroney, Brian, 99, 102-3, 107, 134-35, 200n36

Munro, Jack, 103

Nationair, 169

National Employment Commission Act, 1936, 57

National Employment Service, 59, 67, 154, 158

National Insurance Act, 1911 (UK), 3, 12, 20, 88

National Training Act, 130, 154

National Unemployed Worker's Association, 40

neoliberalism: and actuarial ideology, 158; and Canadian unemployment insurance scheme, 91-92, 146, 159, 167; and employability, 162; and the family supplement, 156; and fiscalization of social policies, 211n44; and free-market approach, xi, 199n16; and free-trade thinking, 164-65; and individual responsibility for unemployment, vii, 93, 128; and job creation, 149; and Liberal Party of Canada, 144; and moral hazard theory, 188n27. *See also* individual responsibility; liberalism

Netherlands, 16, 186n36

New Brunswick, 53, 59, 158

New Brunswick Works, 145

New Deal legislation (Canada), 51-53, 55, 58

New Deal legislation (US), 31, 38, 42, 44, 47, 192n88

New Democratic Party (Canada), 89

new entrants or re-entrants to the labour force (NERE), 96, 135, 155, 182

Newfoundland, 98, 158

nonavailability. *See* availability for work

noncontributory scheme, x, 40, 43, 46-47, 67-68. *See also* contributory system

non-seasonal risk, 79

nonstandard employment: as casual labour, 3-4; as excluded from insurance, 70; extended coverage to, 130, 134, 136, 206n46; government's responsibility in, 84; increase in, 180; organization of, 18; reduction of benefits for, 150-51, 155; and trade agreements, 101

North American Free Trade Agreement (NAFTA), 130-31, 143, 209n100. *See also* Canada-US Free Trade Agreement; free trade

Norway, 16, 186n36

Ogus, Anthony I., 188n30

On to Ottawa March, 43-44

only reasonable solution, 142, 170, 213n17. *See also* voluntary leaving

Ontario, 33, 41, 52-53, 57, 211n51

Organisation for Economic Co-operation and Development (OECD), 128, 150, 154, 199n16, 205n7

Organisation for Economic Co-operation and Development Committee on

Employment, Labour and Social Affairs, 129
Oxford University (UK), 17

Pal, Leslie A., 69
parental benefit program (Quebec), 87, 197n76
parental benefits, 107, 112, 129, 134, 137, 182, 206n41, 211n38. *See also* maternity benefits
Parliamentary Committee on Human Resources Development, 154
part-time employment. *See* nonstandard employment
Patriotic Fund, 36
payroll tax, 52, 130, 164
Pension Appeals Board, 109
pensions, 19, 42, 57, 59, 100. *See also* Canada Pension Plan; Quebec Pension Plan
Petrie, Joseph Richards, 78
Plaxton, C.P., 51-52
Poland, 29
Poor Laws (UK), 2-4, 18-19, 23, 25-26, 33
poverty: and industrialization, 2; and seasonal unemployment, 33; and unemployment, 3, 5-6, 17, 19, 144, 152; war on, 82-83; working-class, 185n2
Powell Duffryn Steam Coal Company, 26
Pratte, Judge, 114
premiums. *See* contributory system
Price, F.G., 41
privatization, 49, 69, 71, 78, 158
Privy Council (Canada), 51-56, 58, 165
Privy Council (UK), 41
public works programs, 4, 17-18, 39, 44, 58
Purvis, Arthur, 57
Purvis Commission, 57-59, 61, 63, 92, 162

qualifying conditions, viii, 77, 96, 128, 130, 134-35, 144, 182
Quebec, 39, 53, 59-60, 77, 83, 100, 109, 111, 134, 150-52, 157-58, 170, 197n76, 201n6, 205n13, 214n3
Quebec City, 60
Quebec Income Security Act, 211n47
Quebec Pension Plan, 86
Queen's University (Ontario), 57, 59, 78

Reagan, Ronald, 164, 212n80
reasonable time, 124-25
Reed, Judge, 111, 139, 176
refusal of suitable employment: and British act of 1911, 27-28; disqualification

for, 81, 88-89, 119, 125, 128, 177; good cause for, 120-21, 121, 124-25; and insurable employment, 65, 79; and labour disputes, 157; and labour market, 63; and Social Security Act, 48
Regina (SK), 43
Relief Camp Worker's Union (RCWU), 43
responsibility. *See* collective responsibility; individual responsibility; social responsibility
right to benefit. *See* benefit entitlement; benefit disentitlement
right to equality, 111-12, 135. *See also* women
rights of the jobless: and 1971 reform, 88, 91, 94, 109; and benefit entitlement, viii, 17, 25, 46, 71, 113; and British act of 1911, 30; and Canada Employment Insurance Commission, 142-43; and Canadian act of 1940, 56, 73; and Canadian labour movement, 67, 72; and Canadian unemployment insurance scheme, 178; and Canadian unemployment insurance system expansion, 74; and case law, 108, 126; and counterreforms of 1990s, 139, 160, 167; and labour disputes, 28; and neoliberalism, 107; political background of, vii; and qualifying conditions, 128; and state involvement, xi, xii-xiii, 12, 179; and unemployment insurance system hijack, 136, 147
right-to-work policy, 12-13, 23, 46
Rinfret, Mr. Justice, 53
risk. *See* non-seasonal risk; seasonal risk; social risk; unemployment risk
risk spreading, 7, 21
risk technology, 7-8, 11
Rogers, Norman, 57, 59
Roosevelt, F.D., 38, 42, 45, 48, 190n16, 192n88
Rouleau, Judge, 169
Rowell, Newton, 33, 51-52, 59
Rowell-Sirois Report. *See* Royal Commission of Inquiry into the Relations between the Dominion and the Provinces
Royal Canadian Mounted Police (RCMP), 43
Royal Commission on the Economic Union and Development Prospects for Canada, 101
Royal Commission of Inquiry on Poor Laws (UK), 17
Royal Commission of Inquiry into the Relations between the Dominion and the Provinces, 52, 58-59, 61

Rueff, J., 71
Russia, 34

St. Gallen experiment (Switzerland), 15, 20, 26, 187n52
St. Laurent, Louis, 51-52
Saskatoon, 39
Saucier, Guylaine, 103
Schachter, Shalom, 112
Scott, Frank R., 53, 57
seasonal benefit system, 76, 79
seasonal risk, 79
seasonal workers: and basic eligibility, 51; and benefit entitlement, 65, 76, 80, 131, 137, 150; and Canadian act of 1940, 70, 75; and Canadian labour market, 31-32, 62; and case law, 113; and counterreforms of 1990s, 182; and employment insurance system, 154; and Gill Report, 81, 85; and intensity rule, 156; and Macdonald Report, 102, 104; and simplistic concept of social insurance, 197n66; and unemployment, 78; and unemployment insurance system expansion, 90; and unemployment insurance system hijack, 113; and variable entrance requirement, 96, 98. *See also* marginal workers
Second World War, 32, 56, 78
self-employment. *See* nonstandard employment
self-financing system, 70, 82, 84-85, 89, 103, 106, 159, 161
Senate (Canada), 131, 134-36, 141
Senate (US), 42
short-term unemployment, 79
sickness benefits, 63, 84, 86-87, 106-7, 137, 182, 211n38
Sirois, Joseph, 59
Smith, Llewellyn, 20-21, 24, 178
Soboda, Frances, 103
Social Aid Act, 1969, 78
Social Insurance Commission, 40
social insurance systems: conceptions of, 9-10, 105-6; contributory system of, 12; European-style, 45; and exclusion of seasonal workers, 197n66; legal framework for, 11; pooling risk within, 107; and redistribution, 172; and responsibility for unemployment, 21, 23, 127; and right to benefit, 161; selective, 149; tripartite funding formula for, 22; universal, 146; and voluntary unemployment, 29
social responsibility, 16, 105
social risk, 1, 8-9, 11, 21, 23, 29, 35, 149
socialism, 4, 6, 17, 19, 37, 41, 67

Société Canadienne des Métaux Reynolds, 116-17
Société de droit administratif (Quebec), 201n7
sound insurance scheme, 71, 78
South Africa, 29
Speenhamland Act, 1795 (UK), 2
stagflation, 91-92
Stangroom, Eric, 62
state involvement: and administration of unemployment insurance, viii-ix, xi, 37, 43; and commercial insurance model, x; in the economic process, 4, 13; and job-creation programs, 150; and market regulation, 10, 91; and neutrality, 26, 81, 100, 108, 119, 138, 163, 168-69; and responsibility for unemployment, 31, 52, 68, 73, 106, 160, 178-80; and social risk, 9; and unemployment compensation, 16, 48, 54, 68, 181
Statistics Canada, 93, 195n10
Stewart, Bryce, 34, 37, 70
Stone, Harlan Fiske (US Justice), 47
structural unemployment, 32, 58
substantial resumption of operations, 116, 138
suitability of employment. *See* refusal of suitable employment; unsuitable employment
Superior Court (Quebec), 143, 214n3
Supreme Court (Canada), xi, 51-53, 56, 109, 112, 163, 166
Supreme Court (Canada), cases: *Abrahams* v. *Canada (P.G.)*, 108, 112-15, 119, 122, 126, 137, 166, 170-71, 177; *Bliss* v. *A.G. of Canada*, 87, 111, 198n77; *Canada Attorney General* v. *Valois*, 115; *Hills* v. *A.G. of Canada*, 108, 115, 119, 126, 137, 166, 169, 188n19; *Martin Service Station* v. *Minister of National Revenue*, 109; *R.* v. *Scheer*, 109
Supreme Court (US), 44, 47-48, 192n88
Sweden, 205n9
Switzerland, 15

Tanguay, Maurice, 121-22, 171
Taschereau, Premier, 41
Tax Court of Canada, 109
temporary unemployment, 70, 83
Tétreault-Gadoury, Marcelle, 112
Thomas, Carole, 169
Thurlow, Chief Justice, 174
Trade Disputes Act, 1906 (UK), 188n48
Trades and Labour Congress of Canada (TLCC), 37, 40, 64
Treaty of Versailles, 35, 41, 43, 52, 187n47

tribunals. *See* administrative tribunals
tripartite funding formula, 11, 22, 50, 65-66, 107, 186n36
Trudeau, Pierre, 82-83, 89

underemployment, 11, 17-18
Unemployed Councils, 46
Unemployed Workmen Act, 1905 (UK), 4, 17
Unemployment Assistance Act, 1956, 77
Unemployment Fund (UK), 28
unemployment insurance abuse, 89, 94, 99, 105
Unemployment Insurance Account (Canada). *See* Unemployment Insurance Fund (Canada)
Unemployment Insurance Act, 1935, 30, 63-64
Unemployment Insurance Act, 1939 (Quebec), 60
Unemployment Insurance Act, 1940, 56-73 *passim,* 75, 100, 112, 165
Unemployment Insurance Act, 1971, 214n4; benefits offered by, 85; and Bill C-105, 208n72; built on humanity, 83; concept of misconduct in, 123-24; and disentitlement, 118; historical overview of, 133*t;* and job-creation programs, 130; and jobless rights, 88-89; and private insurance, 126; reform to premiums of, 159; renumbering of, 205n16; since 1994, 149
Unemployment Insurance Commission (Canada), 65-67, 76-77, 109, 110*t,* 116, 119
unemployment insurance dependency, 72, 83, 97, 128-29, 150-51, 157, 183
Unemployment Insurance Fund (Canada), 52, 60, 66, 79-80, 86, 95, 117, 132*t,* 166, 194n53, 210n31. *See also* Employment Insurance Account (Canada)
Unemployment Insurance Regulations, 207n63
Unemployment Insurance in the 70s, 74, 83-86, 98, 134
unemployment insurance system. *See* Canada, unemployment insurance/ employment insurance system
unemployment rates: basic or natural, 92; and compensation claims, 15; and labour force survey, 195n10; national, 86; provincial, 105; regional, 97, 144, 156, 161; in 1980s, 99; and service expansion, 76; and variable entrance requirement, 94
unemployment risk, 11, 21, 55, 68, 105

unemployment stamps, 66-67
unions: and administrative rulings, 109; boutique, 190n16; and labour disputes, 26, 64; and labour exchanges, 20; and opposition to Bill C-14, 97; Quebec, 214n3; and refusal of employment, 63; and state involvement in unemployment insurance, 22; trade, 13-14, 16, 69, 187n48; and unemployment insurance in Canada, 31, 41; and work-sharing programs, 95
United Kingdom, unemployment insurance system: and compulsory contributions, 186n36; contributory model, 179; development of unemployment insurance scheme, xii, 1, 29-30; and eligibility requirements, 50; jurisprudence, 113, 116, 118, 203n75; and moral hazard theory, 71; and socialist legislation, 41
United Nations, 205n7
United States: and employer contributions, 186n36; extended benefit program, 164; free trade with Canada, 101-2; and influence of British unemployment insurance system, 29; and state intervention, 44, 84; unemployment funds, 15; unemployment insurance system of, 37, 45, 62, 64, 79; voluntary unemployment case law, 212n86; Wagner Act, 1935, 46, 190n16; welfare employment, 151, 162
Universal Declaration of Human Rights (1948), 13
universality, 84, 149, 210
unpredictable unemployment, 70
unsuitable employment, 27, 48, 118, 124
US Constitution, 48

Vaillancourt, Yves, 66
Valcartier (QC), 39
Valcourt, Bernard, 129, 140
Vancouver (BC), 43
variable entrance requirement (VER), 94, 96-98, 105, 134-35, 156
Vermont (US), 165
Victoria conference, 1971, 83
Vietnam War, 82
Vocational Rehabilitation of Disabled Persons (VRDP), 154
vocational training: and actuarial ideology, 129; costs of, 128; economics of, 93; for the employed, 157; extended involvement in, 130, 134, 146; in Gill's report, 80; and job-saving programs, 95-96, 105, 199n16; lack of choice in, 162; and policy making, 140,

207-8n70; reduced support of, 151; reform of, 148; use of UI for, 161

voluntary leaving: and benefit entitlement, 100, 163; case law, 65, 121, 170; disqualification for, 26, 28-29, 89, 98-99, 106, 119-20, 128, 142-43, 156-57, 175-76; jurisprudence, 177; just cause for, 107-8, 119-21, 122-23, 136-37, 139-42, 207n53; and "last employment," 88; penalties for, viii, x, 25, 71, 81, 87, 136, 164-65, 188n30; provisions for, 144-45, 156, 166; and welfare, 152. *See also* only reasonable solution

voluntary unemployment: and 1971 reform, 93; and actuarial ideology, 80, 119, 139; and benefit entitlement, 23, 71-73; and British unemployment insurance scheme, 14, 30; case law, 64, 111, 167, 212n86; deterrents against, 89; and disqualification, 26, 76; and Forget Report, 106; and married women, 77; and moral hazard theory, 188n27; penalties for, 8, 127; provisions on, xi, xiii, 56; as regulatory notion, x

Wagner-Lewis tax-offset plan, 47

Watson, A.D., 41-42, 69, 71

Webb, Beatrice, 17-18, 23

Webb, Sidney, 17-18, 23

welfare, 12, 77, 100, 128-29, 131, 134-35, 145-46, 148, 151-53, 156, 211n47

welfare state (Canada), vii, 74-75, 150, 186n26

western provinces, 40, 150

White, Sir Thomas, 41, 191n51

white paper, 1970. *See Unemployment Insurance in the 70s*

Wilson, Michael, 99

Winnipeg General Strike, 34, 37

Wisconsin (US), 45

Wolfenden, H., 41-42, 69-70

women: and labour market, 85, 182; and manufacturing industries, 196n21; married, 75-77, 80; as nonstandard employees, 155; and pregnancy, 81, 87, 198n77; prejudice against, 87; rights of, 112. *See also* maternity benefits; right to equality

Woodsworth, J.S., 40

work accidents, 9-11, 16

work camps, 39-40, 43, 190n40

work stoppage: and the 85 percent rule, 106, 116-17; disentitlement due to, 113, 137, 201-2n23, 207n63; "exceptional and temporary means," 117, 203n60; and inconsistent disentitlement, 118-19; interpretation in labour disputes, 169-70; and loss of employment, 29, 64; and maternity benefits, 115; regulation of, 76. *See also* labour disputes

Worker's Unity League, 40, 47, 69

workfare programs, 151, 153, 162, 212n72

Working Class Unemployment Insurance Bill, 40

working conditions, 1, 4-5

workmen's compensation, 11, 45, 183, 186n34

work-sharing programs, 95, 99, 130

World Bank, 205n7

youth, 58, 81, 85, 148, 154, 182-83

Zurich (Switzerland), 15

Printed and bound in Canada by Friesens

Set in Stone by Brenda and Neil West, BN Typographics West

Copy editor: Dallas Harrison

Proofreader: Jillian Shoichet

Indexer: Alex Campbell

Law and Society Series
W. Wesley Pue, General Editor

Previously published

Gender in the Legal Profession: Fitting or Breaking the Mould
Joan Brockman

Regulating Lives: Historical Essays on the State, Society, the Individual,
and the Law
Edited by John McLaren, Robert Menzies, and Dorothy E. Chunn

Taxing Choices: The Intersection of Class, Gender, Parenthood, and
the Law
Rebecca Johnson

Collective Insecurity: The Liberian Crisis, Unilateralism, and Global
Order
Ikechi Mgbeoji

Unnatural Law: Rethinking Canadian Environmental Law and Policy
David R. Boyd

Murdering Holiness: The Trials of Franz Creffield and George Mitchell
Jim Phillips and Rosemary Gartner

People and Place: Historical Influences on Legal Culture
Edited by Jonathan Swainger and Constance Backhouse

Upcoming in Spring 2005

Between Justice and Certainty: Treaty Making in British Columbia
Andrew Woolford

First Nations Sacred Sites in Canada's Courts
Michael Lee Ross

Humanitarianism, Identity, Nation: Migration Laws of Australia and
Canada
Catherine Dauvergne

Good Government? Good Citizens? Courts, Politics, and Markets in a
Changing Canada
W.A. Bogart

Unwilling Mothers, Unwanted Babies: Infanticide in Canada
Kirsten Johnson Kramar

Securing Borders: Detention and Deportation in Canada
Anna Pratt

Defending Rights in Russia: Lawyers, the State, and Legal Reform in the
Post-Soviet Era
Pamela A. Jordan